Open Government

Edited by Daniel Lathrop and Laurel Ruma

O'REILLY®

Beijing · Cambridge · Farnham · Köln · Sebastopol · Taipei · Tokyo

Open Government
Edited by Daniel Lathrop and Laurel Ruma

Copyright © 2010 O'Reilly Media, Inc.. All rights reserved.
Printed in the United States of America.

Published by O'Reilly Media, Inc., 1005 Gravenstein Highway North, Sebastopol, CA 95472.

O'Reilly books may be purchased for educational, business, or sales promotional use. Online editions are also available for most titles (*http://my.safaribooksonline.com*). For more information, contact our corporate/institutional sales department: 800-998-9938 or *corporate@oreilly.com*.

Editors: Laurel Ruma and Julie Steele
Production Editor: Sarah Schneider
Copyeditor: Audrey Doyle
Proofreader: Kiel Van Horn

Indexer: Ellen Troutman Zaig
Cover Designer: Mark Paglietti
Interior Designer: David Futato
Illustrators: Nellie McKesson and Rob Romano

Printing History:
February 2010:   First Edition.

ISBN: 978-0-596-80435-0

[V]

1265401084

*A portion of royalties will be donated to
Global Integrity.*

CONTENTS

FOREWORD

It goes without saying that as we step into the future, governments face incredibly complex challenges. Sustaining societies and economies in the face of climate change, energy shortages, poverty, demographic shifts, and security will test the ingenuity of those who wish to see, do, and participate in the public good.

Even though it's the twenty-first century, most governments still reflect industrial-age organizational thinking, based on the same command-and-control model as industrial-age enterprises. Today's bureaucracy and the industrial economy rose hand-in-hand. The economy needed roads, sewers, electrification, railways, and a sophisticated military. As government got bigger, and the revenue of government increased, it became necessary to build more elaborate procedures, structures, and controls, all run by new layers of professional managers. Nonpartisan hiring practices, pay scales, procedures for making appointments, financial systems, and audit processes were put in place. At the time, all of this was judged to be state of the art.

These bureaucracies operated like individual "stovepipes"—with information only flowing vertically and rarely between departments. During the last 40 years, governments, like corporations, applied computers to their work as each agency acquired and built data processing systems to meet their automation needs. The result is that old procedures, processes, and organizational forms were just encoded in software. Huge, unwieldy mainframe beasts not only cemented old ways of working, they required still greater levels of bureaucracy to plan, implement, operate, and control them. Despite best efforts, IT experts have largely failed to resolve the chaos of inconsistent databases, dueling spreadsheets, and other data anomalies that plague many government agencies.

This is not sustainable. Governments face a reality in which they are more and more dependent for authority on a network of powers and counter-influences of which they are just a part. Whether streamlining government service delivery or resolving complex global issues, governments are either actively seeking—or can no longer resist—broader participation from citizens and a diverse array of other stakeholders. Just as the modern multinational corporation sources ideas, parts, and materials from a vast external network of customers, researchers, and suppliers, governments must hone their capacity to integrate skills and knowledge from multiple participants to meet expectations for a more responsive, resourceful, efficient, and accountable form of governance.

The first wave of digitally enabled "e-government" strategies delivered some important benefits. It made government information and services more accessible to citizens while creating administrative and operational efficiencies. But too many of these initiatives simply paved the cow paths—that is, they focused on automating existing processes and moving existing government services online.

It is the next wave of innovation that presents a historic occasion to fundamentally redesign how government operates; how and what the public sector provides; and ultimately, how governments interact and engage with their citizens. It is truly a time when either government will play an active and positive role in its own transformation, or change will happen to it. The transformation process is at the same time exhilarating and painful, but the price of inaction is a lost opportunity for government to redefine its role in society and help launch a new era of participatory government.

The good news is that glimmers of this second wave of innovation are beginning to appear in capitals around the world. Knowledge, information, talent, and energy are being moved, shaped, and channeled in brand-new ways, inside, across, and outside of the boundaries of government. A growing number of governments understand the need to distribute power broadly and leverage innovation, knowledge, and value from the private sector and civil society.

As the excellent essays and case studies in this book reveal, there is a new kind of public sector organization emerging: open government. This is government that opens its doors to the world; co-innovates with everyone, especially citizens; shares resources that were previously closely guarded; harnesses the power of mass collaboration; drives transparency throughout its operations; and behaves not as an isolated department or jurisdiction, but as something new—a truly integrated and networked organization. Today, it's a radical notion, but perhaps it's only as fantastic as the current version of government would seem to a feudal prince from the Middle Ages visiting us now. FDR and Winston Churchill wanted stronger government. Ronald Regan and Margaret Thatcher wanted less. Thanks to the Internet, we can now have it both ways. In the U.S. and many other jurisdictions, government is becoming a stronger part of the social ecosystem that binds individuals, communities, and businesses—not by absorbing new responsibilities or building additional layers of bureaucracy, but through its willingness to open up formerly closed processes to broader input and innovation. In other words, government becomes a platform for the creation of public value and social innovation. It provides resources, sets rules, and mediates disputes, but it allows citizens, nonprofits, and the private sector to do most of the heavy lifting.

All this is happening at a time when an entire generation of baby boomers will retire from government, creating an exodus of knowledge and skills that may never be replaced. In the United States, this demographic shift will see more than 60,000 civil service employees exit annually between now and 2015. Large departments, such as the Department of Defense, will lose 20 percent of their workforces. Many of these people hold executive, managerial, or key administrative positions—replacing them will be nearly impossible.

To make matters worse, recruiting and retaining a younger generation of public servants won't be much easier. Just when government most needs an infusion of fresh-thinking talent, young people are losing interest in public administration as a profession.

Although managers typically fret at the prospect, this attrition may not be such a bad thing. Rather than worry about head counts, governments should look for new ways to ignite innovation. The emerging fiscal and demographic realities are such that most governments will have to do more with less, both today and in the future.

—Don Tapscott
Author of *Wikinomics* and *Grown Up Digital*

PREFACE

What is *open government*? In the most basic sense, it's the notion that the people have the right to access the documents and proceedings of government. The idea that the public has a right to scrutinize and participate in government dates at least to the Enlightenment, and is enshrined in both the U.S. Declaration of Independence and U.S. Constitution. Its principles are recognized in virtually every democratic country on the planet.

But the very meaning of the term continues to evolve. The concept of open government has been influenced—for the better—by the open source software movement, and taken on a greater focus for allowing participation in the procedures of government. Just as open source software allows users to change and contribute to the source code of their software, open government now means government where citizens not only have access to information, documents, and proceedings, but can also become participants in a meaningful way. Open government also means improved communication and operations within the various branches and levels of government. More sharing internally can lead to greater efficiency and accountability.

The subtitle of this book is "Transparency, Participation, and Collaboration in Practice." The terms were borrowed from President Barack Obama's memorandum on transparency and open government, issued his first day in office. In it, he committed the U.S. government to "establish a system of transparency, public participation, and collaboration." (See the Appendix.)

Obama's memo was a signal moment in the history of open government, issued by a president who gained office in part by opening his campaign to allow his supporters to shape its message, actions, and strategy using online tools. The movement to make this happen, which goes back to the earliest days of the World Wide Web, is now generally called "Government 2.0" (Gov 2.0 to its friends).

Just as the Web has fundamentally altered retail, real estate, media, and even manufacturing, Gov 2.0 advocates seek to redefine the relationship between citizens and government officials. It's not about replacing representative democracy with some kind of online poll, but instead engaging the citizen as a full participant rather than an observer of their government.

Take San Francisco, where the city has created an API (application programming interface) to distribute information from its 311 system about city services to developers in a way that they can integrate and distribute that information into new software and web applications (see *http://apps.sfgov.org/Open311API/*). Everyone will be able to get information about citizen requests and issue new requests (such as reporting potholes) directly to city departments via their own web software. The concept breaks down the line between citizens and government—letting someone other than a government official determine how to route citizen requests.

As if this radical transformation were not enough, the Gov 2.0 movement seeks to make a similar transformation within government itself: empowering employees inside governments to go beyond the traditional boundaries and limitations of bureaucracy to act across organizational lines and move from top-down to bottom-up structures of management and decision making.

In this book we have found leading visionaries, thinkers, and practitioners from inside and outside of government who share their views on what this new balance looks like, how to achieve it, and the reforms that are needed along the way.

How This Book Is Organized

Chapter 1, *A Peace Corps for Programmers*
> Matthew Burton proposes a new project to recruit top technologists into government temporarily and harness their knowledge to transform the way government information technology operates. Burton, himself a federal contractor and Web 2.0 technologist, opens this provocative piece by urging the government to fire him.

Chapter 2, *Government As a Platform*
> Tim O'Reilly examines how the philosophy of the open Web applies to transforming the relationships between citizens and government. O'Reilly uses open software platforms as a model for reinventing government.

Chapter 3, *By the People*
> Carl Malamud addresses the third wave of government transformation—the Internet wave—that is now upon us.

Chapter 4, *The Single Point of Failure*

Beth Simone Noveck tackles the issue of closed decision making and open deliberation in this excerpt from her 2009 book, *Wiki Government: How Technology Can Make Government Better, Democracy Stronger, and Citizens More Powerful* (Brookings Institution Press).

Chapter 5, *Engineering Good Government*

Howard Dierking explores applying software design patterns to government. Dierking covers blobs, antipatterns, and the shrinking space between government and citizens.

Chapter 6, *Enabling Innovation for Civic Engagement*

David G. Robinson, Harlan Yu, and Edward W. Felten argue for releasing data in bulk to empower citizens to better connect with their government.

Chapter 7, *Online Deliberation and Civic Intelligence*

Douglas Schuler proposes a new model for online discussion and decision making, modeled on the famous Robert's Rules of Order. Schuler goes on to ask whether we will be smart enough, soon enough, to use online—as well as *offline*—deliberation to help tackle the massive problems that we've created for ourselves.

Chapter 8, *Open Government and Open Society*

Archon Fung and David Weil argue that transparency must be applied across all of society, not just government.

Chapter 9, *"You Can Be the Eyes and Ears": Barack Obama and the Wisdom of Crowds*

Micah L. Sifry looks at the open government promises of the Obama administration and places it in the context of broader notions that underlie the philosophy of open source technology and Web 2.0.

Chapter 10, *Two-Way Street: Government with the People*

Mark Drapeau examines how and why those who favor open government need to provide outside pressure if those inside government who desire change are to able to make it happen.

Chapter 11, *Citizens' View of Open Government*

Brian Reich sketches out what reforms must achieve for regular citizens in order to be effective. Reich reminds Government 2.0 evangelists that, at the end of the day, their reforms must produce definitive benefits to be successful.

Chapter 12, *After the Collapse: Open Government and the Future of Civil Service*

David Eaves take a look at open government and the civil service and argues for experimentation and accepting the inevitable technological shift that is upon government.

Chapter 13, *Democracy, Under Everything*

Sarah Schacht asks what citizens need to do to be full participants in government. Schacht gives prescriptions for both policy makers and regular citizens to solve political gridlock.

Chapter 14, *Emergent Democracy*

Charles Armstrong outlines a new kind of digital democracy in which decisions bubble up from citizens rather than coming down from e-leaders. Armstrong hypothesizes that this new kind of democracy is already coming to businesses and other nongovernmental players, where it will inevitably take hold before being adopted by nation-states.

Chapter 15, *Case Study: Tweet Congress*
Wynn Netherland and Chris McCroskey map the success of Tweet Congress in getting members of Congress to use Twitter and the role of activism-by-web-application in the new ecosystem.

Chapter 16, *Entrepreneurial Insurgency: Republicans Connect With the American People*
Nick Schaper describes the social media strategy the Republican minority in the U.S. House uses to outfox the Democrats who control the chamber. In doing so, this top Republican strategist teaches lessons on how social media can be used by anyone to mobilize citizens.

Chapter 17, *Disrupting Washington's Golden Rule*
Ellen S. Miller explains why radical transparency in government will act as a counterweight to the influence of monied interests in shaping government policy.

Chapter 18, *Case Study: GovTrack.us*
Joshua Tauberer looks at the phenomenal success of his website, which provides public access to data about bills and votes in the U.S. Congress.

Chapter 19, *Case Study: FollowTheMoney.org*
Edwin Bender examines the past, present, and future of online tracking of money to politicians and political parties. Bender gives unsurpassed insight into the good, bad, and ugly of transparency in campaign contributions.

Chapter 20, *Case Study: MAPLight.org*
Daniel Newman looks at how a website has been able to use open web technology and hard work to shed a new kind of light on the relationship among money, power, and legislation.

Chapter 21, *Going 2.0: Why OpenSecrets.org Opted for Full Frontal Data Sharing*
Sheila Krumholz tells the story of why the not-for-profit Center for Responsive Politics released its data about government corruption to the public and embraced the Gov 2.0 movement.

Chapter 22, *All Your Data Are Belong to Us: Liberating Government Data*
Jerry Brito calls on hackers—in the sense of brilliant programmers rather than computer criminals—to liberate government data for the masses. If the government won't make data available and useful, it is up to technologists to do it for them.

Chapter 23, *Case Study: Many Eyes*
Fernanda Viégas and Martin Wattenberg look at the ways Many Eyes, an online suite of visualization tools from IBM, has been and can be used to examine government. Among other insights, these brilliant scientists propose the radical approach to treat all text as data.

Chapter 24, *My Data Can't Tell You That*

Bill Allison looks at the problems with government data collection. Allison, an investigative reporter and open government advocate at the Sunlight Foundation, proposes making those data more useful for citizens.

Chapter 25, *When Is Transparency Useful?*

Aaron Swartz proposes a new paradigm for watchdogging the government. Swartz provides a cogent argument that transparency alone is not enough.

Chapter 26, *Transparency Inside Out*

Tim Koelkebeck looks at the need for the federal government, which he describes as a country within a country, to become internally transparent before it can be anything but opaque to regular citizens.

Chapter 27, *Bringing the Web 2.0 Revolution to Government*

Gary D. Bass and Sean Moulton identify the top obstacles to increased open government that the Obama administration faces and propose solutions. Bass and Moulton give an inside-the-Beltway view on how to make reform take hold.

Chapter 28, *Toads on the Road to Open Government Data*

Bill Schrier looks at what he has learned as CIO of Seattle, Washington, about the practicalities of implementing open government reforms and the problems reformers face.

Chapter 29, *Open Government: The Privacy Imperative*

Jeff Jonas and Jim Harper shine a light on the serious issues of privacy and the brave new world we live in.

Chapter 30, *Freedom of Information Acts: Promises and Realities*

Brant Houston looks at the history and problems of the Freedom of Information Act and similar state laws. Houston goes on to provide a prescription for updating those laws.

Chapter 31, *Gov→Media→People*

Dan Gillmor tackles the thorny issue of the relationship among the government, the press, and the citizenry in the open government universe brought around by the Web.

Chapter 32, *Open Source Software for Open Government Agencies*

Carlo Daffara and Jesus M. Gonzalez-Barahona argue that government must adopt open source software in order to achieve true open government, and that doing so has many social, societal, and economic benefits.

Chapter 33, *Why Open Digital Standards Matter in Government*

Marco Fioretti argues for government adopting open standards in its technology that eschew the lock-in from vendor-specific technologies.

Chapter 34, *Case Study: Utah.gov*

David Fletcher takes a tour through the most transparent state in the United States and explores the history as well as the future of Utah. As Utah's CIO, Fletcher is in the thick of making government open.

Appendix, *Memo from President Obama on Transparency and Open Government*
    The full text of President Obama's memo.

Safari® Books Online

Safari Books Online is an on-demand digital library that lets you easily search over 7,500 technology and creative reference books and videos to find the answers you need quickly.

With a subscription, you can read any page and watch any video from our library online. Read books on your cell phone and mobile devices. Access new titles before they are available for print, and get exclusive access to manuscripts in development and post feedback for the authors. Copy and paste code samples, organize your favorites, download chapters, bookmark key sections, create notes, print out pages, and benefit from tons of other time-saving features.

O'Reilly Media has uploaded this book to the Safari Books Online service. To have full digital access to this book and others on similar topics from O'Reilly and other publishers, sign up for free at *http://my.safaribooksonline.com*.

How to Contact Us

Please address comments and questions concerning this book to the publisher:

> O'Reilly Media, Inc.
> 1005 Gravenstein Highway North
> Sebastopol, CA 95472
> 800-998-9938 (in the United States or Canada)
> 707-829-0515 (international or local)
> 707-829-0104 (fax)

We have a web page for this book, where we list errata, examples, and any additional information. You can access this page at:

> *http://oreilly.com/catalog/9780596804350*

To comment or ask technical questions about this book, send email to:

> *bookquestions@oreilly.com*

For more information about our books, conferences, Resource Centers, and the O'Reilly Network, see our website at:

> *http://oreilly.com*

Acknowledgments

The road to open government is a long one, and over the years many people have contributed to and continue to define its evolution. As John Heywood said, "Many hands make light work."

Daniel Lathrop and Laurel Ruma would like to thank all of the authors for contributing to a fascinating book. The time required to write and revise a chapter is not trivial, and very much appreciated. There were also many other people who worked on this book, including Yasmin Fodil, Sarah Granger, and Kevin Novak, who reviewed and commented on the manuscript. Andy Oram provided invaluable feedback and support. At O'Reilly, Audrey Doyle, Sarah Schneider, Nellie McKesson, Rob Romano, and Julie Steele guided the book through production.

CHAPTER ONE

A Peace Corps for Programmers

Matthew Burton

The federal government should fire me. Like the thousands of other contractors who develop software for government agencies, I am slow, overpaid, and out of touch with the needs of my customers. And I'm keeping the government from innovating.

In recent years, the government has become almost completely dependent upon contractors for information technology (IT). So deep is this dependency that the government has found itself in a position that may shock those in the tech industry: it has no programmers of its own; code is almost entirely outsourced. Government leaders clearly consider IT an ancillary function that can be offloaded for someone else to worry about.

But they should worry. Because while they were pushing the responsibility for IT into the margins, the role of IT became increasingly central to every agency's business. Computing might have been ancillary 20 years ago, when the only computers were the mainframes in the basement. Average employees never had to worry about them. But today, a computer is on the desk of every civil servant. Those servants rely on their computers to do their jobs effectively. Every day, they encounter new problems that could be quickly solved with a bit of web savvy, were there only a programmer there to help.

And they desperately do need help. Imagine not having Google to quickly find information; no Facebook or LinkedIn to find new colleagues; no instant messaging to communicate with those colleagues once you found them. Imagine having to ask for permission every time you wanted to publish content online, instead of being able to do it quickly and easily with a wiki or weblog. This is the state of computing in the federal government.

A TRUE STORY

On top of keeping the government from innovating, the dependence on contractors hurts the country in much more tangible ways. In February 2003, a few weeks into my job as an intelligence analyst with the Department of Defense (DoD), the Federal Republic of Yugoslavia officially changed its name to Serbia and Montenegro. My job was to maintain an enormous database of facilities in Eastern Europe, including labeling each one with a country name. But the tool we used didn't have an option for "Serbia and Montenegro," so on the day of the name change, I emailed the contract officer in charge of the database with a simple request: "This country changed its name. Could you please update the tool to reflect this?"

Doing so would have taken a computer programmer less than five minutes. But instead, he used that time to respond to my email:

"We'll consider it for the next version."

In other words, his current contract—written months prior—didn't account for changes in the geopolitical landscape, so there was no paperwork explicitly authorizing him to make this change. To do it, he would have to wait until the contract was renewed (months or years from now) and the government allotted funds for this five-minute job. It wasn't his fault; he was no doubt aware of how easy it was to make this change. But doing it without permission from either his boss or the government would spell trouble. Yugoslavia didn't exist anymore. Except inside our office, where we had to wait for a contract to make it so.

The government can no longer afford to outsource IT. It is core to the government's business. If the government intends to do IT right, it should wean itself from outsiders like me and start doing the job itself.

What's so wrong with contractors? Nothing, really; the problem is the processes they have given rise to. The pervading philosophy is that government is slow, inefficient, and incapable of quickly adapting to change, while private companies do things better, faster, and cheaper. In many cases, this is true; the government is by no means a well-oiled machine. But software is one thing that contracts do not speed up. Software developed under contract is much slower and much more expensive than any other form of software development still in practice. Here is how the typical IT contract evolves:

1. A low-level government employee complains to her boss about a problem. This could be anything from a bug in an existing piece of software to a gaping hole in her agency's IT security. The boss has no programmers on hand to solve the problem, so he dismisses it.

2. More and more people complain about the problem until it gets attention from higher levels. But even thinking about a solution is expensive—months of paperwork must come

before a contract is awarded and someone finally starts writing code—so the problem remains unsolved.

3. The problem leads to a calamity—a website is hacked, classified information is stolen, or electronic voting booths break down on Election Day—and leaders are finally motivated to solve the problem.

4. Procurement officers write a list of requirements for the ideal solution. Because they have little direct experience with the problem, they survey the workforce to get a sense of what's needed.

5. The workforce's version of the problem is condensed into a document called a Request for Proposals, or RFP. The RFP is then distributed to potential bidders, who will respond with a proposed solution and a bid based entirely on the contents of the RFP. Contractors cannot go directly to the users, the people who know the problem best. The RFP is therefore an indirect, highly edited communiqué from the user to the contractor, a substitute for the invaluable direct interaction between user and coder that guides any successful software product. But it's too late: contractors are from here on out trying to solve what they believe the problem to be, not the problem that really is.

6. The contract is awarded. Months or years after the problem was first noticed, the first line of code is written. Over the coming months, the winning bidder will develop the solution off-site, hidden from the eventual users who could be providing valuable feedback.

7. The solution is delivered. Because the target users had such a small part in the development process, the solution falls short. It is hard to use and comes with an 80-page manual.

It should now be clear why the government is so far behind the times: it isn't allowed to solve its own problems, relying instead on people who do not understand them. Two glaring faults doom the contracting process to failure. First, the development process is vastly different from that of today's most popular software. Modern web applications are persistently watching their users and adjusting their code to make it faster and more user-friendly. Adventurous users can begin using these applications before they're even finished, giving the developers invaluable insight into their users' preferences. Without this constant feedback, the developers risk spending years on a product in private, only to reveal it to the public and find that nobody wants to use it. Such products are so common in government that they have earned their own moniker, named for their eternal home: shelfware.

Second, the paperwork required to simply start coding takes time and money. So, to even consider solutions, the problem has to be severe enough to justify months of bureaucracy. Why go through all that trouble just for a problem that would take a week to solve? The logic makes the taxpayer ill: the bureaucracy actually wants high price tags. The result is an organization full of easy problems that get no attention until they are big, expensive, and ready to boil over.

Tipping Point: The Extinction of Pencils

One such problem that may soon boil over is the terrorist watch list. For years, the list—created to monitor suspected terrorists and keep them from flying on commercial airliners—had inconvenienced innocent travelers. The problems were evident, but they weren't bad enough to justify asking for help.

Then a toddler was kept from boarding a flight. Then a senator. At some point, this problem crossed the threshold, and the government issued an RFP for an improved database to manage the list. The $500 million contract was awarded to Boeing and a smaller company. After months of development, a congressional investigation discovered that the soon-to-be-deployed database could not perform basic searches for names, and was missing huge stores of valuable data. The National Counterterrorism Center had spent half a billion dollars on a tool that, while certainly complex, could not do things that you and I do every day from our home computers.

Why so much money for something that seems so simple? This frame of mind—that technology projects should be big, expensive, and time-consuming—has honest beginnings. Twenty years ago, computing was a niche. The government used computers to encrypt the president's phone calls, simulate nuclear blasts, and predict the weather. The government paid private companies lots of money to build very complex systems. That's OK, because tasks such as these required lots of computing power, so the biggest, baddest, most expensive system was usually the best. It didn't matter that these systems were hard to use, because the only people using them were computer scientists. The builder of the system understood the user—the builder and user may have even worked side by side—and if the user ever needed the system to do something it couldn't, that user probably had the skills to tweak the system. Computers were left to the computer people. Everyone else still used pencils.

But computing is now everywhere. Computers long ago fit on our desktops. Now they fit in our palms. But the government still acts like computers fill basements, and if you could sit down at a government desktop, this outdated mindset would be immediately apparent: on the screen would be websites reminiscent of the mid-1990s, without any of the web-based productivity and collaboration tools that define today's Web. Expensive supercomputers still matter. But so do cheap, light web applications. Small, unassuming tools can change the way an organization does business. Such tools are commonplace online, but they do not get a second look from a government that expects and needs its technology to be expensive. Meanwhile, independent developers are at their keyboards, proving themselves willing to help a government that, as we'll see, is slowly opening its arms to them.

Competition Is Critical to Any Ecosystem

One of the reasons the Web has better tools than the government is competition.

Take airfare as an example. There are countless websites that help you buy plane tickets, each of them constantly improving their tools and layouts to make you happier. And if you aren't happy with those sites, you're free to start your own business and compete with them. But when the government contracts new software, it gets only one product out of it. Instead of many choices, users have only two: use this tool, or use nothing.

Web developers know that the first attempt at an innovation almost never works, and that it takes many attempts before someone gets it right. For every Facebook, there are countless Friendsters. Given one chance, you'll likely end up with one of the latter. If the government wants better software, it has to start creating and acquiring *more* software.

In the past year, two promising government projects have chipped away at this problem. Washington, D.C.'s Apps for Democracy competition* let independent developers build web applications for a shot at prize money. The D.C. government's $50,000 investment bought it 40 tools in 30 days. The District got to keep every contribution but only paid for the really good ones.

Meanwhile, the U.S. Intelligence Community is becoming an unexpected leader in engaging everyday developers. To provide more analytic tools to their workforce, they have released BRIDGE,† an open development platform akin to Facebook's: now, any software developer can build a tool and provide it to intelligence analysts. If the analysts like it, the government buys it. If it's junk, your tax dollars are saved.

This approach worked for Facebook: it gained 30,000 new tools in two years, and got other people to do all the work. Most of these new tools fall into the junk category, but many others are invaluable. The community finds the good ones and makes them more visible. It is the same principle that governs our economy: we buy the dish soap that works, and the bad ones go away. We should expect the same practice from our government, whose very job is the promotion of market economies and democracy. Apps for Democracy and BRIDGE are a welcome departure from contract-based software.

But while these projects are giving government employees more options, they haven't filled in all the gaps. Who will maintain software that was built not by a global firm, but by an independent developer who is juggling multiple projects?

And what about user feedback? Neither of these projects addresses the fact that government software is built by people unfamiliar with government users. Apps for Democracy produced useful tools for D.C. residents, but little for D.C. employees. And applications on the Intelligence Community platform are hobbled by the world's biggest firewall: intelligence analysts use these tools on a top-secret network that doesn't allow them to communicate with the outside world. As long as the government keeps developers outside its walls, those developers have no hope of solving the government's technology problems. The civil service needs an infusion of technical talent. The civil service needs *intel techs*.

* *http://www.appsfordemocracy.org/*

† *http://about.bridge-ic.net*

Creating a Developer Corps

Decades ago, the intel tech (also known as "mission support" at some agencies) was a specialist in the Intelligence Community who helped analysts with now-defunct technologies: setting up the light table to look at satellite imagery, making mimeographs, and so on. Unlike today's tech support staff who sit in the basement or in Bombay, these experts sat among the analysts and were solely dedicated to the analysts' mission. And because they were government employees, they were at the analysts' disposal whenever help was needed.

But then personal computers arrived. Software made the intel techs' tools obsolete. The light tables vanished. The intel techs soon followed. It is the opposite of what should have happened: IT's role in intelligence analysis—and every other government function—has grown tremendously, while the government's in-house technical talent has dwindled. Government employees' need for technical help has never been greater, but there is nobody there to help them.

If they still existed, today's intel techs would be developers. They would be deploying web applications for new needs the moment they arose. They would mash up data and make it easier for both civil servants and private citizens to consume. They would do the things that contractors do today, only immediately—no paperwork necessary—and with users at their side. The intel tech must be resurrected for the Internet age. The government must hire web developers and embed them in the federal bureaucracy.

The government needs to hire the people who have been fueling the web application boom for the past 10 years. They are young programmers who created revolutionary tools from their dorm rooms, and they are small firms with virtual offices who stumbled upon a new way of doing business. The trouble is, most of these people are not compatible with government culture. They like working from p.m. to a.m. They don't like ties. They seek venture capital, not pay grade bumps. Are they supposed to move from one coast to another and indefinitely trade in their lifestyles for something completely different, not knowing when they would return to their old lives? That is asking too much.

But what if these in-house developers weren't standard government hires on entry-level salaries? What if their time in the government wasn't a career, but a mission akin to a term in the Peace Corps or Teach For America? A program marketed and structured as a temporary "time abroad" would let developers help their country without giving up their careers and identities.

Now is the perfect time for such a program. Silicon Valley's interest in D.C. has never been as great as it is now. Technology icons are encouraging developers to quit creating banal tools and instead put their energy into things that matter. And it's working: several prominent Internet entrepreneurs have become full-time civil servants. Many more have contributed software tools to programs such as Apps for Democracy and BRIDGE. Apps for America‡—a federal take on Apps for Democracy sponsored by the nonprofit Sunlight Foundation—received 34 submissions during its first iteration, and 46 more on the second. Geeks want to help government. The government just has to give them the right invitation.

Like the Peace Corps and Teach For America, terms in the Developer Corps would have a time limit. Whether this limit is six months or six years, I do not know. But a limit of some kind is important. First, it will be easier for developers to make the leap if they know they will eventually return to their current careers.

Second, being detached from an agency's pay scale and career plan will give the participants the freedom to experiment and—more importantly—to fail. Failure is a key part of innovation. Technology firms know this, and their employees are used to working in atmospheres that encourage failure. If they don't try new things, they'll be killed by their competition.

Not so in government. Unlike private companies, a government—at least ours—is relatively safe from competition, and thus doesn't feel the need to be constantly reinventing itself. Things are fine how they are. The populace views failed government projects as little more than a waste of taxpayer dollars. No career-conscious government employee wants to take on such a risk. So, to succeed, the Developer Corps' participants must have the same freedom to fail that they did in their former jobs. The knowledge that their terms will end on a set date will quell the fear of failure that plagues the average government employee.

The greatest threat to this program is lack of permission. If red tape keeps developers from being productive, they will end up wasting their time fixing printer jams instead of writing code.

Developers work quickly. They can implement ideas within hours of conceiving them, continuously deploying, checking, modifying, and redeploying their code dozens, hundreds, thousands of times along the way. Doing this never requires anyone's approval. But within each government agency are multiple offices that must vet code before it is deployed: system administrators, information security officers, lawyers, and so forth.

Developers will never get anything done with such thick bureaucratic walls between them and their work. Wasting their talent is the fastest way to destroy the corp's reputation. They must be given authority to code what they please. Not all agencies will grant this authority. Such agencies must not be allowed to participate in the Developer Corps. (Participants in restrictive environments would never get anything done anyway, so there is no harm in barring uncooperative agencies.)

Finally, this program should take a page from a new organization called Code for America (*http://codeforamerica.org*). CFA recruits coders to work with government offices for set terms, but at the municipal level instead of federal. About to enter its inaugural iteration, CFA's participants will work with their respective governments remotely from a shared space in

‡ *http://www.sunlightlabs.com/contests/appsforamerica/*

California. This communal coding environment will let participants enjoy networking events, guest speakers, and the creative energy generated by each other's ideas.

The federal program I've proposed in this chapter should incorporate a similar communal environment. While coders will spend their days at their respective government agencies, group housing will let them discuss their work over dinner and drinks, allowing the creative process to continue after hours. And select days could be dedicated to meetings with government leaders and tech luminaries, visits to other agencies, and networking. Such events will help ensure a D.C. term is a boost to a coder's career instead of diversion from it.

Conclusion

Our government agencies need the ability to develop their own software. Keeping them from doing so prevents them from providing vital services that we all pay for. No story makes the case for this capability better than that of Jim Gray.

Gray was a technology pioneer who, during a sailing trip in early 2007, disappeared off the coast of San Francisco. The Coast Guard searched for him for three days and could not find him. They called off their search.

But a group of determined people kept looking. They had imagery satellites take fresh pictures of a swatch of sea outside the San Francisco Bay. If Gray was out there, he and his boat were now on film. But they were left with hundreds of photos, each big enough to cover a wall. A handful of people could never review the images in time to save Gray. So, a team of software developers converted those large photos into lots of smaller ones, which were then posted to a website where the public could review them. Clicking on a possible sighting sent a report to a flight crew, which then searched the area in question. Noticing that the images were blurry, another team of programmers contributed code that automatically sharpened the images. The entire system was created from scratch in just a few days. And it was done without any help from the government.

This effort was coordinated entirely by private citizens with the help of publicly available technology. Though he was never found, Gray inspired the largest collaborative search party in history. Twelve thousand private citizens reviewed more than half a million images. It is an amazing story of teamwork and ingenuity. Inspiring. Soul-stirring.

But also frustrating: why didn't our government do this the moment Gray was reported missing?

It is tempting to use this story as a case for more self-governance: if the public can do it and the government can't, why not go with it? Instead of equipping the government to do what private citizens already can, let's just do their jobs for them from our home computers.

The Web has made it simple to form ad hoc groups and coordinate their actions, and we will continue to see cases where such groups fill the government's shoes. But such cases will not be the norm. Our populace cannot govern itself just yet. There are too many critical functions that we cannot yet take over. We do not have battleships. We cannot run elections. Some private citizens guard our borders, but that doesn't mean they should.

We will need a formal government for the foreseeable future. Our government should be at least as capable as a quickly organized group of virtual volunteers. It will certainly have the budget for it.

About the Author

 **MATTHEW BURTON** is a web entrepreneur and technology writer. He was an intelligence analyst at the Defense Intelligence Agency from 2003 to 2005, and now advises the Intelligence Community on information sharing and online collaboration. He lives in Brooklyn, NY.

CHAPTER TWO

Government As a Platform

Tim O'Reilly

During the past 15 years, the World Wide Web has created remarkable new methods for harnessing the creativity of people in groups, and in the process has created powerful business models that are reshaping our economy. As the Web has undermined old media and software companies, it has demonstrated the enormous power of a new approach, often referred to as Web 2.0. In a nutshell: the secret to the success of bellwethers like Google, Amazon, eBay, Craigslist, Wikipedia, Facebook, and Twitter is that each of these sites, in its own way, has learned to harness the power of its users to add value to—no, more than that, to co-create— its offerings.

Now, a new generation has come of age with the Web, and it is committed to using its lessons of creativity and collaboration to address challenges facing our country and the world. Meanwhile, with the proliferation of issues and not enough resources to address them all, many government leaders recognize the opportunities Web 2.0 technologies provide not just to help them get elected, but to help them do a better job. By analogy, many are calling this movement *Government 2.0*.

What the heck does that mean?

Much like its predecessor, Web 2.0, "Government 2.0" is a chameleon, a white rabbit term, that seems to be used by people to mean whatever they want it to mean. For some, it is the use of social media by government agencies. For others, it is government transparency, especially as aided by government-provided data APIs. Still others think of it as the adoption of cloud computing, wikis, crowdsourcing, mobile applications, mashups, developer contests, or all of the other epiphenomena of Web 2.0 as applied to the job of government.

All of these ideas seem important, but none of them seem to get to the heart of the matter.

Web 2.0 was not a new version of the World Wide Web; it was a renaissance after the dark ages of the dotcom bust, a rediscovery of the power hidden in the original design of the World Wide Web. Similarly, Government 2.0 is not a new kind of government; it is government stripped down to its core, rediscovered and reimagined as if for the first time.

And in that reimagining, this is the idea that becomes clear: government is, at bottom, a mechanism for collective action. We band together, make laws, pay taxes, and build the institutions of government to manage problems that are too large for us individually and whose solution is in our common interest.

Government 2.0, then, is the use of technology—especially the collaborative technologies at the heart of Web 2.0—to better solve collective problems at a city, state, national, and international level.

The hope is that Internet technologies will allow us to rebuild the kind of participatory government envisioned by our nation's founders, in which, as Thomas Jefferson wrote in a letter to Joseph Cabell, "every man...feels that he is a participator in the government of affairs, not merely at an election one day in the year, but every day."*

As President Obama explained the idea during his campaign: "We must use all available technologies and methods to open up the federal government, creating a new level of transparency to change the way business is conducted in Washington, and giving Americans the chance to participate in government deliberations and decision making in ways that were not possible only a few years ago."

Allowing citizens to see and share in the deliberations of government and creating a "new level of transparency" are remarkable and ambitious goals, and would indeed "change the way business is conducted in Washington." Yet these goals do not go far enough.

Government As a Platform

There is a new compact on the horizon: information produced by and on behalf of citizens is the lifeblood of the economy and the nation; government has a responsibility to treat that information as a national asset. Citizens are connected like never before and have the skill sets and passion to solve problems affecting them locally as well as nationally. Government information and services can be provided to citizens where and when they need them. Citizens are empowered to spark the innovation that will result in an improved approach to

---

* *The Founders' Constitution*, Chapter 4, Document 34 (*http://press-pubs.uchicago.edu/founders/documents/ v1ch4s34.html*).

governance. In this model, government is a convener and an enabler rather than the first mover of civic action.

This is a radical departure from the existing model of government, which Donald Kettl so aptly named "vending machine government."[†] We pay our taxes, we expect services. And when we don't get what we expect, our "participation" is limited to protest—essentially, shaking the vending machine. Collective action has been watered down to collective complaint. (Kettl used the vending machine analogy in a very different way, to distinguish between the routine operation of government and the solution of new and extraordinary problems, but I owe him credit for the image nonetheless.)

What if, instead of a vending machine, we thought of government as the manager of a marketplace? In *The Cathedral & the Bazaar*, Eric Raymond uses the image of a bazaar to contrast the collaborative development model of open source software with traditional software development, but the analogy is equally applicable to government.[‡] In the vending machine model, the full menu of available services is determined beforehand. A small number of vendors have the ability to get their products into the machine, and as a result, the choices are limited, and the prices are high. A bazaar, by contrast, is a place where the community itself exchanges goods and services.

But not all bazaars are created equal. Some are sorry affairs, with not much more choice than the vending machine, while others are vibrant marketplaces in which many merchants compete to provide the same goods and services, bringing an abundance of choice as well as lower prices.

In the technology world, the equivalent of a thriving bazaar is a successful platform. If you look at the history of the computer industry, the innovations that define each era are frameworks that enabled a whole ecosystem of participation from companies large and small. The personal computer was such a platform. So was the World Wide Web. This same platform dynamic is playing out right now in the recent success of the Apple iPhone. Where other phones have had a limited menu of applications developed by the phone vendor and a few carefully chosen partners, Apple built a framework that allowed virtually anyone to build applications for the phone, leading to an explosion of creativity, with more than 100,000 applications appearing for the phone in little more than 18 months, and more than 3,000 new ones now appearing every week.[§]

This is the right way to frame the question of Government 2.0. How does government become an open platform that allows people inside and outside government to innovate? How do you design a system in which all of the outcomes aren't specified beforehand, but instead evolve

---

[†] *The Next Government of the United States: Why Our Institutions Fail Us and How to Fix Them*, Donald Kettl, W. W. Norton & Company, 2008.

[‡] *The Cathedral & the Bazaar*, Eric Raymond, O'Reilly, 1999.

[§] *http://radar.oreilly.com/2009/07/itunes-app-store-incubation-period-increases.html*

through interactions between government and its citizens, as a service provider enabling its user community?

This chapter focuses primarily on the application of platform thinking to government technology projects. But it is worth noting that the idea of government as a platform applies to every aspect of the government's role in society. For example, the Federal-Aid Highway Act of 1956 (*http://en.wikipedia.org/wiki/Federal_Aid_Highway_Act_of_1956*), which committed the United States to building an interstate highway system, was a triumph of platform thinking, a key investment in facilities that had a huge economic and social multiplier effect. Though government builds the network of roads that tie our cities together, it does not operate the factories, farms, and businesses that use that network: that opportunity is afforded to "we the people." Government does set policies for the use of those roads, regulating interstate commerce, levying gasoline taxes and fees on heavy vehicles that damage the roads, setting and policing speed limits, specifying criteria for the safety of bridges, tunnels, and even vehicles that travel on the roads, and performing many other responsibilities appropriate to a "platform provider."

While it has become common to ridicule the 1990s description of the Internet as the "information superhighway," the analogy is actually quite apt. Like the Internet, the road system is a "network of networks," in which national, state, local, and private roads all interconnect, for the most part without restrictive fees. We have the same rules of the road everywhere in the country, yet anyone, down to a local landowner adding a driveway to an unimproved lot, can connect to the nation's system of roads.

The launch of weather, communications, and positioning satellites is a similar exercise of platform strategy. When you use a car navigation system to guide you to your destination, you are using an application built on the government platform, extended and enriched by massive private sector investment. When you check the weather—on TV or on the Internet—you are using applications built using the National Weather Service (or equivalent services in other countries) as a platform. Until recently, the private sector had neither the resources nor the incentives to create space-based infrastructure. Government as a platform provider created capabilities that enrich the possibilities for subsequent private sector investment.

There are other areas where the appropriate role of the platform provider and the marketplace of application providers is less clear. Health care is a contentious example. Should the government be providing health care or leaving it to the private sector? The answer is in the outcomes. If the private sector is doing a good job of providing necessary services that lead to the overall increase in the vitality of the country, government should stay out. But just as the interstate highway system increased the vitality of our transportation infrastructure, it is certainly possible that greater government involvement in health care could do the same. But if the lesson is correctly learned, it should do so not by competing with the private sector to deliver health services, but by investing in infrastructure (and "rules of the road") that will lead to a more robust private sector ecosystem.

At the same time, platforms always require choices, and those choices must be periodically revisited. Platforms lose their power when they fail to adapt. The U.S. investment in the highway system helped to vitiate our railroads, shaping a society of automobiles and suburbs. Today, we need to rethink the culture of sprawl and fossil fuel use that platform choice encouraged. A platform that once seemed so generative of positive outcomes can become a dead weight over time.

Police, fire services, garbage collection: these are fundamental platform services, just like analogous services in computer operating systems. And of course, here we have an "antipattern" from technology platforms: the failure to provide security, for example, as a fundamental system service, leaving it instead to the "private sector" of application vendors, has imposed a huge downstream cost on the technology ecosystem. See Chapter 5 for more on antipatterns.

The question of Government 2.0, then, is this: if government is a platform, how can we use technology to make it into a better platform?

This question allows us to fruitfully extend the platform metaphor and ask: what lessons can government take from the success of computer platforms, as it tries to harness the power of technology to remake government?

Lesson 1: Open Standards Spark Innovation and Growth

Time and again, the platforms that are the most generative of new economic activity are those that are the most open. The modern era in computing began in 1981 when IBM published the specifications for a personal computer that anyone could build using off-the-shelf parts. Prior to the introduction of the PC, IBM had a stranglehold on the computer market. It was a valuable but limited market, with very few vendors serving a small number of very big customers.

After the introduction of the PC, barriers to market entry were so low that Michael Dell, a Texas college student, was able to start what became a multibillion dollar company out of his dorm room. The market for personal computers exploded. IBM had estimated a total of 245,000 PCs would be sold over five years; as we now know, the eventual market size was in the billions, as scrappy little companies like Microsoft worked to put "a computer on every desk and in every home."∥

At the same time, the standardization of the personal computer led to unexpected consequences: software became a higher-margin business than hardware; industry power shifted from IBM to Microsoft.

In its early years, Microsoft triumphed by establishing the best platform for independent software developers. Just as the standard architecture of the IBM PC lowered the barriers to

∥ *http://www.microsoft.com/about/companyinformation/ourbusinesses/profile.mspx*

marketplace entry by hardware manufacturers, the standardized APIs of MS-DOS and, later, Microsoft Windows made it easy for developers to "add value" to the personal computer.

Over time, Microsoft began to abuse their market power as the platform provider to give advantage to their own applications. At that point, the PC software marketplace became less and less vibrant, with most of the profits accruing to a few dominant companies. As a result, many people mistakenly take the lesson from the PC era that owning a platform is the secret of marketplace control and outsized profits.

In fact, by 1995, the PC era had run out of gas. The PC became less and less like a bazaar and more and more like a vending machine. We'd moved from the open personal computer as the platform to the closed and tightly controlled Microsoft Windows as the platform. When one vendor controls the platform, innovation suffers.

What reinvigorated the industry was a new open platform: the Internet, and more specifically, the World Wide Web. Both were radically decentralized—a set of rules for programs to cooperate and communicate, with applications provided by anyone who had a good idea and the skills to write one. Once again, barriers to marketplace entry were low, with multibillion dollar companies created out of college dorm rooms, and tens of thousands of companies competing to provide previously unimaginable new services. The bazaar was back.

We see the same dynamic playing out today in the cell phone market. Cell phone providers have traditionally operated on the vending machine model. Apple changed the rules of the game with the iPhone developer platform. Suddenly, anyone could develop smartphone applications.

The smartphone platform story is perhaps the one most comforting to those inside government. Unlike the IBM PC or the Internet, the Apple iPhone is not a completely uncontrolled Wild West. Apple actively manages the platform to encourage innovation and choice while enforcing clear rules. Some observers believe that over time, the iPhone platform will not prove open enough, and will be superseded by other, more open platforms. But for the moment, Apple appears to be creating an effective balance between control and what Jonathan Zittrain calls *generativity*.#

There are two lessons for government in these stories. The first is the extraordinary power of open standards to foster innovation. When the barriers to entry to a market are low, entrepreneurs are free to invent the future. When barriers are high, innovation moves elsewhere. The second is that vibrant platforms become less generative over time, usually because the platform vendor has begun to compete with its developer ecosystem.

Some readers may take the lesson to be that government plays an important role in antitrust enforcement, keeping a level playing field. Facing the crises of the day, from banking to health care, we see a story in which entrenched players have grown large and have used their resulting

---

The Future of the Internet—And How to Stop It, Jonathan Zittrain, Yale University Press, 2008.

power to remove choice from the marketplace, extracting outsized profits not by creating value but by cornering it.

There may be an "antitrust 2.0" alternative. Rather than simply limiting the size or power of an entrenched player, can government insistence on openness and interoperability be used to cause a "market reset," through which innovation can once again flourish? Antitrust actions against Microsoft were focused on existing business models, yet the real competition for Microsoft came not from other businesses selling software, but from an entirely new class of advertising-based business models that were invented in the initially noncommercial, wide-open spaces of the World Wide Web.

One of the most important ways that government can promote competition is not through after-the-fact antitrust enforcement but by encouraging more innovation. And as has been argued here, the best way to do that is with open standards. So, for example, faced with the race by major players to dominate the emerging world of cloud computing, the government can forestall the risk of single-player dominance by throwing its weight behind open standards and interoperability in cloud computing. And in fact, this is just what we're seeing. The recent General Services Administration (GSA) Infrastructure as a Service (IaaS) solicitation devoted 5 of its 25 questions to vendors to the subject of interoperability:[*]

> 5 Please address the following Interoperability and Portability questions:
>
> 5.1 Describe your recommendations regarding "cloud-to-cloud" communication and ensuring interoperability of cloud solutions.
>
> 5.2 Describe your experience in weaving together multiple different cloud computing services offered by you, if any, or by other vendors.
>
> 5.3 As part of your service offering, describe the tools you support for integrating with other vendors in terms of monitoring and managing multiple cloud computing services.
>
> 5.4 Please explain application portability; i.e., exit strategy for applications running in your cloud, should it be necessary to vacate.
>
> 5.5 Describe how you prevent vendor lock in.

The recent U.S. Department of Defense guidance on the use of open source software by the military is a similar move that uses open standards to enhance competition.[†] The government's move to push for open patient records[‡] also recognizes the power of open standards to promote innovation and bring down costs. And of course, the White House's Data.gov initiative (*http://www.data.gov*), a portal for open APIs to government data, takes this idea to a new level.

---

[*] *https://www.fbo.gov/index?tab=core&s=opportunity&mode=form&id=d208ac8b8687dd9c6921d2633603aedb&tabmode=list&cck=1&au=&ck=*

[†] *http://radar.oreilly.com/2009/10/defense-department-releases-op.html*

[‡] *http://healthit.hhs.gov/blog/faca/*

In considering how open, generative systems eventually become closed over time, losing their innovative spark in the process, there is also a lesson for government itself. Figure 2-1 shows the rising share of the U.S. gross domestic product consumed by all levels of government during the past 100 years.

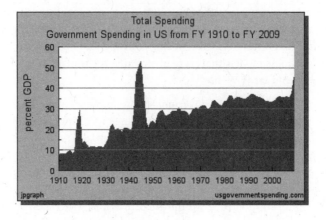

FIGURE 2-1. Government spending as percent of GDP since 1910

As a platform provider, when does government stop being generative, and when does it start to compete with the private sector? When do its decisions raise barriers to marketplace entry rather than reduce them? What programs or functions that were used to bootstrap a new market are now getting in the way? There is no Justice Department that can bring an antitrust action against government; there is no Schumpeterian "creative destruction"[§] to bring unneeded government programs to an end. Government 2.0 will require deep thinking about how to end programs that no longer work, and how to use the platform power of the government not to extend government's reach, but instead, how to use it to better enable its citizenry and its economy.

Lesson 2: Build a Simple System and Let It Evolve

In one of the early classics of software engineering, *Systemantics*, John Gall wrote: "A complex system that works is invariably found to have evolved from a simple system that worked. The inverse proposition also appears to be true. A complex system designed from scratch never works and cannot be made to work. You have to start over beginning with a working simple system."[‖]

Again, the Internet is a case in point. In the 1980s, an international standards committee got together to define the future of computer networking. The Open Systems Interconnect (OSI)

§ *http://en.wikipedia.org/wiki/Creative_destruction*

‖ *Systemantics: How Systems Work and Especially How They Fail*, John Gall, Quadrangle, 1977.

model was comprehensive and complete, and one of the industry pundits of the day wrote, in 1986:#

> Over the long haul, most vendors are going to migrate from TCP/IP to support Layer 4, the transport layer of the OSI model. For the short term, however, TCP/IP provides organizations with enough functionality to protect their existing equipment investment and over the long term, TCP/IP promises to allow for easy migration to OSI.

Au contraire. It was the profoundly simple protocols of the Internet that grew richer and more complex, while the OSI protocol stack became relegated to the status of an academic reference model used to describe network architecture.

Meanwhile, over on the TCP/IP standardization side, there was this wonderful, naive, glorious statement by Jon Postel in RFC 761:* "TCP implementation should follow a general principle of robustness. Be conservative in what you do. Be liberal in what you accept from others." It sounds like something out of the Bible, the Golden Rule as applied to computers. What a fabulous statement of philosophy! "We're not going to specify all of the details of how you interoperate; we're just going to say, 'Please do it.'"

Twitter is another good example of a fundamentally simple system. Jack Dorsey's original design sketch fit on a few lines of paper (see Figure 2-2). Much has grown from that sketch. There are now thousands of Twitter applications, precisely because the core Twitter service does so little. By thinking simple, Twitter allowed its users and an ecosystem of application developers to evolve new features and functionality. This is the essence of generativity.

Of course, in a government context when you say "build a simple system; let it evolve," that sounds like a real challenge. But let's remember that TCP/IP was a government-funded project. It can be done. The first step is getting a philosophy of simplicity into your work, understanding that designing foundations that others can build on is an important part of platform thinking. It's about creating the starting point, something that others can reuse and extend.

Designing simple systems is one of the great challenges of Government 2.0. It means the end of grand, feature-filled programs, and their replacement by minimal services extensible by others.

This quest for simplicity is one of the drivers behind Federal CIO Vivek Kundra's emphasis on Data.gov, a collection of APIs to government data. Kundra realizes that rather than having the government itself build out all of the websites and applications that use that data, providing application programming interfaces to the private sector will allow independent developers to come up with new uses for government data.

"TCP/IP: Stairway to OSI," Robert A. Moskowitz, *Computer Decisions*, April 22, 1986.

* DOD Standard: Transmission Control Protocol report (*http://tools.ietf.org/rfc/rfc761.txt*).

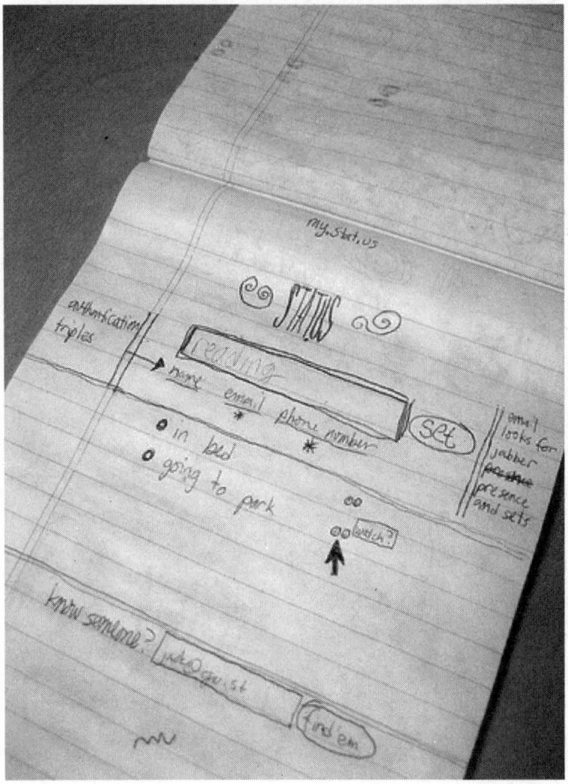

FIGURE 2-2. Jack Dorsey's original vision of Twitter

The rationale for Data.gov was laid out convincingly by David G. Robinson et al. in "Government Data and the Invisible Hand" (see Chapter 6 for an updated take on this), and the emphasis below is mine:†

> In the current Presidential cycle, all three candidates have indicated that they think the federal government could make better use of the Internet.... But the situation to which these candidates are responding—the wide gap between the exciting uses of Internet technology by private parties, on the one hand, and the government's lagging technical infrastructure on the other— is not new. The federal government has shown itself consistently unable to keep pace with the fast-evolving power of the Internet.

> In order for public data to benefit from the same innovation and dynamism that characterize private parties' use of the Internet, the federal government must reimagine its role as an

---

† "Government Data and the Invisible Hand," David G. Robinson, Harlan Yu, William Zeller, and Edward W. Felten, *Yale Journal of Law & Technology*, Vol. 11, 2009 (*http://papers.ssrn.com/sol3/papers.cfm?abstract_id =1138083*).

information provider. Rather than struggling, as it currently does, to design sites that meet each end-user need, *it should focus on creating a simple, reliable and publicly accessible infrastructure that "exposes" the underlying data.* Private actors, either nonprofit or commercial, are better suited to deliver government information to citizens and can constantly create and reshape the tools individuals use to find and leverage public data. The best way to ensure that the government allows private parties to compete on equal terms in the provision of government data is to *require that federal websites themselves use the same open systems for accessing the underlying data as they make available to the public at large.*

Our approach follows the engineering principle of separating data from interaction, which is commonly used in constructing websites. Government must provide data, but we argue that websites that provide interactive access for the public can best be built by private parties. This approach is especially important given recent advances in interaction, which go far beyond merely offering data for viewing, to offer services such as advanced search, automated content analysis, cross-indexing with other data sources, and data visualization tools. These tools are promising but it is far from obvious how best to combine them to maximize the public value of government data. Given this uncertainty, the best policy is not to hope government will choose the one best way, but to rely on private parties with their vibrant marketplace of engineering ideas to discover what works.

Data.gov reflects another key Gov 2.0 and Web 2.0 principle, namely that data is at the heart of Internet applications. But even here, the goal is not just to provide greater access to government data, but to establish a simple framework that makes it possible for the nation— the citizens, not just the government—to create and share useful data.

SERVICE-ORIENTED ARCHITECTURE AT AMAZON

Amazon revolutionized the computer world in 2006 with the introduction of its cloud computing platform: the Elastic Compute Cloud, or EC2; the Simple Storage Service, or S3; and a series of other related services that make it possible for developers to host their applications on the same infrastructure that Amazon itself uses.

Amazon's revolutionary business model included cheap, transparent, pay-as-you-go pricing without contracts or commitments, making launching a web application a completely self-service proposition. But what's perhaps more important was the architectural commitment Amazon had made over the previous five years to building a true service-oriented architecture.[‡] As Amazon Chief Technology Officer Werner Vogels described it in a 2008 *Information Week* interview:[§]

---

‡ *http://webservices.xml.com/pub/a/ws/2003/09/30/soa.html*

§ *http://www.informationweek.com/news/global-cio/interviews/showArticle.jhtml?articleID=212501404*

Each of those pieces that make up the e-commerce platform are actually separate services. Whether it's Sales Rank, or Listmania, or Recommendations, all of those are separate services. If you hit one of Amazon's pages, it goes out to between 250 and 300 services to build that page.

It's not just an architectural model, it's also organizational. Each service has a team associated with it that takes the reliability of that service and is responsible for the innovation of that service…. [W]e found that a lot of those teams were spending their time on the same kind of things. In essence, they were all spending time on managing infrastructure, and that was a byproduct of the organization that we had chosen, which was very decentralized.

So…we decided to go to a shared-services platform and that became the infrastructure services platform that we now know in the outside world as AWS [Amazon Web Services].

Amazon is a bellwether example of why Robinson et al. urge that "federal websites themselves use the same open systems for accessing the underlying data as they make available to the public at large." Amazon's ability to deliver low-cost web services to the public started with its own total embrace of an internal web services architecture, in which Amazon's own applications are based on the same services that they offer to the public.

Lesson 3: Design for Participation

Closely related to the idea of simplicity is the idea of designing for participation. Participatory systems are often remarkably simple—they have to be, or they just don't work. But when a system is designed from the ground up to consist of components developed by independent developers (in a government context, read countries, federal agencies, states, cities, private sector entities), magic happens.

Open source software projects like Linux and open systems like the Internet work not because there's a central board of approval making sure that all the pieces fit together but because the original designers of the system laid down clear rules for cooperation and interoperability. (Yes, there is some oversight: Linus Torvalds and his codevelopers manage the development of the Linux kernel; the Apache Software Foundation manages the development of Apache; the Internet Engineering Task Force [IETF] and the Internet Architecture Board develop and manage Internet standards; and the World Wide Web Consortium manages web standards. But there is little or no official coordination between any of these "local" governance mechanisms. The coordination is all in the design of the system itself.)

In the case of Unix, the original design on which Linux was based, the creators started out with a philosophy of small cooperating tools‖ with standardized inputs and outputs that could be assembled into pipelines. Rather than building complex solutions, they provided building

---

‖ *Unix Programming Environment*, Brian W. Kernighan and Rob Pike, Prentice Hall, 1984.

blocks, and defined how anyone could write additional building blocks of their own simply by following the same set of rules. This allowed Unix, and then Linux, to be an operating system literally created as an assemblage of thousands of different projects. While the Linux kernel, developed by Linus Torvalds, is the best-known part of the operating system and gave its name to the entire system, it is a tiny part of the overall code.

The Internet took a similar approach.

Tim Berners-Lee's first implementation of the World Wide Web is a great example of the Internet approach at work. Berners-Lee was a developer at CERN, the high energy physics lab in Switzerland, trying to figure out how to make collaboration easier between scientists. To do that, he simply wrote some code. He didn't have to get permission from some central design body. All he needed was one other site to install his server. And it grew from there. He built on top of existing platform components, the Internet Protocol, the Transmission Control Protocol, the Domain Name System, which were already part of the TCP/IP stack. What he defined in addition was HTTP, a protocol for web servers and clients to exchange documents, and HTML, the data format of those documents. He wrote a sample client and a sample server, both of which he put into the public domain. The industry has been off to the races ever since.

There were a number of key design breakthroughs in the World Wide Web's "architecture of participation":#

- The HTML syntax for formatting a web page was not embedded in a proprietary document format. Instead, HTML documents are ordinary, human-readable text files. What's more, every web browser includes a "View Source" menu command, which allows users to study and understand the formatting of web pages, and to copy innovative new features. Many early web pages weren't written from scratch, but were modifications of other people's pages.

- Anyone could link to any other page on the Web, without the permission or knowledge of the destination page's owner. This idea was the reversal of one taken for granted in previous hypertext systems, that links must always be two-way—an agreement between the parties, so to speak. If the document on the other end of a link goes away, an error (the famous "404" seen by any web surfer) appears, but no further action is taken. This tolerance of failure is a good example of Jon Postel's Robustness Principle at work.

Another way to frame the idea that anyone could link to any other web page without permission is to say that the Web was open "by default." That is, when developers design software, they make certain choices on behalf of their users about the way that software will work unless the user intervenes to change it. For example, in the design of the World Wide Web, it was possible to make web pages that were private and accessible only after login, but unless proactive steps were taken to hide it, any web page was visible to anyone else on the Internet.

http://www.oreillynet.com/pub/a/oreilly/tim/articles/architecture_of_participation.html

In many ways, the choice of "open by default" is the key to the breakaway success of many of the Internet's most successful sites. For example, early Internet photo-sharing sites asked their users to identify people with whom they'd like to share their photos. Flickr made "public" the default value for all photos, and soon became the gold standard for online photo sharing. Wikipedia allowed anyone to create and edit entries in their online encyclopedia, miraculously succeeding where more carefully curated online encyclopedias had failed. YouTube provided mechanisms whereby anyone could embed their videos on any web page, without coming to the central YouTube portal. Skype doesn't ask users for permission to share their bandwidth with other users, but the system is designed that way. Twitter took off because it allows anyone to follow status updates from anyone else (by default—you have to take an extra step to make your updates private), in stark contrast to previous social networks that required approval.

Cass Sunstein, now head of President Obama's Office of Information and Regulatory Affairs (*https://www.whitehouse.gov/omb/inforeg/*), is no stranger to the importance of default choices in public policy. In his book, *Nudge*, coauthored with economist Richard Thaler, he argues that "choice architecture" can help nudge people to make better decisions.[*] The most publicized policy proposal in the book was to make 401K participation "opt out" rather than "opt in" (i.e., participation by default), but the book is full of many other examples. As Sunstein and Thaler wrote:

> A choice architect has the responsibility for organizing the context in which people make decisions…. If you design the ballot voters use to choose candidates, you are a choice architect. If you are a doctor and must describe the alternative treatments available to a patient, you are a choice architect. If you design the form that new employees fill out to enroll in the company health plan, you are a choice architect. If you are a parent, describing possible educational options to your son or daughter, you are a choice architect.

And of course, if you are designing a government program, you are a choice architect. The ideas of Thaler and Sunstein have great relevance to areas such as agricultural policy (why are we subsidizing corn syrup when we face an obesity epidemic?); job creation (how do we encourage more entrepreneurs,[†] including immigrants?); health care (why does Medicare provide reimbursement for treatments that don't work?); and tax policy (where this concept is of course well understood, and the traditional bone of contention between America's political parties). Venture capitalist John Doerr's suggestion on immigration policy[‡] that we "staple a Green Card to the diploma of anyone that graduates with a degree in the physical sciences

---

[*] *Nudge: Improving Decisions About Health, Wealth, and Happiness*, Richard H. Thaler and Cass R. Sunstein, Penguin, 2009.

[†] *http://www.feld.com/wp/archives/2009/09/the-founders-visa-movement.html*

[‡] *http://blog.actonline.org/2008/11/doerr-staple-a-green-card-to-diplomas.html*

or engineering" is another example of how policy defaults could have an impact on innovation. Pigovian taxes[§] are another application of this principle to government.[||]

In the context of government as a platform, the key question is what architectures will lead to the most generative outcome. The goal is to design programs and supporting infrastructure that enable "we the people" to do most of the work.

A Robustness Principle for Government

President Obama's memorandum calling for transparent, participatory, collaborative government is also just a statement of philosophy (see the Appendix). But it's a statement of philosophy that's fundamentally actionable in the same way that the TCP robustness principle was, or the design rules that are the heart of Unix. And even though none of these things is a formal specification, it is a set of design principles that guide the design of the platform we are collectively trying to build.

It's important to think deeply about what the three design principles of transparency, participation, and collaboration mean in the context of technology.

For example, the word "transparency" can lead us astray as we think about the opportunity for Government 2.0. Yes, it's a good thing when government data is available so that journalists and watchdog groups like the Sunlight Foundation can disclose cost overruns in government projects or highlight the influence of lobbyists (see Chapter 17). But that's just the beginning. The magic of open data is that the same openness that enables transparency also enables innovation, as developers build applications that reuse government data in unexpected ways. Fortunately, Vivek Kundra and others in the administration understand this distinction, and are providing data for both purposes.

Likewise, we can be misled by the notion of participation to think that it's limited to having government decision-makers "get input" from citizens. This would be like thinking that enabling comments on a website is the beginning and end of social media! It's a trap for outsiders to think that Government 2.0 is a way to use new technology to amplify the voices of citizens to influence those in power, and by insiders as a way to harness and channel those voices to advance their causes.

Participation means true engagement with citizens in the business of government, and actual collaboration with citizens in the design of government programs. For example, the Open Government Brainstorming conducted by the White House is an attempt to truly engage citizens in the making of policy, not just to hear their opinions after the fact.[#]

§ *http://en.wikipedia.org/wiki/Pigovian_tax*

|| For an excellent summary of Thaler and Sunstein's ideas on government policy, see *Nudge-ocracy: Barack Obama's new theory of the state (http://www.tnr.com/article/politics/nudge-ocracy)*.

http://www.whitehouse.gov/blog/wrap-up-of-the-open-government-brainstormingparticipation/

Open government APIs enable a different kind of participation. When anyone can write a citizen-facing application using government data, software developers have an opportunity to create new interfaces to government.

Perhaps most interesting are applications and APIs that allow citizens to actually replace functions of government, in a self-service analogue to Craigslist. For example, FixMyStreet (*http://www.fixmystreet.com*), a project developed by UK nonprofit mySociety, made it possible for citizens to report potholes, broken streetlights, graffiti, and other problems that would otherwise have had to wait on an overworked government inspector. This concept has now been taken up widely by forward-thinking cities as well as entrepreneurial companies like SeeClickFix (*http://www.seeclickfix.com*), and there is even a standard—Open311 (*http://open311 .org/*)—for creating APIs to city services of this kind, so that third-party developers can create applications that will work not just for one city, but for every city.

Taking the idea of citizen self-service even further, you can imagine government using a platform like Meetup to support citizens in self-organizing to take on major projects that the government would otherwise leave undone. Today, there are thousands of civic-minded meetups around issues like beach, road, and waterway cleanups. How many more might there be if local governments themselves embraced the idea of harnessing and supporting citizen concerns as expressed by self-organized meetups?

DO IT OURSELVES: AN EXAMPLE FROM HAWAII

One of the most dramatic contemporary examples is a story reported by CNN, "Island DIY: Kauai residents don't wait for state to repair road":[*] "Their livelihood was being threatened, and they were tired of waiting for government help, so business owners and residents on Hawaii's Kauai island pulled together and completed a $4 million repair job to a state park—for free."

Especially striking in the story are the cost and time savings:

> "It would not have been open this summer, and it probably wouldn't be open next summer," said Bruce Pleas, a local surfer who helped organize the volunteers. "They said it would probably take two years. And with the way they are cutting funds, we felt like they'd never get the money to fix it."

> And if the repairs weren't made, some business owners faced the possibility of having to shut down....

> So Slack [owner of a kayak tour business in the park], other business owners and residents made the decision not to sit on their hands and wait for state money that many expected would never come. Instead, they pulled together machinery and manpower and hit the ground running March 23.

> And after only eight days, all of the repairs were done, Pleas said. It was a shockingly quick fix to a problem that may have taken much longer if they waited for state money to funnel in....

---

* *http://www.cnn.com/2009/US/04/09/hawaii.volunteers.repair/index.html*

> "We can wait around for the state or federal government to make this move, or we can go out and do our part," Slack said. "Just like everyone's sitting around waiting for a stimulus check, we were waiting for this but decided we couldn't wait anymore."

Now is the time for a renewal of our commitment to make our own institutions, our own communities, and our own difference. There's a kind of passivity even to most activism: collective action has come to mean collective complaint. Or at most, a collective effort to raise money. What the rebuilding of the washed-out road in Polihale State Park teaches us is that we can do more than that. We can rediscover the spirit of public service, and apply the DIY spirit on a civic scale. Scott Heiferman, the founder of Meetup.com, suggests going beyond the term DIY (Do It Yourself) to embrace a new spirit of DIO: Do It Ourselves!

Citizen self-organization is a powerful concept. It's worth remembering that early in our nation's history, many functions now handled by government were self-organized by citizens: militias, fire brigades, lending libraries, not to mention roads, harbors and bridges. And even today, volunteer fire departments play a major role in protecting many of our communities. Traditional communities still perform barn raisings. Those of us who spend our time on the Internet celebrate Wikipedia, but most of us have forgotten how to do crowdsourcing in the physical world.

EVERYONE HAS SOMETHING TO OFFER

The reflex exerted by government to gather new information, whether in pursuit of spreading around money for housing or planning its next steps in Afghanistan, is to convene an advisory committee of experts. A whole set of laws and regulations, such as the Federal Advisory Committee Act (FACA), controls this process. Such panels are typically drawn from a limited group of academics and industry experts. A list of these advisors would no doubt show a familiar pattern of high-ranking universities.

Recent popular research on crowdsourcing and the wisdom of crowds suggests a totally different approach. Asking everybody for input generates better results than just asking the experts. Certainly, a single recognized expert will tend to offer better facts, predictions, or advice than a random individual. But put a few dozen random individuals together—on the right kind of task—and the facts, predictions, or advice that shake out are better than what the experts alone produce.

The reasons behind the success of crowdsourcing are still being investigated, but the key seems to be this: in a mix of right and wrong answers, the wrong ones tend to cancel each other out, leaving the right ones. This is the secret behind the famous appeals to the audience in the game show *Who Wants to Be a Millionaire*, as well as the success of prediction markets such as the University of Iowa's Electronic Market.[†]

† *http://www.biz.uiowa.edu/iem/index.cfm*

Wikipedia, which invariably makes a central appearance in every reference to crowdsourcing, plays the different opinions of the crowd against each other in more explicit ways. On relatively uncontroversial articles, contributors are expected to discuss their differences and reach consensus. This process is aided by a rarely cited technical trait of web pages: because they present no artificial space limitations, there can always be room for another point of view. On controversial topics, Wikipedia has over the years developed more formal mechanisms, but the impetus for change still wells up from the grassroots.

It's also worth mentioning, in regard to crowdsourcing, the use of low-paid or volunteer labor to carry out simple tasks such as identifying the subjects of photographs. These are called Mechanical Turk projects, in reference to a crowdsourcing technology platform provided by Amazon.com, which is itself named after an eighteenth-century hoax[‡] in which a person pretended to be an intelligent machine; in the modern incarnation, thousands of people are serving as functions invoked by a computer application.

Crowdsourcing has already slipped into government procedures in low-key ways. Governments already use input from self-appointed members of the public on all kinds of things, ranging from reports of potholes to anonymous tips that put criminals behind bars.

One of the key skills required of both technologists and government officials is how best to aggregate public opinion or data produced by public actions to reveal new information or patterns. For example, cities learn a lot about neighborhoods by aggregating crime reports from residents. They could understand their needs for broadband network access much more accurately if they took resident reports into account and didn't depend just on what the broadband vendors told them (because geographic anomalies often cause dead zones in areas that the vendors claim to serve).

In general, people can provide input on several levels:

- Observations such as reports of potholes and crimes
- Feedback on government proposals
- New ideas generated through brainstorming sessions
- Full-fledged applications that operate on publicly available data

Some of those applications may operate on existing government data, but they can also be designed to collect new data from ordinary people, in a virtuous circle by which private sector applications (like SeeClickFix) increase the intelligence and responsiveness of government.

Governments are more likely to use some form of filtering than to rely on public consensus, as Wikipedia does. The combination of free debate among the public and some adult supervision from a government official makes a powerful combination, already seen in the open government brainstorming session mentioned in Lesson 3.

‡ *http://en.wikipedia.org/wiki/Amazon_Mechanical_Turk*

Finally, crowds can produce data without even realizing it—implicit data that smart programmers can collect and use to uncover whole worlds of information. In fact, smart programmers in the private sector have been doing that for years. Lesson 5 covers this trend.

—Andy Oram

Lesson 4: Learn from Your "Hackers"

The secret of generative systems is that the most creative ideas for how a new platform can be used don't necessarily come from the creators of the platform. It was not IBM but Dan Bricklin and Bob Frankston (VisiCalc), Mitch Kapor (Lotus 1-2-3), and Bill Gates who developed the "killer applications" that made the IBM personal computer such a success. It was Tim Berners-Lee, not Vint Cerf and Bob Kahn (the designers of the Internet's TCP/IP protocol), who developed the Internet's own first killer application, the World Wide Web. And it was Larry Page and Sergey Brin, not Tim Berners-Lee, who figured out how to turn the World Wide Web into a tool that revolutionized business.

Such stories suggest how technology advances, as each new generation stands on the shoulders of preceding giants. Fundamental technology breakthroughs are often not exploited by their creators, but by a second generation of entrepreneurs who put it to work.

But advances don't just come from entrepreneurs playing by the rules of new platforms. Sometimes they come from those who break the rules. MIT professor Eric von Hippel has written extensively about this phenomenon, how "lead users"[§] of a product push it to its limits and beyond, showing vendors where their product wants to go, in much the way that rushing water carves its own path through the earth.

There's no better contemporary example than Google Maps, introduced in 2005, nearly 10 years after MapQuest, the first Internet site providing maps and directions. Yet today, Google Maps is the dominant mapping platform by most measures. How did this happen?

When Google Maps was introduced, it featured a cool new AJAX (Asynchronous JavaScript and XML) interface that made it easy to dynamically drag and zoom the map. But there was a hidden feature as well, soon discovered by independent developers. Because JavaScript is interpreted code, it was possible to extract the underlying map coordinate data. A programmer named Paul Rademacher introduced the first Google Maps mashup, HousingMaps.com, taking data from another Internet site, Craigslist.org, and creating an application that put Craigslist apartment and home listings onto a Google Map.

What did Google do? Far from shutting down Rademacher's site and branding him a pirate, Google hired him, and soon put out an API that made it easier for anyone to do what he did.

§ *http://en.wikipedia.org/wiki/Lead_user*

Competitors, who had long had mapping APIs but locked them up behind tightly controlled corporate developer programs, failed to seize the opportunity. Before long there were thousands of Google Maps mashups, and mapping had become an integral part of every web developer's toolkit.

Today, according to the site ProgrammableWeb.com, which tracks mashups and reuse of web APIs, Google Maps accounts for nearly 90% of all mapping mashups, versus only a few percent each for MapQuest, Yahoo!, and Microsoft, even though these companies had a huge head start in web mapping.

There are potent lessons here for governments opening up access to their data via APIs. Developers may use those APIs in unexpected ways. This is a good thing. If you see signs of uses that you didn't consider, respond quickly, adapting the APIs to those new uses rather than trying to block them.

In this regard, consider an instructive counterexample to Google Maps from the government sector. The New York Metropolitan Transit Authority recently attempted to stop the distribution of an iPhone app called StationStops, which provides schedule information for Metro-North trains. After a legal battle, the MTA relented.[||] Other cities, meanwhile, realized that having independent developers build applications that provide information to citizens is a benefit both to citizens and to overworked government agencies, not "copyright infringement and intellectual property theft," as the MTA had originally maintained.

The whole point of government as a platform is to encourage the private sector to build applications that government didn't consider or doesn't have the resources to create. Open data is a powerful way to enable the private sector to do just that.

Data Is the "Intel Inside"

Open data is important not just because it is a key enabler of outside innovation. It's also important to place in the context of current Internet business models. To explain, we require a brief excursion.

One of the central platform lessons of the PC era is summed up in a principle that Harvard Business School Professor Clayton Christensen called "the law of conservation of attractive profits":[#]

> When attractive profits disappear at one stage in the value chain because a product becomes modular and commoditized, the opportunity to earn attractive profits with proprietary products will usually emerge at an adjacent stage.

[||] "M.T.A. Is Easing Its Strict, Sometimes Combative, Approach to Outside Web Developers," *New York Times*, September 27, 2009 (*http://www.nytimes.com/2009/09/28/nyregion/28mta.html?_r=3*).

[#] *The Innovator's Solution: Creating and Sustaining Successful Growth*, Clayton M. Christensen and Michael E. Raynor, Harvard Business Press, 2003.

As the IBM PC—built from commodity off-the-shelf parts—became dominant, hardware margins declined, over time becoming razor thin. But according to Christensen's law, something else became valuable, namely software, and Microsoft was soon earning the outsized profits that once were claimed by IBM. But even in an ecosystem of standard off-the-shelf parts, it is sometimes possible to corner a market, and that's just what Intel did when it broke with IBM's policy that every component had to be available from at least two suppliers, and refused to license its 80386 design to other chip manufacturers. That was the origin of the other half of the famous "Wintel" duopoly of Microsoft and Intel. If you can become the sole source of an essential commodity that is key to an otherwise commoditized product, you too can aspire to a logo like the ubiquitous "Intel Inside."

Reflecting on the role of open source software and open protocols and standards in commoditizing the software of the Internet, I concluded in my 2003 paper "The Open Source Paradigm Shift"[*] that something similar would happen on the Internet. Exactly what that was didn't become clear to me till 2005, when I wrote "What Is Web 2.0?"[†]

If there's one lesson that is central to the success of Web 2.0, it's that data and the algorithms that produce value from it—not the software APIs and applications that were the key to the PC era—are the key to marketplace advantage in today's Internet. Virtually all of the greatest Internet success stories, from eBay, Craigslist, and Amazon through Google, Facebook, and Twitter, are data-driven companies.

In particular, they are companies whose databases have a special characteristic: they get better the more people use them, making it difficult for competitors to enter the market. Once eBay or Craigslist had a critical mass of buyers and sellers, it became far more difficult for competitors to enter the market. Once Google established a virtuous circle of network effects among its AdWords advertisers, it was hard for others to achieve similar results.

The Internet business ecosystem can thus be seen as a competition to establish monopolies over various classes of data. It is indeed data that is the "Intel Inside" of the Internet.

What does this have to do with Government 2.0? If data is indeed the coin of the realm of Internet business models, it stands to reason that companies will find advantage in taking data created at public expense, and working to take control of that data for private gain.

Consider the story of Routesy, an application providing iPhone users with bus arrival data in the San Francisco Bay Area. Like StationStops in New York, it was taken down from the iPhone App Store after a legal complaint. While Muni (the San Francisco transit authority) was supportive of Routesy and believed that its data was public, the contract that Muni had signed with technology provider NextBus allowed NextBus to claim copyright in the data.[‡] If you

---

* *http://tim.oreilly.com/articles/paradigmshift_0504.html*

† *http://oreilly.com/web2/archive/what-is-web-20.html*

‡ "Does A Private Company Own Your Muni Arrival Times?", *SF Appeal*, June 25, 2009 (*http://sfappeal.com/news/2009/06/who-owns-sfmta-arrival-data.php#*).

want to have the kind of responsiveness that Google showed in supporting HousingMaps.com and launching the Google Maps mashup ecosystem, you have to make sure that public data remains public!

Fortunately, the NextBus/Routesy dispute was resolved, like MTA/StationStops, with a win for the public sector. The San Francisco Municipal Transit Authority has now released an XML API to the NextBus data.§

Lesson 5: Data Mining Allows You to Harness Implicit Participation

When thinking about user participation and the co-creation of value, it's easy to focus on technology platforms that explicitly feature the creations of their users, like Wikipedia, YouTube, Twitter, Facebook, and blogs. Yet in many ways, the breakthroughs in Web 2.0 have often come from exploring a far wider range of possibilities for collaboration:

- Open source technology platforms such as the TCP/IP protocol suite and utilities created as part of Berkeley Unix, as well as Linux, Apache, and MySQL, and open source programming languages such as Perl, Python, PHP, and Ruby, all built and maintained by collaborative communities, provided the fundamental building blocks of the Internet as we know it today.

- The World Wide Web itself has an architecture of participation. Anyone can put up a website and can link to any other website without permission. Blogging platforms made it even easier for any individual to create a site. Later platforms like Facebook and Twitter are also enablers of this kind of explicit participation.

- First-generation web giants like Yahoo! got their start by building catalogs of the content assembled by the participatory multitudes of the Net, catalogs that later grew into search engines. eBay aggregated millions of buyers and sellers into a global garage sale. Craigslist replaced newspaper classified advertising by turning it all into a self-service business, right down to the policing of inappropriate content, having users flag postings that they find offensive. Even Amazon.com, nominally an online retailer, gained competitive advantage by harnessing customers to provide reviews and ratings, as well as using their purchase patterns to make automated recommendations.

- Google's search engine dominance began with two brilliant insights into user participation. First, the PageRank algorithm that Larry Page and Sergey Brin created while still at Stanford was based on the realization that every link on the World Wide Web was a kind of vote on the value of the site being pointed to by that link. That is, every time any of us makes a link to another site on the Web, we're contributing to Google. Second, Google realized that it could provide better advertising results not by selling advertisements to the

§ *http://www.sfmta.com/cms/asite/nextmunidata.htm*

highest bidder, but by measuring and predicting user click-through rates on ads. A $10 ad that is twice as likely to be clicked on is worth more than a $15 ad. Google could only deliver these results by understanding that every click on a Google search result is a kind of user contribution. Since then, Google has gone on to mine user participation in many other aspects of its core business as well as in new businesses, including speech recognition, location-based services, automated translation, and much more. Google is a master at extracting value from implicit participation. It makes use of data that its users provide simply in going about their lives on the Internet to provide them with results that quite literally could not exist without them.

Just as Google has become the bellwether company of the Internet era, it is actually systems for harnessing implicit participation that offer some of the greatest opportunities for Government 2.0.

There are great examples to be found in health care. As costs soar, we discover that costs and outcomes aren't correlated. Atul Gawande's *New Yorker* article[||] on this disconnect—outlining how McAllen, Texas, the city with the highest health care costs in the U.S., also had the worst health outcomes—led to what Health and Human Services CTO Todd Park referred to in a conversation with me as a "holy cow moment." Todd is now working on what he calls a "holy cow machine," a set of services that will allow every city to understand how its health care costs and outcomes compare to those of other cities.

We have all the data we need—generated by the interactions of our citizens with our health care system—to understand how to better align costs and outcomes. Taking this idea to its full potential, we need to get beyond transparency and, as Google did with AdWords, start building data-driven feedback loops right into the system. Google's tools for estimating the effectiveness of keyword advertising are available to advertisers, but that's wonky, back-office stuff. The real magic is that Google uses all its data expertise to directly benefit its users by automatically providing better search results and more relevant advertisements. The most amazing thing about Google is how dynamically the prices for its advertising are set. *Every single Google search has its own automated ad auction. The price is set dynamically, matching supply and demand, seven or eight billion times a day.* Only financial markets operate at this kind of speed and scale.

A Gov 2.0 analogue would not just be a "holy cow machine" for transparency; it might, for example, be a new, dynamic pricing system for Medicare. Currently, an outside advisory board makes recommendations to Congress on appropriate Medicare reimbursement rates. As David Leonhardt noted in the *New York Times*, "Congress generally ignores them, in deference to the various industry groups that oppose any cuts to their payments."[#] Leonhardt's solution: an

---

|| "The Cost Conundrum," Atul Gawande, *The New Yorker*, June 1, 2009 (*http://www.newyorker.com/reporting/2009/06/01/090601fa_fact_gawande*).

"Falling Far Short of Reform," David Leonhardt, *New York Times*, November 10, 2009 (*http://www.nytimes.com/2009/11/11/business/economy/11leonhardt.html*).

independent body, akin to the Federal Reserve, empowered to set reimbursement rates in the same way the Fed sets interest rates.

But shouldn't such a body go even further than periodic resets? Technology would allow us to actually manage reimbursements in much the same way as Google dynamically adjusts its algorithms to produce optimal search results and optimal ad placements. Google takes into account hundreds of factors; so too could a Medicare rate-setting algorithm. To take two examples from Leonhardt's article:

> Each year, about 100,000 people die from preventable infections they contract in a hospital. When 108 hospitals in Michigan instituted a simple process to prevent some of these infections, it nearly eliminated them. If Medicare reduced payments for the treatment of such infections, it would give hospitals a huge financial incentive to prevent them....

> There are a handful of possible treatments for early-stage prostate cancer, and the fastest-growing are the most expensive. But no one knows which ones work best.

By measuring outcomes and linking reimbursements to those outcomes—rather than the current "fee for service" model, which encourages unnecessary procedures—Medicare could pave the way to a real revolution in health care.

Because of the political difficulty of such an intervention, it's unlikely that Medicare would be allowed to unilaterally introduce such an algorithmic payment system. As a result, I do suspect that this kind of innovation will come first from the private sector, which will trounce its competition in the same way that Google trounced its competitors in the search advertising market. As a platform provider, though, it's possible to see how government investment in the data infrastructure to measure and report on outcomes could jump-start and encourage private sector investment.

Real-time linkage of health costs and outcomes data will lead to wholesale changes in medical practice when an innovative health care provider uses them to improve its effectiveness and lower its costs. Such a breakthrough would sooner or later be copied by less effective providers. So rather than attempting to enforce better practices through detailed regulations, a Government 2.0 approach would use open government data to enable innovative private sector participants to improve their products and services. And to the extent that the government itself is a health care provider (as with the Veterans Administration) or medical insurer (as with Medicare), it can best move the ball forward by demonstrating in its own operations that it has been able to harness technology to get the job done better and more cost-effectively.

Lesson 6: Lower the Barriers to Experimentation

In a memorable moment during the Apollo 13 moon mission, when mechanical failures required that the mission be aborted and the astronauts rescued using only materials on board the craft, mission controller Gene Kranz famously said, "Failure is not an option." In that case, he was right. But far too often, government programs are designed as though there is only one right answer, and with the assumption that the specification developed by a project team must by definition be correct.

In reality, for most projects, failure is an option. In fact, technology companies embrace failure, experimentation, and rapid iteration.

This has been true long before the latest wave of technology companies. In describing his quest for a working electric light bulb, Thomas Edison said, "I didn't fail 10,000 times. I succeeded 10,000 times in figuring out something that did not work."

You can conceive of the technology marketplace as a series of competitive experiments. But even within a single company, one of the advantages of web-based business models is the ease of experimentation. Companies routinely run A/B tests of new features on subsets of their users. They add and subtract features in real time in a process of constant improvement that I've sometimes called the "perpetual beta."

More recently, thinkers such as Steve Blank and Eric Ries have described an idea that Ries refers to as "the lean startup," in which he describes exploring the market via a series of "minimal viable products," each of which tells you more about what the market really wants.[*]

This is at great variance with typical government thinking, which, by ignoring the possibility of failure, paradoxically creates the conditions that encourage it. Government 2.0 requires a new approach to the design of programs, not as finished products, perfected in a congressional bill, executive order, or procurement specification, but as ongoing experiments.

Quite frankly, this is likely the greatest challenge in Government 2.0, not only because of the nature of the government procurement process, but also because government programs are often dictated by legislation, or by agency regulations that are outside the scope of the agency actually making the decisions. What's more, while the commercial marketplace benefits from Schumpeterian "creative destruction," government programs are rarely scrapped or sunsetted.

This is all the more reason why government programs must be designed from the outset not as a fixed set of specifications, but as open-ended platforms that allow for extensibility and revision by the marketplace. Platform thinking is an antidote to the complete specifications that currently dominate the government approach not only to IT but to programs of all kinds.

A cultural change is also required. Empowering employees to "fail forward fast" accepts and acknowledges that even when an experiment fails, you will still learn something. Software and web culture not only embraces this mindset, but revels in it—you never know which idea will be the million-dollar idea. Once the cost of that experimentation is reduced, you can quickly scrap a product or feature that no one uses and accept that it just wasn't the thing that needed to be built after all.

* http://www.startuplessonslearned.com/2009/10/inc-magazine-on-minimum-viable-product.html

Finally, it is essential for best practices—and even working code—to be shared between agencies of the federal government, between states, and between municipalities. After all, as Justice Louis Brandeis wrote in 1932, "It is one of the happy incidents of the federal system that a single courageous state may, if its citizens choose, serve as a laboratory; and try novel social and economic experiments without risk to the rest of the country."†

HOW PLATFORM THINKING CHANGES THE BIG GOVERNMENT/ SMALL GOVERNMENT DEBATE

It should be obvious by now that platform thinking provides a real alternative to the endless argument between liberals and conservatives that has so dominated U.S. political discourse in recent decades. The idea that we have to choose between government providing services to citizens and leaving everything to the private sector is a false dichotomy. Tim Berners-Lee didn't develop hundreds of millions of websites; Google didn't develop thousands of Google Maps mashups; Apple developed only a few of the tens of thousands of applications for the iPhone.

Being a platform provider means government stripped down to the essentials. A platform provider builds essential infrastructure, creates core applications that demonstrate the power of the platform and inspire outside developers to push the platform even further, and enforces "rules of the road" that ensure that applications work well together.

Lesson 7: Lead by Example

When Microsoft introduced Microsoft Windows, it didn't just introduce the platform; it introduced two applications, Microsoft Word and Microsoft Excel, that showed off the ease of use that came with graphical user interfaces. When Apple introduced the iPhone, it didn't even introduce the platform until its second year. First, it built a device with remarkable new features and a suite of applications that showed off their power.

Despite everything I've said about the importance of a platform provider not competing with its developer ecosystem, it's also a mistake to think that you can build a platform in the abstract. A great platform provider does things that are ahead of the curve and that take time for the market to catch up to. It's essential to prime the pump by showing what can be done.

This is why, for example, Apps.DC.gov, the "App Store" for the city of Washington, D.C., provides a better Gov 2.0 platform model than the federal equivalent Data.gov (see Figure 2-3). Although Apps.gov provides a huge service in opening up and promoting APIs to all the data resources of the federal government, it's hard to know what's important, because

---

† *http://www.whitehouse.gov/blog/2009/11/19/open-government-laboratories-democracy*

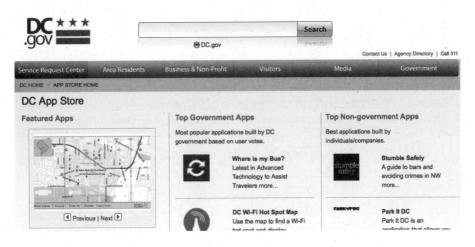

FIGURE 2-3. Apps.DC.gov home page

there are no compelling "applications" that show how that data can be put to use. By contrast, Apps.DC.gov features a real app store, with applications written by the city of Washington, D.C.'s own technology team (or funded by them) demonstrating how to use key features. D.C. then took the further step of highlighting, at a top level, third-party apps created by independent developers. This is a model for every government app store to follow.

It is true that the sheer size and scope of the federal data sets, as well as the remoteness of many of them from the everyday lives of citizens, makes for a bigger challenge. But that's precisely why the federal Gov 2.0 initiative needs to do deep thinking about what federal data resources and APIs will make the most difference to citizens, and invest strategically in applications that will show what can be done.

But the idea of leading by example is far bigger than just Data.gov. Once again, consider health care.

If the current model of "health care reform" were an operating system, it would be Windows Vista, touted as a major revisioning of the system, but in the end, a set of patches that preserve what went before without bringing anything radically new to the table.

If the government wants buy-in for government-run health care, we need the equivalent of an iPhone for the system, something that re-envisions the market so thoroughly that every existing player needs to copy it. I've suggested that an opportunity exists to reinvent Medicare so that it is more efficient than any private insurance company, and to make the VA better than any private hospital system. But being realistic, technology teaches us that it's always harder to refactor an existing system or application than it is to start fresh.

That's why the "public option" proposed in some current health care bills is such an opportunity. Can we create a new health insurance program that uses the lessons of technology—open standards, simplicity in design, customer self-service, measurement of outcomes, and real-time response to what is learned, not to mention access via new consumer devices—to improve service and reduce costs so radically that the entire market follows?

This is the true measure of Gov 2.0: does it make incremental changes to the existing system, or does it constitute a revolution? Considering the examples of Microsoft, Google, Amazon, Apple, and other giants of the technology world, it's clear that they succeeded by changing all the rules, not by playing within the existing system. The personal computer, the World Wide Web, and the iPhone have each managed to simultaneously bring down costs while increasing consumer choice—each by orders of magnitude.

They did this by demonstrating how a radically new approach to existing solutions and business models was, quite simply, orders of magnitude better than what went before.

If government is a platform, and Gov 2.0 is the next release, let's make it one that shakes up—and reshapes—the world.

Practical Steps for Government Agencies

1. Issue your own open government directive. San Francisco Mayor Gavin Newsom has done just that. You might consider his Open Data Executive Directive as a model.‡

2. As Robinson et al. propose, create "a simple, reliable and publicly accessible infrastructure that 'exposes' the underlying data" from your city, county, state, or agency. Before you can create a site like Data.gov, you must first adopt a data-driven, service-oriented architecture for all your applications. The "Eight Open Government Data Principles" document outlines the key requirements for open government data.§

3. "Build your own websites and applications using the same open systems for accessing the underlying data as they make available to the public at large" (Robinson et al. again).‖

4. Share those open APIs with the public, using Data.gov for federal APIs and creating state and local equivalents. For example, cities such as San Francisco (DataSF.org) and Washington, D.C. (Data.DC.gov and Apps.DC.gov) include not only data catalogs but also repositories of apps that use that data, created by both city developers and the private sector.

5. Share your work with other cities, counties, states, or agencies. This might mean providing your work as open source software, working with other governmental bodies to standardize web services for common functions, building a common cloud computing

---

‡ *http://www.sfmayor.org/wp-content/uploads/2009/10/ED-09-06-Open-Data.pdf*

§ *http://resource.org/8_principles.html*

‖ "Government Data and the Invisible Hand," David G. Robinson, Harlan Yu, William Zeller, and Edward W. Felten, *Yale Journal of Law & Technology*, Vol. 11, 2009 (*http://papers.ssrn.com/sol3/papers.cfm?abstract_id=1138083*).

platform, or simply sharing best practices. Code for America (*http://codeforamerica.org*) is a new organization designed to help cities do just that.

6. Don't reinvent the wheel: support existing open standards and use open source software whenever possible. (Open311 is a great example of an open standard being adopted by many cities.) Figure out who has problems similar to yours, and see if they've done some work that you can build on.

7. Create a list of software applications that can be reused by your government employees without procurement.

8. Create an "app store" that features applications created by the private sector as well as those created by your own government unit (see Apps.DC.gov).

9. Create permissive social media guidelines that allow government employees to engage the public without having to get pre-approval from superiors.

10. Sponsor meetups, code camps, and other activity sessions to actually put citizens to work on civic issues.

About the Author

TIM O'REILLY is the founder and CEO of O'Reilly Media, Inc., thought by many to be the best computer book publisher in the world. In addition to Foo Camps ("Friends of O'Reilly" Camps, which gave rise to the "un-conference" movement), O'Reilly Media also hosts conferences on technology topics, including the Web 2.0 Summit, the Web 2.0 Expo, the O'Reilly Open Source Convention, the Gov 2.0 Summit, and the Gov 2.0 Expo. Tim's blog, the O'Reilly Radar, "watches the alpha geeks" to determine emerging technology trends, and serves as a platform for advocacy about issues of importance to the technical community. Tim's long-term vision for his company is to change the world by spreading the knowledge of innovators. In addition to O'Reilly Media, Tim is a founder of Safari Books Online, a pioneering subscription service for accessing books online, and O'Reilly AlphaTech Ventures, an early-stage venture firm.

CHAPTER THREE

By the People

Carl Malamud

Address to the Gov 2.0 Summit

Washington, D.C.

September 10, 2009

When Abraham Lincoln spoke of "a government of the people, by the people, for the people," he was speaking of more than the consecration of a battlefield, he was speaking of a wave of transformation that was changing the way government related to the citizens it served.

This transformation was the second of three waves of change. The first—the Founders' wave—began when printers such as Ben Franklin and pamphleteers such as Thomas Paine dared to involve themselves in civic affairs, publishing their opinions about how government should function, the policies it should follow, daring even to say that the people should go so far as to select their own leaders.

This first wave of transformation culminated when Thomas Jefferson took the White House, riding in on a crest of populist sentiment, a reaction against his more button-down predecessors, George Washington and John Adams. While both Washington and Adams were revolutionaries, they were aristocratic revolutionaries, governing from the top down, an elite who favored the populace with public service by governing them.

John Adams took great pains to instill a sense of dignity (some said majesty) in the new offices of government. He designed an official vice presidential uniform and suggested that Washington be addressed as "Your Excellency." Adams' sense of pomp was such that the

Jeffersonians took to referring to him as "His Rotundity" and a strong sentiment for a more representative and responsive government started to take shape.

When Jefferson moved into the White House after his raucous political campaign, he felt so deeply that his duty was to form a government for all the people of the United States that he abolished the formal dining table in the White House, replacing it with a round one so nobody could sit at the head. Indeed, if you happened to be walking by the White House early in the morning and knocked on the door, you might be greeted by Jefferson dressed in his bath robe, who would likely invite you in for a spot of breakfast.

The first great wave of transformation was a government that spoke, for the first time in modern history, directly to and with its citizens. The second wave—the Lincoln Wave—was just as fundamental.

The same day Lincoln was inaugurated in 1861, a new agency opened its doors, a Government Printing Office with a mission of "Keeping America Informed." Prior to Lincoln, the proceedings of government were reported by the press in a summary and sporadic fashion. The proceedings of Congress were reported by the Congressional Globe, a private enterprise, and the executive and legislative branches were reported only if it struck the fancy of a newspaperman.

The Government Printing Office created the first Official Journal of Government, the Congressional Record, which recorded the floors in a full and mostly true fashion. The Printing Office also began publishing the Foreign Relations of the United States, the official record of the State Department, and Superintendent of Documents John Defrees even served as Lincoln's personal editor for messages of state such as the Emancipation Proclamation.

The Lincoln wave of transformation was one of fully documenting government, publishing the rule book that governs our society. But, it was more, it was also the beginning of a formal process of involving citizens in the workings of government, a process which culminated during FDR's New Deal.

This transformation in the nature of government was spurred by broader changes in society, changes that were breathtaking in scope, but often wreaked a terrible toll on workers and families.

In 1911, in a sweatshop on the 9th and 10th stories of a New York tenement, the nation reached a watershed. The Triangle Shirtwaist factory was a sweatshop crowded with unsafe machinery and combustible materials, with no fire escapes and the exit doors chained shut to keep workers from taking breaks. It was a powder keg that would inevitably explode in a firestorm, and it did. The Triangle Shirtwaist Fire claimed the lives of 146 garment workers.

Standing across the street that terrible day in 1911 was a young woman named Frances Perkins, a social worker and the executive secretary of the New York Consumers League, one of a new kind of civic organization advocating better conditions for factory workers. Perkins watched helplessly as young women, hands clasped in prayer, leapt to their deaths. Later, she recalled "the experience was seared on my mind as well as my heart—a never-to-be-forgotten reminder of why I had to spend my life fighting conditions that could permit such a tragedy."

Equally touched by the tragedy was a hard-boiled politician, Al Smith of Tammany Hall. Smith was horrified and formed a citizen's commission to investigate. When Theodore Roosevelt was asked who should serve as the chief investigator, Teddy thought of the young social worker he had heard so many good things about, saying "with Frances, you can't fail."

Perkins worked alongside a retired fire engineer—who sought her out and insisted on taking part as a volunteer—and with their commission of citizens they created the first fire code, spelling out the minimum standards of safety to be used in factories, offices, and homes. The fire code was adopted by New York City, then spread throughout the nation, joined over time by other fundamental public safety codes governing building, electricity, plumbing, elevators, boilers, and the other technical aspects of our modern society.

When Al Smith took the governor's seat in New York, he brought Frances Perkins with him, installing her on the new Industrial Commission, one of the first state bodies to begin regulating safety in the workplace. Perkins excelled in the post, and when Franklin Roosevelt took the governor's seat from Smith, not only did he ask Perkins to stay on, he promoted her to become one of his senior administrators.

This was an era where commissions and conferences became an important part of government, where citizens were consulted and their opinions heard in order to form a consensus on how government should act. Woodrow Wilson, Warren Harding, and Herbert Hoover used these boards and commissions to decide how to regulate the safety of aeroplanes, finance the creation of roads, and establish new-fangled efficiency mechanisms such as Daylight Savings Time.

This wave of transformation culminated when FDR moved to Washington. By then, these ideas of consultation and documentation had firmly taken root. But in the New Deal, there was chaos.

In 1934, the Assistant Attorney General went to the Supreme Court to argue why two oil companies should be required to obey regulations, only to find out that the government had never published those regulations. Justice Louis Brandeis sternly warned that without systematic publication of the rules, ignorance of the law would become a defense, and a new Official Journal of Government, the Federal Register, was created to serve as the vehicle for systematic publication across all agencies of the regulations and notifications of the executive branch.

To recap this history: The first wave—the Founders' wave—established the principle that government must communicate with the people. Next, the Lincoln wave established the principles of documentation and consultation. We are now witnessing a third wave of change— an Internet wave—where the underpinnings and machinery of government are used not only by bureaucrats and civil servants, but by the people. This change has the potential to be equally fundamental.

This transformation has its roots in unlikely quarters. The military took one of the first definitive steps, when a series of satellite launches by the U.S. Air Force from 1978 to 1993 created a Global Positioning System to guide not only the aircraft and ships of the military services, but opened the system to make navigational information available for private cars, truck fleets, commercial aviation, and even unanticipated applications such as location-enabled telephones and digital cameras. At the same time, the U.S. Geological Survey began releasing high-quality digital maps into the public domain.

With the growth of the global Internet as a communications platform, opportunities arose to offer government information differently. It suddenly became possible, and then trivial, to copy entire databases and serve them in a totally different manner.

The operation of a Global Positioning System, coupled with the release by government of extensive digital maps, is an example of what Tim O'Reilly calls "government as platform," the creation of systems that are used not only by government to fulfill its own tasks, but form the basis for private activities, both for profit and not for profit. (See Chapter 2.)

An example of "government as platform" is a database I helped put on-line in the early 1990s, the Securities and Exchange Commission's EDGAR database of filings of public corporations and other financial institutions. For many years, in order to read SEC reports, one had to go to a special reading room in Washington, asking for specific documents as one would in a closed-stack library or in approaching the service window at the County Clerk's office.

Alternatively, one could subscribe to a few computerized retail information services, and pay the operators $30 to read just one document. In this system, the government produced products to sell, and information was viewed as a profit center for the government and for a few selected concessionaires.

What we found when we placed these so-called products on the Internet—for free—was that these reports were not just fodder for a few well-heeled financial professionals, a commodity used to make the Wall Street money machine function, but instead that these public reports of public corporations were of tremendous interest to journalists, students, senior citizen investment clubs, employees of the companies reporting and employees of their competitors, in short a raft of new uses that had been impossible before.

By exposing the EDGAR database in bulk, the SEC became the platform for a host of new distribution channels, spreading the public filings into the infrastructure and helping to fulfill the SEC's mission of making our markets more efficient and transparent.

"Government as platform" means exposing the core information that makes government function, information that is of tremendous economic value to society. Government information—patents, corporate filings, agriculture research, maps, weather, medical research—is the raw material of innovation, creating a wealth of business opportunities that drive our economy forward. Government information is a form of infrastructure, no less important to our modern life than our roads, electrical grid, or water systems.

What is hopeful in what we are witnessing today is that some quarters of government appears to be embracing this new role instead of fighting it. One of President Obama's first acts was a memorandum that stated that documents should be no longer be guarded and only grudgingly released, but instead that "all agencies should adopt a presumption in favor of disclosure." (See the Appendix.)

While there is much to applaud, not all is sunlight. For too long, access to public information has been a matter of access to inside information, a matter of access to money and power. There is no better illustration of this than access to primary legal materials of the United States: the court cases, statutes, hearings, regulations, codes, administrative decisions, and other materials that define the operating system of our society, the law of the land.

When access to primary legal materials are contracted out to private concerns, as when a state court gives an exclusive contract to a corporation to publish its opinions or when a safety code becomes a revenue opportunity for a nonprofit paying million-dollar salaries, the public domain becomes private property, fenced off to extract value for a few, instead of open as a common good for us all.

We have seen this dramatically in the practice of law, where lawyers in public interest law firms and in government agencies—even the Department of Justice—carefully ration their use of the federal judiciary's PACER database and of the three retail services that monopolize the legal market. They limit their use because of cost considerations, meaning they are more poorly prepared than their adversaries from the private sector.

The costs are not insignificant. The Administrative Office of the Courts has charged the executive branch $50 million simply to access district court records. Law schools all carefully ration their use of PACER because the cost make it unworkable for them to grant law students the ability to read the proceedings of our federal trial courts at will. The Administrative Office of the Courts itself spends $150 million to access U.S. law from private contractors, a small fraction of the $10 billion per year Americans spend to access the raw materials of our democracy.

This is an issue of fundamental importance under our constitution. How can there be equal protection under the law or due process under the law—how can we be a nation of laws, not a nation of men—if the law is locked up behind a cash register, stamped with an unwarranted copyright assertion, and then shrink-wrapped in a license agreement, creating private parcels from the public domain? To purchase in bulk a collection of legal materials costs tens of millions of dollars, a barrier to competition that has resulted in decades of lost innovation for the legal profession.

The fees for bulk legal data are a significant barrier to free enterprise, but an insurmountable barrier for the public interest. Scholars, nonprofit groups, journalists, students, and just plain citizens wishing to analyze the functioning of our courts are shut out. Organizations such as the ACLU and EFF and scholars at law schools have long complained that research across all court filings in the federal judiciary is impossible, because an eight cent per page charge applied to tens of millions of pages makes it prohibitive to identify systematic discrimination, privacy violations, or other structural deficiencies in our courts.

Access to the law, and more broadly, access to the workings of government, the fundamental databases and systems that make up government as a platform for our society, is about more than economic activity, more than improving democracy and justice, it is an opportunity for citizens to help make government more efficient. For example, when we operated the SEC EDGAR database, it was our pleasure to turn all our source code over to the government—and even configure the SEC's routers and loan them hardware—a service we gladly performed at no charge as part of our mission as a 501(c)(3) nonprofit.

I would like to leave you with three propositions that should be true in a democratic society, challenges our government can and should address today:

First, if a document is to have the force of law, it must be available for all to read. Artificial restrictions on access are not appropriate for the law of the land. The federal judiciary, in particular, must make their data much more broadly available or they will find others owning their databases, claiming authority and authenticity that should emanate directly from the courts themselves. This is a foundational issue, one that goes to the very heart of our system of justice.

Second, if a meeting that is part of the law-making process is to be truly public, in this day and age, that means it must be on the Internet. Today, *public* means *online*. When Congress holds hearings, hearings that lead to laws that we must all obey, those hearings must take place in a forum that all may attend and observe. Today, they do not.

If you want to attend a hearing today, you'd best live inside of the Beltway and have the means to hire somebody to guard your place in line. When Congress does webcast, the efforts are half-hearted and of poor quality. Many committees webcast a few select hearings, but then systematically withdraw their archives from the net. Shielding hearings from the public eye reduces the legitimacy of the Congress. Broadcast-quality video from every hearing should be made available on the Internet so our legislative process becomes more visible to all Americans.

Third, the rule of law in our federalist system is a matter that applies to all three branches of the federal government, and also to all 50 states and the local jurisdictions. The principle that primary legal materials should be available to all is a principle that needs to be driven by the leadership of the executive branch and applied to all levels of government.

Our new administration has many noted constitutional scholars—Solicitor General Kagan, Attorney General Holder, President Obama—who must surely understand the importance of making America's operating system open source. Through litigation, legislation, and executive memorandum, the Administration could and should lead a fundamental reform in how we make our laws available to our citizens, turning the private enclaves of today into the public parks of tomorrow.

The promise of the Internet wave is the promise of an opportunity for more efficient government, for more economic activity, and for a better democracy. Artificial and unjust limits on access to information based on money and power can be abolished from our society's operating system, giving us at long last a government that truly is of the people, by the people, and for the people.

About the Author

 **CARL MALAMUD** is the founder of Public.Resource.Org, a nonprofit that has been instrumental in placing government information on the Internet. Prior to that he was the Chief Technology Officer at the Center for American Progress and was the founder of the Internet Multicasting Service, where he ran the first radio station on the Internet.

CHAPTER FOUR

The Single Point of Failure

Beth Simone Noveck

> **The world is full of amateurs: gifted amateurs, devoted amateurs.**
> **You can pick almost any group that has any kind of intrinsic**
> **interest in it, from dragonflies to pill bugs to orb-weaving**
> **spiders. Anybody can pick up information in interesting places,**
> **find new species or rediscover what was thought to be a**
> **vanished species, or some new biological fact about a species**
> **already known.**
>
> —*E. O. Wilson*

The patent system is just one example of how government institutions create single points of failure by concentrating decision-making power in the hands of the few, whether legislators in Congress, cabinet officials in the executive branch, or bureaucrats in agencies. Administrative practices are constructed around the belief that government professionals know best how to translate broad legislative mandates into specific regulatory decisions in the public interest. Governance, the theory goes, is best entrusted to a bureaucracy operating at one remove from the pressure of electoral politics and the biased influence of the public at large.

NOTE

This chapter is an excerpt from *Wiki Government: How Technology Can Make Government Better, Democracy Stronger, and Citizens More Powerful*, Beth Simone Noveck, Brookings Institution Press, 2009.

The Closed Model of Decision Making

The rationale for this closed model of decision making, as explained by such theorists as Max Weber and Walter Lippmann, is rooted in the assumptions of an earlier age. Although citizens may express personal opinions, they are thought to lack the ability to make informed decisions on complex policy matters. Moreover, democratic pessimists warn, government officials must be protected from the factionalized public that Madison so feared in *Federalist 10*. To ward off this danger, centralized power is concentrated in the apolitical professional or, in Weber's words, "the personally detached and strictly objective expert."* Only government professionals possess the impartiality, expertise, resources, discipline, and time to make public decisions. Or so it is assumed. The assumption is not unjustified insofar as the technology has not been available before to organize participation easily. Participation in a representative democracy is largely confined to voting in elections, joining interest groups, and getting involved in local civic or political affairs.

Thus the patent examiner, like her counterparts throughout government, must act as an expert in fields far outside her ken. The process of determining which inventor deserves a patent demands that she analyze and synthesize scientific and technical information about cutting-edge areas of innovation over which she has no real mastery. In any given subject area there are scientists, engineers, and lawyers with greater expertise, as well as laypersons with valuable insights, but the patent examiner has no access to them. In this she is not alone. In a survey of environmental lawyers, for example, only 8 percent of respondents thought that the EPA has sufficient time to search the relevant science before making a decision about environmental policy, and only 6 percent believed that agencies employ adequate analysis in their decision making.† The bureaucrat in Washington often lacks access to the right information or to the expertise necessary to make sense of a welter of available information. This can pose a challenge to good decision making and to creativity in problem solving.

The single point of failure results not just from a lack of time or resources or technology. It goes much deeper than that. Simply put, professionals do not have a monopoly on information or expertise, as the social psychologist Philip Tetlock observes. In his award-winning book *Expert Political Judgment* (Princeton University Press), Tetlock analyzes the predictions of professional political pundits against modest performance benchmarks. He finds "few signs that expertise translates into greater ability to make either 'well-calibrated' or 'discriminating' forecasts."‡ While smart people can explain, they often cannot predict and therefore make decisions based on spectacularly bad guesses.

---

* *Essays in Sociology*, Max Weber, edited by H. H. Gerth and C. Wright Mills, Routledge, 1991.

† "In Defense of Regulatory Peer Review," J. B. Ruhl and James Salzman, *Washington University Law Review*, Vol. 84, 2006: 1–61.

‡ *Expert Political Judgment: How Good Is It? How Can We Know?*, Philip E. Tetlock, Princeton University Press, 2005, p. 20.

Pacifists do not abandon Mahatma Gandhi's worldview just because of the sublime naïveté of his remark in 1940 that he did not consider Adolf Hitler to be as bad as "frequently depicted" and that "he seems to be gaining his victories without much bloodshed"; many environmentalists defend Paul Ehrlich despite his notoriously bad track record in the 1970s and the 1980s (he predicted massive food shortages just as new technologies were producing substantial surpluses); Republicans do not change their views about the economic competence of Democratic administrations just because Martin Feldstein predicted that the legacy of the Clinton 1993 budget would be stagnation for the rest of the decade; social democrats do not overhaul their outlook just because Lester Thurow predicted that the 1990s would witness the ascendancy of the more compassionate capitalism of Europe and Japan over the "devil take the hindmost" American model.§

It turns out that professional status has much less bearing on the quality of information than might be assumed and that professionals— whether in politics or other domains—are notoriously unsuccessful at making accurate predictions. Or as Scott Page, the University of Michigan author of *The Difference*, pithily puts it: "Diversity trumps ability"—this is a mathematical truth, not a feel-good mantra.‖

Moreover, government or government-endorsed professionals are not more impervious to political influence than the impassioned public that bureaucrats are supposed to keep at arm's length. Often the scientists and outside experts who are asked to give impartial advice to government are lobbyists passing by another name. The National Coal Council, made up almost exclusively of coal industry representatives, sits on the Department of Energy's federal advisory committee on coal policy: the department has adopted 80 percent of the Coal Council's recommendations.# White House officials regularly replace experts on agency advisory panels with ideologues and political allies (or eliminate advisory councils altogether). An Environmental Working Group study finds that the seven EPA panels that evaluated proposed safe daily exposure levels to commercial chemicals in 2007 included seventeen members who were employed by, or who received research funding from, companies with a financial stake in the outcome.*

In a published statement titled *Restoring Scientific Integrity in Policy Making*, over 60 preeminent scientists, including Nobel laureates and National Medal of Science recipients, lambasted George W. Bush's administration for having "manipulated the process through which science

---

§ Ibid., p. 15.

‖ *The Difference: How the Power of Diversity Creates Better Groups, Firms, Schools, and Societies*, Scott E. Page, Princeton University Press, 2007.

"Industry-Packed Federal Advisory Board Told DOE to Double U.S. Coal Consumption," Joaquin Sapien, May 19, 2008 (*http://www.propublica.org/article/industry-packed-federal-advisory-board-told-doe-to-double-us-coal-consumpti*).

* "EPA Axes Panel Chair at Request of Chemical Industry Lobbyists," Sonya Lunder and Jane Houlihan, March 2008 (*http://www.ewg.org/reports/decaconflict*).

enters into its decisions."[†] In 2008, 889 of nearly 1,600 EPA staff scientists reported that they had experienced political interference in their work over the last five years.[‡] But if the Bush administration is among the more egregious violators of the presumed wall between politics and institutionalized expertise, its actions only go to show how easy it is for any executive to abuse his power while claiming the mantle of expertise.

Taking a historical view, the journalist Chris Mooney, in his book *The Republican War on Science*, persuasively explains that the marriage of big business to the religious right in the Reagan era has resulted in a systematic abuse of science in regulatory decision making.[§] What began during World War II as an intimate relationship between science and politics—the flames of whose passion were fueled by the competitive jealousy of the cold war and the attentions of an intellectually inclined Kennedy administration—has now waned. The rise of conservatism spurred a movement to create alternative sources for scientific information. Hiding behind the skirt of science, antievolution and antiabortion politics create pressure to misrepresent science to serve political ends. At the same time, the fear by big business that scientific research might impel expensive environmental and consumer regulation further contributes to a distortion of the use of science in policy making. Mooney readily acknowledges that the Left as well as the Right makes decisions on the basis of political value judgments rather than facts. But whereas Democrats, he contends, sometimes conduct politics in spite of science, choosing to ignore the data in pursuit of a normative end, Republicans dress up politics as science and attempt to name such positions "creation science" behind a veneer of scientific legitimacy.

The problem of relying solely on professionals is compounded by the practice of confidential decision making. While federal government agencies are required by law to conduct meetings in the open (and many state governments have similar sunshine laws), this spirit is violated by regular backroom dealings with lobbyists.[‖] Under the Bush administration, the attorney general changed the presumption of disclosure under Freedom of Information Act requests away from the prevailing standard to make it more difficult for agencies to release information and allow agencies to defend decisions to withhold records "unless they lack a sound legal basis."[#] President Obama changed it back. It is not surprising that the American people perceive government to be taking place behind closed doors (three-quarters of American adults

---

† "Restoring Scientific Integrity in Policy Making: Scientists Sign-On Statement," Union of Concerned Scientists, February 8, 2005 (*http://www.ucsusa.org/scientific_integrity/abuses_of_science/scientists-sign-on-statement.html*).

‡ "Interference at EPA: Science and Politics at the U.S. Environmental Protection Agency," Union of Concerned Scientists, April 23, 2008 (*http://www.ucsusa.org/scientific_integrity/abuses_of_science/interference-at-the-epa.html*).

§ *The Republican War on Science*, Chris Mooney, Basic Books, 2005.

‖ Government in the Sunshine Act, P.L. 409, 94th Cong. September 13, 1976.

"The Freedom of Information Act," John Ashcroft, Memorandum for All Heads of Departments and Agencies, October 12, 2001.

surveyed in 2008 view the federal government as secretive, an increase from 62 percent in 2006).* Massive financial bailout measures taken late in 2008 met with concerns that these troubled asset relief programs lacked transparency or monitoring. There have been myriad instances of information being deliberately hidden.

The Bush administration threatened to shut down the award-winning economic indicators website, which combines data like GDP, net imports and exports, and retail sales to make it convenient for viewers to assess the state of the economy.† The administration also announced it would no longer produce the Census Bureau's Survey of Income and Program Participation, which identifies which programs best assist low-income families, and stop publishing its report on international terrorism, making it more difficult for citizens to find important and useful news.‡ The Bush administration has taken down reports about mass layoffs and, by executive order, limited the publication of presidential records.§ Until 1999 the USPTO did not publish patent applications until they were granted.‖ Even today, the office is circumspect about Internet research to avoid compromising the privacy and confidentiality of the decision making process.# The less those outside the government know about its activities, self-evidently, the greater the need to rely on internal experts. When the public cannot see how decisions are arrived at, it cannot identify problems and criticize mistakes. Accountability declines and so does government effectiveness.

New Technologies and Civic Life

Technology enables collective action in civil society and helps some people to route around the logjam created by the single point of failure. Countless civic groups already use new communication and information-sharing tools to promote political action, operate an opposition movement, or mobilize community activism. Collaborative governance needs to be

* "More People See Federal Government as Secretive; Nearly All Want to Know Where Candidates Stand on Transparency," Sunshine Week, March 15, 2008 (*http://www.sunshineweek.org/sunshineweek/ secrecypoll08*) (accessed October 2008); *Nation of Secrets: The Threat to Democracy and the American Way of Life*, Ted Gup, Doubleday, 2007.

† "Bush Administration Hides More Data, Shuts Down Website Tracking U.S. Economic Indicators," Amanda Terkel, February 13, 2008 (*http://thinkprogress.org/2008/02/13/economic-indicators*).

‡ "Bush Admin: What You Don't Know Can't Hurt Us, 2007 Version," Paul Kiel, November 23, 2007 (*http: //tpmmuckraker.talkingpointsmemo.com/archives/004766.php*).

§ Ibid.

‖ American Inventors Protection Act, P.L. 113, 106th Cong. November 29, 1999.

U.S. Patent and Trademark Office, Manual of Patent Examining Procedures, sec. 904.02(c) (8th ed., 2001) ("This policy also applies to use of the Internet as a communications medium for connecting to commercial database providers"); U.S. Patent and Trademark Office, "Patent Internet Usage Policy," 64 Federal Register (June 21, 1999) ("If security and confidentiality cannot be attained for a specific use, transaction, or activity, then that specific use, transaction, or activity shall NOT be undertaken/ conducted"), p. 33,060.

distinguished from this kind of civic action that is independent of government—Change.org instead of Change.gov.

The Carrotmob project (*http://carrotmob.org*) in San Francisco uses the "carrot" of consumer buying power to encourage small businesses to help the environment. Web-based tools are used to organize a consumer "flashmob," which channels business to stores that commit to environmental improvements. Carrotmob organizer Brent Schulkin asked local businesses how much they would be willing to invest in environmental improvements if the group he convened were to organize a buying spree directed toward that business. The result for the winning bodega in San Francisco's Mission District: more than triple the sales of an average Saturday, lots of free advertising, oodles of community goodwill, and a scheme to pay for improvements that, in turn, will save the business money over the long run.

Similarly, Obama Works (*http://www.whyobamaworks.org*), a corps of self-organizing citizen volunteers with no connection to Barack Obama's presidential campaign, used Internet technologies to organize neighborhood cleanups not only on a local scale but also on a national scale. Tech for Obama (*http://www.techforobama.com*) similarly galvanized support for the campaign within the techie community. Supporters, independent of the campaign, even went so far as to create "campaign offices" to recruit volunteers and organize voters. The largest one, in Silicon Valley, California, started on December 15, 2007.* Its Neighborhood Teams project geocoded the records of 1.5 million voters and used them to help over 40,000 neighbors find each other and volunteer in support of Obama. They produced and sent daily email newsletters to 5,000 people. Its 35-person technology team built its own tools to overcome inefficiencies in the organizing process. For its part, the official Obama campaign organized a summer program for Obama fellows (students and recent graduates who were recruited online) to come together and spend six weeks learning basic organizing skills from grassroots leaders. Senator Obama also spoke out publicly about creating a grassroots civic structure that could survive the campaign and continue to work on community issues after the election. In addition to meeting face to face, these volunteers used the Internet to form groups, organize, and bring about social change.

Both Carrotmob and the activities swirling about the Obama campaign are vivid examples of the use of new media technologies to convene and organize groups of people who, working together, can be more effective than any individual acting alone. Other examples include powerful online netroots organizations and blogs, ranging from MoveOn.org on the left to Red State at the other end of the political spectrum.

Civic groups are also taking advantage of new technologies to shine the light of greater transparency on government from afar. These third-party brokers of transparency are helping to do what government is not doing enough of for itself. The Cato Institute's Jim Harper launched the WashingtonWatch (*http://www.washingtonwatch.com*) program to track bills in Congress and estimate their cost or savings, if implemented into law. The Center for Responsive

* Silicon Valley for Obama (*http://www.sv4obama.com*).

Politics started OpenSecrets (*http://www.opensecrets.org*); and the New York Gallery Eyebeam launched FundRace (*http://fundrace.huffingtonpost.com*) (now part of the Huffington Post blog) to make the Federal Election Commission's databases easier to understand and search. PublicMarkup.org (*http://www.publicmarkup.org*) used collaborative editing software, known as a wiki, to mark up the Transparency in Government Act of 2008 and the various economic stabilization and bailout proposals floated during the economic crisis in the fall of that year.[†] MAPLight.org (*http://maplight.org*) shines the light of transparency on money politics by illuminating who contributed to which politician and how he or she subsequently voted.

But while online communities to date may have enabled people to click together instead of bowling alone, they are not yet producing changes in the way government institutions obtain and use information. These purely civic programs are disconnected from the practices and priorities of government. They may circle around political themes and issues but are not tied into institutional processes. They are, therefore, limited in what they can accomplish. A few pioneering programs, such as Connecticut's City Scan program, suggest forms that such change might take were we to redesign rather than try to route around the workings of government.[‡] Launched in the mid-1990s by the Connecticut Policy and Economic Council, CityScan helped city governments in Bridgeport and other municipalities collaborate with local communities to rescue derelict land-use sites. The organization secured a promise from each city to assist with the cleanup of a given number of parcels. Senior citizens and young people used first-generation digital cameras and handheld devices to photograph and track the progress of the work in their own communities. They mapped conditions on a website. The community groups communicated local information about land use that the government would not otherwise have had. They worked alongside the government while holding it accountable.

The government, in turn, worked with the CityScan teams, taking action based on their input and thereby giving relevance and impetus to these volunteer efforts. Technology helped both sides to organize the collaboration and to visualize its success. But the crux of CityScan was not the tools. The practices that CityScan evolved for robust collaboration between groups of citizens and local government are what differentiated this work from that of most civic action.

Collaboration and collective action, of course, are not new. Since the early nineteenth century, members of the august Athenaeum Club on Pall Mall in London have penned questions in a shared book, which was left in the club's leather-chaired drawing room for other members—including Dickens and Thackeray—to answer.[§] The book is still there.

As Stephen Kosslyn, chair of the Harvard Department of Psychology, explains, working together allows people to utilize many different tools. He says that, because we "simply do not

---

† See also "You Can Markup the Bills on the Mortgage Industry Bail Out," Ellen Miller, September 22, 2008 (*http://blog.sunlightfoundation.com/2008/09/22/*).

‡ Connecticut Policy and Economic Council, *http://www.city-scan.org* (accessed October 2008).

§ *The Athenaeum: Club and Social Life in London, 1824–1974*, Frank Richard Cowell, Heinemann, 1975.

have enough genes to program the brain fully in advance," we must extend our own intelligence with what he terms *social prosthetic systems*.‖ At the most basic level, we need to pool our diverse knowledge and skills. Even institutions need prosthetic extensions to make themselves smarter and more effective.

Virtually all activities of public life, including activism and organizing, depend on the work of teams. Until recently, however, most teams have relied heavily on physical proximity.

In the pre-Internet era, when working at a distance was not possible to the same extent (I had to be near you to join you), participation would have demanded a far greater time commitment to a cause. In the decade leading up to the American Revolution, the colonies organized Committees of Correspondence to communicate their practices of self-governance and fortify their opposition to the British.# Through the exchange of ideas about successful ways of working, they coordinated decentralized efforts at resistance across a distance. But they were committed to this all-important cause. Anything less and one would still have had to attend meetings to accomplish shared goals or alternatively pay dues to an organization to work on one's behalf. The ability now to use new technology to organize shared work makes it possible to work in groups across distance and institutional boundaries. Technology can reinforce the sense of working as a group by recreating some of the conditions of face-to-face work environments that build trust and belonging. The ability to organize collective activity puts more power in the hands of individuals by making it possible for people to self-organize and form teams around a boundless variety of goals, interests, and skill sets. And technology can support the formation of larger and more complex teams than previously imaginable.

Not surprisingly, the software community has been in the forefront of efforts to tap these benefits. Harvey Anderson, general counsel of the Mozilla Foundation, which makes the Firefox browser, says of the Mozilla community of volunteer programmers: "Many is better than one." He echoes a common refrain among those who work on open source governance: "Whenever we confront a problem, we have to ask ourselves: How do I parse and distribute the problem? How might we build feedback loops that incorporate more people?"*

The volunteer efforts extend the capacity of the full-time staff at Mozilla. By asking a community to help fix bugs in the software and rewrite the code, the organization begins to rely more and more on its community of volunteers, most of whom are not full time and most of whom may not even be known to the central project leadership. Instead, by articulating a set of common goals the Mozilla Foundation helps disparate groups of people organize

‖ "On the Evolution of Human Motivation: The Role of Social Prosthetic Systems," Stephen M. Kosslyn, in *Evolutionary Cognitive Neuroscience*, edited by S. M. Platek, et al., MIT Press, 2006; "Using Brain-Based Measures to Compose Teams: How Individual Capabilities and Team Collaboration Strategies Jointly Shape Performance," A. W. Wooley et al., *Social Neuroscience*, 2 (2007): 96–105.

"Committees of Correspondence of the American Revolution," Edward Day Collins, Annual Report of the American Historical Association (1901): 245–71.

* "Intellectual Property and Free Expression," lecture, Harvey Anderson, Stanford University, May 27, 2008 (notes on file with author).

themselves and perform practical, concrete tasks toward a shared end.† What begins as a process of information gathering builds steam and ends up creating a culture of engagement. Whereas the Mozilla organization makes the final decision about which software version to release, and when, the centralized organization cannot make these decisions without the help of the community of volunteers upon whom it relies to do the work. As the community comes to be more involved, actual decision making becomes a more amorphous concept, and control becomes dispersed. Everyone in the network has an influence.

Similarly, when a policy problem is divided into smaller parts, so that it can be distributed and worked on by collaborative teams, the drive toward openness and innovation begins. This openness may help government do its job better by bringing better information to the institution. But it can also introduce the institutional priorities to more people so that competition for solutions can emerge. Impelled by government mandate, the private sector and civil society might suggest their own solutions, evolving more robust public-private approaches, which may produce greater legitimacy than government currently enjoys. It may also help to solve complex economic and social problems faster and more efficiently.

New networking technologies, such as those embodied in Peer-to-Patent (*http://www .peertopatent.org/*), provide an opportunity to rethink the closed practices by which agencies gather information and make decisions. In 2007 the U.S. Congress mandated, and the president signed, a complete changeover by 2014 from incandescent bulbs to new, energy-efficient but mercury-containing lightbulbs. Congress instructed the EPA to implement the law into regulations. The agency, however, did not yet have a plan for disposing of the 300 million new mercury-containing bulbs sold in the United States in 2007—a number that will only increase as the mandate approaches.‡ The EPA could have solved this problem at little additional cost by setting up a simple online platform to involve a network of concerned citizens and organizations in identifying both the challenges raised by the new law and possible solutions— a lightbulb clearinghouse. Private sector companies might have stepped up to offer mercury reclamation programs sooner; foundations might have funded prizes to social entrepreneurs who devised effective solutions; interest groups might have run competitions among their members for effective recycling practices; scientists could have pointed out that they were working on the creation of a "nanoselenium" cloth to clean up mercury spills.§ Creating new channels of communication would not only inform and improve information gathering, but it could also lead to improved decision making and greater citizen involvement.

---

† "Summer 2008 Goals," Mitchell Baker, Mozilla Foundation chairman of the board, May 14, 2008 (*http: //blog.lizardwrangler.com/2008/05/14/*).

‡ "Energy Bill Bans Incandescent Lightbulbs." For more on mercury in lightbulbs, see the EPA website (*http://www.epa.gov/epawaste/hazard/wastetypes/universal/lamps/index.htm*). For more on the congressional mandate, see "A U.S. Alliance to Update the Lightbulb," Matthew Wald, *New York Times*, March 14, 2007.

§ "A Cloth to Cut the Mercury Risk from Lightbulbs," Henry Fountain, *New York Times*, July 8, 2008.

Policy makers have been slow to seize these opportunities. Innovation is not emanating from Washington; instead, the practices of government are increasingly disconnected from technological innovation and the opportunity to realize greater citizen participation—and therefore more expert information—in government. At the very least, this means that government institutions are not working as well as they might, producing declining rates of trust in government. (In 2008 the approval rating of both Congress and the president declined below 30 percent and, in some polls, even below 10 percent.)[||] At the very worst, there is a crisis of legitimacy. Clearly, relying on a small number of institutional players to make important decisions is not the only or the best way to confront complex social problems.

One explanation for this government failure lies in the unfamiliarity with technology displayed by many policy makers, including those responsible for its regulation. In the debate over net neutrality, then Senator Ted Stevens of Alaska, vice chair of the Senate Subcommittee on Science and Innovation, infamously referred to the Internet as "a series of tubes."[#] While tubes could arguably be a reasonable metaphor, history has not been kind to Senator Stevens, whose literal remark has now become iconic (it has its own Wikipedia entry) of Washington's ignorance of technology. But lack of technical knowledge is not the only cause of the government's slowness to capitalize on the promise of networked, online groups. An even more fundamental explanation lies in the outdated theory of participatory democracy that drives the design of government institutions.

Participatory Democratic Theory in the Age of Networks

After the advent of the World Wide Web, many anticipated that the Internet would revolutionize government, enabling an increase in political participation: an e-democracy as well as an e-commerce revolution. Pundits heralded a new Periclean Golden Age and celebrated the civic opportunities of the new communications and information technologies.[*] The deliberative ideal of people with diverse backgrounds and differing viewpoints debating and even voting on public issues was about to become a reality. It did not happen.[†]

[||] "Bush's 69% Job Disapproval Rating Highest in Gallup History," Frank Newport, April 22, 2008 (*http:// www.gallup.com/poll/106741/bushs-69-job-disapproval-rating-highest-gallup-history.aspx*); "Congressional Approval Falls to Single Digits for First Time Ever," July 8, 2008 (*http://www.rasmussenreports.com/public _content/politics/mood_of_america/congressional_performance*).

[#] "Series of Tubes" (*http://en.wikipedia.org/wiki/Series_of_tubes*). Also see the Series of Tubes weblog (*http:// www.seriesoftubes.net*) (accessed October 2008). The remark also spawned a graphic, "Series of Tubes as a Tube-map" (*http://www.boingboing.net/2007/07/20/series-of-tubes-as-a.html*).

[*] See, for example, *Internet Politics: States, Citizens, and New Communications Technologies*, Andrew Chadwick, Oxford University Press, 2006.

[†] "A Democracy of Groups," Beth Simone Noveck, First Monday, December 2005. (*http://firstmonday.org/ htbin/cgiwrap/bin/ojs/index.php/fm/article/view/1289/1209*)

The Failure of Direct Democracy

Proponents of direct democracy (sometimes called pure democracy) hoped that the Internet would promote participation unmediated by representative politics by allowing citizens to express themselves through voting (referenda, initiatives, recalls) more often on a wider range of issues.‡ Direct democrats argue for the use of technology to bolster such forms of direct participation as the initiative and referendum as a way to speed up the pace of governance.

During his presidential bid Ross Perot celebrated the direct democratic ideal and advocated that the president communicate directly with the American public via new media and encouraging the public to vote regularly and directly from home on issues.§ Auburn University houses a center dedicated to teledemocracy—large-scale, Internet-enabled, direct democracy.‖ Aficionados of proxy voting like the idea of using the web to allocate one's votes to a trusted interest group of one's choosing to render direct democratic voting better informed and more practical to administer.# A now-defunct Swedish company pioneered online proxy voting in the political arena, a practice in common use in the corporate sector.*

But security and reliability problems have plagued the rollout of both electronic, kiosk-based, voting and Internet-based vote-from-home technologies in the United States. Annual political elections are hard enough to run without introducing yet more possibilities for voter fraud and abuse. Instead, new services, such as Smartvote.ch from Switzerland, use the Internet to inform voting at the polling booth. Smartvote allows the user to plug in opinions in response to questions. The software then tabulates which candidate or proposal is closest to the user's own views. Countless informational websites have sprung up around the electoral process, whether it is the *Washington Post*'s subscription service to inform the reader every time her elected official casts a vote or one of myriad webcasts of online legislative coverage designed to inform and render the political process more accountable by virtue of its being transparent.†

‡ *Direct Democracy: The Politics of Initiative, Referendum, and Recall,* Thomas E. Cronin, Harvard University Press, 2006.

§ "Ross Perot and the Call In Presidency," Charles Krauthammer, *Time*, July 13, 1992, p. 84.

‖ Center for Tele-Democracy (*https://fp.auburn.edu/tann/*). See also Direct Democracy League (*http://www.ddleague-usa.net*).

"How Might Cyberspace Change American Politics," Eugene Volokh, *Loyola Los Angeles Law Review*, Vol. 34, 2001: 1213–20.

* The company was Vivarto Inc., founded by Mikael Nordfors. Its website is still online (*http://www.vivarto.com*).

† "The U.S. Congress Votes Database" (*http://projects.washingtonpost.com/congress/rss/*); "New Opportunities for Involving Citizens in the Democratic Process," Darlene Meskell, USA Services Intergovernmental Newsletter, Vol. 20, Fall 2007: 1–3 (*http://www.usaservices.gov/events_news/documents/USAServicesNewsletterFall-07.pdf*).

But the notion of widespread, push-button democracy in whatever form does little to address how to institutionalize complex decisions in particular cases. It is no wonder that the vision of participation by direct democratic voting has not taken off.

The Timidity of Deliberative Democracy

Deliberative democracy has been the dominant view of participation in contemporary political theory. At its center is the Habermasian notion that the reasoned exchange of discourse by diverse individuals representative of the public at large produces a more robust political culture and a healthier democracy.‡ It has almost become a commonplace that people of diverse viewpoints should talk to one another town-hall-style in public (this despite the fact that some recent empirical research even suggests that talking to people of differing viewpoints correlates to *reduced* participation in community life).§ It is a normative, democratic ideal unto itself and a means to the end of enhancing legitimacy in governance.

With the reduction in the cost of communications since the Internet, the hope had been that new information technologies would result in more widespread deliberation. Early e-democracy thinkers were optimistic that new technology could promote open discourse, equal participation, reasoned discussion, and the inclusion of diverse viewpoints. By allowing diverse participants to come together regardless of the boundaries of geography and time, the Internet could help overcome the hurdle of groupthink—a state in which like-minded people fail to consider alternatives adequately and fall prey to their own ideology.‖ Like direct democrats, advocates of deliberative democracy have also been disappointed. While social-scientific experiments in deliberation proliferate, deliberative theory founders on the practical reality of present-day political decision making. In practice, such conversations have been difficult to achieve, especially on a large scale.#

The weakness of the deliberative approach is not that it reaches too far (as direct democracy may) but that it does not reach far enough. By making talk the centerpiece of its normative aspirations, deliberative democracy's proponents assume that people are generally powerless and incapable of doing more than talking with neighbors to develop opinions or criticizing government to keep it honest. In theory, convening people of diverse viewpoints can have a beneficial impact on policy—assuming that the political system is structured to translate those

---

‡ *Deliberation Day*, Bruce A. Ackerman and James Fishkin, Yale University Press, 2004; *Debating Democracy and Deliberation: New Directions for Democratic Reform*, James S. Fishkin, Yale University Press, 1991; *Public Deliberation: Pluralism, Complexity, and Democracy*, James Bohman, MIT Press, 1996.

§ *Hearing the Other Side: Deliberative versus Participatory Democracy*, Diana C. Mutz, Cambridge University Press, 2006.

‖ *Why Societies Need Dissent*, Cass Sunstein, Harvard University Press, 2003, p. 118.

"Promise and Problems of E-Democracy: Challenges of Online Citizen Engagement," Ann Macintosh and Stephen Coleman, OECD, 2003.

viewpoints into meaningful participation in decision making.* But in practice, civic talk is largely disconnected from power. It does not take account of the fact that in a Web 2.0 world ordinary people can collaborate with one another to do extraordinary things.

The anthropology of deliberative participation leads to practices designed to present the finished work of institutional professionals, spark public opinion in response, and keep peace among neighbors engaged in civic discourse. The goal is not to improve decision making, for "there is no one best outcome; instead, there is a respectful communicative process."† The desire for civilized discussion and dispute resolution lead to a requirement of demographically balanced representation in the conversation. This may ensure inclusion of all affected interests but does not, as Alexander Meiklejohn said, necessarily result in an airing of all ideas worth hearing.‡ Deliberative democracy relegates the role of citizens to discussion only indirectly related to decision making and action. The reality of deliberation is that it is toothless. Perhaps it is, as Shaw once said: the single biggest problem in communication is the illusion that it has taken place.

In 2002, for example, the Civic Alliance to Rebuild Downtown New York (with the help of AmericaSpeaks, a civic group that organizes public deliberation, and the sponsorship of the Lower Manhattan Development Corporation) convened Listening to the City, a demographically representative deliberation exercise that brought 4,500 New Yorkers together in person and 800 online to talk about the first set of designs for the World Trade Center site.§ After hearing a presentation of the proposed plans, the group was highly critical. The high-profile, public nature of the event attracted a front-page story in the *New York Times*. It led directly to officials scuttling the plans and initiating a second round of designs.

The people power, as the populist historian Howard Zinn might say, of a large number of people massing in physical space created political pressure.‖ But people were neither expected nor invited to offer advice and expertise to inform the new plans. In this carefully orchestrated deliberation, they did not have an opportunity to get involved in the cleanup nor to identify problems or solutions to the mounting environmental and economic development challenges in the area. The problem was not presented in ways that could have led to private sector assistance either in the government's effort or as an adjunct to it. Nothing about the weekend changed or improved the way government works. Arguably, the Lower Manhattan

---

* *Democracy Online: The Prospects for Political Renewal through the Internet*, Peter M. Shane, ed., Routledge, 2004.

† "The Right of Public Participation in the Law-Making Process and the Role of the Legislature in the Promotion of This Right," Karen Czapanskiy and Rashida Manjoo, *University of Maryland School of Law Legal Studies*, Vol. 42, 2008: 31.

‡ *Political Freedom: The Constitutional Powers of the People*, Alexander Meiklejohn, Harper, 1960.

§ "Visions of Ground Zero: The Public; Officials Rethink Building Proposal for Ground Zero," Edward Wyatt with Charles V. Bagli, *New York Times*, July 21, 2002, p. A1.

‖ See, for example, *A Power Governments Cannot Suppress*, Howard Zinn, City Lights, 2007.

Development Corporation used the Listening to the City exercise to appear responsive to citizens' concerns while obscuring the real power politics at play, ultimately depriving New Yorkers of the chance to participate rather than simply react.[#]

The political sociologist Michael Schudson writes about the "monitorial citizen," who is too busy to play an active role in government.[*] While it is important and useful that government is responsive to the watchful citizen, this passive vision does not recognize the full potential of ordinary people to share expert information and effort with government. Among members of the public are scientists, engineers, doctors, lawyers, students, teachers, and nonprofessionals with a wide range of experience and enthusiasm who can contribute to an understanding of energy independence by submitting data. Others can analyze information given to them about endangered species or participate in the drafting of policies about transportation. There are expert conferences daily, where instead of presenting disconnected academic papers great minds might also be enlisted to solve pressing social problems. These potential resources for public decision making are largely going to waste.

Distinguishing Deliberative and Collaborative Democracy

There is a difference within participatory democracy between the two related but distinct notions of deliberation and collaboration. Deliberation focuses on citizens discussing their views and opinions about what the state should and should not do. The ability for people to talk across a distance facilitates the public exchange of reasoned talk. But deliberative polls, neighborhood assemblies, consensus councils, citizen panels, and other conversation-centered experiments, whether online or off, have not translated into improvements in decision making practices. The underlying Internet and telecommunications infrastructure is essential to conversing across a distance, but the Internet by itself is not the "killer app." If it were, the history of citizen participation in government institutions, which I describe in Chapter 6 [of *Wiki Government*], would already look very different.

While both deliberation and collaboration may be group-based, deliberative democracy suffers from a lack of imagination in that it fails to acknowledge the importance of connecting diverse skills, as well as diverse viewpoints, to public policy. Whereas diverse viewpoints might make for a more lively conversation, diverse skills are essential to collaboration.

Deliberation measures the quality of democracy on the basis of the procedural uniformity and equality of inputs. Collaboration shifts the focus to the effectiveness of decision making and outputs.

Deliberation requires an agenda for orderly discussion. Collaboration requires breaking down a problem into component parts that can be parceled out and assigned to members of the public and officials.

Starting from Zero: Reconstructing Downtown New York, Michael Sorkin, Routledge, 2003, pp. 57–61.

* *The Good Citizen: A History of American Civil Life*, Michael Schudson, Free Press, 1998.

Deliberation either debates problems on an abstract level before the implementation of the solution or discusses the solution after it has already been decided upon. Collaboration occurs throughout the decision making process. It creates a multiplicity of opportunities and outlets for engagement to strengthen a culture of participation and the quality of decision making in government itself.

Deliberation is focused on opinion formation and the general will (or sometimes on achieving consensus). Consensus is desirable as an end unto itself.[†] Collaboration is a means to an end. Hence the emphasis is not on participation for its own sake but on inviting experts, loosely defined as those with expertise about a problem, to engage in information gathering, information evaluation and measurement, and the development of specific solutions for implementation.

Deliberation focuses on self-expression. Collaboration focuses on participation. To conflate deliberative democracy with participatory democracy is to circumscribe participation by boundaries that technology has already razed. In fact, the distinctions between deliberation and collaboration become even more pronounced in the online environment, whose characteristics are increasingly making collaboration easier.[‡] New technologies make it possible to join ever more groups and teams. Such familiar websites as Wikipedia, Facebook, and even video games like World of Warcraft inculcate the practices of shared group work, be it writing encyclopedia entries or slaying monsters, at a distance.

New technology is also making it possible to divvy up tasks among a group. "Digg-style" tools for submitting and rating the quality of others' submissions have become commonplace ways to sort large quantities of information. Finally, the digital environment offers new ways to engage in the public exchange of reason. With new tools, people can "speak" through shared maps and diagrams rather than meetings. Competing proposals, using computer-driven algorithms and prediction markets, can evolve. Policy simulations using graphic technology can be created. Social networking tools enable collaborative making, doing, crafting, and creating. Yet most of the work at the intersection of technology and democracy has focused on how to create demographically representative conversations.[§] The focus is on deliberation, not collaboration; on talk instead of action; on information, not decision making.

[†] There are numerous proponents of this "strong" theory of civic engagement: *Strong Democracy*, Benjamin R. Barber, Princeton University Press, 1984; *Democracy and Technology*, Richard E. Sclove, Guilford, 1996; *Civic Engagement in American Democracy*, Theda Skocpol and Morris P. Fiorina, eds., Brookings, 1999.

[‡] "Digital Speech and Democratic Culture: A Theory of Freedom of Expression for the Information Society," Jack M. Balkin, *New York University Law Review*, Vol. 79, 2004: 1–58.

[§] The ideal type of citizens' group is one that is "composed of representatives of all strata of its community; it would be unbiased, courteous, well-organized, adequately financed, articulate." *Citizens Groups and Broadcasting*, Donald Guimary, Praeger, 1975, p. 148.

The Argument for an Open and Collaborative Democracy

The case for an open and collaborative vision of democratic theory is bolstered by three arguments: collaboration as a distinct form of democratic participation, visual deliberation, and egalitarian self-selection.

First, collaboration is a crucial but not well understood claim of democratic practice. There is a belief that the public does not possess as much expertise as people in government. Furthermore, the technology has not previously existed to make collaboration possible on a large scale. These spurious assumptions have produced an anemic conception of participatory democracy. Participation has generally referred to once-a-year voting or to community deliberation, in which neighbors engage in civil dialogue and public opinion formation on a small scale. New social and visual technologies (sometimes referred to as Web 2.0) are demonstrating that people are knowledgeable about everything from cancer to software and that, when given the opportunity to come together on a network and in groups, they can be effective at solving problems (not only deliberating about them). We must therefore distinguish between deliberation and collaboration as forms of participatory practice, exploring many examples of ordinary people joining together to do extraordinary things coordinated via the Internet. Peer-to-Patent is a paradigmatic case of database programmers and wind-farming experts working with patent examining professionals to make a better decision.

Second, the medium matters. To enable collaboration at scale requires designing the practices to make participation manageable and useful and then enabling those practices by means of technology. While the forms of participation will differ when information gathering or priority setting or data analysis are required, the technology should always be designed to reflect the work of the group back to itself so that people know which role they can assume and which tasks to accomplish. This second insight is what I term visual deliberation. In traditional deliberative exercises, strict procedures for who can talk govern the public conversation. But collaboration depends, instead, on having tools that convey the structure and rules of any given collaborative practice. This kind of social mirroring can be communicated through software. Peer-to-Patent uses visualizations to communicate the workflow by which information goes from the government institution to the public and back again. The website helps to convey what it means to review a patent application. It exploits rating and reputation techniques that help each group work together as a group, even across a distance. Hence, designing new democratic institutions also depends on designing the appropriate collaborative practices and embedding that design in software.

Third, collaboration is a form of democratic participation that is egalitarian—but egalitarian in a different way than the traditional understanding of the term. Typically, mass participation like voting is thought of as being quite democratic because everyone can participate in the same way. By contrast, Peer-to-Patent is not mass participation. It demands highly technical expertise. Successful participation depends upon the participant's interest in and knowledge of patents. If Peer-to-Patent were the only example of collaborative participation, it would not be egalitarian. But Peer-to-Patent multiplied by a thousand would be more institutionally diverse and complex. If the patent expert and the doctor and the teacher each have a vehicle for engagement, contexts would be created in which they each uniquely possess expertise and derive meaning.

In other words, people do not have to participate in the same exercise. One person may want to work on Peer-to-Patent, another may want to get involved in health care debates. One person may want to work on energy policy, another may want to organize a corps of energy "scouts" to go door-to-door and help neighbors evaluate their energy usage. The ability to self-select to participate in the arena of one's choosing is what makes collaborative democracy egalitarian. A person may be an expert on wetlands because she possesses professional credentialing. Another person may be an expert on wetlands because she lives near one. Perhaps it is a level of know-how or the enthusiasm to commit more time that generates status in other domains. For every project, there is a different kind of expertise, which could be sought. Experts will flock to those opportunities that exploit their intelligence. In this choice lies the equality of opportunity.

What does open and collaborative democracy look like in practice? In the old way of working, the bureaucrat might decide to repair a bridge in response to an opinion poll or vote that randomly obtains feedback. Or the bureaucrat might publish a fully developed plan to repair the bridge, ostensibly soliciting comment in response to a notice of proposed regulation, attracting participation by formal interest groups and lobbyists but not ordinary citizens, who can never hope to match the power and influence of corporate interests. Community groups might use the web to lobby for bridge repair but with no greater opportunity to get involved in detailed decisions. The government or a nongovernment organization (NGO) might organize a face-to-face deliberative discussion about the bridge and hope to use the event to trigger a newspaper article that will influence the decision. A similar online discussion may or may not attract attention.

Under a collaborative strategy, the bureaucrat establishes the process then frames and asks the questions that will get targeted information from bridge users (the truck driver, the commuter), from an engineer, and from the informed enthusiast. The public can contribute evidence and data to help inform specific decisions, analyze data once gathered, and share in the work of editing, drafting, and implementing policies. Alternatively, if officials articulate the priority of bridge safety, they might spur private sector businesses, nonprofits, and individuals to develop their own strategies, such as organizing a volunteer corps of bridge safety inspectors who log their work on a shared website. Citizens are no longer talking about the process: they are the process.

The future of public institutions demands that we create a collaborative ecosystem with numerous opportunities for experts (loosely defined as those with expertise about a problem) to engage. There is a Plum Book, which lists government jobs, and there is a Prune Book, which lists the toughest management positions. The pluot is supposed to be the sweetest variety of plum (or plum plus apricot). Yet there is no "Pluot Book" cataloging opportunities for part-time participation in government! When participatory democracy is defined to include diverse strategies for collaboration, when these thousands of opportunities to self-select come to light, a Pluot Book may well be needed.

Challenges for Collaborative Democracy

Critics might suggest that there already exists an architecture of participation, involving a wide array of actors in policy-making processes. Corporations participate through lobbyists and notice-and-comment rule-making. Nongovernmental organizations, too, funnel information to government through think tanks, white papers, and publications. Interest groups lobby and enlist their members to respond—usually through postcards and email—in rulemaking and legislative policy making. Scientists and others participate in deliberative, small-group, federal advisory committees that give advice to officials. And more public deliberation exercises, when they take place, help to generate opinion formation.

What is lacking, though, are effective ways for government to be responsive to the public, as opposed to corporate interests, large stakeholders, and interest groups. These citizen participation strategies suffer from the problem of "capture"—excessive political influence. Nominees are often subjected to ideological litmus tests. Lobbyists use their ability to participate to stall rather than inform the regulatory process. The use of notice-and-comment periods (in response to agency-proposed rule-making), which solicit individual participation, is typically late in the process, when policies are all but finalized. And people are too busy anyway to do the work of professionals in government.

What will prevent new, networked publics from becoming as entrenched as the lobbying culture that has produced the failures of current politics is that collaborative democracy seeks to proliferate many smaller opportunities for openness. The EPA doesn't need 100,000 people to work on the issue of asbestos or mercury. While some issues attract a huge number of people, obscure (yet important) decisions are made every day in government that could be made better if technology were used to open participation and oversight to a few dozen experts and enthusiasts—those that blogger Andy Oram calls the microelite: the 5 or 10 or 100 people who understand a discrete question and who are passionate about getting involved in a particular way.‖ Collaborative democracy is about making it easier for such people to find the areas where they want to work and contribute.

Some will counter that more active involvement in government by self-selecting private citizens would only increase the risk of corruption. Their fear is that opening up channels of participation would create a whole new class of online lobbyists and campaigns that participate to serve their own financial interests. Perhaps. But if the practices of twenty-first-century government were designed to split up tasks into many small fact-gathering and decision

---

‖ "In Search of Microelites: How to Get User-Generated Content," Andy Oram, November 14, 2007 (*http://radar.oreilly.com/2007/11/in-search-of-microelites-how-t.html*).

making exercises, technology would diversify against that risk. It is harder to corrupt a system with many parts. This approach would also make it easier for busy people to participate. And if government decisions were designed to be made in groups, group members would keep each other honest and blow the whistle if corruption occurs.

The primary challenge when engaging in deliberation is to avoid capture and corruption by those who speak with the most influence. In a collaborative governance environment the greatest challenge is one of design: organizing the work most effectively to tap outside expertise. The bureaucrats who design the collaborative processes might be tempted to set them up in such a way as to promote participation by particular vested interests over others. But open processes that enable people to evaluate one another's participation help to preclude the risks. At the very least, technology makes it possible to organize decision making in ways that might overcome abuses familiar from the offline world. If governance is thought of as a granular and focused set of practices, ways can be designed to delegate greater power to citizens to gather facts, spend money, and participate in making decisions.

Giving ordinary people—as distinct from corporations and interest groups—the right and ability to participate enables them to form new groups better suited to address new problems. Alone, there is not much any one person can do to bring about change or to participate meaningfully and usefully in a policy-making process. But working together a group can take meaningful action. Online groups can also change their collective goals in response to pressing problems more quickly than traditional organizations that lock in their own institutional and individual priorities.

Government need not—it must not—fear new technology and the opportunity it creates to invite participation from those with the experience in the field. Reinventing democracy as collaborative democracy will create work for government. Having a blog requires someone to respond to comments. Posting a wiki demands following the changes as they evolve. Creating a web form to invite input from the public necessitates honing in on the right questions and listening to the resulting answers. Participation will require staffing and technology to manage. But a collaborative culture does not place the burden on government or the public alone to address complex social problems. Instead, by organizing collaboration, government keeps itself at the center of decision making as the neutral arbiter in the public interest and also benefits from the contributions of those outside of government. Joseph Nye explains the collaborative imperative for governments:

> The very nature of leadership has changed in today's interdependent, globalized world. In information-based societies, networks are replacing hierarchies, and knowledge workers are less deferential. Business is changing in the direction of "shared leadership" and "distributed leadership," with leaders in the center of a circle rather than atop a hierarchy.... Modern leaders need an ability to use networks, to collaborate, and to encourage participation. They need to be able to make decisions within rapidly changing contexts. They need to attract followers into new identities—both individual and social—and provide meaning in a disruptive world of

globalization. In short, they need to use the soft power of attraction as well as the hard power of force and threat, both at home and in foreign policy.#

In other words, collaboration offers a huge potential payoff in the form of more effective government. Effective government, in turn, translates into better decision making and more active problem solving, which could spur growth in society and the economy.

Let's say that the Environmental Protection Agency wants to pass a regulation protecting a certain endangered species. As currently designed, public input comes too late for anyone but a lobbyist to effectively have a say. But the Internet makes it possible to design methods for soliciting better expertise sooner from private citizens. Or imagine that the United States Postal Service wants to cut its energy bills by 30 percent over the next three years. An online best-practices website would enable the USPS to generate many solutions from crowds of people. Those crowds could include self-selected experts across federal, state, and local government as well as motivated members of the public. Imagine that a series of economic events triggers a crisis of confidence in the economy. Technology could make it possible to track economic data in a more transparent, collaborative, verifiable way.

Innovation in the practices of governance will require investment. But if government can design effective mechanisms—law, policy, and technology—to build the bridge between institutions and networks, it can enhance its legitimacy and value. Look what happened to the entertainment industry. Fearing a loss of ad revenue from consumers' home taping, the movie studios and television broadcasters initially feared the new tools. They (unsuccessfully) sued the makers of the Betamax personal video recorders (the precursor of the DVD and the VCR) in an effort to put the consumer electronics companies out of the Betamax business altogether.* People wanted to watch movies at home and would not be stopped. Eventually, the home video rental market, far from threatening the incumbents, flourished and vastly increased their markets.

Similarly, in response to the advent of digital technologies that reduce the cost of making and distributing nearly perfect copies of music, the record labels proposed legislation to criminalize new forms of copyright infringement. They began suing twelve-year-olds and grandmothers for illegally sharing music files via peer-to-peer networks and filed suit to put the makers of these new digital technologies out of business.† But the law is out of step with society's music

---

"Picking a President," Joseph Nye, *Democracy Journal*, Fall 2008: 19–28.

* Sony Corp. of America. Universal City Studios, 464 U.S. 417 (1984).

† Prioritizing Resources and Organization for Intellectual Property Act of 2008 (ProIP Act) S. 3325. "Big Content Gloats as Bush Signs Pro-IP Act," Nate Anderson, Ars Technica, October 14, 2008 (*http:// arstechnica.com/news.ars/post/20081014-bush-signs-pro-ip-act-big-content-gloats.html*); "RIAA Settles with 12-Year-Old Girl," John Borland, September 9, 2003 (*http://news.cnet.com/2100-1027-5073717.html*); "RIAA versus Grandma, Part II: The Showdown That Wasn't," Eric Bangeman, December 16, 2007 (*http:// arstechnica.com/tech-policy/news/2007/12/riaa-versus-grandma-part-ii-the-showdown-that-wasnt.ars*). See also MGM Studios Inc. v. Grokster, Ltd., 545 U.S. 913 (2005) (peer-to-peer file-sharing case), and also *http: //arstechnica.com/old/content/2005/06/5042.ars*.

consumption practices: while traditional business models wane, iTunes, eMusic and other alternatives innovate and embrace the power of new technology. Instead of cheating or routing around the music laws, these new entrants are helping to reengineer and reshape the industry. If institutions don't work with the networks, networks will work around them, rendering government practices increasingly disconnected, ineffectual, and brittle.

About the Author

BETH SIMONE NOVECK is the United States Deputy Chief Technology Officer for open government. She directs the White House Open Government Initiative at *http://www.whitehouse.gov/open*. She is on leave as a professor of law and director of the Institute for Information Law and Policy at New York Law School and McClatchy visiting professor of communication at Stanford University. Dr. Noveck taught in the areas of intellectual property, technology, and first amendment law and founded the law school's "Do Tank" (*http://dotank.nyls.edu*), a legal and software R&D lab focused on developing technologies and policies to promote open government. Dr. Noveck is the author of *Wiki Government: How Technology Can Make Government Better, Democracy Stronger, and Citizens More Powerful* (Brookings Institution Press, 2009) and editor of *The State of Play: Law, Games and Virtual Worlds* (NYU Press, 2006).

CHAPTER FIVE

Engineering Good Government

Howard Dierking

Looking back over the history of the United States, it is not just remarkable to see how 13 former colonies of the British Empire could come together to form what became the longest continuously functioning government in recorded history, but it is also incredible that such a durable government was set up as a republic. Until the United States, history records few examples of even moderately successful republics, and even those moderate successes were aided by factors external to the specific system of government employed. How, then, did the framers of the U.S. Constitution succeed in creating a republican-style government where so many had failed?

Simply put, by good design.

When looking back through the Constitution and the Federalist Papers, we can observe that the founders took many novel approaches in crafting the structure of the United States. Indeed, Alexander Hamilton went so far as to describe these approaches as based on the new "science of politics."* The Constitution was the embodiment of this new science and served as a lightweight framework, providing enough prescription to ensure basic stability in the republic, but little more, so as to enable the government to adapt over time and thus ensure the longevity of that stability.

In many ways, the framers of the Constitution were like the software designers of today. Modern software design deals with the complexities of creating systems composed of

---

* Federalist 9.

innumerable components that must be stable, reliable, efficient, and adaptable over time. A language has emerged over the past several years to capture and describe both practices to follow and practices to avoid when designing software. These are known as *patterns* and *antipatterns*. This chapter will explore known software design patterns and antipatterns in context of the U.S. Constitution and will hopefully encourage further application of software design principles as a metaphor for describing and modeling the complex dynamics of government in the future.

The Articles of Confederation and the Stovepipe Antipattern

Software design patterns and antipatterns can be classified by the general type of problem they describe or solve. Patterns in a category known as *enterprise architecture* make a good place to begin exploring the connection between the worlds of government and software, as they tend to be concerned more with the management of overall systems than with lines of code. What follows is an exploration into how the Articles of Confederation, the first constitution of the United States, represents a classic example of an antipattern known as the *enterprise stovepipe*. From that comparison, we will explore strategies for overcoming an enterprise stovepipe and will then see how the Constitution is in fact a historical illustration of those strategies.

> **N O T E**
> An antipattern is much like a regular pattern in that it describes observable phenomena that tend to occur with some frequency. However, antipatterns go further to define specific types of patterns which generally yield negative outcomes. Put another way, an antipattern describes a pattern that should be stopped.

The First Constitution

Drafted during the early part of the American Revolution, the Articles of Confederation became the first constitution for the new confederacy of 13 states. Though the original draft of the Articles provided for a strong federal government, the sentiments of the time resulting from the war for independence from Great Britain ultimately yielded a governmental structure that consisted of a loose confederation of independent states, bound together by a "firm league of friendship."† While the Articles did provide provision for a federal government, the language used to define its goals was undermined by the language used to describe the constraints on its ability to achieve those goals. For example, in describing the role and ability of the federal government to assess and levy taxes on the states to provide for the cost of war, including the recently fought Revolutionary War, Article 7 establishes the following:

† Articles of Confederation, Article III.

All charges of war, and all other expenses that shall be incurred for the common defense or general welfare, and allowed by the United States in Congress assembled, shall be defrayed out of a common treasury, which shall be supplied by the several states, in proportion to the value of all land within each state, granted to or surveyed for any Person, as such land and the buildings and improvements thereon shall be estimated according to such mode as the united states in congress assembled, shall from time to time direct and appoint. The taxes for paying that proportion shall be laid and levied by the authority and direction of the legislatures of the several states within the time agreed upon by the united states in congress assembled.[‡]

The problem in the preceding example is simply that while the federal government is charged with a responsibility, its ability to fulfill that responsibility is up to the sole discretion of the various state legislatures. This example is representative of a more general pattern that can be seen throughout the 12 Articles. Moreover, history shows that the federal government established under the Articles was simply ignored by the states, resulting in an embarrassingly long delay in accepting the Treaty of Paris and the inability of the federal Congress to pay back debts accumulated during the Revolutionary War, including payment to soldiers of the Continental Army.

The Stovepipe Antipattern

From a software architect's perspective, the Articles of Confederation created a governmental system that is best represented by an antipattern known as a *stovepipe enterprise*.[§] This term derives from the metaphor of the exhaust pipes that sit atop a potbellied, wood-burning stove. Because burning wood releases byproducts that corrode metal, these exhaust pipes would require constant patching, and this patching would generally use whatever material was on hand, ultimately resulting in a chaotic patchwork of fixes.

In software architecture, a stovepipe enterprise is formed as the result of multiple application development efforts that are conducted in isolation from one another. This development approach yields a patchwork of systems built using different development methods and different technologies, and many times having overlapping or competing functionality (see Figure 5-1).

As a result, any form of integration, whether it is integrating individual systems within an enterprise or integrating with systems external to an enterprise, is difficult or altogether impossible.

Internal integration is equivalent to navigating a minefield of systems with similar terms representing different concepts, or multiple terms for the same concept. Additionally, many such systems in a stovepipe enterprise provide many of the same business processes, but use completely different rules in accomplishing those processes. Therefore, integrating one system

[‡] Articles of Confederation, Article VIII.

[§] *AntiPatterns: Refactoring Software, Architectures, and Projects in Crisis* (Wiley, 1998).

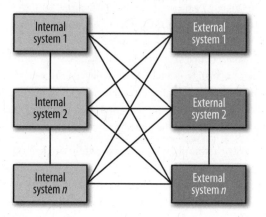

FIGURE 5-1. Example of a stovepipe enterprise

within a stovepipe enterprise to any other system requires, at the very minimum, finding the correct system with which to integrate, resolving differences in technology, resolving differences in terminology, and ensuring that both systems have a sufficient level of understanding about the internal processes of each other.

If you multiply these consequences by the total number of systems that must generally integrate in even the most trivial-sized enterprise, you can see that the net result of a stovepipe enterprise is at best an extremely high cost of maintenance. More realistically, however, the likely result is that automated integration will not be attempted at an enterprise level, and more costly manual integration tactics will prevail. Additionally, the lack of a single interface point for external integration may inadvertently lend itself to an environment where individual systems begin integrating outside the enterprise, effectively broadening the enterprise stovepipe to a multienterprise stovepipe. In this context, the stovepipe antipattern can bring with it the unintended consequence of tying the entire enterprise to expectations set by one of its parts.

Order from Chaos: The Standards Reference Model

The core problem behind a stovepipe enterprise is that there is effectively no underlying framework to provide basic guidance around integrating systems in an enterprise. Put another way, there is no architecture. Each system attached to the stovepipe is designed independently of, and evolves separately from, the other systems in the enterprise. The solution for reversing this antipattern is found in both laying down a common set of standards around how applications are to be constructed and integrated, and creating a set of core infrastructure components to provide determinism across systems in terms of management and integration, as well as to provide consistency for integrating with external enterprises. In software architecture terms, this solution is known as a *standards reference model* (see Table 5-1).

TABLE 5-1. An example standards reference model

Document	Purpose	Scope
Open Systems Reference Model	Defines a list of target standards for any development project	Enterprise
Technology Profile	Defines a more concise list of standards for a specific development project	Enterprise
Operating Environment	Defines guidelines around system release and installation	Enterprise
Systems Requirements Profile	Defines a summary of key requirements for a family of related systems	System family
Enterprise Architecture	Provides a complete view over a system or family of systems	System family and system
Computational Facilities Architecture	Defines the abstract integration points for a system or family of systems	System family
Interoperability Specifications	Defines the technical details for a Computational Facilities Architecture	System
Development Profile	Records the implementation plans to ensure successful integration between systems	System family

As should be evident, the standards reference model is composed of multiple levels of standards based on relevant organizational scope, and it proceeds from abstract to concrete. This is an important point to note, because in any sizable organization, failure to establish proper scope boundaries when attempting to solve a stovepipe antipattern can result in another antipattern known as the *blob*, whereby a single entity evolves to assume a large set of responsibilities outside of those to which it was originally purposed.

> **NOTE**
>
> A blob or god class is the result of a poorly maintained software system where a single unit of program code grows to assume responsibility—in part or in whole—for nearly every aspect of system behavior. The result is that this unit of code becomes large and brittle (a change to one section can have dire unintended consequences to other sections), and the system does not evolve.

Some of the various scopes commonly associated with a standards reference model include the enterprise scope, the system family scope, and the system scope. To prevent the creation of an inflexible architecture, each scope must balance flexibility with prescription. For example, it is generally unreasonable to assert a code or system-scope directive at the enterprise scope, since such an assertion would be dependent on far too many additional predicates relating to hardware, operating systems, and various other tools. Rather, many times at this scope, the appropriate standard is simply to identify the possible standards that are available for use by various system families, and define a process for augmenting that list. As one proceeds from the enterprise scope to the specific system scope, the various standards can become incrementally more concrete, since at those lower scopes, there is also much more known about the objects of those standards. This scoped approach enables the standards reference model, and the order that follows suit, to scale to very large enterprises.

The Constitution As a Standards Reference Model

By the time of the Philadelphia Convention in 1787, the delegates along with the majority of the leaders of the time were well aware of the consequences from the lack of strong union under the Articles of Confederation. However, there was a great deal of debate surrounding the available alternate forms of governance. The fundamental problem was one of how to create a stronger, more permanent union between the states and provide for the welfare of all citizens while not putting the fundamental principles of liberty and self-governance at risk. Many at the time argued that a move toward a stronger central government, which had initially been written into the Articles of Confederation and later removed, was seen as an inevitable path toward the form of despotism over which the war for independence from Great Britain was fought. On the other hand, structuring the government as a single republic was also seen by many, including Federalists such as Alexander Hamilton, as simply an alternate path toward despotism. In arguing for the government laid out in the Constitution, Hamilton acknowledged that throughout history, many famous republics "were continually agitated, and at the rapid succession of revolutions, by which they were kept in a state of perpetual vibration, between the extremes of tyranny and anarchy."[||] Hamilton is referring here to the historical example referenced by many opponents of the proposed constitution of the ancient Greek and Roman republics. Such governments were ultimately unable to prosecute an effective government or control the rise and growth of internal factions. Additionally, a more general criticism of republican government in that day came from men such as Montesquieu, who argued that a traditional republican form of government could remain effective within only a small populace.

The framers argued ardently that such prior models could overcome their historical limitations thanks to significant improvements such as the "regular distribution of power into distinct departments—the introduction of legislative balances and checks—the institution of courts composed of judges, holding their offices during good behavior—the representation of the people in the legislature by deputies of their own election."[#] These were the elements that greatly shaped the U.S. Constitution and created a framework for the establishment of a confederated republic with a federal government strong enough to carry out the duties for which it was established, but engineered in such a way as to prevent a majority or minority faction from subverting the general welfare.

|| Federalist 9.

Ibid.

The confederated republican government codified in the Constitution and argued for in the Federalist Papers is similar in nature to a standards reference model. Similarly, it proceeds from the abstract definition of goals to the establishment of the various components of the federal government as well as their relationship to one another and to the state legislatures. In reference model terms, it establishes itself as the core set of standards against which all concrete standards are evaluated. It then proceeds to define more concrete participants of the systems—specifically, the three branches of the federal government. Additionally, it defines in concrete terms the relationships that the branches are to have with one another and with the states (see Table 5-2).

TABLE 5-2. Constitution as a standards reference model

Section	Purpose	Scope
Preamble	Defines the core principles to which any system of proposed government must conform	Union
Articles 1–3	Establishes the principals of the federal government	Federal
Article 4	Defines the relationship between the federal government and states and among the states themselves	Federal and state
Articles 5–7	Defines procedures for amending (extending) the Constitution, establishes it as the ultimate legal authority, and defines ratifying procedures	Federal and state

Like a standards reference model, the Constitution provided a unifying vision and a common set of rules by which other acts of legislation could be evaluated. Additionally, it defined the fundamental interoperability points between the various principalities that had a role to play in government, but then deferred to those principalities to the determination, promulgation, and interpretation of those responsibilities. As a framework, these lightweight qualities are what enabled the United States to reach the geographic scale that it did and even survive near collapse in the face of secession nearly 100 years later.

Continued Maintenance: The Blob and Confederacy

While the stovepipe antipattern represents just one high-level example, you can hopefully see at this point that many of the patterns that have emerged in software design have applicability in the structuring and maintenance of government. Looking into the future, another antipattern worth investigating is known as the *blob* or the *god class*.

The Blob

One of the most widely used paradigms in designing software is known as *object orientation*. At a very high level, this approach describes the organization of source code into discrete units called *classes* whose purpose is to encapsulate related data and behaviors for a given abstraction.

For example, were one to model the U.S. governmental structure using an object-oriented approach, the resultant classes might look something like Figure 5-2.

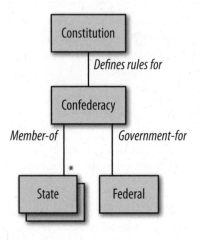

FIGURE 5-2. The U.S. government as an object model

One of the benefits of using the paradigm—and much of the reason for its popularity in designing modern systems—is that it naturally breaks up complexity into manageable units of code which can be verified and maintained independently without causing a ripple effect throughout the entire system. As we can observe, this was certainly an expected benefit that would result from the Constitution's design of a confederated republican government, as Hamilton articulates by quoting Montesquieu:

> Should a popular insurrection happen, in one of the confederate States, the others are able to quell it. Should abuses creep into one part, they are reformed by those that remain sound. The State may be destroyed on one side, and not on the other; the confederacy may be dissolved, and the confederates preserve their sovereignty.[*]

As with any endeavor, a great set of tools or paradigms does not by itself yield a well-designed system. In the world of object-oriented design, constant effort must be exerted to ensure that the classes defined most accurately represent the abstractions that they are meant to describe and that the system's code is most appropriately divided among the classes in accordance with previously defined goals such as independent testing and maintainability. Should the software designer become lax in this effort, an antipattern known as the blob or the god class can emerge.

The blob antipattern is generally the result of a system designed using object-oriented tools, but without the discipline of object-oriented thinking. It reveals itself in a design "where one

[*] Ibid.

class monopolizes the processing...."[†] Looking at this antipattern in terms of responsibilities, the blob class assumes a significant majority of the responsibilities in the system, and generally relegates the other classes to dependent supporters.

The problems inherent in this type of system are many, and all stem from the fact that nearly every capability that the system supports is tightly associated at the code level—a term in software design known as *coupling*—with every other capability in the system. Therefore, any change to one capability requires modifying the blob class, which would then impact every other capability for which the blob has assumed responsibility. This creates a situation that is inefficient at best due to the amount of energy that must be exerted to manage changes or new capabilities. At worst, it dramatically increases the likelihood that changes to the blob will unintentionally break a seemingly unrelated part of the system.

The solution for keeping an object-oriented system from devolving into a blob antipattern is constant expenditure of effort to ensure that all system logic meets two basic criteria: high cohesion and low coupling. High cohesion describes ensuring that all code that is logically related is physically grouped together in the same class. This enables a discrete area of functionality in a system to be more comprehensible, and more importantly, testable. Low coupling describes the removal of as many dependencies as possible between the aforementioned cohesive units. This enables each unit to evolve independently while significantly reducing the risk that the evolution of one unit will unintentionally cause the failure of another. Additionally, it has the added benefit of enabling the designer to more confidently evaluate the efficiency of each unit without the distraction of the efficiency or inefficiency of related units.

The blob and government

The blob antipattern many times develops when a system is relatively small in size. The entire system can be known in whole, and so the necessity of solid design is less obvious than in large systems, where the sheer number of capabilities provided makes such principles a necessity. The framers of the Constitution also understood these principles in context of the size and scope of government. For example, in articulating how an extensive republic is more beneficial to guarding the public interest, James Madison argues that by extending the sphere:[‡]

> ...you take in a greater variety of parties and interests; you make it less probable that a majority of the whole will have a common motive to invade the rights of other citizens; or if such a common motive exists, it will be more difficult for all who feel it to discover their own strength, and to act in unison with each other. Besides other impediments, it may be remarked, that where there is a consciousness of unjust or dishonorable purposes, communication is always checked by distrust, in proportion to the number whose concurrence is necessary.

[†] *AntiPatterns: Refactoring Software, Architectures, and Projects in Crisis* (Wiley, 1998).

[‡] Federalist 10.

Madison argues here that the size of the union was one of the very things that would shield it from the rise of despotism at the hands of any group of citizens, whether they are in the majority or the minority. On this point, I believe that additional reflection is warranted. Madison seems to define size predominantly in terms of geography, and as such, the difficulty that he describes in specific groups being able to discover their own strength seems to be somewhat predicated on the geographic disbursement and isolation of the various members.

In the present age, we live in a society where access to any person or any piece of information is never more than a few button or mouse clicks away. Size, according to its utility as described by Madison, cannot be measured in square miles or even number of people, but in the speed with which individuals can connect with one another. And by this definition, the sphere has in effect grown smaller. This increases the risk of the blob antipattern developing in government by way of the blurring and sometimes outright dissolution of the scope boundaries established explicitly in the Constitution and implicitly as envisioned in the Federalist Papers. A governmental blob can take many forms; however, media and the press can serve as a good indicator for where the concerns of citizens are most closely placed. And this indicator is not encouraging as we are witnessing the continued decline of local news outlets due to either consolidation or outright closure. This places the responsibility of all news—and by association, all perceived concerns of government—to national news organizations, who as a product of seeing a high return on investment for each news story they pursue, will naturally focus their attentions at the federal scope. A shift in the focus of the citizenry from an inherently local to federal scope, coupled with a smaller society as a result of advances in technology, creates an environment where it becomes easier for political factions to mobilize and where their effects can be far more reaching and destructive.

Conclusion

While this chapter is not intended to provide comprehensive treatment of republican government and Constitutional history, nor a complete catalog of software design patterns, it has hopefully demonstrated that there is a strong correlation between the two, and has effectively put forth software design as a new metaphor for exploring the dynamics of government. Further, as we are currently in a period of widespread reform efforts, the lessons and mitigation paths described in antipatterns, such as the blob, can help to ensure that reform efforts continue to yield a sustainable and maintainable republic.

The next logical step, and the subject of future research, will include taking aspects of the U.S. governmental system and actually modeling them in software. Such an endeavor will more concretely demonstrate the patterns outlined in this chapter, along with many others. More importantly, however, it will create an executable model that can be modified and tested based on the application of new patterns. As the evolution of technology continues to change some of the fundamental dynamics of our society, it is likely that the very same technology will be necessary to enable our government to evolve as well.

About the Author

 **HOWARD DIERKING** works at Microsoft as a program manager on the MSDN and TechNet Web platform team, where he is focused on principles of collective intelligence as they relate to content. Howard has a degree in political science from Samford University and has spent the majority of his professional career as a software developer and architect. His continued research interests include software design and development process as well as political philosophy and macroeconomics.

CHAPTER SIX

Enabling Innovation for Civic Engagement

David G. Robinson
Harlan Yu
Edward W. Felten

Until recently, government data made its way to the Internet primarily through central planning: civil servants gathered the raw data generated by their work, processed and analyzed it to make maps, reports, and other informative products, and offered these to citizens seeking insight into school performance, crime in their neighborhoods, or the status of proposed laws. But a new, more dynamic approach is now emerging—one that enlists private actors as allies in making government information available and useful online.

NOTE

A portion of this chapter was previously published as "Government Data and the Invisible Hand," *Yale Journal of Law & Technology,* **Vol. 11, 2009 (***http://papers.ssrn.com/ sol3/papers.cfm?abstract_id=1138083***).**

Citizen Initiatives Lead the Way

When the Web was born, computational and network resources were so expensive that building large-scale websites required substantial institutional investment. These inherent limits made government the only free provider of much online civic information, and kept significant troves of data off the Web entirely, trapped in high-end proprietary information services or dusty file cabinets. Government officials picked out what they thought to be the most critical and useful information, and did their best to present it usefully.

Costs for storage and processing have plummeted, but another shift, less well known, is at least as important: the tools that let people develop new websites are easier to use, and more powerful and flexible, than ever before. Most citizens have never heard of the new high-level computer languages and coding "frameworks" that automate the key technical tasks involved in developing a new website. Most don't realize that resources such as bandwidth and storage can be bought for pennies at a time, at scales ranging from tiny to massive, with no upfront investment. And most citizens will never need to learn about these things—but we will all, from the most computer-savvy to the least tech-literate, reap the benefits of these developments in the civic sphere. By reducing the amount of knowledge, skill, and time it takes to build a new civic tool, these changes have put institutional-scale online projects within the reach of individual hobbyists—and of any voluntary organization or business that empowers such people within its ranks.

These changes justify a new baseline assumption about the public response to government data: when government puts data online, someone, somewhere, will do something innovative and valuable with it.

Private actors of all different stripes—businesses and nonprofit organizations, activists and scholars, and even individual volunteers—have begun to use new technologies on their own initiative to reinvent civic participation. Joshua Tauberer, a graduate student in linguistics, is an illustrative example. In 2004, he began to offer GovTrack.us, a website that mines the Library of Congress's (LOC) THOMAS system to offer a more flexible tool for viewing and analyzing information about bills in Congress (see Chapter 18). At that time, THOMAS was a traditional website, so Tauberer had to write code to decipher the THOMAS web pages and extract the information for his database. He not only used this database to power his own site, but also shared it with other developers, who built popular civic sites such as OpenCongress and MAPLight (see Chapter 20), relying on his data. Whenever the appearance or formatting of THOMAS's pages changed, Tauberer had to rework his code. Like reconstructing a table of figures by measuring the bars on a graph, this work was feasible, but extremely tedious and, ultimately, needless. In recent years, with encouragement from Tauberer and other enthusiasts, THOMAS has begun to offer computer-readable versions of much of its data, and this has made tools such as GovTrack easier to build and maintain than ever before.

Providing for Reuse and Innovation

Making government data public should always include putting it online, where it is more available and useful to citizens than in any other medium. But deciding that certain data should be published online is the beginning, not the end, of an important series of choices.

All publishing is not equal—instead, the way data is formatted and delivered makes a big difference. Public sector leaders interested in supporting this trend should look for the formats and approaches that best enable robust and diverse third-party reuse. Such a publishing strategy is powerful because it allows citizens themselves to decide how best to interact with civic data. Government-produced reports, charts, and analyses can be very valuable, but it is essential to also publish the underlying data itself in a computer-friendly format that makes it easy for the vibrant community of civic technologists to make and share a broad range of tools for public engagement.

Innovation is most likely to occur when data is available for free over the Internet in open, structured, machine-readable formats for anyone to *download in bulk*, meaning all at once. Structured formats such as XML make it easy for any third party to process and analyze government information at minimal cost. Internet delivery using standard protocols such as HTTP can offer immediate access to this data for developers. Each set of government data should be uniquely addressable on the Internet in a known, permanent location. This permanent address can allow both third-party services, as well as ordinary citizens, to refer back to the primary unmodified data source as provided by the government.

Public government data should be provided in this format in a timely manner. As new resources are added to a given data set, or changes are made, government should also provide data feeds, using open protocols such as RSS, to notify the public about incremental additions or changes. However, a feed that provides updates is of limited value unless the existing body of information that is being modified can itself be downloaded in full. These principles are not ours alone—they are consistent with a number of other recommendations, including the Open Government Working Group's list of eight desirable properties for government data (*http:// resource.org/8_principles.html*).

In an environment with structured data, questions about what to put on the home page become decisions for the public affairs department. Technical staff members in government, whose hard work makes the provision of underlying data possible, will have the satisfaction of seeing their data used widely—rather than lamenting interfaces that can sometimes end up hiding valuable information from citizens.

Third-party innovators provided with government data in this way will explore more advanced features, beyond simple delivery of data. A wide range of motivations will drive them forward, including nonprofit public service, volunteer enthusiasm, political advocacy, and business objectives. Examples of the features they may explore include:

Advanced search
  The best search facilities go beyond simple text matching to support features such as multidimensional searches, searches based on complex and/or logical queries, and searches for ranges of dates or other values. They may account for synonyms or other equivalences among data items, or suggest ways to refine or improve the search query, as some of the leading web search services already do.

RSS feeds

RSS, which stands for Really Simple Syndication, is a simple technology for notifying users of events and changes, such as the creation of a new item or an agency action. The best systems could adapt the government's own feeds (or other offerings) of raw data to offer more specialized RSS feeds for individual data items, for new items in a particular topic or department, for replies to a certain comment, and so on. Users can subscribe to any desired feeds, using RSS reader software, and those feeds will be delivered automatically to the user. The set of feeds that can be offered is limited only by users' taste for tailored notification services.

Links to information sources

Government data, especially data about government actions and processes, often triggers news coverage and active discussion online. An information service can accompany government data with links to, or excerpts from, these outside sources to give readers context into the data and reactions to it.

Mashups with other data sources

To put an agency's data in context, a site might combine that data with other agencies' data or with outside sources. For example, MAPLight.org combines the voting records of members of Congress with information about campaign donations to those members. Similarly, the nonprofit group Pro Publica offers a map showing the locations of financial institutions that have received funds from the Treasury Department's Troubled Asset Relief Program (TARP).

Discussion forums and wikis

A site that provides data is a natural location for discussion and user-generated information about that data; this offers one-stop shopping for sophisticated users and helps novices put data in context. Such services often require a human moderator to erase off-topic and spam messages and to enforce civility. The First Amendment may make it difficult for government to perform this moderation function, but private sites face no such problem, and competition among sites can deter biased moderation.

Visualization

Often, large data sets are best understood by using sophisticated visualization tools to find patterns in the data. Sites might offer users carefully selected images to convey these patterns, or they might let users control the visualization tool to choose exactly which data to display and how. Visualization is an active field of research and no one method is obviously best; presumably sites would experiment with different approaches.

Automated content and topic analysis

Machine-learning algorithms can often analyze a body of data and infer rules for classifying and grouping data items. By automating the classification of data, such models can aid search and foster analysis of trends.

Collaborative filtering and crowdsourced analysis

    Another approach to filtering and classification is to leverage users' activities. By asking each user to classify a small amount of data, or by inferring information from users' activities on the site (such as which items a user clicks), a site might be able to classify or organize a large data set without requiring much work from any one user.

Exactly which of these features to use in which case, and how to combine advanced features with data presentation, is an open question. Private parties might not get it right the first time, but we believe they will explore more approaches and will recover more rapidly than government will from the inevitable missteps. This collective learning process, along with the improvement it creates, is the key advantage of our approach. Nobody knows what is best, so we should let people try different offerings and see which ones win out. For those desiring to build interactive sites, the barriers to entry are remarkably low once government data is conveniently available. New sites can easily iterate through many designs, and adapt to user feedback. The people who ultimately benefit from these investments are not just the small community of civic technologists, but also the much larger group of citizens who seek to use the Web to engage with their government.

Data Authenticity Down the Line

Once third parties become primary interfaces for crucial government information, people will inevitably ask whether the presented data is authentic. Citizens may wonder whether some of the sites that provide data in innovative ways are distorting the data. Slight alterations to the data could carry major policy implications, and could be hard for citizens to detect.

To lower the barrier for building trustworthy third-party sites, government should provide authentication for all published bulk data sets so that anyone who encounters the data can verify its authenticity. Since government is the original publisher of the data, and citizens seek assurance that a third party has not altered the data, government is the only party that can provide a useful digital signature for its data. While other publishing tasks can be left open for many actors, only government itself can provide meaningful authentication.

The ideal way to provide such authentication is through National Institute of Standards and Technology (NIST) standard "digital signatures." Government should sign entire data sets, which will allow any downloader to check that the "signed" data set was published by the government and not altered in transit. The advantage of digital signatures is that it allows third parties to republish a trustworthy mirror of the same signed data set. Innovators who download the signed data set, from either a third-party source or the government's own server, can trust that it is authentic if its attached signature is valid. Enabling trustworthy third-party mirrors can significantly reduce the government's server and bandwidth costs associated with hosting the primary copy.

But just authenticating at the data-set level is not enough. Government must also make it possible for citizens to verify, down to a reasonable granularity, the authenticity of individual elements that were picked out from the larger set. If signing individual elements is overly burdensome, government can alternatively publish individual data elements over a secure web connection (HTTPS). A third-party website offering crime statistics, for example, could link to specific data elements on the secure government website. This would make it easy for citizens to verify that the statistics for their own neighborhoods represent authentic government data, without having to download and verify the entire bulk data set on which the website is built.

There are a number of ways to support data authentication at each level—digital signatures and secure web connections are just two possibilities—and each agency, perhaps with the input of outsiders, should determine which option provides the best trade-off between efficiency and usability in each circumstance.

Why Bother with Bulk?

An alternative approach to bulk data, and one that is sometimes mentioned as an equivalent solution, is for government to provide a data application programming interface (API). An API is like a 411 telephone directory service that people can call to ask for specific information about a particular person or business. The directory operator looks up the answer in the telephone book and replies to the caller. In the same way, computers can "call" an API and query it for specific information, in this case, from a government database that is otherwise inaccessible to the public, and the API responds with an answer once it is found. Whether a third-party website uses an API or hosts its own copy of the government data is an architectural question that is not likely to be directly observable by the website's end users.

APIs can be excellent, disappointing, or anywhere in between, but generally speaking, providing an API does not produce the same transformative value as providing the underlying data in bulk. While APIs can enable some innovative third-party uses of data, they constrain the range of possible outcomes by controlling what kinds of questions can be asked about the data. A very poorly designed API, for example, might not offer access to certain portions of the underlying data because the API builder considered those data columns to be unimportant. A better API might theoretically permit access to all of the data, but may not allow users to get the desired data out efficiently. For instance, an API for local spending might be able to return lists of all projects by industry sector, but might lack the functionality to return a list of all projects funded within a particular zip code, or all projects contracted to a particular group of companies. Because of API design decisions, a user who wants this information would face a difficult task: she would need to find or develop a list of all possible sectors, query the API for each one, and then manually filter the aggregate results by zip code or contractor.

APIs and finished, user-facing websites face the same fundamental limit for the same reason: both require a designer to decide on a *single monolithic interface* for the data. Even with the best of intentions, these top-down technical decisions can only limit how citizens can interact with the underlying data. Past experience shows that, in these situations, interested developers will struggle to reconstruct a complete copy of the underlying data in a machine-readable way, imposing a high cost in terms of human capital and creating a risk of low data quality. The task would be like reconstructing the phone book by calling 411—"First, I want the last names starting with Aa...." Moreover, APIs and websites are likely more expensive for government to develop and maintain, as compared to simply publishing copies of the raw data and allowing third parties to host mirrors.

If government releases the data first in bulk, citizens will not be restricted to just the approved interfaces. Since APIs, like websites, do serve a useful purpose in efficient data delivery, developers will build their own APIs on top of bulk data sets that best suit their own needs and those of downstream users. Indeed, a number of nonprofit groups have already built and are now offering public APIs for data the government has published in bulk form. OMB Watch, for example, combines multiple government contract and grant databases into a single "FedSpending" API that other developers use for their own sites. The National Institute on Money in State Politics offers a "Follow the Money" API which provides convenient access to its comprehensive state-level campaign finance data set (see Chapter 19).

Conclusion

Government should seek to ease any friction that limits developers' ability to build these tailor-made solutions. Only with bulk data can government harness the creativity and innovation of the open market and leverage the power of the Internet to bring all kinds of information closer to citizens. In the long run, as the tools for interacting with data continue to improve and become increasingly intuitive, we may reach a state in which citizens themselves interact directly with data without needing any intermediary.

Of course, beyond publishing data, government might also decide to build finished websites, and to build APIs. But publishing data in bulk must be government's first priority as an information provider. The success of a government is measured, ultimately, by the opportunities it provides to its citizens. By publishing its data in a form that is free, open, and reusable, government will empower citizens to dream up and implement their own innovative ideas of how to best connect with their government.

About the Authors

DAVID G. ROBINSON is a J.D. candidate in the class of 2012 at Yale Law School. Before arriving at Yale, David helped launch Princeton's Center for Information Technology Policy, serving as the Center's first associate director. He holds an A.B. in philosophy from Princeton, and a B.A. in philosophy and politics from Balliol College, Oxford, where he was a Rhodes Scholar.

HARLAN YU is a Ph.D. student in computer science and the Center for Information Technology Policy at Princeton University. His research is in information security, privacy, and technology public policy. His recent work in open government includes the development of RECAP, a tool that helps the public liberate federal court documents from PACER (Public Access to Court Electronic Records). He received his B.S. in electrical engineering and computer sciences (EECS) from UC Berkeley in 2004 and his M.A. in computer science from Princeton University in 2006.

EDWARD W. FELTEN is professor of computer science and public affairs, and director of the Center for Information Technology Policy, at Princeton University. His research interests include computer security and privacy, civic technologies, and technology policy. He received his Ph.D. in computer science and engineering from the University of Washington in 1993.

CHAPTER SEVEN

Online Deliberation and Civic Intelligence

Douglas Schuler

In addition to the prosaic—but nevertheless crucial—tasks related to the everyday necessities of staying alive, people and communities must also face—at least indirectly—a wide range of staggering challenges, such as pandemics, environmental degradation, climate change, starvation, war, militarism, terrorism, and oppression. Unfortunately, many of the world's inhabitants are very young or have other good reasons (such as extreme poverty) for their lack of opportunity, motivation, knowledge, or skills to face these challenges.

This, in essence, is the situation in which we find ourselves: a world seriously out of order and a world society that for many reasons may be less equipped to deal with these challenges than it needs to be. This is precisely the issue that the concept of "civic intelligence" is intended to highlight: *will we be smart enough, soon enough*?

Definitions and Assertions

Before we go any further, it seems best to present the four concepts that are at the core of this chapter—civic intelligence, democracy, open government, and deliberation—and show how they are related to each other.

1. *Civic intelligence* is a form of *collective* intelligence directed toward shared challenges.* Its presence or absence will determine how effectively these challenges are met. Civic intelligence exists to a greater or lesser degree in all societies.

   Because the government and other elite groups are not capable of addressing the problems we're faced with, a deeper form of civic intelligence built upon rich interactions between citizens distributed throughout the world will be required. This intelligence won't emerge solely from a series of votes or other algorithmic techniques no matter how clever they are.

   Thinking in terms of civic intelligence helps us to pose an interesting thought experiment: as the challenges facing us become more complex, numerous, fierce, and unpredictable, do we have the necessary collective intelligence to meet them?

2. *Democracy* in its ideal sense is the form of political organization that most closely embodies civic intelligence.

   Many people seek a precise definition of democracy to guide their thinking in this area. But the meanings of social concepts are not chiseled in granite. In its most general form, democracy means governance by the people. Democracy takes different shapes in different contexts. Democracy is also defined by inclusive and transparent processes, although access to these processes is sometimes blocked and the processes themselves are often corrupted by the political or economic elite.

   Many descriptions of democracy focus on the outcome and the formalized process for getting there. One common aspect of arguments in support of democracy is the prospect of an outcome that is better because of more involvement in its creation, almost exclusively through voting. Rarely heard is the idea that participation in a democratic process can actually make individuals more qualified for citizenship and hence can build a type of civic intelligence that is better for the entire commonwealth. This is the case that John Dewey, the prominent American public intellectual, developed: that democracy should be seen as a *way of life*, not as a duty to be duly discharged every four or so years.

   Democracy exists at the intersection of practicality and idealism. As a society attempts to move closer to an ideal democratic state, it generally becomes more difficult to maintain its practical nature. On some level, democracy, like any system, must be implemented (and maintained); it consists of institutional processes and material machinery and uses resources. Is democracy more expensive in terms of resource investment (including time and money) than other forms of government? How much is democracy *worth*?

3. *Open government*, an idea whose meaning is currently being constructed, offers a provocative set of ideas for reconstructing government in ways that could increase and improve the abilities of democratic societies to deal effectively, sustainably, and equitably with its issues. In other words, open government, if implemented thoughtfully, could

---

* "Cultivating Society's Civic Intelligence: Patterns for a New 'World Brain'," Douglas Schuler, *Community Informatics*, Leigh Keeble and Brian D. Loader (eds.), Routledge, 2001. *Liberating Voices: A Pattern Language for Communication Revolution*, Douglas Schuler, MIT Press, 2008.

improve our democracy and our civic intelligence while keeping the costs to acceptable and appropriate levels.

Some people take comfort from the seemingly solid ideological position that asserts that "less" government is always good. This position tacitly acknowledges that other institutions (e.g., large corporations) will assume more power (though likely of a different kind). President Obama rightly reframes that question not as a choice between *less* or *more*, but between *better* or *worse* government. And if the goal isn't necessarily *less* government, the goal is certainly not *no* government. After all, *Road Warrior* makes a better movie than an exemplar for an ideal society. The goal is to change the nature of governance, particularly the relationship of "ordinary citizens" to the government, not the abandonment of social norms. The main reason that governance should be opened up to "ordinary" people is not because it's more just. And while opened-up governance is likely to be less corrupt than opaque governance, opened-up governance is simply the only feasible way to bring adequate resources (such as local knowledge and creative problem-solving capabilities) to bear on the challenges that we now face.

Open government without a corresponding increase in an informed, concerned, and engaged citizenry is no solution; in fact, it makes no sense. Paradoxically, the first place to focus attention when attempting to develop a more open government is on the people being governed. Open government might mean totally distributed governance; the end of the government as the sole governing body. For that reason, one of the most critical questions to ask is what capabilities and information do *citizens* need most to meet the challenges they face?

4. *Deliberation* is a process of directed communication whereby people discuss their concerns in a reasonable, conscientious, and open manner, with the intent of arriving at a decision. Deliberation takes different forms in different societal contexts and involves participants of myriad interests, skills, and values. It is generally more formal than collaboration or discussion. While some people may balk at this "tyranny of structure," it is the shared awareness of the structure that provides legitimacy and impetus toward meaningful discussion and satisfactory decision making.

Deliberation occurs when people with dissimilar points of view exchange ideas with the intent of coming to an agreement. Less successful outcomes—that are not *failures*—include agreeing to disagree, or even attaining a better understanding of other viewpoints. At any rate, deliberation is distinct from other communication modalities such as individual reflection, repeating and reinforcing shared viewpoints, acquiring a viewpoint solely through exposure to mass media, or working to defeat a person, idea, or enterprise, not via merits of one's own argument or the lack of merits of the other, but by any (nonviolent) means necessary, including character assassination and lying.

Significantly, deliberation is an important capability within the more general capability of civic intelligence. After a decision is made, there is presumably an opinion or frame, activity or plan that is shared by a larger number of people. The intended product of deliberation is a more coherent vision of the future. It can also result in increased solidarity within a group.

The Context of Deliberation

Deliberation, of course, makes sense only within a social context and is meaningful only when it's actually linked with multiple "levels" of society, including, ultimately, the potential to be a factor in social change. This "context of deliberation" can be depicted visually in an hourglass form (see Figure 7-1). Although somewhat abstract, this depiction illustrates the necessary social attributes of a society in which deliberation can be said to function adequately. (And a society without deliberation can't really be considered a democracy society.) The lower half of the hourglass shows that deliberation depends on the desire and the ability of the people to deliberate, and that the venues within which people can deliberate are available. The upper half of the hourglass shows that deliberation is an instrument of democracy only when the possibility of interacting with—and influencing—the rest of society exists. This means that "social access points" such as newspapers, educational systems, public forums, government institutions, and the like that can help carry the content and the decisions of a deliberative body to a wider audience in society also exist. This in turn relies on the receptivity of people and institutions to actually adopt the findings of the deliberation.

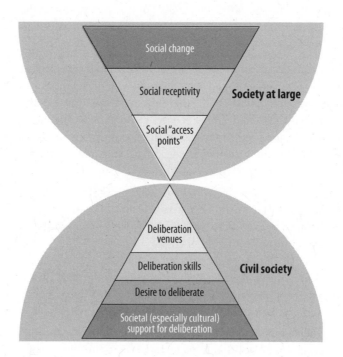

FIGURE 7-1. Context of deliberation

Democracy, Deliberation, and the Internet

Since its inception, the Internet has been touted as a medium with revolutionary potential for democratic communication. Although other media including broadcast television and radio have not lived up to their democratic potential, it is too early to dismiss the Internet as being solely a tool of the powerful. The Internet is actually a "meta-medium" that can be used to host a variety of traditional media as well as new hybrids.[†] Its extreme mutability, coupled with the potential of establishing communication channels between any two (or more) people on Earth, accounts for its enormous—and radical—potential for democratic communication. Certainly, civil society recognizes this and has been extraordinarily creative in using the Internet for positive social change.[‡] On the other hand, many people don't have full access to the Internet or have the time to access it. These vast differences help provide another dimension to the have/have-not continuum, and to the degree that governance moves into the digital realm this distance becomes a measure of digital disenfranchising.

Although a very large number of approaches to communication exist in cyberspace, one critical function—deliberation—seems to have been forgotten. Groups need to deliberate, and for many reasons they aren't always able to meet face to face. In fact, as many problems that we face are global in nature, the groups that are affected by the problems or who otherwise are compelled to address the problems must reach across local boundaries to address their shared concerns. The need for computer support for online *deliberation* can be shown by the fact that many online discussions seem to have no resolution at all; they often dribble off into nothingness, leaving more frustration than enlightenment in their wake. Worse, many online discussions degenerate into "flame wars" where online feuds make it difficult for the nonfeuders to get any work done.

Online Civic Deliberation

Online deliberation is the term for a network-based (usually Internet) computer application that supports the deliberative process. People have been thinking about how computer systems could be used for collaboration, negotiation, and deliberation for some time. Douglas Engelbart's work in this field was pioneering.[§] At present, few examples exist, although this number is slowly increasing. There have been many innovative deliberative approaches

---

[†] "Community Computer Networks: An Opportunity for Collaboration Among Democratic Technology Practitioners and Researchers," Douglas Schuler, *Technology and Democracy: User Involvement in Information Technology*, David Hakken and Knut Haukelid (eds.), Centre for Technology and Culture, University of Oslo, 1997.

[‡] "Appropriating the Internet for Social Change: Towards the strategic use of networked technologies by transnational civil society organizations," Mark Surman and Katherine Reilly, New York: Social Sciences Research Council Information Technology and International Cooperation Program, 2003.

[§] "Coordinated Information Services for a Discipline- or Mission-Oriented Community" (*http://www .dougengelbart.org/pubs/augment-12445.html*), Douglas Engelbart, 1972.

involving face-to-face interactions. These include the consensus conferences developed by the Danish Board of Technology (DBT) (*http://www.tekno.dk/*), deliberative polling,[||] and Citizen Summits (e.g., *http://americaspeaks.org*). The DBT is currently coordinating the Worldwide Views on Global Warming project (*http://www.WWViews.org*) with approximately 50 countries to engage their citizens in deliberation about climate change: other deliberative projects are also targeting climate change, including MIT's Collaboratorium[#] and the Global Sensemaking project (*http://www.globalsensemaking.net*). While I do not have the space here to discuss them, people have experimented with video teleconferencing, live television, special-purpose-outfitted rooms, and so forth to assist deliberative processes. These efforts, however positive some of the results may have been, are often stymied by high costs and other challenges and have yet to be adopted widely.

There are several reasons for the relatively small effort in this area. For one thing, deliberation applications are difficult to design and implement. This is one of the main reasons why few applications are available. (Of course, this reflects the "chicken and egg" nature of this situation. *If the applications don't exist, people won't use them. If people don't use them, programmers won't develop them....*) For this reason, we must develop deliberative systems in a co-evolutionary way, working cooperatively with the communities that are most interested in using them. Moreover, there is seemingly little money to be made with online deliberation. E-commerce, for example, has larger target populations, is easier to program, and is more lucrative. The difficulty of demonstrating the benefits of deliberation using current approaches may contribute to this lack of support.

Deliberation is also difficult to do. It is time-consuming, it is confusing in many cases (due to content as well as the formal nature of the process), and the "payoff" is often perceived by would-be participants to be far less than the effort expended. For this reason, the percentage of people who actively engage in deliberation in a regular civic or formal sense is very low— even lower than voting, a discouraging fact considering voting's low bar and its declining rates of participation. A third reason is that government bodies from the smallest towns to the highest national and supranational (e.g., the European Union) levels seem unable (or, perhaps more accurately, unwilling) to support public deliberation in a genuine way, whether it's online or not.

The hypothesis is that if it were easier to participate in deliberative sessions and—most importantly—the results of their efforts were perceived as worthwhile, citizen deliberation would become more popular. If deliberation actually was incorporated into governance and

---

[||] "Experimenting with a democratic ideal: Deliberative polling and public opinion," James Fishkin and Robert Luskin, *Acta Politica*, Vol. 40, Number 3, 2005: 284–298.

[#] "Supporting Collaborative Deliberation Using a Large-Scale Argumentation System: The MIT Collaboratorium," Mark Klein and Luca Iandoli, Directions and Implications of Advanced Computing: Conference on Online Deliberation, Todd Davies and Seeta Peña Gangadharan (eds.), San Francisco: Computer Professionals for Social Responsibility, 2008.

became valued by society at the same time, a closer approximation of the vision of democracy as a way of life envisioned by John Dewey would be achieved.

Support for Online Civic Deliberation

Development of a network-based application that could help nonprofit, community-based organizations convene effective deliberative meetings when members couldn't easily get together for face-to-face meetings could be very useful. While the goal is not to replace face-to-face meetings, it is hypothesized that the use of an online system could potentially help organizations with limited resources. Ideally, the technology would increase the organization's effectiveness while reducing the time and money spent on its deliberative meetings. In general, judging the success of any approach to deliberation includes considering access to the process, the efficacy of the process (including individual involvement and the process as a whole), and integration with the social context (including legal requirements, etc.). Of course, these criteria overlap to some degree and influence each other.

Motivated by a long-term desire to employ computing technology for social good, particularly among civil society groups who are striving to create more "civic intelligence" in our society, I proposed that Robert's Rules of Order could be used as a basis for an online deliberation system.[*] The selection of Robert's Rules of Order was supported by its widespread use—at least in the United States—and the formalized definitions of its rules. Robert's Rules of Order is one version of the familiar form of deliberation often known as *parliamentary procedure*. Proposals are put forward to the assembly with *motions* ("I move that we hire Douglas Schuler as our executive director") that must be *affirmed* ("seconded") by another person in the assembly before the proposal can be discussed, possibly amended, and voted on (or *tabled*—dismissed at least temporarily) by the assembly.

ABOUT ROBERT'S RULES OF ORDER

Robert's Rules of Order was developed over a 40-year period by Henry Robert, beginning in the late 1800s. Robert's "rules" defined an orderly process for face-to-face meetings in which the goal was to make decisions fairly. One of the most important objectives was to ensure that the majority could not silence the minority—every attendee would have opportunities to make his ideas heard. At the same time, however, the minority could not prevent the majority from ultimately making decisions. One of the interesting observations about the Robert's Rules process is that it seems to be useful at

---

[*] "A Civilian Computing Initiative: Three Modest Proposals," Douglas Schuler, *Directions and Implications of Advanced Computing*, Ablex Publishing, 1989. "Cultivating Society's Civic Intelligence: Patterns for a New 'World Brain'," Douglas Schuler, *Community Informatics*, Leigh Keeble and Brian D. Loader (eds.), Routledge, 2001. *New Community Networks: Wired for Change*, Douglas Schuler, Addison-Wesley, 1996. *Robert's Rules of Order, Newly Revised*, Henry Robert, Perseus Books, 1990. "Online Civic Deliberation and E-Liberate," Douglas Schuler, *Online Deliberation: Design, Research, and Practice*, University of Chicago Press, 2009.

a variety of scales: groups with just a handful of members can use them as well as groups numbering in the hundreds or even more. Robert's Rules of Order is now used by thousands of organizations around the world every day, and in fact, its use is legally mandated in many government and civil society meetings.

Robert's Rules of Order is a type of "protocol-based cooperative work" system. It is related to Malone's "semi-structured messages" work[†] and the work done by Winograd and Flores[‡] (which was built on the "speech act" work of John Austin.[§]) Those examples all employ "typed messages." The message "type" is, in effect, a descriptor of the message content, and because it is discrete it is more easily handled by computer applications than natural language. There are several reasons why a strict regimen over communication may be imposed. Generally, this is done is cases where there is contention for resources. In the case of deliberation, the scarcest resource is the time available for speaking. This is generally true in situations when explicit objectives and/or formal constraints are placed upon the venue—in a courtroom or with a legislative body, for example.

E-Liberate is created

In 1999, a team of students at The Evergreen State College developed the first prototype of an online version of Robert's Rules of Order that was ultimately named *e-Liberate* (which rhymes with the verb *deliberate*; see Figure 7-2). The objective of e-Liberate was to move beyond chat, premature endings, and unresolved digressions. The initial objective was to support groups that were already deliberating and to try to mimic their *existing* processes—*as closely as possible*. This approach was intended to minimize disruption by integrating the online system as unobtrusively as possible into their work lives. E-Liberate is intended to be easy to use for anybody familiar with Robert's Rules of Order.

Online deliberation offers some advantages and disadvantages over face-to-face deliberation. The system employs a straightforward user interface which is educational as well as facilitative. The interface shows, for example, only the legal actions that are available to the user at that specific time in the meeting. (For example, a user can't second a motion that she submitted or when there is no motion on the table to second.) Also, at any time during a session an "about" button can be clicked that presents an explanation of what each particular action will accomplish, thus providing useful cues that aren't available in face-to-face meetings. In addition, the software checks if meeting quorums exist, conducts voting on motions, and

---

[†] "Semi-structured messages are surprisingly useful for computer-supported coordination," *ACM Transactions on Office Information Systems*, Thomas Malone, et al., 1987.

[‡] *Understanding Computers and Cognition*, Terry Winograd and Rodrigo Flores, Addison-Wesley, 1987.

[§] *How to Do Things with Words*, J. L. Austin, Harvard University Press, 1962.

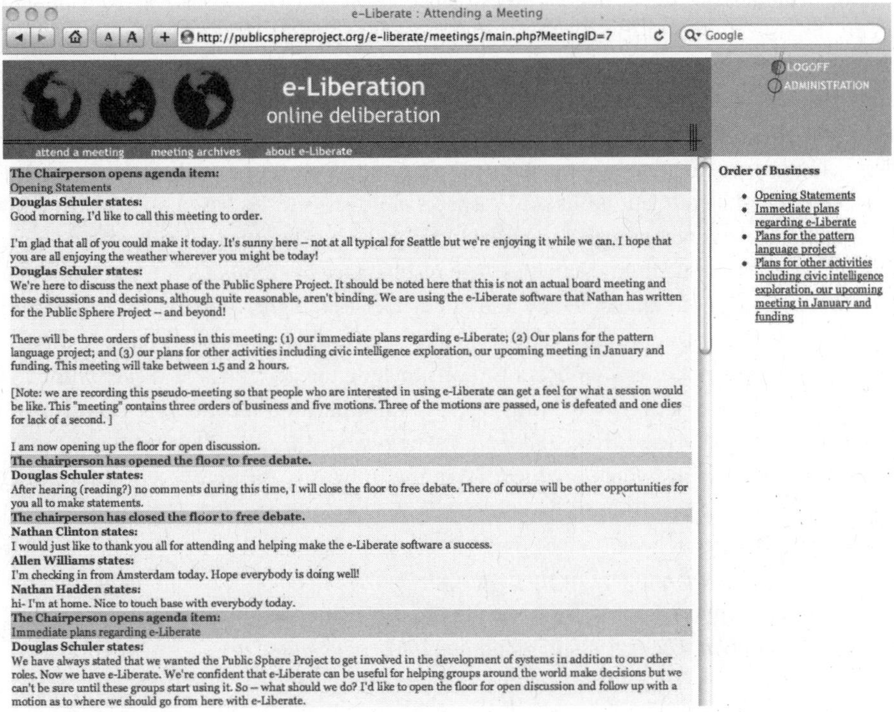

FIGURE 7-2. E-Liberate meeting in progress

automatically records (and archives) the minutes. See *http://publicsphereproject.org/e-liberate/ demo.php* for a transcript of an entire sample meeting.

The developers of e-Liberate have begun working with groups that are interested in using the system to support actual meetings. We are enthusiastic about the system but are well aware that the current system is likely to have problems that need addressing. It is for that reason that we continue to host meetings with groups and gather feedback from attendees. We plan to study a variety of online meetings in order to adjust the system and to develop heuristics for the use of the system. Our plan is to make e-Liberate freely available for online meetings and to release the software under a free software license.

For many years, Fiorella de Cindio and her group at the University of Milan have been developing community collaborative tools in association with the Milan Community Network (Rete Civica di Milano, or RCM) effort. The openDCN approach is to work toward an integrated ensemble of online services that is useful for community members and citizens.‖ The evolving

---

‖ "Deliberation and Community Networks: A Strong Link Waiting to be Forged," Fiorella De Cindio and Douglas Schuler, *Communities and Action: Prato CIRN Conference*, 2007.

environment builds on the idea of *spaces* to organize these services.[#] Thus, the *community* space supports discussion, brainstorming, the City Map application, and other capabilities; the *deliberation* space supports interactions that are more structured and formal; and the *information* space links the other two spaces in a variety of ways. The openDCN effort is informed by theory but always with the objective of promoting effective, inclusive, and widespread citizen participation. The openDCN developers created a deliberation module that was inspired by e-Liberate but omits some aspects of Robert's Rules based on usability studies. This basic module has been tested in several locations around Italy, generally around Agenda 21 participatory urban planning activities. The results have been mixed, but the work has helped bring many potential challenges and opportunities to light. A change in the leadership of a municipal administration, for example, is likely to result in profound changes, often withdrawal of support. Other significant projects include the *georeferenced discussion* used on a site sponsored by the South African Ministry of Communication for the 2010 soccer world championship (*http://www.e-soccer.opendcn.org/*). The *informed discussion* has been used to support a group of friends who were together in the university during the years around 1968 and want to maintain their friendship online (*http://www.68cittastudi.retecivica.milano.it/*), while the *citizens consultation* has been used by the Milan School Trade Unions to collect feedback from workers on a negotiated agreement (*http://flc-cgil.retecivica.milano.it/*). Additionally, openDCN has been used to support teaching and learning in the virtual community course at the university (*http://jlidcncv.lic.dico.unimi.it/* and *http://desire.dico.unimi.it/*).

Findings and Issues

Our experience with online deliberative systems is limited. What follows is a discussion of issues that the developers of any deliberative system should address.

Role of the Chair

The first set of issues is related to the role of chair, which Robert's Rules of Order explicitly specifies for every meeting. The specific role of the person so designated includes enforcing "rules relating to debate and those relating to order and decorum," determining when a rule is out of order and to "expedite business in every way compatible with the rights of members."[*] These responsibilities apparently rule out a meeting conducted solely among peers. The main reason that a chair is needed at all is due to the fact that the rules alone won't suffice. There are a variety of situations in which the chair's input is needed, notably when human judgment is required. Another reason that Robert called upon the services of a chair in his deliberative universe is that meeting attendees may attempt to "game" the system by invoking

---

[#] "A Two-room E-Deliberation Environment," Fiorella De Cindio, et al., *Directions and Implications of Advanced Computing: Conference on Online Deliberation*. San Francisco: Computer Professionals for Social Responsibility, 2008.

[*] *Robert's Rules of Order, Newly Revised*, Henry Robert, Perseus Books, 1990.

rules, which although strictly legal, violate the spirit of the meeting. We initiated a form of "auto-chair" in e-Liberate after we ascertained that the chair could actually be an impediment to progress and seemed to be less necessary in the online environment—at least in some situations. When an attendee requests the floor, he is automatically "recognized" by the automated proxy of the chair.

Distributed Meeting Attendees

A second set of issues is introduced when meeting attendees are unseen and distributed. These issues arise when a process that is used in face-to-face environments is adapted to be used in an online environment. For example, how do we know when a quorum is present? This is part of the larger issue of how we know who's online. Establishing the identity of a person who is interacting, sight unseen, via the Internet is important and is certainly not trivial. In some cases—as in online voting—there are opportunities for fraud that may sometimes prove irresistible. We also would like to know whether, for example, members are offline by choice or whether they want to participate but are unable to connect. And if they're not connected and/or not paying attention to the meeting at any given time, does that mean that they're not in attendance and, consequently, a quorum may no longer exist?

Social Environment Requirements

The third set of issues is related to the legal and other aspects of the social environment in which the system operates. In addition to establishing whether a quorum exists, a variety of other requirements include the timely distribution of the notice of the meeting, who can attend, and what type of access must exist for members and must be translated in suitable ways into the digital medium. All of these issues are interrelated and influence each other in obvious and subtle ways. For example, since attendees are no longer at a single shared location, where they would be (presumably) attending solely to the business of the assembly, the question of meeting duration comes up. Should meetings be relatively intense affairs where all attendees are interacting and business is conducted in one or two hours or should/could the meeting be more leisurely, perhaps stretching over one or two weeks? The distribution of attendees across time zones highlights a variety of "problems" that humankind's Earth-based orientation and social institutions (such as the "workday", the "workweek," and family obligations) place in the way of Internet-enabled "always-on" opportunities. These problems add considerable complexity to an already complex undertaking, and for now it suffices to say that addressing these issues will require social as well as technological approaches. Finally, we can only raise the issue of how well e-Liberate performs when used by larger groups. The only way to understand and learn about that is to host meetings with larger numbers of people—50, 100, 1,000—and observe the results and interview the participants.

E-Liberate's Role

At present, e-Liberate supports online deliberative meetings, discrete sessions that aren't linked in any way to each other. But deliberation is an ongoing process—not a sporadic, context-free occurrence that has neither history nor consequences. This fact suggests, among other things, the need to integrate deliberative technology with other collaborative technology such as brainstorming or collaborative editing. It is hypothesized that developing software that could support a variety of protocols, along with the ability to inspect and modify the rule base, would make new deliberative projects plausible without necessarily changing the functionality of the basic Robert's Rules core. It may be possible to develop a variety of "plug and play" modules that could support exploration in the area of "deliberation in the large" in which individual meetings or sessions ("deliberation in the small") are linked. The ongoing nature of deliberation also suggests that an online tool that helps maintain institutional memory would be especially useful (including the retrieval of agenda items that had been postponed in prior meetings). In many collective enterprises, it is common to break the larger group into smaller working, distributed subsets such as committees or consortia, and the system should support that.

There are also several capabilities related to integration with other services such as email, fax, videoconferencing, and so forth. Invitations and other notices are already sent electronically to e-Liberate participants and there are other times when email communication should be invoked. We also plan to look into document sharing (e.g., the organization's bylaws) among participants and support for image presentation during meetings.

Finally, as I alluded to earlier, we live in an era in which problems aren't always confined to one country. The need for international and other cross-border initiatives in which the participants are not elites is critical. The expression "deliberation in the small" can be used to describe a single meeting. Although a single meeting is the foundation of deliberative discourse, it's only a molecule in the universe of social learning, or what could be called deliberation *in the large*.

Addressing the broader issues of deliberation in the large can be faced in several ways, from a piecework bottom-up approach, linking, for example, environmental groups in some way, perhaps via an e-Liberate-like system, perhaps not. The other, somewhat orthogonal, approach is to design and implement (and evaluate and critique, etc.) new systems that explicitly address this issue in a more top-down way. Our approach readily combines both approaches and allows for others not yet identified. We are proposing a loosely linked, collaborative enterprise that combines both theoretical and applied research, information and communication technology (ICT) design and implementation, public and popular education, and policy work. We are looking into deliberation in the large as an important thought experiment that should be taken up in a broad social dialog.[†] Part of this is related to inherent rights of people (to communicate, deliberate, participate, etc.), and part of this is related to the necessity of global communications on issues such as climate change.

Conclusion

The online environment offers many opportunities for collective problem solving. Online deliberation (especially in conjunction with other collaborative approaches) has immense potential whose surface is only now being scratched. Although deliberation is not as easy to do as, say, online shopping, it is a cornerstone of democracy and of the civic intelligence required in the twenty-first century.

Currently, there are few opportunities for individuals to help address shared problems. We believe that focusing on civil society—both its organized and its unorganized constituents—is a rich, rewarding, and deserving area for multisector collaborative ventures. The time is ripe for loosening the restrictive boundaries between institutional bodies and other groups of people worldwide: the current governors must be willing to share or abandon some of the power they currently hold, while the people must be willing to assume increased responsibility for governing tasks, thus becoming more fully realized citizens.

A host of risks are associated with these deliberative proposals. Yet the risk of not acting is the most dangerous. Focusing attention on online deliberation presupposes a faith, partially supported by evidence, which states that humans of diverse social stations can deliberate together. We may yet employ our vast technology to the task of obliterating ourselves and life on earth. This possibility should surprise no one: throughout history, humankind has exhibited an enthusiastic genius for establishing hells on earth that surpass the misery of those conceived by our poets, artists, and theologians. On the other hand, the ability to deliberate together may be our most powerful—yet neglected—natural resource. And in our embrace of open governance, we may discover that it is the key to civic intelligence.

I want to thank Fiorella de Cindio for many helpful suggestions with this chapter and for many fruitful discussions and collaborations over the years.

† "'Tools for Participation' as a Citizen-Led Grand Challenge," Douglas Schuler, Directions and Implications of Advanced Computing: Conference on Online Deliberation, San Francisco: Computer Professionals for Social Responsibility, 2008.

About the Author

 **DOUGLAS SCHULER** is president of the Public Sphere Project and a member of faculty at The Evergreen State College. Trained in computer science and software engineering, Douglas has been working on the borderlines of society and technology for more than 20 years. He has written and coedited several books, including *New Community Networks: Wired for Change* (Addison-Wesley, 1996; *http://www.publicsphereproject.org/ncn/*) and *Liberating Voices: A Pattern Language for Communication Revolution* (MIT Press, 2008), a civic intelligence undertaking with 85 contributors (*http://www.publicsphereproject.org/patterns/*).

CHAPTER EIGHT

Open Government and Open Society

Archon Fung
David Weil

Perhaps more than any other national leader, President Obama has stressed his commitment to "creating an unprecedented level of openness in Government" (see the Appendix).* His administration has followed up these words with impressive actions—expanding the quality and quantity of data available on USASpending.gov, laying the groundwork for making the economic stimulus and recovery expenditures public, and creating a high-level process— *itself* conducted in a highly inclusive way—to develop open government policies under the Office of Science and Technology Policy.

Transparency's Moment?

Complementing these federal initiatives, a host of skilled civic organizations—composed of groups such as Sunlight Foundation, OMB Watch, and the League of Women Voters—now comprise a capable transparency movement that both presses for greater openness in government and develops tools to enable citizens to take advantage of that openness. Coming somewhat later to the issue of transparency, these groups and others have caught the eye of important funders at philanthropies such as the Open Society Institute, the Omidyar Foundation, and the Ford Foundation.

---

* "Transparency and Open Government," President Barack Obama, Memorandum for the Heads of Executive Departments and Agencies, January 21, 2009 (*http://www.whitehouse.gov/the_press_office/ TransparencyandOpenGovernment/*).

These developments converge in a perfect storm (the good kind) that may in several years result in a federal government that is much more open to public scrutiny than it has ever been. Indeed, this government may in time become more open than any other major government in the world. This would be a remarkable democratic achievement.

Enthusiasts of transparency, which most readers of this book are, should be aware of two major pitfalls that may mar this achievement. The first is that government transparency, though driven by progressive impulses, may draw excessive attention to government's mistakes and so have the consequence of reinforcing a conservative image of government as incompetent and corrupt. The second is that all this energy devoted to making *open government* comes at the expense of leaving the operations of large private sector organizations—banks, manufacturers, health providers, food producers, drug companies, and the like—opaque and secret. In the major industrialized democracies (but not in many developing countries or in authoritarian regimes), these private sector organizations threaten the health and well-being of citizens at least as much as government. The remedy for this second pitfall is to marshal forces in government and the civic sector into a movement for an *open society*. The aim of this chapter is not to celebrate the current hopeful moment for transparency, but to draw attention to these blind spots and to suggest some correctives.

The Dark Side of Open Government

The principle that government—not just its laws and policies, but the reasons and processes of decisions that generated those policies and the flows of money that fund their implementation—should be open seems not just unobjectionable, but an essential component of democratic government. Without that freedom of information, citizens cannot hold their government accountable, evaluate officials' claims, and hold them responsible when they veer too far from the tether of democracy.

This reasoning becomes problematic when transparency focuses primarily—or even exclusively—on accountability. Campaign finance disclosure, contracting disclosure, and much of the freedom of information activity aims to create a "gotcha" game in which the information provided by open government measures is used by journalists, advocacy groups of the right and left, and political opponents to catch official wrongdoing. This cat-and-mouse game forms a civic check-and-balance mechanism that is fundamental to curbing the misbehavior of the powerful. In this regard, our society is fortunately blessed with many independent journalists whose personal interests and professional ethos press them to sniff out official malfeasance. The American public, going back to the time of Tocqueville and before, have had a skeptical strain in their view of government, particularly the possibilities of malfeasance. When pollsters asked whether "this country is run by a few big interests looking out for themselves" or whether it is run "for the benefit of all the people" in 2004, 54% of respondents thought that it was run by a few big interests.† Open government efforts can thus plug into a media apparatus and public political culture that together make a very effective "gotcha" machine.

But the larger responsibility of citizens is not just to judge when officials behave badly, but also to provide feedback on their performance in more nuanced ways, including registering approval when government performs well—when it protects people's interests and solves public problems effectively and justly. Unfortunately, the current discourse of transparency—focused as it is on accountability and issues such as corruption—produces policies and platforms that are particularly sensitive to government's mistakes but often are blind to its accomplishments. Transparency in this sense is like a school report card that only reports when a student is sent to detention, plays hooky from class, or fails courses, but does not register when she earns As in her course. The systems of open government that we're building—structures that facilitate citizens' social and political judgments—are much more disposed to seeing the glass of government as half or even one-quarter empty, rather than mostly full.

Thus the progressive impulse for transparency—shared famously by Justice Brandeis as well as most of the authors of this volume—may well produce conservative or even reactionary effects of delegitimizing government activity quite broadly as public disclosure feeds more and more stories of government waste, corruption, and failure. To illustrate, consider current efforts to disclose federal stimulus spending activity. Much of that disclosure aims to make public the flow of funds through contracts, enabling journalists and citizen-auditors to "follow the money." This is a worthy contribution to forming public judgments about the stimulus package. But its main thrust provides less information on project progress, its capacity to provide employment to parts of the labor force particularly hard hit by the recession, or the public value created by the spending (e.g., how much local users of an improved transportation line benefit from decreased commuting time or more predictable service). Instead, the approach tends to focus on costs and not the commensurate public benefits arising from the spending. Imagine if Amazon or Internet Movie Database (IMDb) reviews only allowed users to point out problems with books and movies but not to highlight what they thought was artful and creative about them. People who looked at Amazon and IMDb reviews would think that the overall quality of books and movies was very poor indeed. That's what stimulus transparency—and much government disclosure generally—does.

The solution to this problem is not to reduce government transparency, but rather to create a fuller accounting of it. Instead of focusing solely on disclosure systems that produce accountability, we should press for disclosure systems that allow citizens to identify and express their evaluation of government activities as they would private products and services. One promising set of examples of this is public accounting systems developed by a number of local

---

† The American National Election Studies (*http://www.electionstudies.org*), *The ANES Guide to Public Opinion and Electoral Behavior* (University of Michigan, Center for Political Studies). In a similar vein, Tocqueville famously noted, "The American Republic will endure until the day Congress discovers that it can bribe the public with the public's money." (Alexis de Tocqueville, *Democracy in America* [1838, reprinted by Harper Perennial, 1988].)

governments that provide a platform for citizens, civic groups, and other organizations to provide ongoing feedback on the service provision of specific government agencies or key providers such as the police.‡

But these fledgling examples need to be ramped up, particularly given the escalating scale and scope of government activity in response to the economic crisis. Disclosures about federal economic stimulus activities, for example, need to be organized around projects rather than contracts—that is, on the users who ultimately benefit from expenditures. They might report many dimensions of performance—such as the number of jobs created and the quality of those jobs. And they might enable residents in local communities to rate those projects—as they rate books, movies, and hotels on commercial sites—on criteria such as how they are serving specific public needs and the quality of services provided.§ Americans might be justified in feeling pretty good about the stimulus in areas with many five-star projects and suspicious where there were lots of projects with just one or two stars. In essence, we need transparency that provides a full accounting of the benefits as well as the costs of government activities. The information technologies are readily available;‖ what we need is the political drive to foster a more complete form of open government.

The Missing Diagnosis

A broader and more important question for transparency advocates is this: what is the problem for which transparency is the solution? One natural answer to this question is that transparency is the solution to the particular challenges of democratic *government*. Governments exercise enormous power—including the power to put people in jail and seize their possessions. Democratic governments are also supposed to express the will of the people. Transparency can both check power and help to make government responsive. A quite different answer to this question, however, is that many large organizations in society—not just national governments, but also corporations, social service agencies, and public service providers—create harms and risks to individuals, and transparency is a general method that can help citizens understand these harms, protect themselves, and press organizations of all kinds to behave in more socially responsible ways.

---

‡ See, for example, "What Exactly Is City Stat?", Bob Behn, *The Operator's Manual for the New Administration*, Rowman and Littlefield Publishers, 2008.

§ One interesting example of the elements of such a system was created by the nonprofit news organization ProPublica on its website. The "Stimulus Progress Bar" and associated materials provide ongoing tracking of the progress of stimulus spending across the country (see *http://www.propublica.org/ion/stimulus*).

‖ Many of the burgeoning information technologies developed by the private sector could be readily adapted to this task. This has been recognized by a growing number of organizations, including an offshoot of Google, Google Public Sector (*http://www.google.com/publicsector*), which focuses on developing new applications for public sector organizations.

From this second perspective, should transparency enthusiasts invest their energies in *open government* or in creating an *open society* in which organizations of all sorts—in particular, private corporations—are much more transparent? The answer to this question depends on a sober evaluation of the social facts on the ground; where do the risks and harms to citizens come from? In societies where government is the major force, where it has few mechanisms for public accountability, and where other organizations are, by comparison, innocuous—China, Iran, and nations with still-embryonic forms of democratic governance where the boundary between public and private spheres is opaque and often corrupt—transparency should aim primarily to make government more open.

The United States and other industrialized democracies, however, possess quite a different organizational ecology. Governments at the federal, state, and local levels are large and powerful, to be sure. But the well-being of citizens—their employment; the purity of the food they eat and the air they breathe; whether their waterways are fishable and swimmable; their housing prices, mortgage rates, and credit charges; the reliability and safety of transportation; even the very soundness of the economy—also depends on the actions of large and often secretive organizations in the private sector, such as banks, manufacturers, and other corporations.

Therefore, a very substantial part of the energies of transparency advocates should be redirected toward making corporations and other organizations in society meet the same standards increasingly demanded of open government. This shift requires the transparency movement to reorient itself in several substantial ways. Government assumes a different role in the political imagination. Rather than a looming specter of threat that society must tame through transparency, government becomes an ally of society whose strength is required to make businesses transparent. In many cases, private and civic organizations will not disclose information voluntarily, and the force of law and policy—and the kind of authority that can come only from government—will make them do so. Complementing a citizen's right to know about general processes within government, measures to create an open society produce information that is geared at reducing specific risks and harms, such as health threats, pollution, and economic risks.

Targeted Transparency

To open government partisans, the open society agenda may seem quite foreign; where to begin? Fortunately, laws and policies that compel corporate disclosure have emerged in various policy domains in recent decades. In other work, we have called these measures "targeted transparency" because they aim not just to provide general information, but rather to achieve specific public objectives such as better schools, high-quality hospitals, and safer consumer products.[#]

Full Disclosure: The Perils and Promise of Transparency, Fung, Graham, and Weil, Cambridge University Press, 2007.

In 1997, for example, the Los Angeles County Board of Supervisors adopted an ordinance that requires restaurants to post highly visible letter grades (A, B, C) on their front windows that are based on the results of County Department of Health Services inspections. This transparency system makes it much easier for patrons to avoid restaurants with dirty kitchens or otherwise unsafe practices. There is substantial evidence that the system has worked. Revenues at "C" restaurants declined and those of "A" restaurants increased after the policy was implemented. Over the course of a few years, the number of "C" restaurants decreased and the number of "A" restaurants increased. Perhaps most importantly, fewer people are getting sick from food poisoning after the implementation of the report card system. Studies estimate that hospitalizations from foodborne illnesses have decreased from 20% to 13%.[*] This transparency innovation has spread to several other cities and two states.

At a larger scale, Congress passed a law in 1975 (and has updated it several times), called the Home Mortgage Disclosure Act (HMDA), that compels banks to disclose detailed information about their mortgage lending. HMDA requires banks and other lending institutions to amounts, geographic distribution, and other characteristics of their mortgage applications, including race, gender, and income of applicants. Advocacy groups such as National People's Action and community-based organizations have used data produced by HMDA to show how many lenders discriminate and to help negotiate fairer lending practices with those institutions. Furthermore, banking regulators used the data both to establish the extent and patterns of discrimination as well as to conduct their enforcement efforts under laws such as the Community Reinvestment Act.[†]

These are just two examples of how methods of transparency have been applied to the actions and products of private sector organizations. Transparency has also been used—sometimes quite effectively and sometimes less so—to address problems such as automobile safety, nutrition and health, hospital safety, credit risk, environmental quality, and workplace health and safety.

Analyzing the effectiveness of transparency incentives is important because measures that succeed can reduce critical public risks and improve public services. Those that miss the mark can distort incentives in ways that waste resources and expose people to risks they do not fully comprehend. In addition, some transparency systems in areas of health care and for certain consumer products are gaining momentum as information and communication technologies increase the capacity of citizens and consumers to use them to make more informed choices—

---

[*] Ibid, pp. 192–194.

[†] Ibid, pp. 203–205. HMDA and CRA have also been cited recently as one of the precipitating causes of the subprime mortgage meltdown. In our view, transparency surfaced wide-scale and pernicious discrimination in bank lending practices. How much it also contributed to the inappropriate use of subprime and other forms of complex mortgage instruments during the housing boom—versus other factors such as the securitization of mortgages and the agency problems arising within the housing finance sector that allowed brokers to approve borrowers with little capacity to meet the terms of their mortgages—requires separate treatment.

and to circle around corporate secrets and political obstacles to collaborate on their own transparency efforts. Technology is also transforming the capacity of entities that create public risks to pick up signals from consumers' changed choices and respond by reducing those risks.

A Matter of Politics

These efforts to make the private sector of society, as opposed to government, more transparent have emerged in fits and starts. Unlike the open government movement, there is no focused and organized effort to create an open society through these kinds of measures. Instead, they have emerged bit by bit in particular fields. Health advocates see some advantage in pressing for hospital disclosure in one place. In another, environmentalists press for toxics disclosure as part of their antipollution efforts. Worker advocates push for disclosure of chemical exposures in the workplace somewhere else. Furthermore, targeted transparency often emerges as a response to some kind of crisis. Congress, for example, passed a law requiring automobile manufacturers to disclose the propensity of their cars to roll over in 2000 after a series of widely reported fatal SUV accidents earlier that year. The current economic crisis is engendering its own calls for transparency in regard to regulating the financial sector, including more responsible disclosure of risks to potential borrowers for home loans to redress information failures in the subprime mortgage market, and better disclosure of systemic risks from complex securities.[‡]

These dynamics limit the reach of targeted transparency because of common political dynamics. As with open government, efforts to make private organizations more transparent often face substantial opposition. It is no surprise that the California Restaurant Association opposed the Los Angeles health grade report system. Generally, companies and other associations will act in the political arena to oppose laws and policies that compel them to provide information to the public.

Conclusion

The contest between these groups and transparency advocates is usually rigged against transparency. In the open society domain, transparency laws and policies usually create requirements upon some small group of organizations—restaurants, car manufacturers, hospitals, and the like—to tell the public information that most organizations wouldn't voluntarily disclose. At a minimum, it is cumbersome to comply with these requirements. Often, disclosure can harm some of these organizations by highlighting their bad behavior and

[‡] For example, a Federal Trade Commission study conducted in 2007 demonstrates that the methods of disclosure used by banks to provide information on standard 30-year mortgages are often misunderstood by mortgagees, to say nothing of the more complex features of subprime loans. See James M. Lacko and Janis K. Pappalardo, "Improving Consumer Mortgage Disclosures: An Empirical Assessment of Current and Prototype Disclosure Forms," Federal Trade Commission Bureau of Economics Staff Report, June 2007.

embarrassing them. On the flip side, those who benefit from greater social transparency—sometimes consumers, investors, citizens, and the public at large—are much more numerous and diffuse. As a matter of practical politics, it is usually far easier for smaller groups of concentrated interests to organize to oppose or undermine transparency policies than it is for the much larger groups of consumers and citizens to organize to support and defend those very same policies. Political scientists and political economists have called this the problem of "asymmetric organization." The dynamic explains why so many disclosure policies end up being toothless and ineffective.§

For these reasons, the current sophisticated movement for Open Government should expand its agenda and become a movement to Open Society. In American society, the threats to citizens individually and to society generally come as much—perhaps much more—from powerful private sector actors as from government. Therefore, it is appropriate, even urgent, that the champions of transparency and disclosure train their sights on all of these threats: those coming from economic and civic organizations as well as those coming from government. They should build on the burgeoning lessons of IT-enabled social networks to create responsive, evolving, and vibrant transparency platforms. Absent such a broader movement of targeted transparency to create an open society, many of the real sources of social risk—those that have been responsible for widespread food contamination, the meltdown of the housing market, the broader economic crisis, and the exploitation of the poor through usurious lending practices—will remain shrouded in secrecy, mysterious to citizens, and beyond the reach of democratic control.

§ For a full discussion of political sustainability, see *Full Disclosure*, Chapter 5.

About the Authors

ARCHON FUNG is the Ford Foundation Professor of Democracy and Citizenship at the Harvard Kennedy School. His research examines the impacts of civic participation, public deliberation, and transparency upon public and private governance. His recent books include *Full Disclosure: The Perils and Promise of Transparency* (Cambridge University Press, with Mary Graham and David Weil) and *Empowered Participation: Reinventing Urban Democracy* (Princeton University Press). His current projects examine democratic reform initiatives in electoral reform, urban planning, public services, ecosystem management, and transnational governance. He has authored 5 books, 3 edited collections, and more than 50 articles.

DAVID WEIL is a professor of economics and Everett W. Lord Distinguished Faculty Scholar at Boston University School of Management. He is also codirector of the Transparency Policy Project at the Kennedy School of Government at Harvard University. His research spans regulatory and labor market policy, industrial and labor relations, occupational safety and health, and transparency policy. He has written three books, including the recently released *Full Disclosure: The Perils and Promise of Transparency* (Cambridge University Press, 2007) and the award-winning *Stitch in Time: Lean Retailing and the Transformation of Manufacturing* (Oxford University Press, 1999). In addition, he is author of more than 75 scholarly and popular articles and publications.

CHAPTER NINE

"You Can Be the Eyes and Ears": Barack Obama and the Wisdom of Crowds

Micah L. Sifry

On his first full day in office, President Barack Obama issued an executive memorandum that may someday be seen as signaling the most important shift in how government works in the United States since the rise of the New Deal. His subject? Not jobs or health care or the environment, but "transparency and open government." In five succinct paragraphs, he promised to create an "unprecedented level of openness in Government" (see the Appendix). "We will work together to ensure the public trust and establish a system of transparency, public participation, and collaboration," he wrote, arguing that it would "strengthen our democracy and promote efficiency and effectiveness in Government."

Most significantly, he declared that in addition to making government more transparent, it should become more participatory and collaborative:

> Public engagement enhances the Government's effectiveness and improves the quality of its decisions. Knowledge is widely dispersed in society, and public officials benefit from having access to that dispersed knowledge. Executive departments and agencies should offer Americans increased opportunities to participate in policymaking and to provide their Government with the benefits of their collective expertise and information…. Executive departments and agencies should use innovative tools, methods, and systems to cooperate among themselves, across all levels of Government, and with nonprofit organizations, businesses, and individuals in the private sector.

Obama's language was dry, but the message is clear: in essence, he is pointing toward a third way between the stale left-right dichotomy of "big government" versus "smaller government." Effective government, Obama is suggesting, may be found by opening the bureaucracy to direct public monitoring, engagement, and, where viable, collaboration. Is Obama calling for the federal government to embrace the wisdom of crowds? The signs certainly abound.

Change.gov Shows How to Change the Gov

The most robust moves came early, undertaken by Obama's transition team during the weeks after the election but before his inauguration, when his team's use of the Web wasn't yet fully constrained by government traditions and legal hurdles. A number of valuable experiments came in quick succession.

First, on Change.gov, the official transition website, visitors were invited to "Join the Discussion" on topics such as health care reform, the economy, and community service, and rate the comments made by others. Several thousand people participated.

Then the transition team launched "Open for Discussion," a gigantic online forum where people were invited to post questions and to vote the best ones up.* Over the course of two rounds, more than 120,000 people voted nearly 6 million times on more than 85,000 questions. In both cases, top administration officials offered answers to a handful of the top-voted issues.

Finally, there was the "Citizens' Briefing Book," an attempt at making sure that at least some iconoclastic ideas from the public made their way, unfiltered, directly into the president's hands. More than 125,000 people voted on more than 44,000 submissions, and several months later, the White House Office of Public Engagement released a 32-page PDF along with a video showing Obama holding the report.†

"You Can Be the Eyes and Ears"

But the transition website was just the beginning. Early in his administration, Obama made several declarations about how his approach to government, and in particular the giant "Economic Recovery" spending plan that was the major legislative priority of his first months in office, would be informed by direct public participation in the process. In one online video, he told his supporters that this program would be conducted "with unprecedented transparency and accountability." Clearly aware that his critics were already predicting "big government" would waste hundreds of billions in taxpayer dollars, he added:

* http://www.whitehouse.gov/open/innovations/OpenforQuestions/

† http://www.whitehouse.gov/blog/Meet-the-Office-of-Public-Engagement-and-the-Citizens-Briefing-Book

I'll appoint an aggressive Inspector General and a cabinet level oversight board to make sure your money is spent wisely. More importantly, I'll enlist all of you. As soon as this plan is signed into law, Recovery.gov goes live and you'll be able to see precisely where your tax dollars are going. Because this is your democracy, and as I said throughout the campaign, change never begins from the top down. It begins from the bottom up.

A day later, on February 9, 2009, while selling his recovery plan at a town hall meeting in economically devastated Elkhart, Indiana, Obama went further in explaining his vision for using the social Web to crowdsource the watchdogging of government spending:

We're actually going to set up something called Recovery.gov—this is going to be a special website we set up, that gives you a report on where the money is going in your community, how it's being spent, how many jobs are being created so that all of you can be the eyes and ears. And if you see that a project is not working the way it's supposed to, you'll be able to get on that website and say, "You know, I thought this was supposed to be going to school construction but I haven't noticed any changes being made." And that will help us track how this money is being spent.... The key is that we're going to have strong oversight and strong transparency to make sure this money isn't being wasted.

"I'll enlist all of you." "You can be the eyes and ears." These are the words of someone who clearly understands the power and wisdom of a crowd, and the axiom that all of us are smarter than any one of us.

Recovery.gov Site Still Under Construction

But it's one thing for the president to promise to involve the public in a fundamentally new way in their government, and another to get government agencies and leaders to actually change how they do business. As of the fall of 2009, the implementation of Obama's vision remained sketchy at best.

For starters, Recovery.gov, which in Obama's own words was meant to play a central role in collecting, displaying, and tracking how billions in new monies are spent, was for most of the year just a placeholder of a website showing only top-line data and graphics on what was supposed to be happening, not an actual data trove for citizen engagement.

The inspector general in charge of that program, Earl Devaney, admitted that it would take at least until the fall before the site contained much detailed information, but after a $9.5 million crash contract to redesign the site, it still wasn't inspiring much confidence among transparency advocates. The revised site did contain tools enabling fairly granular data lookups and nifty maps showing where funding and jobs were supposedly occurring, but the lack of recipient reports made those tools relatively hollow. Similarly, users were encouraged to post reports of possible fraud, waste, or abuse, but the site didn't make those reports available in any fashion. In addition, Devaney promised to reach out to "citizen inspectors general" on social networking sites such as Facebook and Twitter, to help him surface problems, but compared to Obama's early promises of civic engagement, Devaney's words seemed mostly like gestures without strong follow-up.

Online Town Hall or "Participation Theater"?

In terms of involving the public in a meaningful discussion of policy priorities, the Obama administration clearly chose to crawl before it walked, let alone ran. Or to use a less clichéd metaphor, Obama's early moves were marked by an odd dichotomy: one leg of his administration seemed ready to race ahead, trying out new interactive experiments, while the other leg seemed to want to stand in place and control the discourse.

For example, twice in the first six months of 2009, Obama held an interactive "online town hall" where the public was invited to submit questions in advance and the president responded during a live webcast done in tandem with an in-the-flesh town hall meeting.

First, in late March, his new media team held an online town hall about the economy where for two days anyone could post a question on the White House website or vote one to the top of the pile. Then Obama held a live webcast from the White House where he pointedly responded to most of the top-voted questions. Nearly 93,000 people submitted more than 100,000 questions, and more than 3.6 million votes were cast on them. Tens of thousands watched the event live online. The forum was generally deemed a success, but it hit one discordant note when Obama made fun of the fact that questions about legalizing marijuana did surprisingly well in the online voting. "I don't know what this says about the online audience," he chuckled, ignoring the fact that somewhere between 40% and 50% of U.S. voters favor the reform.[‡]

Then, in early July, the president held another online town hall meeting on health care reform, but despite using sites such as YouTube, Facebook, and Twitter to invite the submission of questions from the public, this event was far less interactive than his first. Obama said he'd answer some of the "more popular" questions, but there was no mechanism established to determine which ones were indeed popular. Instead, his staff chose which questions he would be asked to respond to, producing an event that was less spontaneous and less town-hall-like than if all the questions had come from citizens live at the event using no technology at all. Reporters at the daily White House briefing peppered Press Secretary Robert Gibbs with critical questions about the event, attacking it as a sham. My colleague at Sunlight Foundation, Ellen Miller, called it "transparency theater," though the more precise term would be "participation theater."

The seeming reluctance of the Obama operation to allow the public to inject its own preferences into a White House media event is rooted in a traditional understanding of how important it

---

‡ See *http://www.pollingreport.com/drugs.htm*. For example, 46% favor the legalization of small amounts of pot for personal use (*Washington Post* poll from April 2009), and 44% are in favor of making the use of pot legal (Gallup poll from October 2009).

is to always control your message. But back in 2008, candidate Obama seemed unfazed by the prospect of involving the public in such events in a more free-form fashion. When the Open Debate Coalition, a cross-partisan group of reform advocates, was pushing for the use of "bubble-up" style public question filtering for the national debates, in particular for the one "town hall"-style debate, Obama declared his support for the concept (as did his opponent, Senator John McCain). Obama wrote:

> Town hall debates such as the October 7 debate provide an excellent opportunity to utilize technology to give voters more of a role in determining which questions are selected and asked. For example, during the MTV forum in which I participated last year, the Internet community voted to ask a question regarding my position on network neutrality, which I support. I support the use of such technology in debates as the Coalition proposes in its letter.

It remains to be seen whether President Obama will listen to candidate Obama on this issue.

Open Data and Open Government

Fortunately, the progress of Obama's call for a more open, participatory, and collaborative government isn't dependent on change solely in how the White House manages its most precious political asset, the president and his ability to communicate directly with the American people. Obama's call for change, coupled with the hiring of several leaders in the fields of open data and open government, has set off ripples across the federal government. CIOs and web managers in hundreds of departments and agencies are embracing this change in tone, and policy, to engage in all kinds of new approaches. A long list of agencies are now using YouTube, Facebook, MySpace, and dozens of less well-known but equally potent Web 2.0 platforms, thanks to efforts by the White House new media team and the U.S. Government Accountability Office (GAO) to negotiate acceptable terms of service with these third-party services. At least 68 agencies have official Twitter accounts (those were the ones the White House was following from its official Twitter account). And several agencies, such as the U.S. Environmental Protection Agency (EPA), have begun to roll out their own initiatives to make their piece of government more transparent.

The biggest developments of note were the launch of Data.gov and IT.usaspending.gov by White House CIO Vivek Kundra, and the "open government initiative" launched by the Office of Management and Budget (OMB) and the Office of Science and Technology Policy (OSTP) and led by deputy CTO Beth Noveck. Each of these efforts represents the finest distillation of Obama's principles into practice, and their emergence in the first six months of his administration is a sign of real promise.

Kundra's work in opening up raw government data in structured, machine-readable form is positively revolutionary. Literally hundreds of thousands of data streams are coming online at Data.gov, and in the process a whole new kind of public engagement with public information is being enabled. His willingness to launch the site before all these data sets were identified, and to also enable users to openly rate the quality of the data on the site, are subtle but significant shifts in how government conducts information technology (IT) projects, moving away from control and perfection and toward iteration and interaction. This is also the case with IT.usaspending.gov, which showcases user-friendly "dashboards" to help the public (as well as government leaders) track tens of billions in IT spending. "We want to tap into the ingenuity of the American people to show us a better, innovative path," Kundra told a rapt audience at the Personal Democracy Forum in June 2009, as he described his approach to iterative website development.

A similar willingness to give up partial control and invite freewheeling public participation has characterized Noveck's leadership of the Open Government Directive. For several weeks between late May and early July 2009, the public was invited to participate in a series of open online conversations about Obama's day-one transparency memorandum. The goal, in Noveck's words, was to create a "structured dialog" aimed at the "co-creation of government" with "many people participating in the process."

The process started with an online brainstorm using IdeaScale, a third-party platform that enables Digg-style voting to bubble up popular suggestions. In a short period of time, about 4,000 people had posted more than 1,100 ideas and thousands of comments, and cast more than 30,000 votes to help rank them. Then the public was invited to comment on a series of detailed blog posts. And finally, participants were given the opportunity to actually help draft each of 16 distinct sections of the draft directive, using the collaborative writing tool Mixed Ink. A total of 375 participants wrote 305 different drafts across those 16 topics, and voted 2,256 times on those drafts to help produce some promising policy language.

This open process wasn't without its bumps. Especially in the early stages, the OSTP site was bombarded with comments from members of the public with their own narrow concerns, including people who believe Obama's birth certificate is invalid. These "birthers" were, in many cases, driven to Noveck's site by right-wing websites and bloggers, and for a time their voices appeared to drown out those of people genuinely interested in proposing improvements in government transparency practices. To a casual visitor of the site, it might have appeared that it had been hijacked. But Lena Trudeau, vice president of the National Academy of Public Administration, which hosted that phase of the process, said it was an overall success.

She did tell *Federal Computer Week (http://www.fcw.com/Articles/2009/07/20/FEAT-Lena-Trudeau -QandA.aspx)*, however, that after an initial burst of participation by members of the public who wanted to contribute constructive suggestions, the IdeaScale phase of the initiative hit some turbulence. She noted, "Part of the theory behind the site was that the community would help moderate it. Well, the challenge that you have is, when a large part of the constructive community goes away, you're left with people who may not have the full context of what you are trying to accomplish or they may have their own agendas. And that's just something we need to know and understand if we are going to be using more of these tools and approaches in the policy evolvement process."

Co-creation, Co-optation, or Collision?

It remains to be seen just how far the administration will go toward implementing Obama's vision of change fostered by making government more open, participatory, and collaborative. In part, this is because he is juggling many difficult priorities at once. In part, this is because he and the innovators he has appointed to pioneer these changes are traveling uncharted territory. And finally, by offering to involve and empower the public in "co-creating" government, Obama is unleashing an inherently disruptive force.

As his administration's early experiments with crowdsourcing have shown, hundreds of thousands of Americans are eager to take up his call to participate in new ways—and that's without his having pushed hard to publicize the opportunity. What happens when those numbers climb into the millions, and people who have been invited to have a voice now expect to be listened to?

It isn't just that online collaborative platforms for public input and participation can be gamed, and thus special interest groups or semiorganized pranksters can seemingly hijack such sites to make mischief. Ideally, the more often government enables such interaction to happen, the less meaningful those disruptions will become. It's when the chance to participate is kept rare that the value of gaming these sites is at its highest.

The more difficult issue for advocates of opening up a process of "co-creating" government is what may happen when newly empowered citizens inevitably collide with entrenched interests. Obama's vision of enlisting the public in a new, socially conscious and transparent process of improving how government works—"You can be the eyes and ears"—may be exhilarating, but it also may lead to all kinds of unexpected consequences. The subcontractor who is skimming recovery funds that are supposed to be spent on building that new school may be a cousin of the local mayor, who may be tied to the Democratic Party, or his workers may belong to a construction union that endorsed the president's election. In other words, local e-democracy, Obama-style, could easily crash head-on into local power politics.

We don't know yet how this story will play out. But the evolving history of the social Web offers one encouraging hint. From Wikipedia to Craigslist to Amazon to Google, the Web keeps rewarding those actors who empower ordinary users, eliminate wasteful middlemen, share information openly, and shift power from the center to the edges. Applying those same principles to government will undoubtedly be messy, but Obama has one thing going for him: it is where technology is already taking us.

About the Author

 **Micah L. Sifry** is cofounder and editor of the Personal Democracy Forum (*http://www.personaldemocracy.com*), a website and annual conference that covers the ways technology is changing politics, and TechPresident.com (*http://www.techpresident.com*), an award-winning group blog about how the American presidential candidates are using the Web, and how the Web is using them.

CHAPTER TEN

Two-Way Street:
Government with the People

Mark Drapeau

During the 2008 elections in the United States, then-candidate Barack Obama's campaign made excellent use of new media to not only raise an unprecedented amount of money, but also market him as the candidate that would bring change to the country. Inspired by this, citizens prominently used new media such as YouTube, Flickr, and Twitter to share their experiences during Obama's inauguration week celebration in Washington, D.C. And after President Obama took office, his first orders of business were to reveal a modern White House website and to issue a memo[*] directing the federal government to be more transparent, participatory, and collaborative (see the Appendix).

But the wheels of government do not turn merely because the president gives an order—even when that order comes from a leader as popular as Obama. Disagreements between people in the executive and legislative branches over policy, strategy, and tactics can delay progress for months, if not years; not to mention outside pressure from think tanks, special interest groups, and super-empowered individuals. Engaging in spirited debate is the core of democracy, but it periodically feels like participating in a nationwide traffic jam.

[*] "Transparency and Open Government," President Barack Obama, White House Memorandum for the Heads of Executive Departments and Agencies, January 22, 2009 (*http://www.whitehouse.gov/the_press _office/TransparencyandOpenGovernment/*).

Pockets of Excellence: The Goverati

An interesting byproduct of leaders encouraging government to be more transparent, participatory, and collaborative is that people are increasingly if inadvertently taking matters into their own hands. Encouraged by high-profile uses of social software, government employees previously hidden in "pockets of excellence" have used personal blogs, microsharing, and other new communication technologies to promote their ideas with wider audiences than ever before, in the process circumventing to some extent their normal chains of command. And outsiders who have become enthusiasts regarding changing the way the government operates have increasingly been sharing their ideas, hosting events, and creating websites and applications that use government data to help people.

These evangelists for a transparent, participatory, and collaborative Government 2.0 are a group of people I previously dubbed the Goverati.[†] They are a unique and empowered band of insiders and outsiders using an understanding of government, a passion for technology, and a gift for communication to change governance and help people. Two things set the Goverati apart from other special interest groups that want to lobby or change government:

- The technologies they are encouraging the government to use are the very things that enable them to better communicate their messages to their audience, increase their reach, and gain recognition for their work. Practicing what they preach, they endorse technologies they use themselves (and criticize ones they dislike). Their personal passions feed back onto their mission in a positive way, and their messages come across as more authentic because of it.

- The Goverati are a loosely organized groundswell lacking formal organization or a designated leader. There are catalysts within the movement, to be sure; but while some persons have emerged as temporary thought leaders, many of them disagree with each other over various issues, and no one clearly leads the tribe by himself. Nevertheless, modern communication technology has enabled the decentralized[‡] Goverati to network with each other and empowered them to become very effective at educating people about the topic of Government 2.0 and its potential. As author Robert Waterman, Jr., would say, the Goverati is an "adhocracy"—a highly adaptive organization cutting across normal bureaucratic lines to capture opportunities, solve problems, and get results.[§] Adhocracies can be seen as everything bureaucracies are not, and they are perhaps what are needed most at a time when the world is grappling with many serious issues.

[†] "Government 2.0: The Rise of the Goverati," Mark Drapeau, ReadWriteWeb, February 5, 2009 (*http://www.readwriteweb.com/archives/government_20_rise_of_the_goverati.php*).

[‡] *Starfish and the Spider: The Unstoppable Power of Leaderless Organizations*, Ori Brafman and Rod Beckstrom, Penguin, 2006. *Here Comes Everybody: The Power of Organizing Without Organizations*, Clay Shirky, Penguin, 2008.

[§] *Adhocracy*, Robert H. Waterman, Jr., W. W. Norton & Co., 1993.

An interesting subphenomenon, perhaps crucial to the growing influence of the Goverati adhocracy, is that while some members have decades of experience in government, technology, or both, others have relatively little. Nevertheless, some fresh thinkers in this area, typically from Generation X, have become extraordinarily talented at using social technology to spread their views or innovate using pilot projects. Cynics sometimes judge this pattern as abuse of intellectual personal branding or even annoyingly viral self-promotion; regardless, a new class of influencers‖ has risen from the bureaucratic ooze to network and partner with experienced and prominent leaders.

GovLoop and BRIDGE: Networks for Government Employees

In perhaps the best-known example of a relatively young member of the Goverati having a major impact, an informal Government 2.0 social network named GovLoop (*http://www.govloop .com*) was developed by a U.S. government employee in his spare time on the popular platform Ning. In the span of just one year,# it gained more than 12,000 members at all levels of government inside and outside the United States, and its rate of growth seems to be accelerating as excitement about Government 2.0 spreads. Its membership includes advisors at the highest levels of the Obama administration. Incredibly, GovLoop was made possible simply because one passionate, empowered young person filled a void that employees felt they needed but that the government left empty. Now members of the government are some of its biggest fans.

Government taking the lead from citizens about the benefits of using social software is also evident on a more individual scale, as government leaders both in the United States and elsewhere continue to embrace new media tools, both personally and professionally. The examples set by senior leaders at the top of the hierarchy are trickling down throughout government, empowering others to start new projects or revive old ones shelved as unimportant in a more stovepiped era. One excellent new example of this is BRIDGE, which is an unclassified U.S. Intelligence Community virtual environment that debuted in 2009 to allow analysts to network with subject matter experts outside government.* Not long ago, collaboration between intelligence analysts and outsiders on national security challenges in an online environment would have been unthinkable to many; now, open collaboration is becoming the default place to start new projects.

‖ Interestingly, this phenomenon may be responsible for the fast-growing influence of the Goverati. According to a new research paper ("Effective Leadership in Competition," Hai-Tao Zhang et al., 2009 preprint: *http://arxiv.org/PS_cache/arxiv/pdf/0907/0907.1317v1.pdf*), relatively few new leaders within a large group can shift the balance of power by distributing their ideas broadly and retaining allegiances well. Social media can facilitate exactly that when used well.

"Celebrate the 'Summer of Gov' in Washington, DC and San Francisco," Mark Drapeau, Examiner.com, July 10, 2009 (*http://www.examiner.com/x-13483-DC-Technology-and-Politics-Examiner~y2009m7d10 -Celebrate-the-Summer-of-Gov-in-Washington-DC-and-San-Francisco*). See also *http://govloop.com*.

* BRIDGE was funded by the deputy director of National Intelligence for Analysis. Information about how BRIDGE is helping the U.S. Intelligence Community connect with outside subject matter experts who understand emerging technologies is available at *http://about.bridge-ic.net/index.html*.

Web-based social networking innovations such as GovLoop and BRIDGE may result in the public-facing parts of government appearing more personable. At a time when citizens are thinking about government more than ever, this can almost certainly be a good thing. As evidenced by the Goverati, however, this is a partnership of sorts—the government has the ability to be more personable toward citizens, and citizens have the ability to more easily tell the government what they think. The technology to make this possible is available. Decisions about who will take advantage of it, and when and how to utilize it, vary considerably. This two-way street is fraught with obstacles.

Reversing the Obscurity of Public Servants

There is, however, pushback on the ideals of Government 2.0, for many different reasons ranging from lack of understanding about emerging technologies to ordinary resistance to change within a very large bureaucracy. It is often said that battles in government are usually won by the most persistent party; decentralized organizations such as the Goverati have the ability to work on many things at once, adapt quickly to changing situations, replenish members and even leaders who move along to other passions, and reinforce their influence by using social media to spread their ideas. Increasingly, large (more than 500 attendees) events such as Government 2.0 Camp, Personal Democracy Forum, and Gov 2.0 Summit—formally organized independent of the government, but with government's participation—are viewed as opportunities for networking and hearing the best ideas. Whereas the government previously held events to tell citizens about what it was doing, the government now more often finds itself in the position of taking advice from a subset of those very citizens who have more reach with their thoughts than ever before. And there is nothing wrong with this meta pattern. Who declared that government had to have all the answers? Citizens are smart, too.

In the not-so-distant future, when a citizen is asked to name an individual government employee, the ideal end state should be that a person working in a microniche of interest to her (finance, farming, health, etc.) immediately comes to mind. Unfortunately, interesting and talented people working inside the government are often not known to the public despite the great importance of their work to everyday life. This state of affairs is mostly a vestige from the days when communications were controlled by professionally trained public relations staff members dealing with mainstream media. This was understandable—equipment was expensive, channels were few, and citizens trusted authenticated, official sources for their information. But this media structure that worked well for half a century is now outdated. Reversing the obscurity of public servants[†] should be a principal goal of an open, transparent government.

---

† "Government 2.0: How Social Media Could Transform Gov PR," Mark Drapeau, MediaShift, January 2009 (*http://www.pbs.org/mediashift/2009/01/government-20-how-social-media-could-transform-gov-pr005 .html*).

In the Web 2.0 world‡ where the Internet is used as a platform, every individual is empowered to be not only a consumer of information, but also a producer of it. Published words, pictures, and video are searchable, discoverable, sharable, usable, and alterable. The bloggers formerly known as kids in their parents' basements have morphed into a powerful society class of listeners, questioners, writers, editors, publishers, and distributors; some bloggers have even become household names. Interestingly, this is beginning to happen not only outside the government but also within it. Take "Blogger Bob" from the U.S. Transportation Security Administration's blog (*http://www.tsa.gov/blog/*); true, he isn't as famous as Tom Clancy, but he's been empowered by his organization to write with a personal viewpoint that showcases the personality of a human being rather than the coarseness of official jargon.

The developed global citizen is not an empty vessel waiting to be filled with press releases and government website updates. Even a sophisticated government website such as that of the White House can expect to attract only a subset of citizens a subset of the time, because there are simply too many avenues of information flowing toward these people formerly known as a captive audience. No matter how compelling the government information, they are not waiting to hear about it. Nor are they necessarily waiting to hear from the *New York Times*, the BBC, or any other mainstream organization. From the government's viewpoint, rather than assuming citizens are eagerly awaiting government information, it is more productive to imagine them as interwoven networks of individuals having conversations over dinner with their families, in their workplace cafeteria, and on social media websites.

Such online and offline social networks are an increasingly important and powerful force in the lives of adults.§ But while governments have to some degree embraced new media in the form of publishing official blogs and reading comments, or using Twitter and Facebook to accumulate "fans" and answer questions, they appear in many cases less adept at deploying individuals to become trusted members of microniche citizen networks based around the topics on which they work. Asking people to tune in to a live news chat on Facebook is not much different from asking them to tune in to a televised news conference. Come-to-us is not being replaced by go-to-them, and yet trusted people within communities of interest have become filters for the multimedia vying for citizens' attention.

Bureaucracies cannot have conversations with citizens; only individual people who work within the bureaucracy can. Ideally, such people having conversations can become "lethally

---

‡ "What Is Web 2.0: Design Patterns and Business Models for the Next Generation of Software," Tim O'Reilly, September 30, 2005 (*http://oreilly.com/web2/archive/what-is-web-20.html*).

§ "Social Networks Grow: Friending Mom and Dad," Amanda Lenhart, January 14, 2009 (*http://pewresearch .org/pubs/1079/social-networks-grow*).

generous" trusted community members.‖ How does one know whether someone has achieved that status? I posit that such lethally generous community leaders are known to the community by name. In other words, when a citizen who is passionate about environmental issues or health care reform or veterans' benefits is asked to name a government staffer working on those topics, he should be able to answer, because that staffer is also a trusted member of his community of interest.

Harnessing Social Capital

Anecdotally, few government employees consider "marketing" part of their job, and similarly most citizens don't think of "lobbying" as part of theirs. But when every person can be a writer, publisher, and distributor, everyone cannot be immune from these responsibilities. Granted, both private sector companies and government agencies have rules about what you can and cannot write about your job, and not everyone wants to participate. But many people have already chosen to opt-in to publishing blogs using WordPress, belonging to social networks such as Facebook, and sharing real-time experiences on Twitter. The key question is how do organizations channel such preexisting social communication talents of their workforce for better networking between government and citizens?

Social capital within large organizations should be harnessed, not punished. Such people engaged in communities of interest may very well be more in touch with grassroots conversations# than the public affairs office of an agency, which traditionally tends more toward unidirectional outward information flow. These employees may also already be trusted members of a community of interest, flush with knowledge and generous with assistance. It's difficult to think of good reasons to not use such preadapted social engagement to the government's advantage.

Government "social ambassadors" should be fully accessible, transparent, authentic, and collaborative leaders that inspire people to cooperate and engage with their government and with each other for the sake of common concerns. As part of their missions, government brand ambassadors should conduct community-based research to better understand the grassroots interests of the average person, which are sometimes misunderstood or overlooked. Listening to and participating in online conversations is quickly replacing polling as a way to understand what communities of interest are actually interested *in*.

‖ The term *lethally generous* with regard to social media usage was coined by author Shel Israel and means that rather than adopting a command-and-control strategy, someone seeking to be a thought leader in a community should participate in its conversations and add the most value possible. See *http://redcouch .typepad.com/weblog/2008/10/using-lethal-ge.html*.

Good online community managers tend to have a unique combination of skills, including those of a magazine editor, orchestra conductor, teacher, and parent. See "What do you need in a community manager?", Simon Young, June 5, 2009 (*http://www.marketingmag.com.au/blogs/view/what-do-you-need-in -a-community-manager-1295*).

Conclusion

With government social ambassadors using new media to more effectively reach out to communities of citizens, and with citizens using those same tools to lobby* their government, a two-way channel of information flow—a two-way street, if you will—may slowly become a "government with the people." While governments certainly face challenges in using social technologies, experts estimate that the benefits of using these tools to engage the public outweigh the negatives.† Social technologies can make networking and engagement with the public simple and powerful, make informal research faster, identify influencers in useful microniches, provide mechanisms for combating negative publicity, and measure public sentiment to help inform public policy and improve governance.

About the Author

MARK DRAPEAU is currently adjunct faculty in the School of Media and Public Affairs at The George Washington University in Washington, D.C. Until recently he was a research fellow at the Center for Technology and National Security Policy at the National Defense University. He is a cofounder of the Government 2.0 Club, a cochair of the O'Reilly Media/TechWeb-produced Gov 2.0 Expo, and a frequent guest speaker and writer on topics related to government, social media, technology, and society. Previously, in his career as a laboratory scientist, he held postdoctoral fellowships from NIH and AAAS and studied the genetics and neurobiology of animal behavior. He has a B.S. in biology from the University of Rochester, and a Ph.D. in ecology and evolutionary biology from the University of California, Irvine.

---

* The recent White House experiment called the "Open Government Initiative" is a good example of how social technologies are empowering citizens to contribute to the government policymaking process. It was directed by the Office of Science and Technology Policy. See *http://blog.ostp.gov/2009/06/22/open -government-directive-phase-iii-drafting/#TB_inline?height=220&width=370&inlineId=tb_external*.

† "Social Software and National Security: An Initial Net Assessment," Mark Drapeau and Linton Wells II, Defense and Technology Papers, National Defense University, April 2009 (*http://www.ndu.edu/ctnsp/Def _Tech/DTP61_SocialSoftwareandNationalSecurity.pdf*). See also "Social Networking and National Security: How to Harness Web 2.0 to Protect the Country," James Jay Carafano, Heritage Foundation Backgrounder, May 18, 2009 (*http://www.heritage.org/Research/NationalSecurity/bg2273.cfm*).

CHAPTER ELEVEN

Citizens' View of Open Government

Brian Reich

The American public has lost trust in its government, its elected leaders, and the media institutions that have covered it for so long. But the public hasn't dismissed or forgotten the role it can play in informing and improving the world. With the tools now available to us, the opportunities are greater—and the stakes higher—than they have ever been. We have the potential to reengage the public in its democracy and for the nation to flourish as never before. The question is: how will it happen?

Our society has changed, dramatically, over the past few decades. We talk about it all the time in the context of business (flattening), media (speeding up), and community (connecting). But what about government?

While the audience used to watch the government operate, now we are in the middle of it. Technology and the Internet have given elected officials new ways to reach constituents. Citizens have unprecedented opportunities to access information and, at the same time, myriad ways to see issues obscured. Information is accessible and available to all who are interested. And there are new tools for communities to come together and explore different ways to address the serious challenges that exist in our society.

Still, for most Americans, technology and the Internet haven't changed government. Our leaders remain out of touch. Politicians appear to care more about being reelected than they do about fixing real issues. Not only do the struggles that everyday Americans face still exist, but in many cases the speed at which our society now moves seems to have only made things worse.

The promise of open government is great. Technology can help to improve how policies are made and implemented, open the halls of power, hold elected officials more accountable, and reengage citizens in the functioning of our democracy. But technology won't fix government by itself. Making information available isn't enough. For the promise of open government and the benefits of transparency to truly be felt, we need to change the way we think, act, and organize. We need to change the way we talk about public service and listen to what the public needs. Everything we know about government, and how it operates, must be reconsidered.

The First "We President"

With the explosive growth of the Internet, the pervasive use of mobile technologies, and the seemingly ubiquitous accessibility of people across the globe, President Obama began his presidency with a historic opportunity to communicate more directly with the American public—and with the entire world. The world, in turn, had an opportunity to monitor, inform, and influence the Obama administration's actions and policies. It was the beginning of a new era for our nation and for our government.

In many ways, this put President Obama in a stronger position than any previous president, allowing him to more easily engage citizens in the process of leading the nation. His administration had new tools to help overcome the communication obstacles and unseat the entrenched interests that exist in government, as well as bypass traditional barriers erected by the media when governments engage their constituents. Moreover, President Obama brought with him a massive and loyal network of supporters and volunteers who, throughout his campaign, were inspired to play a role in supporting their government and were empowered to participate in finding solutions to the challenges facing our nation.

It is no accident, of course, that President Obama took office with such a strong foundation from which to lead—through its use of technology and the Internet during the campaign, the Obama campaign has, in the words of the *New York Times*' Adam Nagourney, "rewritten the rules on how to reach voters, raise money, organize supporters, manage the news media, track and mold public opinion, and wage—and withstand—political attacks, including many carried by blogs that did not exist four years ago" (*http://www.nytimes.com/2008/11/04/us/politics/04memo .html*). For the first time in history, it's possible for hundreds, thousands, or even millions of people to have a single conversation. But the Internet is far more than just a way to raise money or mobilize supporters. It's a way to shrink the distance between people and politicians.

This new era of leadership and engagement presents many obstacles. For starters, would the president be able to transfer the knowledge and experience from the campaign to the hard work of governing? President Obama and his administration can deliver their message as never before, by bypassing traditional channels or choosing to create their own direct channels to the public. At the same time, the risks of trying to control what is said (and how it is delivered) range from an unchecked president to a disappointed and disillusioned electorate who won't support his agenda or help to reelect him in four years.

With all the issues that demand attention from the president—a global economic crisis, two wars, a broken health care system, and failing schools, among others—would the Obama administration have time to engage the population and welcome their contribution?

And could the public, with so many distractions and a low tolerance for the partisanship that has long defined politics in Washington, move beyond their established beliefs and overcome their lack of interest to take advantage of the opportunity to be involved when the solutions aren't as easy to figure out as they might expect?

The answer to all these questions, so far, is largely no.

Our society is increasingly powered by a bottom-up, grassroots-fueled, emergent process that can be applied to the production and distribution of information or the organization of people in support of real action. The act of a citizen or group of citizens playing a role in the process of making policy, passing legislation, or implementing a program on the local level is an advancement of our democratic principles at work. The intent is clear: by providing independent, reliable, accurate, wide-ranging, and relevant information and opportunities for participation, we bolster our democracy. That information and participation is now available to everyone who can connect—communities, businesses, government agencies, pundits, journalists, and everyday people. Using technology and the Internet to foster that discussion, and convert the interest of those involved into meaningful, measurable action, requires a different approach and skill set, however.

People want a place, digital or otherwise, where they can gather and learn about the community in which they are a part, a place where they can get in touch with the issues. The Obama campaign turned the Internet into a gateway for millions of ordinary Americans to participate in the political process, and now the administration fully expects these people to continue on their own, acting locally, to bring about change in our communities. The Obama campaign also demonstrated through its online campaign efforts that they had trust and confidence in their community. That trust and confidence, when shown at the national level by the candidate and his team, transformed people from supporters into participants. People were actively thinking about why they supported Obama and how to express that.

Now that opportunity exists on the local level as well, and it must be applied to the substance of government work. It's not just Obama supporters who are feeling the need for change, and who have access to these tools. The opportunities offered by the Internet are available to all who seek to engage on issues and deliver change. What is missing is the participation of the media and the audience together to make it happen.

The Internet Has Made Us Lazy

Technology and the Internet have given us greater control over our own media experience—what information we get and share, how we spend our time, and to whom we are connected. We are more diverse as a society, more informed as individuals, and more involved as communities. Government, however, hasn't changed much in this new, fast-paced digital era. And change is slow.

Because the pace of change is not aligned with the rhetoric that calls for new approaches, we have lost sight of what real change in government looks like. The creation of sites such as Recovery.gov, the launch of the White House blog (*http://www.whitehouse.gov/blog/*), and the inclusion of the online audience in the president's town hall meetings have received a lot of attention—and the White House deserves a lot of credit for being open and welcoming. But what has really changed about government?

The websites for the federal government (and some state and local governments) have absolutely improved—they feature better design and usability for starters, and more information and access to elected officials is coming every day. More and more data is filtering out, and everyone from think tanks to media to individual citizens is mashing things up in creative and compelling ways. Perhaps most importantly, the public now has someone who is on the inside listening. This is progress.

Still, the release of data alone is not an accomplishment. When the discussions at a town hall meeting are divisive and inflammatory—or worse—the fact that more people are participating in those discussions than in previous years is not so important. And while millions of people sign petitions online every day with one click of a mouse, those petitions rarely (if ever) change minds or impact the outcome of a vote in Congress.

Because we can use the tools that are now widely available online to conduct campaigns, send notices, and raise awareness of issues—more efficiently and cost-effectively than ever before— we have lost sight of what real impact looks like, how to change behavior, and how success should be measured. We've settled for low open rates for emails and names on an email list as signs of success instead of demanding more from our leaders, and ourselves, and working harder to make things happen.

Lots of things aren't changing. There are still too many layers of bureaucracy; technology is supposed to make things more efficient, but we aren't seeing that in government yet. Most/all of the legislation that is passed/signed into law doesn't do enough to address the core issues it is designed to address, and there is little evidence that better legislation is going to emerge from the current Congress anytime soon. The implementation of policies remains largely out of the reach of average people. And perhaps most dangerous of all, the public's opinion of and perceptions about Congress, the president, and other elected officials remain largely negative.

Put another way, the Internet has made us lazy, and has obscured our focus on what truly matters. The activities that have defined the opening of government and the release of government information are overshadowing the discussion of whether any real impact is being had. Too much attention has been paid to the process of making our government more transparent and not enough consideration has been given to whether the goals of transparency are truly being achieved.

Toward a Findable Government

During a recent presentation at the New America Foundation, Google chief executive Eric Schmidt said, "The vast majority of information is still not searchable or findable either because it's not published or it's on websites which the government has put up which no one can index." He was referring to the U.S. government, one of the world's largest depositories of data, which has been unwilling or unable to make millions of its web pages accessible to search engines.

According to the *Washington Post (http://www.washingtonpost.com/wp-dyn/content/article/2008/12/10/AR2008121003241.html)*, "a wide array of public information remains largely invisible to the search engines, and therefore to the general public, because it is held in such a way that the web search engines of Google, Yahoo!, and Microsoft can't find it and index it." The *Post* added, "The National Archives expects that its entire database containing descriptions of its holdings will be available to Google by January…the EPA has made some sites accessible…and the Smithsonian has sent Google the links for 78,000 pages."

We are barely scratching the surface.

The idea of searchable government information is appealing, but incomplete. Beyond just being able to locate this information, aligning what users want when searching for government agencies or regulations (and such) is the key to success. Accessibility is not enough. We need to make this information "findable." As I wrote in *Media Rules!,**** findability and meeting user expectations in the connected age is critical:

> Your ability to be located and to become rooted in the consciousness of your target audience is perhaps the greatest challenge you will face as an organization. Call it your Findability factor.

> Findability is not only about being found on the Internet, having your name and address in the Yellow Pages, or placing a billboard where all can see. Findability is the likelihood that someone encountering your organization can get the relevant, timely, and compelling information they expect throughout their interaction with you. If they do, they are far more likely to remember you and return again. If they don't, that person from your audience will make a judgment about you that puts you at the bottom of their priority list. And when they go out looking for someone to sell them something or to answer their question in the future, they will have plenty of other, better choices to look to for help.

> Organizations that support their audience in finding the information they want and need have a lot to gain. Organizations that don't, or can't do that, invite increased competition. Most organizations fail miserably when it comes to findability, because they don't consider the interests of their audience over their own interests. The good news is that it is not that difficult to make yourself more findable.

---

* *Media Rules! Mastering Today's Technology to Connect With and Keep Your Audience*, Brian Reich and Dan Solomon, Wiley, 2008.

The challenge of making government information more findable will require cooperation between the government and search engine operators, and shifts in behavior and perspective from both. At present, the government produces information it believes serves its audience and search engines are trying to make that information available. Findability is about making that information relevant, on top of everything else, and currently neither the government nor Google seems all that interested in meeting that standard.

Much of what is produced and made available by government offices and agencies is of little or no interest to the broad audience of constituents it is designed to serve. It is written in a format, or with a tone, that appeals to only a narrow band of experts. And it is distributed at a time and place when few citizens are paying attention. The search engines, meanwhile, aggregate the information effectively, but the multitude of choices quickly becomes unreasonable for the audience to wade through. It's wonderful to know that thousands of pages of results have been returned on your query, but in practicality, it doesn't help you find what you need in most cases.

The search engines deserve to be commended for their commitment to making government information accessible (though the cynical part of me thinks they are just interested in the increased revenue that comes from search ads aligned with queries). And the government's interest in opening its doors more to the public is commendable. However, if they don't commit to creating a more findable government, and begin to move with that goal in mind, the likely impact of having government websites and documents newly available across the Web will have only limited value.

Advanced Citizenship

It is absolutely necessary that we talk about the future of government in a connected society— but we have to do it in order of priority. First, we must clearly define what we want from our government; how it will support the citizenry, and what kinds of services it will provide. Second, we need to look at what is working in government, and what fails to live up to our expectations. Third, we have to ask ourselves how to improve or change those issues. And then, only then, should we be talking about what technology to use, what data standards to create, and the like.

The conversation about the future of government is stalled until we can have a real conversation about how to change what government does. If we can get that conversation started, the rest will flow (more) easily from there.

That is why everything needs to change.

When I talk about everything changing, I am not just talking about functional change—the fact that almost everyone owns a cell phone or people spend a lot more time shopping online than they used to, the rise of social networks, the speed at which information moves, or the lack of time we have to process everything. Those are important data points, evidence of the change that we are seeing. I am talking about how our expectations are changing, in terms of the information we spend time with (or want to spend time with), the access we hope to have (to people, or anything else), the level of participation we might demand or our willingness to collaborate on things we used to do alone, and of course, our increased awareness of the need for something to have a real, meaningful, measurable impact to warrant our attention.

Unfortunately, while many people recognize that the world is changing and that what we are doing isn't working anymore, few are willing to embrace what that means in terms of how they need to communicate and operate. When I tell people that their marketing isn't as successful as it used to be, heads nod, but nothing changes. When I suggest to people that their audience (be they customers, or voters, or donors, or readers) won't engage in the same ways as before, people scribble notes, but they don't put into practice any of the things they need to adapt.

Do you know why nothing changes? Because change is hard. It's difficult for people to change course. It's difficult for people to look past the short-term metrics and instead focus on long-term impact. And I understand that. And when things are difficult, we tend not to do them.

Whenever I hear that change is difficult, I think of a speech that the (fictional) president of the United States (played by Michael Douglas in the moving *The American President*) gave:

> Everybody knows America isn't easy. America is advanced citizenship.

> You gotta want it bad, 'cause it's gonna put up a fight. It's gonna say, "You want free speech? Let's see you acknowledge a man whose words make your blood boil, who's standing center stage and advocating, at the top of his lungs, that which you would spend a lifetime opposing at the top of yours. You want to claim this land as the land of the free, then the symbol of your country can't just be a flag; the symbol also has to be one of its citizens exercising his right to burn that flag in protest." Show me that, defend that, celebrate that in your classrooms.

> Then you can stand up and sing about the land of the free.... We've got serious problems, and we need serious men, and if you want to talk about character, Bob, you'd better come at me with more than a burning flag and a membership card. If you want to talk about character and American values, fine. Just tell me where and when, and I'll show up.

It is just a movie, but the message is clear. Change requires a lot of effort. But change is also possible.

There remain so many opportunities to invite supporters to contribute ideas and policy suggestions. There remain so many issues where a simulation or calculator would help to clear up much of the confusion. Feedback from people across America is now more welcome in the conversation, but it rarely seems to be integrated. The tools exist, and they will only improve. But before we put more energy into facilitating conversation, we must elevate the dialogue. Before we make choices about which platform to use in sharing information, we need to understand more about the challenges that citizens across the country share. And before we claim more progress as a result of a new website launching or a new store of data being released, we must ask the audience whether their lives have been improved and whether they are seeing progress.

Conclusion

We have barely scratched the surface of what is possible and what is necessary if we are going to truly repair the damage that has been done to our democracy over the years. I have high hopes for how the Obama administration will use technology and the Internet to open the process of running this country and give all of us a little opportunity to change and improve things ourselves. I also have high expectations for us, as citizens, that we will answer the call and take the opportunity to become more involved. Government is truly the best place to experiment with the uses of technology and the Internet to increase participation and drive deeper levels of engagement by citizens around issues.

Truly, anything is possible in today's age, so it's time we throw out the old playbook and try something entirely new.

About the Author

BRIAN REICH is the managing director of little m media, which provides strategic guidance and support to organizations around the use of the Internet and technology to facilitate communications, engagement, education, and mobilization. He is well known for his expertise in new media, Web 2.0, social networks, mobile, community, e-commerce, brand marketing, cause branding, and more. Reich is the author of *Media Rules!: Mastering Today's Technology to Connect With and Keep Your Audience* (Wiley, 2007), and serves as director of community and partnerships for iFOCOS, the media think tank and futures lab that organizes the We Media community, conferences, and awards. He is the managing editor of WeMedia.com. He is also the editor of Thinking About Media (*http://www.thinkingaboutmedia.com*) and contributes as a Fast Company expert.

CHAPTER TWELVE

After the Collapse: Open Government and the Future of Civil Service

David Eaves

Across North America and around the world, citizens and public servants—influenced by social media, Web 2.0, open source software, and other social and technological developments—see growing pressure on governments to evolve. Seeking to respond to increasing citizen expectations around service delivery and effectiveness, these reformers envision governments that act as a platform: that share information (particularly raw data), are transparent in their operations and decision making, enable and leverage citizen-led projects, are effective conveners, and engage citizens' requests, ideas, and feedback more intelligently.

Government as a platform holds enormous possibility. But most present-day government institutions are not designed with this role in mind. More importantly, their cultures usually reflect the corporate values of a hierarchical system: centralized decision making, risk aversion, a strong delineation between insiders and outsiders, and deference to authority and specialization. In short, our governments are analog systems, not just in their structure and processes, but also in their values and culture. Understanding first the exogenous forces that are driving governments to evolve, and second how these forces will affect and manifest themselves within government, is essential to successfully managing the transition from Government 1.0 to Government 2.0. This is the goal of this chapter.

Based on my experiences working with civil services, as well as open source communities in the public policy and software space, the first half of this chapter describes four core shifts that are pushing governments from hierarchy to platform: Shirky's Coasean collapse, the long tail of public policy, patch culture, and finally, the death of objectivity. In the second half of the chapter I outline the preconditions to shifting government from an analog/hierarchical structure to a digital/network structure, some strategies for extending the network to include citizens, and some ideas for the basis of a new culture to support public servants. My experience has been that most public servants, particularly those who are younger, are not only dedicated but keen for new models that would enable them to serve the public and their political masters more effectively. Many recognize that getting government to serve as platforms in a digital world will be a difficult transition. We have many allies for change, and so we also have a collective responsibility to provide them with language and frameworks to describe why government will change, as well as suggest a map for how to manage it effectively.

The Coasean Collapse

At the beginning of *Here Comes Everybody*,* Clay Shirky cites the work of Ronald Coase, who in 1937 published his famous paper, "The Nature of the Firm." In it, Coase answered a question that had vexed economists for some time: what is the value of hierarchical organizations? Why don't people simply self-organize in a manager-free environment to create goods and deliver services? Coase theorized that managing transaction costs—the costs of constantly negotiating, coordinating, and enforcing agreements among collaborators—creates efficiencies that favor organizations. Interestingly, as transaction costs fall moderately, large firms can become larger still, but a greater number of smaller organizations also emerge as the costs to coordinate the production of niche products drop.

Shirky, however, takes Coase's thesis to its logical conclusion and asks the question that ultimately forms the basis of his book:

> But what if transaction costs don't fall moderately? What if they collapse? This scenario is harder to predict from Coase's original work, as it used to be purely academic. Now it's not, because it is happening, or rather it has already happened, and we're starting to see the results.

So what happens to some of the world's largest and most important institutions— governments—when transaction costs collapse?

The most important outcome of the Coasean collapse is that self-organizing groups can perform activities—more effectively and cheaply—that were previously the preserve of large hierarchical institutions.

One of the most compelling examples of an emergent network within government is the advent of the DIRECT Launcher project. A few years ago several NASA engineers and scientists became increasingly concerned about the direction of the planned replacement for the Ares I and Ares V rockets. Specifically, they believed senior decision makers were overlooking designs that could achieve the projects' objectives more quickly, safely, and cheaply. Ultimately, these

---

* *Here Comes Everybody: The Power of Organizing Without Organizations*, Clay Shirky, Penguin, 2008.

scientists and engineers began to meet in secret, working together online to scope out and design an alternative rocket. As word spread, non-NASA employees joined the group, providing additional support. According to Wikipedia, as of September 2008 the DIRECT team consisted of 69 members, 62 of whom are NASA engineers, NASA-contractor engineers, and managers from the Constellation Program. A small number of non-NASA members of the team publicly represent the group.

This is a classic Coasean collapse scenario—not in the marketplace, but in a government bureaucracy. A group of individuals, thanks to lowered transaction costs, have created a virtual, unofficial "skunk works" capable of *designing a rocket* that many argue outcompetes that of the large bureaucracy to which many of the participants belong. The network is more effective and efficient than the hierarchy. It is also more nimble: the capacity to involve outsiders is especially important as the NASA employees fear they could lose their jobs. The external volunteers—some with significant expertise—are free to represent and advocate for the project's design.

So how serious is DIRECT Launcher? Serious enough that on January 9, 2008, President Obama's transition team met with the project's representatives.[†] Subsequently, on May 7, 2008, the administration announced the launch of the Augustine Panel, an independent review of planned U.S. human space flight activities. It is very hard to imagine that this review was not a result, at least in part, of the DIRECT Launcher initiative.

The lesson here is that the structure of government will change. Today there are more efficient means of coordinating activities, sometimes exponentially so, than the large bureaucracies of government. To be clear, this is not an argument to end government. But it does suggest that if governments are too slow or too unresponsive, citizens—or even government's own employees—may find new ways to tackle projects that, due to high coordination and transaction costs, were previously exclusive to the governments' domain.

But the Coasean collapse isn't just making self-organizing easier, both within and outside government. It poses a still larger challenge to government: it blurs the line between the value of "insiders" versus that of "outsiders." In a world where expertise is spread across government agencies, not to mention among institutions outside government (to say nothing of Charles Leadbeater's Pro-Ams or even just hobbyists), the Coasean collapse allows for an even greater shift: it opens access to the long tail of public policy.

The Long Tail of Public Policy

In his 2006 book *The Long Tail*,[‡] Chris Anderson describes the shift from the traditional retail economics of "hits," created by limited and expensive shelf space, to the digital economics of niches that emerge when retailers can stock virtually everything. In these digital marketplaces,

† *http://www.popularmechanics.com/science/air_space/4298615.html*

‡ *The Long Tail: Why the Future of Business Is Selling Less of More*, Chris Anderson, Hyperion, 2006.

according to Anderson, "the number of available niche products outnumber [and collectively outsell] the hits by orders of magnitude. Those millions of niches are the Long Tail, which had been largely neglected until recently in favor of the Short Head of hits."§

The same long tail principles in consumer markets apply to citizen interests in public policy.

It is a long-held and false assumption that citizens don't care about public policy. The belief is understandable: many people truly don't care about the majority of public policy issues. There are a few geeks, such as myself, who care passionately about public policy in general, just like there are some people who are baseball geeks, or model train geeks, or nature geeks. But we shouldn't restrict ourselves to thinking that a community must be composed only of the hardest-core geeks. While there are hardcore baseball fans who follow every player in the league, there are still a significant number of people who follow only a favorite team. Similarly, there are many people who do care about *some* public policy issues or even just *one* policy issue. They've always been there: some are active in politics; others volunteer; many are dedicated to a nonprofit organization. Most simply keep up with the latest developments on their pet issue—present, perhaps, but silent unless the immediate benefits become more apparent, or the transaction costs of participating are lowered. They form part of the long tail of expertise and capacity for developing and delivering public policy that has been obscured by our obsession for large professional institutions (see Figure 12-1).

I first encountered the long tail of public policy in 2001 while volunteering with a nonprofit called Canada25. Canada25's mission was to engage young Canadians aged 20–35 in public policy debates. From 2001 through 2006 the group grew from a humble 30 members to more than 2,000 people living across the country and around the world. These members met on a regular basis, talked policy, and every 18 months held conferences on a major policy area (such as foreign policy). The ideas from these conferences were then filtered—in a process similar to open source software development—into a publication which frequently caught the attention of the press, elected officials, and public servants.

Did Canada25 get Canadians aged 20–35 interested in public policy? I don't know. At a minimum, however, it did harness an untapped and dispersed desire by many young Canadians to participate in, and try to shape, the country's public policy debates. While most people assume interest—and expertise—in public policy resides exclusively within civil service‖ and possibly some universities and think tanks, we discovered a long tail of interest and expertise which, thanks to collapsing transaction costs, was able to organize.

The Coasean collapse has made accessing and self-organizing within the long tail of public policy possible. While essential to moving government to a platform model, it poses enormous cultural challenges. Governments are built on the assumption that they know more, and have greater expertise, than the public. Public servants are also oriented toward managing and

---

§ *http://www.thelongtail.com/the_long_tail/about.html*

‖ In Canada, this is called public service, but in the United States it's commonly known as civil service.

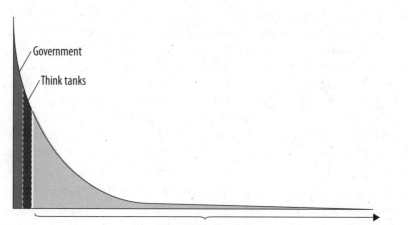

FIGURE 12-1. The long tail of public policy

controlling scarce resources, not to overseeing and engaging an abundant but scattered community. Most of all, governments' culture still values presenting a final product, not works in progress. In short, opening up the long tail of public policy requires a government that is willing to shift from a "release" it uses internally, to the "patch culture" a growing number of citizens are becoming accustomed to.

Patch Culture

One of the traits of open source software, but also of the Internet and virtually everything that resides on it, is that, because of its digital nature, nothing is ever finished. There are always mistakes to be corrected, new uses and applications to be adjusted for, or extensions and improvements to be added. The expectation is not "This is finished and will remain as so forever," but rather "Here is this service/idea/document/et cetera, at this moment in time: feel free to use it, or tell us what you think."

In short, the Internet has rewired our relationship with everything around us and has given rise to a new ethos: the patch culture. Without a doubt, patch culture is strongest among coders who participate in open source communities. While the number is growing, there are still relatively few people who can see a bug or imagine a feature and code up the patch themselves and submit it. But the ethos of a patch culture has spread far beyond this community. People regularly notify me about typos or errors on my blog, and I see people who extend or rethink pieces I've written; I do the same, remixing, editing, and extending the works of others. (How many people have I cited in this chapter so far?)

The great thing about a patch culture on the Web is that once users understand that nothing is final and everything can be improved, this worldview quickly shifts from the online to the offline space. The emergence of services such as FixMyStreet.com is recognition that any infrastructure, online or offline, has bugs and that there is value in identifying them—and possibly even in self-organizing to repair them. The upside is that although people will still "complain" when it comes to a government service, a piece of infrastructure, or even a bill destined for debate, more and more people will look to "comment" or to offer suggestions or solutions. Still better—but more demanding—is that they will expect someone to act on their suggestion, or more interestingly, if no one acts on it, they may create "the patch" themselves.

This is precisely what OpenCongress (*http://www.opencongress.org/*) is doing. The founders of OpenCongress could have spent years lobbying Congress to more effectively share information about how its members are voting and working. Instead, they chose to patch the system by creating their own site, one that, by aggregating information about Congress, brings greater transparency (and, in theory, accountability) to the institution. Lawrence Lessig's Change Congress (*http://change-congress.org/*) is another example of patch culture. Once again, Lessig could have spent years lobbying Congress to adopt new rules (a completely valid approach to patching the system), but instead he has proposed an "add-on" or "plug-in" to the rules, a more aggressive rule set that members of Congress can select to adopt. His hope is that, if enough members choose to use this plug-in, the patch will be adopted into the core source code—the laws and rules that govern Congress.

Patch culture is also an outcrop of a deeper shift that has been taking place among Western democracies for the past several decades: the decline of deference. If one is going to be able to "patch" one's government or community, one needs access to the underlying code. This means not only access to the basic raw data (like that being released by cities such as Vancouver, Washington, D.C., San Francisco, and Nanaimo, BC), but also access to understanding how decisions get made, how resources get allocated, and how the underlying system of government works. There was a time when citizens trusted objective professionals and elected officials to make those decisions on our behalf, and where the opacity of the system was tolerated because of the professionalism and efficiencies it produced. This is no longer the case; the Internet accelerates the decline of deference because it accelerates the death of objectivity. It's not that we don't trust; it's just that we want to verify.

The End of Objectivity

In the 2008 Bertha Bassam Lecture (*http://www.tvo.org/TVOsites/WebObjects/TvoMicrosite.woa?bi ?1234040400000*), David Weinberger points out that over the past several centuries we have come to equate credibility with objectivity and impartiality, but that the rise of the Internet is eroding this equation (italics added by me):

> Because it shows us how the sausage is made, Wikipedia is far more credible. Yet this is exactly the stuff that the Britannica won't show us because they think it would make them look

amateurish and take away from their credibility. But in fact *transparency*—which is what this is —*is the new objectivity*. We are not going to trust objectivity. We are not going to trust objectivity unless we can see the discussion that led to it.

Replace "the Britannica" in this quote with "civil service" or "the government" and you see the problem. The values of civil service presume that objectivity and impartiality lead to credibility. Indeed, in many Western democracies this is a core value of civil service: to provide "objective" advice to partisan elected officials. Increasingly, however, this model is breaking down. One reason why demand for open data has resonated within and beyond the tech community is that people aren't satisfied with seeing the final product; they want *the right* to see how, and with what, it was made.

Governments will argue they are open, but this is in only a relative sense when compared to private corporations (as opposed to open source projects). Take, for example, Freedom of Information (FOI) requests (*http://www.tbs-sct.gc.ca/tbsf-fsct/350-57-eng.asp*) infrastructure in Canada. Put aside the fact that this system is simultaneously open to abuse, overwhelmed, and outdated. Think about the idea of FOI. The fact that information is by default secret (or functionally secret since it is inaccessible) is itself a powerful indication of how fundamentally opaque the workings of government remain. If information growth is exponential, how much data can the government not only manage but effectively assess the confidentiality of on a regular basis? And at what cost? In a world where open models function with great efficiency, how long before the public loses all confidence?

Why does this matter? Because successful platforms are very rarely those that are opaque and self-appointed as credible. Quite the opposite: platforms for innovation work because they are transparent, are accessible, and can be remixed. And yet reorienting governments from an authority model based on objectivity to one based on transparency is possibly one of the single greatest obstacles.

The combination of these four forces—the Coasean collapse, the long tail of public policy, patch culture, and the death of objectivity—is reshaping how governments operate and their relationship with citizens, and is presenting them with an opportunity to establish themselves as platforms for innovation. But they simultaneously serve as enormous challenges to the status quo. Virtually everyone I speak to in government talks about the stress of change and uncertainty they currently experience. This is hardly surprising. Sociologist William Ogburn once noted that social stresses can arise out of the uneven rates of change in different sectors of society. Today, the gap between the government and the private sector (particularly the tech sector) has become enormous.

From the inside, the transition from a civil service that is corporate and opaque to one that is transparent, open, and platform-oriented risks looking like it will be gut-wrenching, challenging, and painful. Reengineering processes, metrics, worldviews, roles, and, above all, a 100-year-old culture and values set *deeply* embedded within civil service is scary. We all fear change, particularly if we fear that change might erode our influence. Ironically, however, it is the resistance that will erode power and influence. Those governments, and especially those civil services, that embrace these shifts and develop appropriate strategies will discover that they are still influential—just in new and unforeseen ways.

Two Preconditions to Government As Platform: Capacity for Self-Organization and Collaboration

Presently, much of the talk around Web 2.0 and social media focuses on how governments can better serve and connect with citizens. I, too, share optimism about these technologies (which I'll discuss later). However, this focus is presently misplaced. At the core of these discussions is a belief that government need not react to the four shifts I outlined earlier. Instead, the dominant perspective seems to be that a social media "shell" will protect governments from these changes and allow business to carry on as usual. Ask NASA how well that strategy is working out.

The first part to becoming a platform is ensuring that *government employees* are able to connect, self-organize, and work with one another. Any effort to improve citizen engagement will ultimately fall flat unless we first tackle how government itself operates.

Take Facebook as an example. Frequently, the debate in many countries rests on whether governments should ban access to Facebook, or, in more sophisticated environments, how the government uses Facebook to engage citizens. But both discussions miss the real issue.

If government is going to serve as a platform, it must first embrace the Coasean collapse. This means accelerating, not preventing, the capacity of public servants to self-organize. More specifically, it means allowing them not only to connect, but also to be able to assess and determine *with whom* to connect. It is a little-known fact that few governments have comprehensive directories where employees can find one another. For example, in Canada, the Government Electronic Directory Services (GEDS) lists the name, title, work address, and phone number of every federal employee (and is thus miles ahead of most countries). Ironically, however, if you know any of those search parameters, you probably didn't need the search engine to begin with. People need to connect based on interests, knowledge, or experience—precisely the type of search Facebook enables. Facebook is *the* (silo) killer app. It allows public servants to find expertise and self-organize around issues—such as security, health, and the environment—that cut across departments or agencies. Indeed, the U.S. government's security community, which takes its work very seriously, has already embraced the effectiveness and efficiency of a network structure. In December 2008 it created A-Space, a Facebook-like application for intelligence analysts. Thomas Fingar, the deputy director of national intelligence for analysis, says the technology "can also help process increasing amounts of information where the number of analysts is limited."#

http://www.ft.com/cms/s/0/6e2648ea-5014-11dc-a6b0-0000779fd2ac.html?nclick_check=1

In addition to finding one another, public servants must have a place to share their work before government as a platform can take form. This again requires an enormous cultural shift. Public servants have to be trusted to share information internally within departments, externally across departments, and eventually (and most controversially) externally with the public.

The shift centers on the fact that, at the moment, most governments continue to exist in a pre-Coasean-collapse universe. They almost exclusively use hierarchies to filter information and allocate resources. Those at the top see only what those immediately below believe they need to (or should) see. This places an enormous burden and responsibility on those in the middle of the organization. They literally control the flow of information within government departments. This means senior officials regularly make critical decisions in the absence of all sorts of information. More specifically, these senior decision makers—and the interests and concerns they perceive as paramount—are separated from the raw information by myriad middle managers, whose reasons for filtering information may vary. Collaborative tools such as wikis offer us an escape from this problem. Recently, Natural Resources Canada, a ministry of the Canadian government, started conducting deputy minister briefing notes on a wiki. This means anyone in the department, no matter how junior, can add or correct information in the briefing note. As a result, anyone can see who is adding (and who is removing) information from the briefing note and an open debate over what should be filtered can emerge. Suddenly, a ministry is tapping into its internal long tail of expertise, in terms of both the information supplied and the filters applied.

Still more exciting is GCPEDIA, a massive wiki accessible to all 300,000 federal Canadian public servants, where anyone can share his work and invite others to comment. Will everyone participate? Likely not. But those who do will have proposals whose ideas will be better vetted and informed, even if only a minority comment. Such wikis could themselves emerge as a platform, one that could increasingly serve as a common space, even a community, where public servants—and possibly some members of the public—can connect, exchange ideas, and update one another on their work.

Let me reiterate: the challenge of embracing the Coasean collapse and accessing the long tail of public policy across and outside government is not technical, it is cultural. Enabling public servants to self-organize, solve problems, and share information runs counter to the corporate/hierarchical cultures that frequently dominate government agencies. There is good reason for this: most governments center on an accountability model that holds ministers responsible for what takes place within their institutions. But this does not mean that the minister or her direct representative must approve every interministerial meeting or sign off on every internal communiqué. Most importantly, few government agencies will have access to all the information they need. Drawing on the long tail, be it within government or outside, will be necessary. And remember, virtual networks will form within governments. They are simply too efficient a way to operate. The only question is whether they will emerge by design, as in the case of the intelligence community, or in opposition to structures that refuse to yield, such as with DIRECT Launcher.

Extend the Network

Once governments have figured out how to create platforms for their own employees, we can begin to think about how to enable citizen participation. One thing that is frequently frustrating is that we treat these types of approaches as new (and thus different or scary). The fact is that governments have been accessing a long tail of information from the public for a long time. Indeed, municipal 911 services are an excellent example. Here is a system that, to a limited degree, is already a platform. It relies on constant citizen input and is architected to be participatory. Indeed, it works only *because* it is participatory—without citizen input, the system falls apart. Specifically, it aggregates, very effectively, the long tail of knowledge within a community to deliver, with pinpoint accuracy, an essential service to the location it is needed at a time it is needed. Better still, people are familiar and comfortable with it, and virtually everyone agrees it is both an essential component of modern government service as well as one of the most effective (see Figure 12-2).

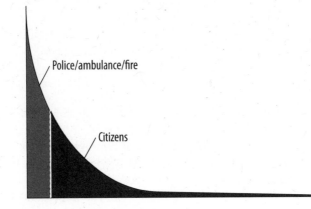

FIGURE 12-2. Citizen participation and emergency services

Imagine the curve in Figure 12-2 represents all of the police, fire, and ambulance interventions in a city. Many of the most critical interventions are ones the police force and ambulance service determine themselves. For example, the police are involved in an investigation that results in a big arrest, or the ambulance parks outside an Eagles reunion concert knowing that some of the boomers in attendance will be "overserved" and are likely to suffer heart attacks.

Although investigations and predictable events may account for some police/fire/ambulatory actions (and possibly those that receive the most press attention), the vast majority of arrests, firefights, and medical interventions result from plain old 911 calls made by ordinary citizens. True, many of these are false alarms, or are resolved with minimal effort (a fire extinguisher deals with the problem, or a minor amount of drugs is confiscated but no arrests are made). But the sheer quantity of these calls means that while the average quality may be low, the calls still account for the bulk of successful (however defined) interventions. Viewed in this light,

911 is a knowledge aggregator, collecting knowledge from citizens to determine where police cars, fire trucks, and ambulances need to go.

As we look to governments to replicate this type of success across other areas, to tap into both the long tail and the emerging patch culture, two important lessons spring to mind:

It is a self-interested system
> While many 911 callers are concerned citizens calling about someone else, I suspect the majority of calls—and the most accurate calls—are initiated by those directly or immediately affected by a situation. People who have been robbed, are suffering from a heart attack, or have a fire in their kitchen have a high incentive to call 911. Consequently, the system leverages our self-interest, although it also allows for Good Samaritans to contribute as well. We need to enable citizens to contribute when and where it is most convenient and urgent *to them*.

It is narrowly focused in its construct
> The 911 service doesn't ask or permit callers to talk about the nature of justice, the history of fire, or the research evidence supporting a given medical condition. It seeks a very narrow set of data points: the nature of the problem and its location. This is helpful to both emergency response officials *and* citizens. It limits the quantity of data for the former and helps minimize the demands on the latter.

These, I believe, are the secret ingredients to citizen engagement of the future: one where we focus on gathering specific, painless information/preferences/knowledge from citizens to augment or redistribute services more effectively.

The genius of 911 is that it understands the critical nature information plays in a system. It has the credibility to draw important information in, and it rewards those who share appropriate information by moving it quickly through the network. As a result, the right resources, in the right place, can be allocated to the task.

The Next Civil Service Culture: The Gift Economy

One of the exciting outcomes of the four shifts is that, like the Internet, they commoditize information. As public servants are able to network and self-organize, information will flow more freely. This, for example, is what occurs with the deputy minister briefing notes at Natural Resources Canada. This freedom of information further increases if governments tap into the long tail of public policy and ask citizens to submit "patches" to the system. As public servants are better able to access one another through social media and find information through wikis, the nature of power and influence within that system begins to shift. While hierarchy will not disappear from government, a networked civil service will evolve a new culture.

Presently, the information economy in many governments is scarcity-based. Information can be hoarded—and deployed to maximize the influence of its owner—because of government, silos, the sheer size of those silos, and the hierarchical structure that controls and filters the flow of information. But something frequently happens to scarcity economies when their underlying currency becomes abundant: they transform into gift economies. For an example, consider Eric Raymond's description of the gift economy that operates within an open source system:[*]

> Gift cultures are adaptations not to scarcity but to abundance. They arise in populations that do not have significant material-scarcity problems with survival goods.... Abundance makes command relationships difficult to sustain and exchange relationships an almost pointless game. In gift cultures, social status is determined not by what you control but by *what you give away*.

As public servants are better able to locate and share information across silos, the incentives around hoarding will begin to shift. For many in civil service, gift economies become more prevalent than scarcity economies. Sharing information or labor (as a gift) within civil service increases one's usefulness to, and reputation among, others within the system. Power and influence in this system thus moves away from the ability to control information, and instead shifts to a new set of skills: the ability to convene, partner, engage stakeholders, act creatively, and analyze.

And here is both the most important lesson and the most exciting implication for governments as platform. The traits that make people successful in a gift economy culture overlap with the type of culture that makes platforms successful. Platforms work first because people want to use them: because they are both useful and easy to use. But they sustain themselves when those who manage them recognize they are a *shared* space. A government platform that seeks out patches and gifts from the long tail of public policy, treats internal and external input equally, and is persistently transparent in how the platform is being managed will be a government that thrives in the twenty-first century. Such a culture is not a foregone conclusion. Today there are open source and online communities where, because of choices made by early participants, ideas are shared, people are dealt with respectfully, and contributions are acknowledged. There are also less functional communities where positive values and behaviors are not modeled. The key here is that governments have an opportunity now, as they manage the shift, to create an underlying culture that will support a sustainable platform people will want to build upon.

Conclusion

Without a doubt, the early twenty-first century is both a stressful and an exciting time to be a government employee. The constant fear of gotcha journalism, the increased centralization of bureaucracy, as well as the perpetually rising expectations of citizens and taxpayers mean that many public servants often work under conditions that many would find too exhausting and too draining to tolerate. This chapter's outline for how this entire world could (or will) shift

---

[*] *The Cathedral & the Bazaar: Musings on Linux and Open Source by an Accidental Revolutionary (http://oreilly.com/catalog/9780596001087/)*, Eric S. Raymond, O'Reilly, 2001.

could be seen as either liberating or completely overwhelming. Happily and sadly, it will be a little bit of both. I believe that the four shifts I shared here are inevitable. Enabled by technology and demanded by the public, the way governments operate will change.

The good news is that this transition need not be as painful as many believe, and it carries with it enormous opportunities for improving the mission of government. I once remember hearing a story about when computers were introduced into a government department. At first, people ignored them; then, when only secretaries knew how to use them, they feared them and lobbied against them. Today, however, if you walk into a government department and suggest removing all the computers, every public servant will insist you are crazy. Today we think networks in government, long tails of public policy, gift economies, and the death of objectivity can all be either ignored or fought against. Neither is a viable strategy. Governments need to be ready to experiment and embrace these shifts. And it can be a shift. In this chapter, I outlined achievable and incremental actions governments can and are taking. Indeed, in my experience, in every government there are individuals or groups that are already experimenting and innovating. This change is not beyond our capacity; indeed, in many cases the shift has already begun.

About the Author

DAVID EAVES is a public policy entrepreneur, an open data activist, and a negotiation consultant. A fellow with the Centre for the Study of Democracy at Queen's University, he is a frequent speaker to students, executives, and policy makers on issues relating to public service sector renewal, open government, and Canadian public and foreign policy, and writes daily on these subjects at *http://www.eaves.ca*. He advises the Mayor and Council of Vancouver on open data and open government and serves as an international reference group member of the Australian Government's Web 2.0 taskforce. As a negotiation consultant, he provides strategic advice, coaching, and training to leading companies around the world in industries such as financial services, health care, information technology, energy, and telecommunications. Originally from Vancouver, British Columbia, David completed a Bachelor of Arts in history at Queen's University in 1998 and a Master's of International Relations at Oxford in 2000.

CHAPTER THIRTEEN

Democracy, Under Everything

Sarah Schacht

Not everything is political, but increasingly, everyone is.

In a democratic country with a growing population, everything's a resource, an allocation, a public good or ill. There was a time when some things just *were*, and I am barely old enough to remember that time. We now seem to live in a country that is wrestling between issues of scarcity and nimiety—in which we feel compelled to voice our concerns, complaints, and opinions. Not so long ago, there were simple things that *weren't* political, such as school lunches, urban trees, and fish in the oceans. Now, even the most mundane elements of our world have causes, campaigns, and advocacy platforms (e.g., there has been an international movement, spearheaded by cooking guru Jamie Oliver, to make children's lunches healthier and more sustainable).

Many Voices, Many Messages, One Government

Enabled by technology, our concerned voices are piling onto the democratic process in record numbers. But the underpinnings of the legislative process are weakening; accessible legislative information and healthy dialogues between citizens and legislators are difficult to come by. And while we view the bureaucratic process of building legislation as arcane, we rarely glimpse how anachronistic the technology within the process is—from minutes stored in microfiche to bills released online to the public days after they were available in person. The tools of our modern legislative process are old and ill-fitting. If we listened well enough, I think we'd hear the sound of our democratic process cracking under the weight of our new demands.

That sound, for me, was the voice of a U.S. Capitol security guard saying to me, "Oh, there's nothing left to see here, now. We're closed." Closed? Who was the Capitol closed to, and why did this guard assume I was a tourist?

It was 4:25 p.m. on a hot, humid, summer afternoon in the nation's capital in early July 2008. I was dressed in heels, skirt, and blouse, and had just tromped through three government buildings to get my two gallery passes to watch Senate and House proceedings. Outside the Capitol dome where I'd served as a House intern, I stood at the mouth of the velvet rope as the door to the dome closed. Proceedings in the House and Senate were still underway—but I didn't have access that day.

I wasn't a tourist. I hadn't come to "see" government like a specimen under glass. I was here to observe the U.S. legislative process, but Congress views most constituents who make the pilgrimage to D.C. as tourists, not participants. Congress built a $621 million tourist center at the Capitol, investing relatively little in making its process and information as accessible.

Standing outside the Capitol in the heat of a D.C. summer, I was just another tourist shut out of Congress in person and online.

If I had chosen to visit Congress via Thomas.gov that afternoon, I would've found bill information lagging about 48 hours behind what was actually happening in Congress. I would never know that members of Congress and their staff have a more modern, organized, thorough congressional website accessible only to them (on the House and Senate intranet). If I was passionate about an issue, I would've cranked out an email or forwarded a form letter to my congressperson. And it would've gone into a stack of several thousand emails my representative received that day, one of millions collected in Congress each week; my voice would add to the electronic cacophony of voices of other Americans, a barely manageable, never-ending stream of advocacy that requires our nation's elected officials to spend more time in document management than in dialogue with constituents. My efforts would be largely ineffective; frustrated, I might choose to believe that my voice didn't matter at all. Like the 57% of Americans who believe that they don't have a say in government, I would feel marginalized, when more likely I'd just be caught up in a poor document management system.[*]

I'm not suggesting that we build a new and improved legislative process, one robustly equipped to handle our every whim. I'm suggesting that we need delicate, distributive tools for placing political pressure on our democratic process. If we're all going to be actively involved in government, we should gain techniques and tools to tread lightly on a system that has served us so well.

---

[*] 2009 National Conference on Citizenship (NCOC) report, finding that 43% of Americans feel like they have a say in government.

My Idea

Nine years ago, I was a college student who loved politics and was very optimistic about citizens' abilities to change laws and influence policy. It was my job to help organize fellow students to keep tuition low, expand affordable child care on campus, and generally represent them in the state legislature. In 2000, we had the Internet, we had Washington state's legislative website, and we had email, form letters, and so on. But none of it made participation in the legislative process more effective for citizens.

After a failed attempt to quickly rally opposition to a new tuition increase bill, I felt powerless. As I sat at my desk, I felt like something about public participation in the legislative process was broken. Just then, an email popped into my inbox. It was an update for skiers like me; it told me the exact number of inches of snow on every mountain in the Pacific Northwest. I thought, "How can I know the snowpack at the top of a mountain, but not what's going on in my state legislature?!?"

It hit me that the only thing standing between citizens and full engagement in the legislative process was the lack of tools for monitoring legislative information and communicating effectively within the process. Individuals needed personalized tools to help track *exactly* what *they* cared about, and to notify them in time to take action. They needed better ways to communicate with legislators—form letters were a poor substitute for skilled citizens. I couldn't anticipate that this idea would take me on an eight-year odyssey through every element of politics and technology. Eventually, it led me to founding Knowledge As Power, an online nonprofit service that helps citizens become informed and effective within the legislative process. Here's what I learned along the way.

Constitutional Guidance: Avoid Secrecy Via Access

During the revolutionary period in the United States, Americans struggled with the secrecy of English-controlled legislatures. Legislative secrecy was cited early in the Declaration of Independence for why the United States chose to secede. The fourth point of grievance the founders cited was "He has called together legislative bodies at places unusual, uncomfortable, and distant from the depository of their public records, for the sole purpose of fatiguing them into compliance with his measures." This means that neither elected legislators nor citizens could access their laws or the legislative process, making it difficult for these proceedings to be accurate or accessible.

Americans' frustration with inaccessible public records led to the country's rights to press freedom and Article 1, Section 5 of the Constitution, mandating public distribution of legislative information. The country's founders strongly believed in the public's right to information (excluding what was absolutely necessary for national security). In fact, our modern inequality of access to legislative information runs counter to what the country's founders deemed necessary to a healthy democratic process. At the Constitutional Convention in 1787, James

Wilson remarked, "(Americans)…have the right to know what their Agents are doing or have done, and it should not be in the option of the Legislature to conceal their proceedings."

While the writers and signers of the Constitution probably never imagined the communications technology we have available today, it seems clear that they believed clear records on legislative, budgetary, and agency information were necessary for maintaining an active, informed citizenry and an accountable government. And to maintain that informed citizenry, individuals and organizations would need to access legislative information to leverage power in the legislative process. When we glance over some of the least sexy portions of the Constitution, the founders' dedication to public records becomes apparent.

Article 1, Section 5, Clause 3:

> Each House shall keep a Journal of its Proceedings, and from time to time publish the same, excepting such Parts as may in their Judgment require Secrecy; and the Yeas and Nays of the Members of either House on any question shall, at the Desire of one fifth of those Present, be entered on the Journal.

Article 1, Section 7:

> But in all such Cases the Votes of both Houses shall be determined by Yeas and Nays, and the Names of the Persons voting for and against the Bill shall be entered on the Journal of each House respectively.

Yet the information services that legislatures provide often fail to meet the public's need for timely, accessible information. The modern "journal" has become legislative websites, a basic information technology that should meet the information needs of citizens, activist groups, and elected officials. Yet government information sources are often too complicated, poorly organized, or legalistic for average citizens to use. Websites for state legislatures seem geared toward professional lobbyists, staffers, or agency officials, not public participation. Many of these "online journals" share limited or delayed information (such as Thomas.gov), are missing portions of the legislative record, or allow inconsistent access to information across houses of the legislature. Worse, some governments charge individuals for access to timely, accurate, detailed legislative information. The state of Arkansas, through a private corporation called Arkleg, charges $250 for legislative information per session. The state of New York has an entire legislative office charging $2,500 per year for accurate legislative information. Even if the information is available to the public, it is written in legalese; 80% of Americans read and write at an eighth grade level, while legalese requires a law degree to read accurately.

James Madison said, "A popular government, without popular information or the means of acquiring it, is but a prologue to a Farce or a Tragedy, or perhaps both. Knowledge will forever govern ignorance, and a people who mean to be their own Governors must arm themselves with the power knowledge gives." I think many of our legislatures need to examine whether they are living up to the high standards for public information and citizen inclusion that the founders envisioned. Given the technology available to us today, there's really no excuse to fall short.

Meeting Modern-Day Needs

In 2005, between work on a presidential campaign and college, I'd spent lots of time researching and designing ways for the public to more easily track legislative information. Determined to tailor Knowledge As Power, the nonprofit I would found, to meet the needs of citizens and legislators, I took an internship in Congress. I wanted to see the problems our legislative process faces from the inside out. What I found was startling, but not surprising.

Within the congressional intranet, I could gain access to every bit of legislative or committee information I needed to understand the content, context, and trajectory of a bill. If something was in hard copy in a committee room, I could get it digitally on the intranet site. However, if I visited Thomas.gov, Congress's public site, I'd have to sift through poorly organized information that ran at a 24- to 48-hour lag to its congressional counterpart. Hard-copy documents available in committee rooms were not available on Thomas.gov. I couldn't help but question why there were two separate sites with unequal access to information. If legislators and their staff members need robust, well-designed information to do their jobs, wouldn't citizens need at least as much to do theirs?

Thomas.gov, like many state and local government sites, uses clunky search tools that don't match up legalese terms with the plain-English terms Americans commonly use for political topics. Without guidance or skill, citizens find it hard to discover the legislative information they're looking for. Bill documents are often stored as PDFs, which makes it difficult to search across bill documents for terms. Worse, antiquated document management systems, typically adopted between 1995 and 2000, are expensive to modernize, trapping legislative information in systems that cost-cutting governments cannot afford to update. Systemic problems with government information distribution obscure the legislative process from citizens, making it difficult for them to participate fully or hold their legislators accountable.

Revealing Obscured Government Data

I experienced a prime example of an obscured government on a research trip to Albany, New York, in the spring of 2009. I spent two whirlwind days in New York's capital learning the ins and outs of the state's legislative information management. Two days in Albany had me feeling like I'd gone back in time, to somewhere around 1972. Albany's mismatched modern architecture juts out of the hillside on which the medieval-castle-like state capitol sits. Walking into the lobby room between the Assembly and Senate chambers, I was shocked to see that it's actually full of lobbyists. Sharply dressed in suits and shined shoes, they anxiously awaited Assembly or Senate leaders to show up. They huddled in conversation on the large wood and green velvet couches. In a corridor nearby, offices of New York newspapers bustled with actual reporters who seemed straight out of central casting. If you've toured or worked in other legislatures, you'd be shocked by the scene in New York. The state is an anachronism—nobody's lobbyists congregate in the lobby area, and the press barely exists inside legislative bodies anymore. Hallways of government are usually quiet and empty—everyone is working online from somewhere else. I'd discover that lobbyists congregated at the capitol to get an edge on valuable legislative information, a precious commodity in New York.

Sitting in the Assembly's gallery, I looked out on a small sea of state Assembly members engaged in voting on bills. I opened the Assembly's bill tracking website, pulling up publicly available information on each bill that came before the Assembly. What I found online was shocking; there was no mention of any of these bills coming up for vote that day—no schedule, no notice, nothing beyond the first draft of a bill and maybe one other copy from committee. What I'd find out on my tour of Albany's legislative system is that the only people who knew bills were coming up were those in the Assembly, the partisan-appointee clerks[†] who control the release of legislative information, and the lobbyists who paid the state $2,500 to access the full record of New York legislation from the Legislative Research Service (LRS).[‡] New York may be the most expensive state to gain access to accurate legislative information, but it's joined by other states that view access to legislative information as a means to political power or increasing the legislature's funding.

Over the next day, I found that the New York State LRS sells legislative information at a per-session subscription of $2,500, with the funding going to supporting offices within the bill drafting and publication process of the state. I found that transcriptions of minutes from Senate votes and debates were copied onto microfiche with 35-year-old machines and filed in drawers, and only one computer was available for looking up where the transcripts were in the file drawers. For copies of transcripts, a citizen would need to request them at twenty-five cents per page—perhaps not exorbitant fees, but certainly prohibitive of timely access to records. I went from one office to the next, learning that information about the state's legislation was spread across several offices, each of which was bogged down in old technology, or stuck in red-tape rules with which the majority party could refuse to release information. New York may be at the extreme end for lack of transparency and accessibility, but the state is not an anomaly. Governments across the United States and the globe are struggling to modernize their technology and become more transparent. Luckily for the citizens of New York, the state Senate's new CIO, Andrew Hoppin, and his crackerjack team of techies came on board in February of 2009 and began taking the Senate toward transparency and modern technology.

Recently, I caught up with Hoppin to find out what progress his office has made in the New York State Senate. The improvements his office has made in just 12 months are a lesson for all governments. The Senate's quick shift toward transparency, information modernization, and open information policies have radically improved the information publication within the

---

† New York's legislative clerical staff would typically be nonpartisan support staff in other state legislatures. However, in New York, these staff (like those who manage updates to legislation public records) are selected by the majority party, allowing for information management by a party's staff.

‡ LRS is not affiliated with political parties, but rather is under the "Legislative Bill Drafting Commission" appointed by both houses of the Legislature. LRS's sale of the legislative information provides revenue for general bill drafting services.

state, catapulting them from a 1970s framework with a dash of late-1990s website technology to a full-fledged modern legislative body.

Hoppin and his crew are part of the political-appointee structure of the New York State legislature; unlike many legislatures, the administrative and clerical staff work for the party in power. With the 2008 election of a new Democratic majority, the New York Democratic Senators made a commitment to transparency and modernization. Making good on their promises, they brought Hoppin in to modernize the Senate (it should be noted that the Assembly and the Senate are not guided by the same technology or transparency policies— they set their own agendas). Quickly, Hoppin assembled a fresh team of techies with a bent toward doing things inexpensively while utilizing open source tools and well-adopted data standards. The team researched how information flowed through the Senate and (something I often suggest to governments) found where the information was in its earliest data form.

An example of that early data is the Senate's transcripts, typed up by Candy, of Candy Co., a one-woman transcription wonder with a locked-in contract for transcription services with the Senate. Her transcripts went through a process in Microsoft Word to be published only on the Senate intranet[§] and into the microfiche process I described earlier, resulting in microfiche rolls of transcripts that were neatly tucked into a file drawer and made accessible to those who made a pilgrimage to the office to pay for copies. To add those transcripts to the online records of the Senate, Hoppin's office posted them at the gorgeous and comprehensive *http://nysenate.gov/ legislation*.

Through Knowledge As Power's research in 2009, I noticed a trend amongst legislatures of all sizes—either their electeds or the techies realized their technology wasn't sufficient to meet the needs of a modernized constituency seeking greater access and transparency. Without partners in technology *and* policy, modernization stagnated and often resulted in governments remaining locked into old technology or spending a lot of money contracting out to inadequate third-party software systems.

The New York State Senate, in less than a year, with legislative leadership and a fresh technology team, overcame what I would call the most complicated, tension-filled, overly politicized legislative environment and anachronistic technology I've ever seen. They are quickly progressing toward more transparency, access, and modernization.

Now, the New York State Assembly—and other legislatures—have an example to follow.

THE SHRINKING NEWS

Though we have access to millions of political blogs, activist websites, RSS feeds, text messaging, and so on, I still believe that the legislative process needs rigorous, impartial news sources. The process can be so detailed and complex that you need a news service to delve into details and bring

§ Accessible only within the Senate's shared database.

them to the public. Yet these news sources are increasingly difficult to find. Faced with sinking ad revenue and dwindling audiences, TV, print, and radio news media allocate smaller budgets and fewer staff members to legislation and government news. With large cuts in reporting staffs and heavier reliance on "wire" news, citizens receive very limited coverage of local government or legislative news. As fewer political "beat" reporters dig into research-driven stories, citizens are more likely to hear about the passage of a controversial law in Congress than about local school district budget cuts. Since only the big stories make headlines, there's less information for citizens to notice, or take action on. An example of this phenomenon comes from a 2008 article in the *Los Angeles Times* highlighting a new string of newspaper job cuts:

> Consolidation among papers in the Los Angeles area...affected coverage of government. Where six or eight reporters once routinely covered the Board of Supervisors and county agencies, now there are only two or three on the county beat, said Joel Bellman, a longtime spokesman for Supervisor Zev Yaroslavsky. "I think people are losing any understanding of what local government does and how it figures in people's lives," Bellman said. "There is the paper there, but there is no substantive understanding of the government beat anymore. We simply fade away like the Cheshire Cat."

In the founding fathers' days, you'd miss important law-making information (and the chance to take action on it) because of censorship; today, it's because of corporate cost-cutting.

For Knowledge As Power, we've realized that providing legislation-tracking services to citizens isn't enough. Citizens need context for legislation, and if traditional news media or new media sources aren't going to provide that context, we will. So, in January 2010, we introduced KAPblog, a nonpartisan "context-building" journalism source on the Washington State Legislature. KAPblog complements our work at KnowledgeAsPower.org, as we endeavor to build a model for increasing citizens' activity in—and understanding of—the legislative process.

Improving Communication without Being Crushed by Email

In the spring of 2005, I moved from one Washington to the other, where I worked on Capitol Hill and researched the communications patterns of Congress. I wasn't a professional researcher and I didn't have institutional backing. I was an intern. An old one. At 25, I was intensely interested in how the highest-end users of constituent feedback—senators and congresspeople—managed the influx of email and phone calls from constituents. So, I worked days in a congressman's office, spent free time in the Congressional Research Service, and asked pretty much any legislative staffer I met out to coffee or drinks (they preferred drinks). As an intern in Congress, I was on the frontline between constituents' communications and the legislator's office. Virtually every email, phone call, fax, and letter goes through an intern's hands. Though the office I was in was exceptional in its dedication to communicating with constituents, you couldn't help but feel that most offices were so overwhelmed by the sheer numbers that they weren't able to hear what their constituents were saying. It was a daily, constant roar and the only sound that stood out was the rare, individual voice.

Research backs up these observations. From the Congressional Management Foundation (CMF) report in 2004:

> Quality is more persuasive than quantity. Thoughtful, personalized constituent messages generally have more influence than a large number of identical form messages. Grassroots campaigns should consider placing greater emphasis on generating messages of higher quality and reducing form communications.

The surprising thing I noticed was that these communications would go through four to six other staffers' hands before returning to a constituent as a hard-copy form letter. It was quite likely that you'd receive thousands of emails in a single day. Each name was matched up with a name in the voter file, contained in a clunky email system built by Lockheed Martin. Even phone calls would be typed into emails—to the same legislator's office—so that hopefully, the system would auto-group emails on the same topic. In this process, a sample of letters (mostly form letters) were scanned for major common points, and then responded to with a form letter. Each legislative staffer had to execute a long list of tasks each day, in which he spent more than half his time just dealing with the quantity of feedback (my estimate from observing and asking legislative staff members to estimate).

Though research such as CMF's has found that legislative staff members highly doubt the legitimacy of form letters, they still value hearing from their constituents. What I noticed, again and again, was that when people called or wrote an email, you could tell when they weren't feeding you a line straight from an advocacy group. They were genuinely concerned about an issue—it affected their lives—and the polite conviction in what they said was gripping. As much as issue groups like to send millions of form letters, it was these personal, repeated voices that caught the attention of legislators and their staff members. When I told staffers, "It seems like we're getting a lot of individuals emailing/calling about this bill," they'd respond, "Like an advocacy push?" and I'd respond, "No, these seem like real people—and they're from all over the district." That's when staffers took notice.

In 2004, the CMF found that citizens sent more than 200 million emails to Congress. State legislatures don't have it much easier. Through my personal research interviewing Washington state legislative staff members in 2006, I found that they received 800 to 1,300 emails in their Outlook inboxes each week. Sometimes they receive peaks of 8,000 to 16,000 emails per day. While I shadowed a state senator for a day during legislative session, she took a 30-minute break between meetings to read through constituents' emails. As she wrote quick, personal responses to constituents, she mumbled, "What *are these*?" She'd just received 1,000 emails from labor union members in Michigan who wanted her to support an anti-Walmart bill. She said, "You know, it's hard enough [to manage email] without hearing from thousands of [citizens] from another state." With just one legislative staffer to manage all the office's duties, the email load contributes 20 to 50 hours per week of work.

How to Improve Civic Engagement

It's easy to be cynical about members of Congress and your local elected officials, to believe that they don't care about what you think. But my experience from talking with hundreds of them and their staff members is that they genuinely do care—they're just overwhelmed and fatigued by the sheer number of impersonal communications they receive. They'll sheepishly admit that it's easier to deal with one lobbyist than 20,000 form letters from constituents. I can't blame them. What I *can* do is build a better system for open government and civic participation.

We don't need to build a new and improved legislative system, one robustly equipped to handle our every whim. We need delicate, distributive tools for placing political pressure on our democratic process. If we're all going to be actively involved in government, we should gain techniques and tools to tread lightly on a system that has served us so well.

How do we do that? Via a few simple strategies in the short term and a few in the long term.

Short-Term Solutions for Citizens

These simple strategies won't solve everything in our legislative process, but they'll serve to prop up a participatory structure as we build larger solutions to the challenge of widespread civic engagement.

Be knowledgeable

Advocacy groups would have you believe that all you need to do to "make your voice heard" is to send off their form letter or sign their petition. This isn't true; you're more likely to be effective if you're speaking with your own voice, at the right times, and speaking with some experience or knowledge of the position you're advocating. This doesn't mean you need to hold a PhD in advocacy; you just need to do a few online searches (or use KnowledgeAsPower.org) to find out the following:

- Who are my legislators and when are they in session? Do they prefer email or would they rather I enter a letter in their web form?

- Why does this issue matter to me? How am I affected by it? If you're not affected, state the basic rationale for why you care. Cite a statistic or example, but don't write a midterm paper on it. You should be able to explain your position on the issue with a few sentences.

- Who, if anyone, is already advocating for my issue? Instead of seeing them as a vehicle for delivering your messages, find out from them how you can become better educated on the issue or more meaningfully involved.

Focus on quality over quantity

Don't believe the advocacy group deploring you to "Sign our petition!" or "Send this letter NOW!!!" While they might be pushing for a bill, they're also just trying to build their membership lists and demonstrate their group's influence. In the meantime, those mass mailings make your communications impersonal and ineffective. Instead, send a two-paragraph, personal email to your legislator explaining who you are and why you are affected or care about this issue. Send it to your elected officials only when a bill is in their house. Send it as early in the legislative session as you can. Even better, talk with your legislators outside of any legislative session. Make a follow-up call or two to "thank or spank" your legislator for her vote and be exceedingly polite when you make that call. Finally, don't feel like you have to advocate on everything; find a few issues that are really important to you and stick with them. With less effort, you'll find yourself making more of an impact, having more expertise on the subject, and feeling more confident in your role as a citizen. In the meantime, legislators will actually be able to hear you and the other people who live in your district.

Clearly identify your emails

Mark your email subject headings with a standardized subject headline. Instead of saying, "Vote YES on the Fluffy Bunny Bill!!" use the following basic advocacy headline (BAH) format to make finding and reading your email easier for your elected officials:

Chamber Bill Number-Position-Zip Code-Zip Plus 4 Number

In real life, this looks like:

HB1234-PRO-98115-5542

which means:

"Hi, I'm emailing you about House Bill number 1234, I'm pro on the bill, and I live in your district in this neighborhood in the 98115 zip code area."

Or:

SB6987-Amend-90015-2345

which means:

"Hi, I'm emailing you about Senate Bill 6987. I'm in favor of amending a portion of the bill. I live in your district in this zip code, and in a particular neighborhood."

Use BAHs to help your email slip into overflowing inboxes, receive more personalized responses delivered faster, and give the impression, "I know what I'm doing here." For more examples of BAHs, see KnowledgeAsPower.org.

Forego the use of form letters

Activist groups need to participate in electronic advocacy more delicately. Although using form letters with members does result in more letters sent, it also means fewer letters are read, more communications get lost in the shuffle, and members of those groups become politically anemic. They should use BAHs in subject headlines, cease their arms race to send more form letters via web-form-breaking technology, and begin teaching their members how to engage at a higher-quality level with their own elected officials.

Long-Term Solutions for the Government

The following long-term solutions will require us to build strategic, standardized solutions to legislation tracking, constituent communications, and activism.

Use XML to disseminate data

The United States should adopt a modern standard for disseminating its legislative and government information. This standard should be computer-readable (file formats such as PDF are easily read by humans, but computers just see them as a file, whereas computer-readable data allows computers to quickly organize and aggregate data); I suggest that the country go with the current standard, XML. While there are variations on XML—web services, RESTful web services, even XSL—this basic file format can allow for simple distribution of government information. Although each government in the United States functions like a small business that picks and chooses its in-house technology, the country should strongly consider making a national standard format for all governments to share their public information within. Not only would this make information much more accessible to individuals, groups, and government entities, but it would save them money and time. Private companies have thrived on selling reorganized government information, costing taxpayers millions of dollars— needless, expensive services that could be eliminated by standardizing government information into a format anyone can use.

New, low-cost services could spring up via the nonprofit and government sectors, helping all those involved in government do so with greater ease at lower cost. In the meantime, it would speed up the dissemination of legislative information and create greater government transparency. A great example of this standard being implemented is in my home state of Washington, where the state's Legislative Service Center developed a low-cost web service, which is available for free to agencies within government and independent organizations (such as Knowledge As Power).

Use open source tools

Government, nonprofits, and the private sector should band together to release open source tools for updating document management systems and distributing their information in XML. This effort could be supported by innovative foundations and philanthropists who value transparency and want to leave an indelible legacy of open government. Updating internal document management technology and creating bridges to release outdated document formats in XML will take investment; governments shouldn't have to choose between transparency and basic services in their budgets.

Conclusion

At the age of 29, I've been in the "open government" field for almost a decade. When I started envisioning the tools necessary for an informed, effective citizenry, I felt like I was the only person focusing on this area. I thought it'd be possible to build technology to help governments be more open and enable citizens to participate effectively. It's great to finally feel like I'm part of a group of people working for open government; none of us are fighting for this issue alone. I see our work toward open government as an opportunity to fulfill our vision of what the United States should be.

I dream of a day when personalized, online legislative information gives individuals the capacity to be meaningfully involved in the lawmaking process and still tuck the kids in at night. I want legislators, elected by their constituents, to talk with their constituents again—I want it to be easier to hold a town hall meeting than to schedule a meeting with a lobbyist. I crave equality of access to information so that whether you live in the House of Representatives or in a small town, you have the same information at your fingertips, at the same time. I hope that instead of playing "gotcha" with governments and hoping sunlight sanitizes everything, small groups of dedicated citizens will scrub away, rebuild, and strengthen the dilapidated portions of our laws and society. This vision of the United States is one in which individuals intimately know their capacity to make change, knowledge that no government, pundit, or poorly designed government website can take away from them. It's a vision of Americans fulfilling our potential as a democratic society.

About the Author

SARAH SCHACHT is the founder and executive director of Knowledge As Power (*http://www.knowledgeaspower.org*), an online nonpartisan system that helps individuals effectively participate in the legislative process. She's been a Republican and a Democrat, has worked on presidential campaigns and in Congress, and her mission now is to help "average" individuals become powerful citizens.

CHAPTER FOURTEEN

Emergent Democracy

Charles Armstrong

The Internet is already bringing important changes to our political and governmental systems. But while we pursue the immediate benefits, we must take care not to overlook deeper implications that could have greater long-term significance.

In this chapter, I argue that the Internet has changed a fundamental aspect of democratic systems which has persisted for 7,000 years. This change may presage a period of democratic innovation on a scale comparable to classical Greece. It will lead to democratic systems that are more fluid, less centralized, and more responsive than those we know today; systems where people can participate as little or as much as they wish and where representation is based on personal trust networks rather than abstract party affiliations.

This is Emergent Democracy.

Democracy As a Scaling Mechanism

To understand Emergent Democracy we need to take a brief look at how communities have governed themselves through history. There have been a great many forms of government over the millennia, but my focus here is the evolution of the particular subset we call democracy; a continuous thread of systems where power is spread through a large portion of the community.

There is no single definition of democracy. The original Greek δημοκρατία means simply "rule by the people." Each society and epoch has defined democracy differently, reflecting its unique preoccupations and aspirations. Democracy is a mechanism to distill the will of a people, a way to remove ineffective governments, a means of resolving conflicting interests in a community without recourse to violence and a thousand other things.

For the purposes of this chapter, I'm going to add yet another definition to the catalog. Looked at in the sweep of human history, democracy can be understood as a scaling mechanism for self-government. Small groups are able to govern themselves efficiently without any need for formal structure. But the larger a group gets, the less efficient this becomes. From this perspective, a democratic system is an exoskeleton enabling a group to self-govern at a larger scale.

This definition promotes democracy as a system, a social machine manifested in a body of fixed and unambiguous rules. This positions democracy firmly as a product of postliterate society and a world where rules can be written down. Yet examples abound of preliterate societies and unstructured groups where decision making is shared between the members. While it's problematic to call these democracies, they are certainly democracy's direct ancestors. Our story starts with them.

Informal Self-Government

Our ability for informal collective self-government is one of humanity's most virtuosic achievements. Because it functions almost entirely subconsciously, we barely appreciate the wonders we perform each day through nuances of speech and microgesture. Each of us is a cell in a collective intelligence machine of marvelous complexity and efficiency. Look beneath the surface of a typical village and you will find a continuous jostle of demands, alliances, and opinions in play. Without any formal structure, voting, or central management, this hubbub of tiny individual signals translates into collective decisions that are strategically intelligent and widely respected as legitimate.

However, this phenomenon works only in communities of a similar size to those in which the behavior evolved. In his oft-quoted 1992 article "Neocortex size as a constraint on group size in primates," Robin Dunbar suggested that humans are able to maintain social relations with around 150 other people, but struggle to exceed this. The archeological evidence also suggests that for most of our 2 million years on Earth we existed in hunter-gatherer communities ranging in size from a dozen to a couple hundred people. This was the setting in which our social mechanisms for collective governance evolved. Beyond this size, their efficiency declines precipitously.

The scaling barrier was first breached during the tenth millennium BC when the earliest agricultural societies developed independently in Melanesia, Mesopotamia, and sub-Saharan Africa. Nobody knows what triggered the switch to agriculture. Perhaps it was a change in the climate as the last ice age retreated, or perhaps a critical combination of technological developments.

Whatever its cause, the shift to agriculture changed the balance between population and food supply which had persisted previously. Communities of several thousand people developed; a size which had no precedent. It's no coincidence that specialized roles and hierarchy start to become visible in these societies. As populations grew and informal collective governance began to creak, it started to be supplemented by humanity's first innovations in formal structured governance.

This seems most often to have taken the form of tribal heads and councils of elders. Having spent a little time in modern tribal societies I believe these formal elements functioned as focal points within an established mesh of informal interactions rather than wholesale replacements for informal self-government. Some anthropologists have described these models as "primitive democracy," hinting at its transitional position.

Increasing Scale, Increasing Formalization

The agricultural revolution entered a new phase in the late sixth millennium BC with the appearance of the first city-states in southern Mesopotamia. This transition led once again to larger populations. By the end of the fifth millennium BC, the Sumerian city of Uruk had upward of 10,000 inhabitants. These are the societies where written language first appeared, perhaps responding to a need for accurate recordkeeping and taxation in an increasingly complex hierarchic society.

With literacy also came the possibility of fixed laws and of democracy itself. Several legal codes survive from this period. It seems that a large proportion of male citizens of Uruk were entitled to participate in an assembly which could make legal judgments, advise the king, and in extreme cases even remove him. Raul Manglapus, the Philippine statesman and writer, has argued that what developed in those Mesopotamia city-states constituted the first democracies. It is a sobering reminder of our short memory and historical arrogance to reflect that democracy was born in what is now Iraq thousands of years before it ever blossomed in Europe or North America.

Regardless of how we label it, the governance systems that developed in these first city-states represents a leap in the formalization of authority, citizenship, and participation compared to the pre-urban agricultural societies.

The next milestones in scale and formalization come in the middle of the first millennium BC when sophisticated democratic systems were established in northern India, in a number of Greek city-states and in the Roman republic. By the sixth century BC, Athens had a population of several hundred thousand people of whom some 10% were male citizens entitled to participate in government. The Athenian system was vastly more intricate than anything that had come before; appropriate to a community 10 times larger than any that had employed self-government previously. Meanwhile, the Roman model employed a multitiered system of election and representation, governing a population that exceeded 10 million people by 100 BC.

The consistent pattern that becomes visible in this evolutionary chain stretching from the earliest hunter-gatherer communities to the Roman republic is that as communities increased in size, so the balance shifted from informal to formal decision making and citizen participation in government declined. This line continues right up to modern times. The Constitution of India of 1949 extended democracy to a society which then numbered half a billion people and has since doubled. Conducting an election at this scale takes several weeks. The Indian government addresses mostly the same preoccupations and needs as those which faced the first hunter-gatherer communities. But a price is paid for this extraordinary increase in scale.

Limiting Factors and the Internet

Since the first legal codes were written in Mesopotamia 7,000 years ago the fundamental trade-off with democracy has been that it enables a society to self-govern at a large scale, but at the price of a reduction in agility and problem-solving capacity.

Underlying this trade-off are three limiting factors:

- The need to associate citizens and state interfaces with a fixed geographical location in order that information can reliably be exchanged between them
- The need to build in time lags between each stage of a multistep process because information could move no faster than a galloping horse
- The need for people to come together at the same place at the same time for formal debate and decision making

These constraints have been part of every democracy from Solon's time to the present day. They underlie many of the rigidities and inefficiencies of what I shall call Static Democracy. Involving citizens in decision making on any scale is so burdensome as a result of these factors that highly formalized representational systems have become the norm. Most states rely on focus groups and market research as a surrogate for widespread citizen involvement. Even occasional participative mechanisms such as referenda are too costly and disruptive to be practical. Meanwhile, the operation of a representative assembly itself requires a huge superstructure of formal processes with an associated apparatus for monitoring and enforcement. This maintains equity in debate and decision making but slows the process to a glacial pace.

A few years ago, it occurred to me that the Internet has rendered all three of these limiting factors obsolete. The combination of ubiquitous connection, storage, and processing opens the door to complex many-to-many interactions which can be molded dynamically by logical systems. But the democratic fabric with which we're familiar is so impregnated with assumptions founded on these three limiting factors that it's hard for us to imagine anything different. Nobody has ever experienced a democratic system that wasn't tied to those three factors. What would it look like?

By obviating these limiting factors the Internet calls into question the iron trade-off between scale and fluidity. In the absence of these constraints, it's possible to conceive of large-scale democratic systems an order of magnitude more complex than existing ones that harness our complex social behavior for collective decision making rather than disabling it. Imagine the jostle and opinion-clustering process that operates in a village, but functioning in a society of 1 billion people. A system that operates in this way represents a new kind of democracy which the phrase "Emergent Democracy" captures nicely.

The distinction between emergent and planned systems has a rich intellectual history. In economics, Friedrich Hayeck made the distinction between *taxis* and *cosmos* with the former concept representing mechanical, designed structure and the latter organic, spontaneous structure. In systems theory, emergence is seen as a central mechanism of self-organization, enabling complex behavior to result from the interaction of a large number of relatively simple agents.

The phrase "Emergent Democracy" itself has a little history. Joi Ito and others employed it in 2003 in a somewhat different sense to describe the way public opinion flowed and coalesced via blogs and other web communication platforms. Indeed, it was a conversation with Joi that got me thinking about Emergent Democracy again.

Building an Emergent Democracy

In the summer of 2008, I formed the Themis project with CIRCUS foundation to experiment with constitutional and technical systems for Emergent Democracy. The project brought together a variety of people involved with democratic innovation for a series of workshops in London.

Underlying Principles

We started by identifying six principles which would provide a foundation to develop a constitution for Emergent Democracy:

1. The formal system is capable of modeling a level of fluidity and complexity similar to informal self-government.

2. Citizens are linked to electronic, not geographical, addresses.

3. All formal interaction between citizens and the state is conducted electronically.

4. Discussion and decision making are continuous processes, not restricted to discrete times or places.

5. Dependence on nonautomated processes is minimized.

6. The formal system is deliberately incomplete; informal processes cross the boundary into formal mechanisms only when there's a good reason for them to do so.

The first principle is the central one. An Emergent Democracy is a formal system, but one which can adapt and reform the same way our underlying social behavior does. This entails bureaucracy an order of magnitude more complex than a Static Democracy. For the formal system to even approximate the fluidity of informal self-government there need to be mechanisms capable of reflecting the continuous recrystalization of authority and opinion in connection with different issues. The constitution itself also needs to be able to evolve constantly. This degree of complexity and constant change would be impossible to realize in a paper-based democratic system, even at the smallest scale. Only by translating a constitution into software does it become feasible. This fusing of a constitutional rule system and an electronic processing system is a defining characteristic of Emergent Democracy.

The second and third principles sever the paper-bureaucratic umbilical cord between the state and citizens, removing the built-in time lags. The fourth departs from the "same time, same place" foundation of Static Democracy, replacing discrete processes with continuous ones.

The fifth principle recognizes that an emergent system will be impeded if it has to interoperate with external bureaucratic systems (such as manually drafted contracts or regulatory structures) that continue to function in the conventional manner. Any such dependencies will undermine the fluidity and responsiveness of the system.

The sixth principle reflects the perennial tendency in systems design to try to encompass every conceivable circumstance within the engineered framework. In the case of Emergent Democracy, it is better if discussion and consensus-forming are permitted to happen "offstage" and cross into a formal mechanism only at the point a formal record is needed or a consensus can't be achieved without a vote.

The Themis Constitution

Building on these principles, the Themis Constitution is a simple participative democracy where each citizen has an equal right to propose and vote on group decisions. The constitution contains multiple references to an electronic governance system through which citizens can access definitive records, participate in decision making, and join communities of other citizens interested in particular topics. Even amendments to the constitution are initiated on the electronic governance system and the constitution is automatically updated if they succeed.

The Themis Constitution incorporates a rather unconventional representative system. In line with the first and fourth principles it was clear any representative model would need to introduce minimal rigidity and reflect informal behavior as closely as possible. That ruled out cyclic elections, fixed-term appointments, restricted candidate lists, and party-based voting.

In the purest sense, a representational system is a way of concentrating authority within a wider group. My experience with small communities has been that influence is held by different people in particular subject areas; also, that the distribution of authority can change remarkably quickly in response to events. In the absence of formal hierarchy, this mainly seems to function through a web of peer-to-peer trust relations. Such systems respond very efficiently to changing circumstances, increasing the concentration of authority at times of crisis so that decisions are made and implemented rapidly, but distributing authority more evenly at other times, creating space for more debate and disagreement. Static Democracy lacks this ability to flex. Powers which become centralized during a crisis tend not to be relinquished once the crisis has passed.

I spent a lot of time thinking how a representative system could be engineered to model similar characteristics. The solution I came up with was a fluid proxying system. Every citizen retains the right to participate actively in debate and decisions when they want to. But if they don't want to get involved, they can assign their vote to someone they trust, who is then able to cast two votes. There's no permanence in this. If someone doesn't like how his vote is being used he can withdraw the proxy at any moment and either participate himself or give it to a different person. Proxies can in turn be pooled. A citizen holding six proxies can assign all of them to another person whom he trusts. In this way, authority is dynamically concentrated through people's trust networks, able to ebb and flow freely. Based on this proxying system, a second, more sophisticated Themis Constitution was drawn up.

A fluid representative system of this kind would, of course, be completely impractical in a Static Democracy. It would be impossible to update records fast enough to know with certainty how many proxies each person held at a particular point in time. Only with the shift to an electronically managed Emergent Democracy do solutions of this kind become feasible.

One Click Orgs and Virtual Corporations

After completing the Themis Constitution, the next task was to develop its accompanying electronic governance platform. Guided by the philosophy of Michael Young (my late mentor), I thought we should set out to develop something of immediate practical value rather than an academic test bed. From my experiences with the School for Social Entrepreneurs, I knew that social ventures encounter a scaling barrier at the point they need to open a bank account or create a formal governance structure. It seemed to me that providing a website where groups could automatically generate a simple legal structure and group decision-making system would probably be useful.

In October 2008, I put out an invitation for software engineers and others interested in building such a platform. The first project meeting took place a week later, and development of the One Click Orgs prototype commenced.

At a public meeting at Berlin's Chaos Communications Congress in December 2008, the One Click Orgs project simultaneously became the world's first virtual organization and its first Emergent Democracy. Two nonprofits, the Bar Camp London Planning Association and Rewired State, followed suit and constituted themselves on the prototype system during spring 2009. The full v1.0 system was completed toward the end of 2009 and deployed to 20 organizations as part of a beta program.

After seeing the platform in operation for a year, it functions much as anticipated. Groups make most decisions by consensus without touching the formal governance system. In the One Click Orgs project group, formal proposals have mostly been submitted when a member judges a decision to be unusually significant. For instance, when we picked the Affero GPL v3 as the regime under which we'd release the code, this was formalized with a vote. Another situation where votes have been used is to resolve fuzziness. We spent several weeks debating whether the platform was ready to release to beta groups. In the end, one of the members initiated a vote which was successful. An authoritative decision had been made, so we proceeded with the release.

Many questions remain to be answered. As soon as we started work on the system, we began to discover edge cases and paradoxes that needed figuring out. Linking the constitution to an electronic system casts the significance of bugs in a new light. Rather than causing minor inconvenience, a bug can potentially bring an entire organization to a grinding halt. Also, if we failed to think through how different constitutional mechanisms could interact, there was a risk that users would create logical paradoxes that could likewise cause the organization to seize up. Even simple things such as system upgrades needed to be rethought. Most upgrades will involve a combination of functional and constitutional elements, but any change to a constitution will require a vote. Therefore, we must provide an automated mechanism to offer groups "upgrade resolutions," which, if passed, will trigger the relevant changes to system and the constitution.

The experience of One Click Orgs suggests there may be a natural affinity between Virtual Corporations and Emergent Democracy. Each innovation consists of mapping legal-bureaucratic processes onto electronic logical systems. The former may turn out to be the natural container for the latter.

Currently, the One Click Orgs platform provides a self-contained Emergent Democracy wrapped in what's technically an unincorporated association. Legally, this is the amoeba of the organizational world, conjured into being by the mutual agreement of its members. The next step is to extend the platform to provide incorporated structures suitable for businesses and larger projects.

David Johnson at the Center for Democracy and Technology and Oliver Goodenough at Harvard's Berkman Center drafted a set of recommendations which in June 2008 led Vermont's State Legislature to pass an "act relating to miscellaneous tax amendments." Despite its unassuming title, this established Vermont as the first jurisdiction in the world where fully fledged virtual corporations could be formed, with no requirement for a physical address or face-to-face meetings. Other legislatures around the world are now considering similar amendments. Such developments pave the way for a new generation of virtual organizations running on One Click Orgs and other platforms. Some of these organizations will be Emergent Democracies.

The Road to Emergent Democracy

We tend to associate democracy with nations, cities, and other state entities. But through history, democracy has played an equally important role in trading leagues, religious groups, nongovernmental organizations, and other nonstate entities. My hunch that virtual corporations may turn out to be a critical delivery mechanism for Emergent Democracy fits this picture.

Anyone seeking a living example of what a complex Emergent Democracy might look like could do worse than look at the crowdsourced encyclopedia Wikipedia. This is an extraordinarily sophisticated collaboration where consensus progressively forms from a mass of divergent views and agendas with minimal central control. While the community strongly deprecates polling as a tool and such votes as take place are not binding, Wikipedia demonstrates many of the characteristics of an Emergent Democracy. Moreover, it is triumphantly, improbably successful. James Wales is sometimes (inaccurately) quoted as saying that Wikipedia is not an experiment in democracy. That may never have been its main purpose, but from a certain perspective, that's exactly what it is. Wikipedia is a democratic machine for agreeing the truth.

Looking at how Emergent Democracy is likely to, well, emerge I think the state will probably be its very last port of call. As with any experimental process, the wave of democratic innovation I predicted at the start of this chapter requires the ability to fail over and over again. Far too much is at stake in national politics for failure to be acceptable.

Therefore, in the next few years I expect to see a ferment of experimentation in settings where the stakes are lower. As successful models for Emergent Democracy start to crystallize, some will become widely adopted by nonprofits, activist groups, clubs, businesses, and others who seek to govern themselves in a more participative manner. I also expect to see existing online communities adopting legal structure and governance. We will see World of Warcraft guilds and Facebook groups gaining legal personality, systems of government, control over assets, and the power to form contracts with the outside world.

There will also be a wave of innovation driven by businesses seeking increases in agility. This may see shareholding and remuneration tied to automated mechanisms alongside participation and voting rights, or employee contracts translated into dynamic electronic structures. Businesses' main interest will be the removal of procedural burdens that slow response times in a conventional organization.

Only after Emergent Democracy has become well established in many other areas might it start to be brought into the machinery of the state. Perhaps there will be a few tentative experiments in parish councils and other peripheral structures. Next, experiments may be considered at county or regional level. But realistically, it will be decades before we see aspects of Emergent Democracy in the government of nation states.

However, national governments may begin to see an impact somewhat sooner than this. Grassroots campaigning groups may be among the earliest adopters of Emergent Democracy. As a tool for interested citizens to debate policy questions and agree on common positions, Emergent Democracy will be a powerful aid. This connects with Joi Ito's picture of a society where blogs and social networking platforms power planet-wide tides of opinion which coalesce around points of consensus. It also overlaps with Clay Shirky's view of electronic systems as enablers of concerted action from disparate communities. The distinct feature of Emergent Democracy is its incorporation of formal decision-making machinery able to give focus and force to the concerns of thousands of citizens.

I can imagine an intriguing situation developing where governments elected through Static Democracy find themselves engaging with mass citizen groups operating with Emergent Democracy. It's hard to imagine a conjunction that would highlight the differences between the systems in a more revealing fashion.

About the Author

 **CHARLES ARMSTRONG** is an ethnographer, a writer, and an entrepreneur based in London, UK. He serves as chief executive of Trampoline Systems, the social analytics consultancy named by IDC as one of the world's top 10 innovators in business software. Charles is also director of One Click Orgs, the pioneering platform for virtual organizations. Both of these ventures are spin-outs from the think tank CIRCUS foundation, which he leads.

Charles studied social and political sciences at St. John's College, Cambridge, and was subsequently mentored by Lord Young of Dartington, one of the architects of Britain's post-war society. His thinking on emergent structure and self-government was strongly influenced by research with communities in the Isles of Scilly, Ghana, and Stromboli.

Charles is a fellow of the School for Social Entrepreneurs, a board member of the Fundacja TechSoup, and an advisor to various social and commercial ventures. He speaks at symposia around the world, pursues photo-ethnographic studies, and occasionally performs with baroque keyboard instruments or electroacoustic noise generators.

CHAPTER FIFTEEN

Case Study: Tweet Congress

Wynn Netherland
Chris McCroskey

"We the Tweeple of the United States, in order to form a more perfect government, establish communication, and promote transparency, do hereby tweet the Congress of the United States of America."

Open government empowers citizens to participate. Participation means more than just voting. Participation means applying your unique set of talents to improve the government that works for you. It means pausing in that moment when you ask yourself "Why does the system work this way?" or "Wouldn't it be great if people could do such and such?"—and when you ask the real question: "What can I do about it?" That's exactly how Tweet Congress came about.

Tweet Congress: Build an App, Start a Movement

TweetCongress.org provides a directory of all congressional Twitter users and aggregates their *tweets*, short microblogging updates of up to 140 characters in length. The mission of Tweet Congress is to promote transparency on Capitol Hill. We lobby members of Congress to forgo the usual PR blasts and use Twitter and other forms of social media to engage their constituents in more meaningful, conversational *dialogue*.

The Idea

On a Friday afternoon in December 2008, we stumbled across our congressman, Rep. Michael Burgess, R-Texas, on Twitter (*@michaelcburgess*). We thought it noteworthy that a politician not running for national office would be using social media in this way, so we tweeted it out to our Twitter followers. While looking for our Texas senators on Twitter, we had the idea of building a list of every tweeter in Congress, saving other folks the legwork of finding them. We wanted a single site that would allow people to find, follow, and engage on Twitter the people they had sent to Washington.

Building the App

To let people find their elected officials we needed to:

- Find everyone from Congress who was on Twitter.
- Find or build a lookup service that let users find their reps by searching by zip code.

As a double bonus, a search on ProgrammableWeb.com led us to Sunlight Labs. Not only does Sunlight Labs provide an application programming interface (API), a way for web applications to expose functionality to other applications, but it also had a list of 30 Twitter usernames for members of Congress. We had our seed data!

Thoroughly well-documented APIs from Twitter and TwitterCounter.com meant we could present data from Twitter and follower stats from TwitterCounter on our own app with minimal effort.

Open source fuels open government

It's important to highlight the importance of open source software in creating Tweet Congress. To those unfamiliar with the concept, open source software is software distributed as source code, allowing others to freely modify and build on it. Our web application framework, Ruby on Rails, is an extremely popular open source tool for creating web applications. Our database engines, MySQL and MongoDB, are also open source. We used a Ruby language wrapper for the Twitter API from John Nunemaker (*@jnunemaker*) and a wrapper for the Sunlight API from Luigi Montanez (*@LuigiMontanez*), both also open source projects.

We mention each of these only to show how cheaply we were able to develop Tweet Congress. Our only costs were our time, a hundred bucks a month in hosting fees, and a few dollars for some stock art to create the logo. We were successful only because many, many people created great software, most with no clue how it was going to be used.

Be someone else's foundation, set your app free

If you're considering building your own open government application, the good news is you've got a leg up. At latest count, ProgrammableWeb.com reports 31 publicly available APIs with all sorts of juicy bits of government data (*http://www.programmableweb.com/apis/directory/1?apicat =Government*).

After you've added value on top of that open source software and free API data, pay it forward. At Squeejee, we open-sourced a version of Tweet Congress as Floxee Community Edition, allowing others to build their own Twitter directories by starting from our baseline. We also offer a hosted version at Floxee.com (for the less technically inclined), and we work with public policy organizations at the state level to build their own state versions of Tweet Congress. TweetIllinois.org demonstrates how the idea is spreading to state legislatures.

Our experience in software development has taught us that most problems are people problems, not technical problems. Tweet Congress proved this to be the case as well. The first version of the site was completed over that first weekend, and then the real work began.

Starting the Movement: We Are All Lobbyists Now

Early on, we were embarrassed that our state, Texas, a state with 34 members of Congress, had only three elected officials on Twitter. So, we started locally and began the task of calling each congressional office and lobbying them on behalf of Twitter and Tweet Congress. To our frustration (but not surprise), we found it impossible to get past the gatekeepers and speak directly to members of Congress or senators. We did, however, find most of the press secretaries we spoke with receptive to using Twitter to engage voters. We immediately saw a jump in the adoption of Twitter by elected officials in Texas. Many saw it as an opportunity to get their message out to constituents, unfiltered by old media. Some reps, however, did not immediately see the value.

When we phoned Rep. Luis Ghomert's office in Texas's First District, we explained the benefits of Twitter to his press secretary and how we provided the ability for constituents to easily find elected officials on Tweet Congress. "We just aren't going to be interested in 'the Twitter,'" she said. We tried to explain that this was a great new tool for the congressman to use to communicate with his constituents, and again we were cut off. "We just aren't interested," she repeated. We thanked her for her time and we ended the call.

At this point, we decided to enlist our own Twitter followers to help our cause. After all, one of the realities of social media and open government is that *we are all lobbyists now*. At that time, we had about 3,000 followers. When we sent out a tweet that declared Rep. Ghomert was not interested in "the Twitter," it caught fire and was quickly tweeted again and again, reaching upward of 8,000 people within minutes! We wish we could report that Rep. Ghomert is now a social media user, but it's clear that some elected officials ignore the medium with that kind of reach at their own peril.

Inflection Point

We continued to promote Tweet Congress mainly from our own *@tweetcongress* Twitter account. As our list of reps grew, so did our own following (almost 10,000 Twitter users as of this writing). Some positive press from the media, including *The Economist*, *USA Today*, and Mashable, helped lend some credibility to our cause, but the inflection point happened on a Tuesday night in February 2009.

When President Obama gave his first address from the House Chamber, the media picked up on a large number of members of Congress thumbing away on their BlackBerry devices. While many thought they were texting, it soon became apparent that they were live-tweeting their response to the president's speech. As the buzz spread across Twitter, word soon spread that Tweet Congress provided the only place to see all the congressional tweets in one spot. Suddenly, we had an influx of new people, previously unreached, who wanted to find and engage their reps on Twitter.

So, Who Gets It?

Rep. John Culberson (*@johnculberson*), R-Texas, and Senator Claire McCaskill (*@clairecmc*), D-Mo., set the standard for Twitter use in Congress. Conversational and tech-savvy, they have been great supporters of our mission at Tweet Congress to get elected officials in Washington on Twitter.

John Culberson is a political Twitter Rock Star. He will talk to anyone on the Hill who wants to listen about the benefits of using Twitter. An early adopter, Congressman Culberson is and has been the most active tweeter in Washington. Not only does he use Twitter effectively to communicate his daily activity and work in Washington, but he also believes that he should, since he is accountable to the voters who sent him to the Hill.

In our software development business, we wouldn't dream of employing someone and not have some accounting of her time. Yet this is business as usual in Washington. We encourage all elected officials to imitate John Culberson in his use of Twitter for this purpose.

Another shining example is Claire McCaskill. Claire (we use her first name only because that's how approachable she is on Twitter) is probably the most human of all politicians you'll see on Tweet Congress. Her updates are insightful, concerning not only politics but also her personal life. You can't follow *@clairecmc* and not like her. Senator McCaskill updates followers about time spent with her family and about her mother. Some people think this is trivial and just want politics, but we think Senator McCaskill understands that being a great communicator means connecting with people on an emotional level. Senator McCaskill has more than 28,000 followers. The people who follow her sought her out and want to hear what she has to say. She also understands that instead of enlisting support every six years, with Twitter she maintains a relationship between election cycles. She will have thousands of people who feel like they know her personally when they go to the polls.

Impact

Tweet Congress has had a tremendous impact on how social media is used in government. For instance, one of the great things we've seen on Tweet Congress is what we like to call "the TC effect."

The TC Effect

When we add new people to the Tweet Congress directory, they immediately see a jump in new followers. When we added Senator Jim DeMint (*@jimdemint*) of South Carolina to Tweet Congress in late January 2009, we saw his follower count explode. DeMint had 652 followers in September 2008. On January 23, 2009, the day we added him to the Tweet Congress list, he had 2,165 followers. A week later, he had more than 4,000 followers. Today, Senator DeMint has almost 23,000 followers and is the third most-followed Twitter user in Congress.

We don't claim to take all the credit for Senator DeMint's meteoric rise in popularity, but we like to think we had a little something to do with it. People are hungry to communicate with their elected officials and those officials should be just as hungry to let their constituencies know how they are representing them (see Figure 15-1).

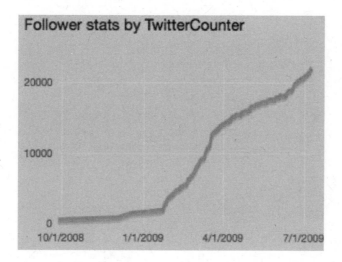

FIGURE 15-1. Senator DeMint's Twitter follower numbers

A Valuable Resource

Since Twitter indexes tweets for only the previous six days, Tweet Congress has become a resource as the only archive for congressional tweets. Both the public and the media use our site to see what folks in Congress are tweeting about a particular subject. Since we also extract links from tweets and display any photos and videos in them, a better resource for seeing a day in the life of your congressperson simply does not exist.

Conclusion

Perhaps the biggest impact Tweet Congress has made has been on us personally. We have developed scores of relationships with people we most likely would have never known otherwise, including members of Congress, their staff members, D.C. social media personalities, talented software developers, and very passionate, engaged citizens.

The site has also opened doors for us professionally that might not have been opened had we not pursued the idea. We were honored to win the Activism category at the 2009 South by Southwest Web Awards. This led to a speaking engagement at RailsConf in Las Vegas, an industry conference. This led to the opportunity to write the chapter you're reading. We were humbled by all three opportunities and mention them here only to encourage you, the reader, to take a chance on an idea, no matter how small. You never know what might come of it.

About the Authors

WYNN NETHERLAND loves the creative side of building software, from brainstorming with clients to designing the solution to executing the idea. The author of two programming books, he has more than 10 years of web application development experience. With a passion for building great user interfaces, he is a rare programmer that feels equally comfortable in a text editor, a command-line shell, or Adobe Photoshop. He's had the opportunity to help create some very cool things, like Tweet Congress, which took home a SXSW Web Award in 2009.

CHRIS McCROSKEY is a director at Rockfish Interactive, a full-service interactive marketing agency located in Bentonville, Arkansas. Prior to joining Rockfish, Chris was active in the worlds of social media and politics. He is the cofounder of Tweet Congress, a website that initially began as a grassroots effort to encourage politicians on Capitol Hill to begin tweeting with constituents. Tweet Congress went on to win the Web Award at the annual SXSW Conference in Austin, Texas and garnered coverage from various publications and websites including Politico, Mashable, *USA Today*, and *The Hill*. Chris is an active speaker on the topics of social media and politics and has spoken at the National Conference of State Legislatures, World Affairs Council, and the U.S. Department of State International Visitors Program.

CHAPTER SIXTEEN

Entrepreneurial Insurgency: Republicans Connect With the American People

Nick Schaper

When it comes to politics and government on the Internet, it's the Democrats' Web—the GOP just browses it, right? From Howard Dean's campaign pioneering online fundraising to candidate-then-President Obama's team's top-to-bottom integration of the Web, the conventional thinking is that the left has lapped Republicans in the race to digital dominance. As many of you reading this may know, this perception is hardly the true picture, particularly in Congress. In fact, when I go into work every day, I see a very different story unfolding.

Significantly outnumbered and looking for new, more efficient ways to engage the American public, the current minority party in Congress has moved aggressively into the social media space to not only promote their message but also shine more light on the workings of the majority's activities. This creative use of the Web to circumvent traditional channels and deliver a clear, unfiltered message to the American people is the hallmark of what has been dubbed *entrepreneurial insurgency*.

Entrepreneurial Insurgency and Congress

The term itself was coined by Republican Policy Committee Chairman Rep. Thaddeus McCotter of Michigan at an elected leadership retreat in January 2009. A major theme of that retreat was how to communicate more effectively using emerging and established social media tools. While there, members of Congress and staff members exchanged ideas and previous experiences in using the Web on their campaigns or in an official capacity. As we spoke, we found that nearly everyone had some personal experience in social media (many of us were surprised to find that my boss, John Boehner, had been quietly maintaining his own personal Facebook page), and everyone had unique stories of how it had helped them connect with family, friends, and constituents.

While this certainly wasn't the first time House Republicans discussed putting more focus on the Web, I believe this was a turning point in how the new media piece fits into the larger messaging puzzle. It was about this time when it was decided that our digital outreach was going to be a consideration in every major effort that we would undertake. Far from an afterthought or simply the domain of the "tech guys," an aggressive engagement online was not only going to help us tell the story, sometimes it would be the story itself.

It was also about this time that we began to see some very interesting things happening in terms of who was using social media in Congress. This chapter discusses Twitter and YouTube in Congress and how they fit into the larger push for increased transparency in government. That's not to say that these are the only tools being used. Thankfully, due to some recent rule changes (more on that in a bit), it is now permissible for representatives to publish official content nearly anywhere on the Web, providing that the content itself conforms to established regulations prohibiting fundraising, overtly political language, and other nonofficial activities. Members have taken full advantage of this opportunity and have been experimenting with everything from mobile streaming video to SMS text with great success.

Congress Tweets, Too

So, some of you may have heard of Twitter. I say that with more than a little tongue-in-cheek sarcasm, as you'd be hard-pressed to turn on your television or computer or walk down the street without hearing multiple pleas from news anchors, celebrities, musicians, and your friends and neighbors to "follow" them on the trendy microblogging service. For a technology that in many ways subverts the traditional media, the media has an undeniable love affair with Twitter, twitterers, and tweets. Oprah is on Twitter, my dad joined Twitter, and...the U.S. House cafeteria is on Twitter? If you're anything like me (and by me I mean *@nickschaper*), you may be suffering from occasional bouts of Twitter-publicity fatigue.

Not to worry, I won't be bothering you with yet another description of Twitter. What I do want to explore is a phenomenon that has gone largely unnoticed to those outside the beltway new media world: far more Republican members of Congress are using Twitter than Democrats. Not exactly an earth-shaking revelation in and of itself, but the fact remains that one of the newer, shinier tools in the new media shed is solidly the domain of the GOP in Congress. Figure 16-1, from TweetCongress.org, depicts the number of Republican and Democrat users in the U.S. House and Senate. As you can see, Republicans outnumber Democrats on Twitter by more than 2 to 1. (For more on Tweet Congress, see Chapter 15.)

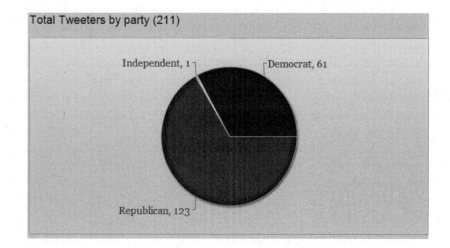

Total Tweeters by party (211)

Independent, 1

Democrat, 61

Republican, 123

FIGURE 16-1. Number of congressional Twitter users

The minority has taken to Twitter because it exemplifies the entrepreneurial insurgent mindset. As a simple tool that has the power to not only reach thousands, but also receive their feedback and quickly judge public sentiment, Twitter is a powerful device. Using Tweetreach.com I recently observed the spread of a tweet sent from Leader Boehner (*@gopleader*); see Figure 16-2. The tweet itself was simply highlighting a *Politico* article noting the party disparity on Twitter I've described. In less than a matter of minutes, Tweetreach estimated more than 60,000 impressions of the link we transmitted to our modest list of 7,000 or so followers. Not too bad for fewer than 140 keystrokes.

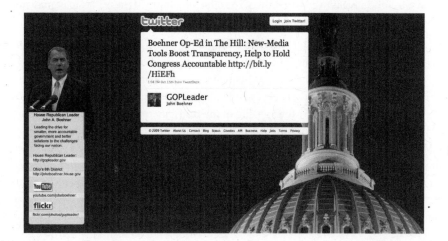

FIGURE 16-2. @gopleader Twitter account

"So what?" many will say. So Republicans figured out how to use Twitter, big deal. They've got only a few thousand followers anyway, and are they even *tweeting themselves*? Because as so many in the twittering class will tell you, if a politician isn't sending his own tweets, reviewing all his replies, following all his followers, and keeping up with #musicmondays and #followfridays, then he's not doing it right, right? #wrong.* Like people all over the world, members on both sides of the aisle are using Twitter in ways that reflect their styles. Some are intensely personal, others just like to share links to what they're reading, and still others have their RSS feeds running the entire operation on autopilot. I reject the notion that there is a right way to use Twitter and other popular social media tools. Certainly, some are more effective than others, and we all surely have much left to learn. But the fact that an institution known best for 200 years of tradition is finding new ways to connect with the electorate should be encouraging to all of us.

So, maybe Twitter is the exception—the talk radio of the new media landscape. By many expert accounts, it might not even be with us in a year or two (as an aside, I'm certain that most who smugly note the company's huge user base and lack of plan to monetize would be quite happy to have such problems). But what if Twitter isn't the only example?

I YouTube, You YouTube

For years now, members of Congress have been posting hours of video to their websites and eventually their YouTube channels. As technology has made video recording and editing more accessible to staff members, multimedia content from floor speeches to news appearances to video podcasts are thankfully now a fixture of most congressional websites. As a free, easily accessible, wildly popular public forum, YouTube was almost immediately a hit in the halls of Congress. That's not to say there weren't some bureaucratic hurdles to overcome before Congress was officially allowed to get their YouTube on. Some of these obstacles may not have been overcome if it weren't for the help of activists around the country.

In July 2008, Congress decided it was time to amend the antiquated regulations that guided members' official communications. As new Internet usage rules were being considered in the House Administration Committee, a leading member of the committee drafted a proposal that had the potential to prohibit nearly everything discussed in this chapter, including YouTube, Twitter, and Facebook. Asked by the Speaker of the House to recommend how best to proceed, Rep. Michael Capuano (D-Mass.) proposed the creation of an "acceptable" list of websites that would be developed and maintained by members of the committee and their staff. Faced with the prospect of bureaucrats picking winners and losers—while almost certainly stifling innovation by drastically slowing the institution's ability to react to evolving technology— concerned citizens of all political persuasions spoke out on the need for each member to decide for himself how to best communicate with his constituents. Eventually, the committee adopted

---

* Twitter users create trends and sort phrases by adding a hashtag before a term.

a decidedly more open policy based on recommendations drafted by committee Republicans (*http://www.theopenhouseproject.com/2008/10/03/franking-reform-a-happy-ending/*).

With the change in rules and the bipartisan launch of the YouTube House and Senate Hubs, designed specifically as a destination for constituents looking for their elected officials' videos, members are free to chronicle every minute of their day on Capitol Hill (and many do). As more time passes, though, we are beginning to see some very intriguing original content emerge. Members and their staff began to understand that video sharing communities such as YouTube are more than just a depository for floor proceedings and press conferences. Some of the most senior members of the House and Senate brought handheld cameras into their offices and introduced the staff to their constituents and others around the Web by simply pressing the Record button and being themselves. Realizing that social networks are meant to be a discussion, not a speech, representatives put the call out asking their constituents how they could better serve them, or to help by offering their insight on the issues before them in Congress.

Gathering Effective Tools

Like Twitter, the minority party has come to know YouTube as one of the most effective weapons of the entrepreneurial insurgency. When the content is compelling (and that is no small caveat), YouTube—along with Twitter, Facebook, and others—ensures that many thousands of eyes will see it in minutes. When Rep. Dave Camp, R-Mich., pressed a Democratic witness on job creation in the proposed stimulus package, the video was seen nearly 100,000 times in a matter of hours. When Republican Whip Eric Cantor asked Americans via YouTube to submit their questions and ideas about how to get the economy going again, the video saw more than 150,000 views and dozens of responses. When Leader Boehner, furious at having not been allowed to read the 1,200-page stimulus package, threw the bill onto the House floor, the 36-second video spread like wildfire. As I write this, that short video of Boehner has been viewed nearly half a million times.

Encouraged by their success, Republicans have moved quickly to take advantage of advances in low-cost video production software and camera equipment. Creating a for-web video composed of unique content directed at the online community is now a common component of our messaging strategy that has helped to break through some of the noise and deliver a clear message.

In a May 2009 analysis by web video industry watcher TubeMogul Inc., it was shown that congressional Republicans' YouTube channels had nearly 2 million more views than their colleagues in the majority (*http://www.washingtontimes.com/news/2009/mar/20/gop-bests-its-rival-for-youtube-views/*). And while Republicans had uploaded fewer overall videos, their average view count was more than double that of their counterparts (1,572 to 750). That same report found that eight of the top 10 congressional channels on YouTube belonged to Republican members.

Social Media and the Fight for Transparency

Social media is helping to bolster another crucial movement that has found many strong advocates in the minority party. Transparency initiatives led by citizens, advocacy organizations, and elected officials themselves have benefited dramatically from the widespread adoption of sites such as Twitter, YouTube, and Facebook. It has never been easier to find out who your elected officials are, what they're doing, and how you can contact them. Aside from tracking elected officials themselves, we are beginning to see more and more public information made available online in an easily usable format. Beginning as an oft-repeated campaign promise, the Obama administration has devoted significant resources to the development of websites such as Data.gov (*http://www.data.gov*) and Recovery.gov with a stated goal of providing complete transparency in how federal money and resources are being allocated. By all accounts, the jury is still out on the effectiveness of these sites, particularly Recovery.gov. Recovery.gov, already in its second redesign and carrying a staggering price tag approaching $18 million, has come under increasing scrutiny lately for not performing some of its basic promised functionality.

One interesting example of this intersection of social media and transparency was observed during the initial stages of the White House's Open Government Initiative (*http://www .whitehouse.gov/open/*). Seeing a unique opportunity to start a discussion on transparency in government spending with the president and the American people, Leader Boehner and our office submitted an idea to a public online forum created by the White House. The Boehner-submitted idea (see Figure 16-3), a 72-hour mandatory minimum public review proposal on spending legislation, was already backed by a wide range of outside groups including Sunlight Foundation and the nonpartisan American Legislative Exchange Council (ALEC), a coalition of reform-minded state legislators. Leader Boehner's submission also asked that President Obama make good on his promise to provide for five days of public comment on all legislation before being signed into law. (According to the Cato Institute, since taking office President Obama is one for 39 in providing that review period.)

In announcing the Open Government Initiative, the administration welcomed any and all ideas on increasing openness and transparency, saying:

> We are seeking innovative approaches to policy, specific project suggestions, government-wide or agency-specific instructions, and any relevant examples and stories relating to law, policy, technology, culture, or practice.

This seemed to be an ideal forum for the 72-hour/five-day reviews, especially considering the established support of the public, and the president himself. Thousands of Americans agreed, and at the conclusion of the scheduled voting period, the idea received more votes than any other. So, surely the White House took the idea into consideration, right? Not so much. When ideas from the "brainstorm" phase were chosen to move forward for further development, it was apparent that administration officials handpicked them with no regard for public support or merit. In the White House blog post "Wrap-Up of the Open Government Brainstorming:

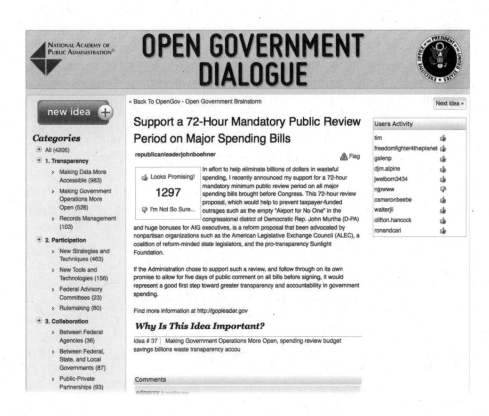

FIGURE 16-3. The White House Open Government Dialogue

Transparency" (*http://www.whitehouse.gov/blog/Wrap-Up-of-the-Open-Government-Brainstorming
-Transparency/*), White House Deputy CTO Beth Noveck indicates that the process may not be
nearly as broad in scope as had been previously stated:

> We took the voting into account when assessing your enthusiasm for a submission, but only
> somewhat in evaluating relevance…. There were plenty of great ideas that we read but that
> unfortunately did not make sense to bring into the next phase, including those…outside the
> purview of the Executive branch.

So, to the nearly 1,200 supporters of Leader Boehner's submission, the thousands of supporters
of Sunlight Foundation's Read the Bill initiative (*http://readthebill.org/*), American taxpayers
seeking more accountability in government spending, and yes, even the president, who has
been a vocal supporter of the concept in the past, administration officials had a message: it
didn't "make sense" to discuss this idea any further.

That attempt at eliciting citizen opinions illustrates an internal struggle that I see happening in
offices and agencies all over Washington. In the quest to increase participation and openness,
what do you do when inconvenient ideas and comments are submitted (e.g., marijuana
legalization)? What do you do if they highlight some of your shortcomings? This is still one of

the most formidable barriers to entry into social media for elected officials. Worried about unflattering comments slipping by, many representatives highly censor or turn off the comments on their YouTube and Facebook pages. Others, as we observed earlier, simply choose not to bother at all. As time passes and we come to expect more interaction from our representatives, I have a feeling that fewer of those who decide to stifle that communication will be in Washington to regret it.

I would be remiss to not acknowledge how much easier it is for the minority party to call for increased transparency, without the direct ability to effect change. I have been told many times that when Republicans regain the majority, expectations will have been set very high. Some have asked whether we will be able to produce the degree of openness we have demanded from our colleagues across the aisle. I'm happy to report that aided by the entrepreneurial insurgent tactics I've discussed, Republicans are making sure those questions will be answered in the next two to three years.

I'm not saying that Republicans will win back the majority because of their enthusiasm for social media and aggressive promotion of transparency. But I am certain that this is important. These numbers show that the Right is willing to step outside its comfort zone to engage new constituencies and continue to fire up established ones. For a sign of how times have changed, look no further than Senator John McCain, who was excoriated for his lack of a mobile device and for not being computer savvy, but now sits atop the Twitter heap in Congress with close to 1.5 million followers.

And while the Right is leaping out of its box, the Left seems quite content in it. And why shouldn't they be? Our first wired commander in chief and the First BlackBerry have more than enough innovation to go around. That seems to be the hope of Democrats in Congress. For instance: to date, not one member of House Democratic leadership feels that Twitter will add anything to his messaging.

> **NOTE**
>
> **It is worth noting that House Speaker Nancy Pelosi did announce her entrance into tweeting (*http://twitter.com/speakerpelosi*) in *US News & World Report (http://www .usnews.com/blogs/washington-whispers/2009/01/30/on-capitol-hill-twitter-is-catching -on.html*). She quickly racked up about 500 followers (including yours truly), but has yet to send one tweet. So, it's at least safe to say that Pelosi is aware of Twitter.**

Conclusion

Despite the political party, the importance of understanding the power of social media tools—regardless of which one is the most popular at the time—far exceeds the usefulness of each individual device. If we have learned anything over the past 10 years it is that digital media is advancing faster than any one brand (with perhaps one small exception) can anticipate. Technology will continue to evolve, and when it does politicians who cut their teeth on Twitter and Facebook won't miss a beat when the next opportunity to connect with voters and constituents hits the scene.

I don't claim to be unbiased in my appraisal of these recent trends. But it is hard to ignore the success in which a far-outnumbered party has been able to mount a number of very successful offensives. But my feelings won't be hurt if you completely discount everything I've observed here. In fact, especially to my friends on the other side of the aisle, I wouldn't worry much about any of this. Nothing to see here.

About the Author

NICK SCHAPER currently serves as director of new media for House Republican Leader John Boehner (R-OH). As a part of one of the most active and innovative communications teams on Capitol Hill, Nick focuses on developing new ways to expand Boehner's messaging online while assisting other members of the GOP Conference and their staff in executing effective, forward-thinking media strategies. Under Boehner's direction, Nick and his colleagues have orchestrated House Republicans' aggressive use of digital and social media in promoting GOP solutions. Nick previously served as director of congressional affairs for Adfero Group, where he helped more than 100 members and candidates harness the power of contemporary new media tools.

CHAPTER SEVENTEEN

Disrupting Washington's Golden Rule

Ellen S. Miller

NOTE
**This chapter was written before the Supreme Court's decision on Citizens United
v. Federal Election Commission changed the campaign finance landscape.**

Washington's golden rule is different from the one we all learned growing up: "Do unto others
as you would have them do unto you." In fact, Washington's golden rule—"He who has the
gold, rules"—works in opposite fashion.

That's not news. The fact that big money drives government decisions, that it has created a
mercenary culture in which nearly everything appears to be for sale, has been true of our
nation since its founding. Whether it's information, access to lawmakers and elected officials,
legislation, or government spending, an exclusive group of moneyed insiders have outsized
influence. There are, of course, many channels for money to influence outcomes, most notably
campaign contributions and lobbying expenditures. There are also a multitude of ways this
group of insiders gets rewarded—contracts to consulting firms, special earmarks for
government spending, targeted tax breaks, and corporate subsidies. But the result is the same:
those who give, get. Ordinary people—"outsiders"—are excluded from this cozy little game.

But now there is a new challenge to this very old way of doing things.

With the rise of the Internet and the social Web, the outsiders are becoming "insiders"—or, to
be clearer, the barriers to entry are falling, the gatekeepers are losing their power to control

access, and thus the golden rule is being disrupted. Thomas Jefferson once remarked, "Information is power." In large part, the highly paid "insider" lobbyists in Washington work to help their clients to not just gain access to lawmakers, but perhaps as importantly, shape, obtain, and make sense of crucial government information. Lobbyists are the ones who can get their hands on copies of proposed legislation hot off the printing press before anybody else. They can help craft language for an earmark funding a pet project and make sure it gets sponsored by a lawmaker and dropped into some massive spending bill. They can interpret the minutiae of some government agency's contracting rules and shepherd a client through the thicket. Indeed, the need for this kind of assistance has become so de rigueur that even state and local governments have sometimes taken to hiring highly paid lobbyists to help them negotiate the mysteries of Washington. With a government opaque to all but the "insiders," outsiders—read, ordinary people—rarely have a chance to engage.

In a generation that is growing up with the Internet, however, the "outsiders" have a different kind of expectation: they expect information to be fully available 24/7, and they expect technology to allow them to engage with their friends, communities, and elected officials. If you can sit thousands of miles away from Washington, D.C., in a coffee shop with free WiFi found via a few clicks on Google Maps; if you can then do simple searches about particular health care statistics on where you live, such as the number of people who lack health care insurance and how much cash local hospitals and clinics are getting from Medicaid and Medicare; if you can dig around to see how much campaign cash your senator and representative have taken from the health care industry and how they have voted on key health care issues—well then, you have essentially become your own lobbyist, gathering the information you need to make your case to your elected representatives. If your lawmaker is on Twitter or Facebook or whatever the next revolution in the social web will be, you can communicate directly with your representatives and hold them accountable for their actions. This information shift works in both directions, by the way. Thanks to emerging technology, lawmakers and government officials will have access to increasingly sophisticated tools that help them aggregate and analyze the views of their constituents and connect directly to you. They also will not need to rely as much on intermediaries for information on what people care about. A systemic change in how Washington works is now possible.

We are only just beginning to see the potential benefits of this new age. James Madison, father of the U.S. Constitution, wrote:

> A popular Government, without popular information, or the means of acquiring it, is but a prologue to a farce or a tragedy; or, perhaps both. Knowledge will forever govern ignorance; and a people who mean to be their own governors must arm themselves with the power which knowledge gives.

A more transparent government will not be the panacea for all that ails us. Our democracy will remain as messy as the founders expected and ensured it would be. But in this revolution there is finally the potential to subvert the "golden rule" of Washington—to turn government inside out.

The Bad Old Days: When Insiders Ruled

When it comes to transparency of information, there have never been any good old days. Even now, as the Obama administration is laying out an ambitious transparency agenda, we are just beginning to understand how little information is made available online—the modern-day definition of transparency. But just as in the age of the automobile it's difficult to grasp what it was like to plan a trip across the country by stagecoach and train, or how impossible it was to get an idea to a faraway audience before the printing press, in the time of Twitter, Facebook, YouTube, Google, and more, it's easy to forget the really bad old days of truly opaque government.

It helps to take a time machine back via the Sunlight Foundation's Transparency Timeline (*http://www.sunlightfoundation.com/projects/transparency-timeline/*). Much of the openness about Congress's doings that we now take for granted was hard to come by.

What were they talking about?
> If you wanted to follow congressional debate but couldn't make it to the nation's capital to see it in person, you were out of luck. It wasn't until the 1820s that Congress made its debates public, long after the fact, in the "Annals of Debates." It was nearly 100 years after the Declaration of Independence, in 1873, that Congress finally established the *Congressional Record*. It would be another 122 years (1995) before the text became available online for anybody with a computer and modem to access.

Who was giving them campaign cash?
> Big campaign donors have always known how much money they gave to politicians—but the rest of us didn't. While some scattershot rules required disclosure of limited information about campaign contributions, it took the biggest political scandal of all time—Watergate—for Congress to start disclosing comprehensive information about who was funding campaigns. Until 1995, however, this information was available only in cumbersome hard-copy files. In 2001, the U.S. Federal Election Commission (FEC) required House candidates to file campaign reports electronically. Even to this day, U.S. senators refuse to file their campaign finance records electronically. Instead, the FEC has to take hard-copy records and have staff members type information into a database, causing a substantial delay in transparency and at substantial cost to taxpayers.

Are they invested?
> It wasn't until the late 1970s that members of Congress began disclosing their personal finances, including the gifts they received and travel they took on the dime of outside sources. Even then, the information was available only in clunky paper formats. It would have to wait until 2006, until the Center for Responsive Politics (CRP) began making these forms available in PDF format on its website. More recently, CRP has made them available in searchable format (see Chapter 21).

Of course, it's not just Congress that has specialized in opacity. Myriad government agencies, at taxpayer expense, collect and produce dizzying amounts of data about our economy, food and drug safety, and environment—indeed, every aspect of our lives. Yet in the past, most of this information remained piled up in dusty docket rooms deep inside cement edifices. Taking this data and making it available at a high price for those that could pay became a highly lucrative business.

It was only little more than a decade ago, for example, that the U.S. Securities and Exchange Commission (SEC) began making corporate financial data—annual reports and other filings—available online. Before that, this information was the province of a small group of politically connected database vendors. Carl Malamud, public domain advocate and founder of Public.Resource.Org, essentially shamed the government into making this information available. He did this by putting the information up on the Internet himself. Once the site became popular, he told the SEC that he would take it down, but would first train the agency on how to continue to provide the data itself. The SEC bowed to the public pressure he marshaled, and now we have EDGAR, where anybody can look up corporate filings for free. Malamud ran a similar campaign to get the U.S. Patent Office to put the text of patents online.

This Is the Mashable Now

In the past, it was a victory simply to get Congress and government agencies to disclose information on paper. Then came the Internet, which, particularly in its beginnings, meant government could conduct a "paper-style" kind of disclosure—with unwieldy PDFs, for example. Now we're in a new era, with increasing amounts of information made available in raw, machine-readable format. Every day, new experiments bloom that are helping to turn outsiders into insiders.

For years, the CRP (*http://www.opensecrets.org*) was a lonely voice, doing the hard work of collecting and coding campaign contribution and lobbying data, and making it publicly available online for reporters, researchers, and activists. Now, thanks to support from Sunlight, CRP has made this data available via APIs and downloadable databases so that anybody can take it, enhance it, and link it to other information. Already, the group MAPLight.org has taken this campaign finance data and mashed it up with congressional votes so that anybody can find out quickly how money may have influenced a lawmaker's actions (see Chapter 20). Now, creative developers are creating new interfaces, such as "Know thy Congressman" (a winner in the Sunlight Foundation's Apps for America contest; *http://know-thy-congressman.com/*), which combines CRP's information on campaign contributions with data from elsewhere on earmarks and biographical and legislative information. New venues bring this information alive for different audiences. For example, remember during the 2008 elections the wild popularity of The Huffington Post's "FundRace" feature, fueled directly from FEC downloads, which people could use to look up who had given contributions to a particular presidential candidate via an interactive map? Millions of people went to check on their neighbors' political giving histories.

What Malamud did for the SEC and the Patent Office, he also recently did for congressional video. His campaign reached a tipping point after C-SPAN tried to stop House Speaker Nancy Pelosi from posting C-SPAN hearing footage on her website. Bloggers, led by Malamud, protested online. In March 2007, C-SPAN responded by liberalizing its copyright policy and opening up its archives. The result is that now bloggers, citizen journalists, and anyone can post any federally sponsored event covered by C-SPAN online without fear of copyright reprisals, allowing websites such as Metavid.org to focus more on the application layer, building interfaces for remixing, contextualizing, and participating with the audio/video media assets of our government. As a result, it's now possible for anyone to find, annotate, tag, clip, and display a snippet of video of lawmakers speaking from the floor of Congress on a particular bill or topic.

Providing this kind of information isn't just an exercise in entertainment. It helps citizens become more involved and hold government accountable. In 2005, a coalition of bloggers known as the "Porkbusters" was behind efforts to help expose Alaska's so-called "Bridge to Nowhere." This transportation project in Alaska to connect the tiny town of Ketchikan (population 8,900) to the even tinier Island of Gravina (population 50) cost some $320 million and was funded through three separate earmarks in a highway bill. The same group helped expose which senator—former Sen. Ted Stevens, R-Alas.—had put a secret hold on a bill creating a federal database of government spending, cosponsored by none other than then-Sen. Barack Obama, D-Ill., and Sen. Tom Coburn, R-Okla. Recently, the Sunlight Foundation launched Transparency Corps, where people can volunteer small amounts of time to help enhance the transparency of government data. The first project underway—Earmark Watch (*http://www.earmarkwatch.org/*)—is helping to digitize earmark data, which lawmakers are making available but only in awkward formats. Armed with easily searchable data, citizens will be better equipped to track government spending on these projects.

OpenCongress.org is another example of making information more available so that citizens can digest and act on it. Through this site—which provides baseline information about federal legislation along with social networking features—users can sign up for tracking alerts on a bill, a vote, or a lawmaker and link up with other people who are interested in monitoring the same topics, monitor and comment on legislation, and contact their members of Congress. In 2008, more than 45,000 people posted comments on legislation extending unemployment benefits; first they used the OpenCongress platform as a way to press their representative to vote for the legislation; then, once it was enacted, they turned their comment thread into a de facto self-help group for people looking for advice on how to get their state unemployment agency to release their personal benefits. (Who needs lobbyists when you have the power of many?) This spring the OpenCongress Wiki launched, providing web searchers an entry on every congressional lawmaker and candidate for Congress by pulling together their full biographical and investigative records. And that's open for anyone to edit.

We're starting to see change from without become change for within, as government starts to move toward a more modern, twenty-first-century understanding of its obligations to provide up-to-date, searchable online information to the public. For example, FedSpending.org was the first publicly available database on all government spending, created by the nonprofit OMB Watch with support from Sunlight. Through it, citizens can find out not only how much money individual contractors get, but also what percentage of those contracts have been competitively bid. The database has been searched more than 15 million times since its inception in the fall of 2006. Its creation helped to prompt passage of the Coburn-Obama bill mandating that the U.S. Office of Management and Budget (OMB) create a similar database. But instead of spending $14 million appropriated for that task on re-creating the wheel the OMB ultimately struck a deal with FedSpending.org to license the software to build the backbone of what is today USASpending.gov, which provides citizens with easy access to government contract, grant, and other award data.

Now, with the launch of Data.gov, the Obama administration is taking government transparency to a new level. The site is still early in its development, but the idea is sound: to provide a one-stop shop for all government data. If successful, it will ultimately make hard-to-find, obscure databases, once the province only of experts, much more accessible. We can't imagine yet what new uses people will come up with for this information.

What Comes Next

Despite admirable advances in transparency, we have a long way to go. We in the transparency community are working toward a time when there will be one-click, real-time disclosure. That would mean that a person could search corporations such as Exxon and find out, in an instant, the campaign contributions made at both the federal and state levels by its Political Action Committee (PAC) and executives; who does its lobbying, with whom they're meeting, and what they're lobbying on; whether it's employing former government officials, or vice versa; whether any of its ex-employees are in government; and whether any of those people have flown on the company's jets. We will also know what contracts, grants, or earmarks the company has gotten, and whether they were competitively bid.

When we look up a senator, we will find an up-to-date list of his campaign contributors—not one that is months out of date because the Senate still files those reports on paper. The senator's public calendar of meetings will be online, so we can see which lobbyists are bending his ear, as will a list of earmarks the senator has sponsored and obtained. We will know what connections the lawmaker has to any private charity that people might be funneling money to. Also online will be an up-to-date list of the senator's financial assets, along with all of the more mundane things, such as a list of bills sponsored, votes taken, and public statements made. Notably, all of this will be made available in a timely fashion.

We would like to see information about Congress linkable to agency data. That way, we could find out, easily, whether a lawmaker who received mega contributions from electric utilities and voted a certain way on an energy bill also has plants in his district and how much pollution they emit. We could see how many people in a congressional district were sickened by the latest outbreak of *Salmonella* or *E. coli*, how that representative voted on food safety legislation, and whether he attended a fundraiser hosted by a lobbyist for a big food conglomerate.

Making information available was the first big step: being able to connect the dots is the next crucial one. To make sense of information, we need to be able to analyze how one data set relates to another as easily as we search Google Maps for that coffee shop with free WiFi. The more connections we can make between seemingly disparate data, the more outsiders are invited inside, and the golden rule is subverted. A small contractor who wants to get into government work has a better chance. Citizens can help watchdog and cut down on wasteful spending. People can find out about traffic fatalities in their neighborhoods, government-sponsored clinical drug trials, and whether there's been a safety complaint about the toy they were planning to buy their kid. The barrier for entry into policy debates will be much lower.

Sure, we will always need experts who have deep experience to help explain what information means, to give it context. But in the future, it will be a lot easier for journalists, academics, public interest advocates, bloggers, and citizens directly to help *conduct* these analyses themselves. That will mean a healthier debate and, as a result, a fairer and more vibrant democracy.

"The old paternalism said the world was way too complex, and that we should trust the elders who have got the credentials to make the right decisions," said David Weinberger, author of *Everything is Miscellaneous: The Power of the New Digital Disorder,*[*] at the 2009 Personal Democracy Forum conference. "But we're beyond a paper-based democracy now. The facts that are being given to us are intended to keep us unsettled, because in the hyperlinked world of difference, being unsettled, existing in chaos and constructive difference and never-ending argument, is a far better approximation of reality than the paper-based world could ever give us.... Transparency is the new objectivity."

The old paternalism is dying, but there is more work to be done, because it's in the interest of big money to try to get around transparency efforts and work outside of public view. Transparency alone will not create a democratic nirvana. But there is no denying that the outsiders are becoming the new insiders, with the potential to rattle the status quo in fundamental ways. In the immortal words of the venerable Yoda, "Always in motion is the future."

---

[*] *Everything is Miscellaneous: The Power of the New Digital Disorder*, David Weinberger, Times Books, 2007.

About the Author

 **ELLEN S. MILLER** is the cofounder and executive director of the Sunlight Foundation, a Washington-based, nonpartisan nonprofit dedicated to using the power of the Internet to catalyze greater government openness and transparency. She is the founder of two other prominent Washington-based organizations in the field of money and politics—the Center for Responsive Politics and Public Campaign—and is a nationally recognized expert on transparency and the influence of money in politics. Her experience as a Washington advocate for more than 35 years spans the worlds of nonprofit advocacy, grassroots activism, and journalism.

CHAPTER EIGHTEEN

Case Study: GovTrack.us

Joshua Tauberer

More than 10,000 bills are on the table for discussion in the U.S. Congress at any given time. The most important bills can be 500 pages long or longer, and they can be rewritten several times on their way to becoming law. And with its 200 committees and subcommittees, Congress is overwhelming to anyone who is watching. The sheer volume of information coming out of Congress is itself a threat to government transparency. How can a representative be accountable if his legislative actions are too numerous to track? How can one take a stand on a bill if it is impossible to find? How can one know the law when it takes days to read a single bill?

Technology is a key player in government transparency. It's our own defense against the threat of government information overload. Looking for a bill? Do a search. Following a bill? Get a computer to track its changes.

Innovating the public's engagement with Congress has been the motivation behind GovTrack.us, the free Congress-tracking website that I built and have been running since 2004 (mostly in my spare time). GovTrack gathers the status of legislation, voting records, and other congressional information from official government websites and then applies the latest technology to make the information more accessible and powerful. Today the site reaches around 1 million people each month—visitors to GovTrack directly as well as visitors to other sites that reuse the open legislative database that GovTrack assembles. Figure 18-1 shows a screenshot of the GovTrack website.

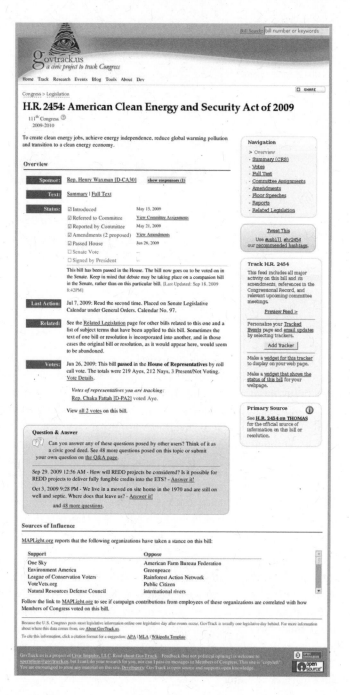

FIGURE 18-1. The GovTrack website

Opening Legislative Data

Back in 1994, the newly elected Speaker of the House, Republican Newt Gingrich, pushed forward a revolutionary idea: use the Internet to keep the public as informed about the inner workings of Congress as the members of Congress were. And so the Library of Congress (LOC) immediately built THOMAS (*http://thomas.loc.gov*), where the public could, and still can today, find the status and text of all legislation in Congress (see Figure 18-2). As it still runs on 1990s technology, THOMAS's innovation stops at keyword search. This is where GovTrack begins.

GovTrack integrates and cross-references more information than is on THOMAS, including voting records, biographical information on members of Congress, geographic information on congressional districts, and cost estimates from the Congressional Budget Office. By bringing everything into one place and cross-referencing the data, GovTrack is also able to compute novel statistics about the legislative history of each member of Congress, including an ideological score based on cosponsorship patterns and leader-follower scores based on who cosponsors whose bills. The site's presentation is tuned for a wide audience, and it allows users to personalize their view into Congress. It's also a community of wonks helping each other understand Congress. And the legislative database that powers the site is shared openly with other websites that mix and mash the information in new ways.

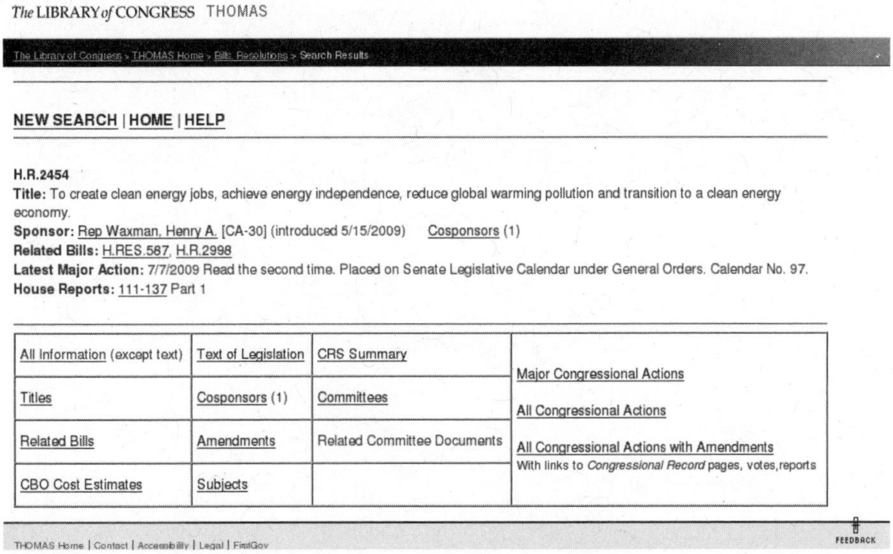

The LIBRARY *of* CONGRESS THOMAS

The Library of Congress > THOMAS Home > Bills, Resolutions > Search Results

NEW SEARCH | HOME | HELP

H.R.2454
Title: To create clean energy jobs, achieve energy independence, reduce global warming pollution and transition to a clean energy economy.
Sponsor: Rep Waxman, Henry A. [CA-30] (introduced 5/15/2009)   Cosponsors (1)
Related Bills: H.RES.587, H.R.2998
Latest Major Action: 7/7/2009 Read the second time. Placed on Senate Legislative Calendar under General Orders. Calendar No. 97.
House Reports: 111-137 Part 1

All Information (except text)	Text of Legislation	CRS Summary	
			Major Congressional Actions
Titles	Cosponsors (1)	Committees	
			All Congressional Actions
Related Bills	Amendments	Related Committee Documents	All Congressional Actions with Amendments
			With links to *Congressional Record* pages, votes, reports
CBO Cost Estimates	Subjects		

FEEDBACK

THOMAS Home | Contact | Accessibility | Legal | FirstGov

FIGURE 18-2. THOMAS.gov, the Library of Congress's legislative tracking website

The site's RSS feeds keep visitors up-to-date on what is happening in Congress. There are literally tens of thousands of feeds on GovTrack, one for every bill, member of Congress, and topic area. Users can create personalized feeds by picking up "trackers" throughout the site:

the site then creates a customized feed based on the user's choices that is updated whenever legislative activities occur related to the trackers the user chose, such as a new bill being introduced or a vote taken. The tracked events can also be sent by email.

GovTrack applies technology that didn't exist in 1994 to legislative information:

- A congressional district map uses the Google Maps API to help visitors find their representatives by allowing them to zoom to street level (see Figure 18-3).

- Changes are tracked to bills as they move through the legislative process: text comparisons can be made between any two versions of a bill. (This is based loosely on the GNU diff program, a Unix command-line tool for comparing text files.)

- Permanent URLs trace back to particular paragraphs in bills, and there are a few embeddable widgets that can be used on other websites.

- Twitter hashtag recommendations for bills help us all tap into conversations happening elsewhere on the Web.

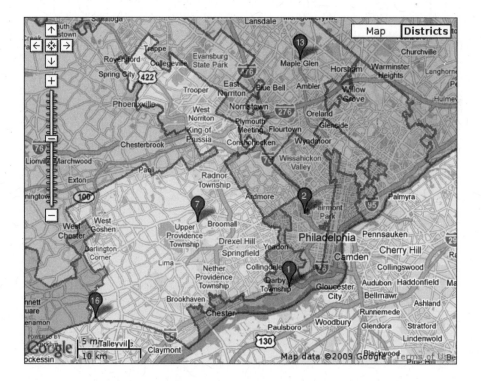

FIGURE 18-3. GovTrack's congressional district map is a mashup of Google Maps and cartographic data from the Census Bureau

Screen Scraping Congress

The best part is that the site runs itself. Almost all of the information GovTrack collects was already put online *somewhere* by the government. It's just scattered, difficult to understand, and harder yet to aggregate for the purposes of analysis. But this means that building a website such as GovTrack doesn't require continual manual labor to enter bill information into the system. Instead, I've programmed the site to periodically go out to government websites and fetch the information they have. It scans for new bill status daily, which is about as often as the THOMAS website is updated. The first goal, then, of GovTrack was to build a database of legislative information.

This was no small task, however, since most of the government websites weren't designed to share data with other websites. A human being might be able to make sense of a web page on THOMAS, but a computer doesn't know what's what on a web page. That didn't stop me, though: I just *told* the computer how to extract data from pages on THOMAS—how to look inside the HTML of the page, find keywords such as *sponsor*, then look to the right and pick out a name, and finally look up that name in my own database of congressional names to match it to the member of Congress it refers to (in past years, several have had the same name, which makes it trickier). This process is called *screen scraping*. My screen scrapers are a collection of small programs, or Perl scripts, that rely heavily on regular expressions and essentially manually written finite state machines to parse the structure of the pages.

It's not fun, and it's not perfect. Screen scraper scripts are not particularly difficult to write, but writing them does require a lot of trial and error. Because there is no guide to *everything* one can expect to see on THOMAS, I could only hope that I had considered all of the cases. I found out several years after finishing the bill status screen scraper that a bill can be sponsored by a person as well as by a committee. This was a surprising case that I hadn't anticipated. If a page on THOMAS displays something the screen scraper wasn't expecting, the screen scraper might bail with an error message, but it also might not notice and miss information on the page or, worse, misunderstand what is on the page, leading to inaccurate information being displayed on GovTrack. And when government websites change small details about how they format pages, the screen scrapers can get hung up and won't see the keywords they are looking for.

Fortunately, then, government websites change as often as…well, often they don't change.

This wouldn't be necessary if all of the legislative information was made available to the public as a database that a machine could process, such as a spreadsheet. That would eliminate the need for screen scraping and help make sites such as GovTrack more timely and reliable. And it would be cheap and easy for Congress to do because *it already has the databases.*

WHY DO THIS?

I wish I could say I had all this insight about innovating civic engagement when I first started building GovTrack in 2001. In the beginning, I thought the point of technology in civics was to help the public hold elected officials directly accountable; that if the public could get a better glimpse of what was happening in Congress they would be able to take that information to the polls. The site's first slogan was "Knowledge About Government Is Power" and it included an image of the all-seeing eye found on the back of a $1 bill, which represented the public keeping an eye on Congress.

I realize now that it may have been a bit foolish to think legislative information would yield accountability. The information overload we face is not just a matter of size. A 700-page anything is a problem, yes, but with a bill we're facing 700 pages of precise legal text with references to parts of law you've never heard of on issues few people have enough expertise to truly understand. Then there are amendments, and procedural motions, and a whole other level of detail to consider. We elect representatives to read and draft bills so that we don't have to. Accountability is important, but a type of accountability where citizens weigh in on each vote is impossible.

It is also unnecessary. The type of corruption we actually find in Congress is not as obvious as members of Congress wittingly voting against their constituents while the constituents aren't looking. If money has an influence, it is well before the time of a vote. It is who gets elected, how they get on powerful committees, and what bills get introduced.

The goals of GovTrack have changed over time accordingly. The focus now is on addressing the great divide between what most people think goes on in Congress and how it really works. We are taught in school that members of Congress write laws. Yet the most important bills seem to go through the process so quickly that no one could possibly have had time to parse them. A congressman's chief of staff recently told me that there was "no" general process by which a bill becomes a law. We've all been taught the parliamentary flowchart, but is its relevance to what actually goes on so insignificant? We need to find out.

When I started GovTrack I felt downright righteous that government data should be free. That's "free" in the sense of the open source movement, meaning available to all and without restrictions on how it can be used or shared with others. The LOC had the data I wanted, but didn't share it. Commercial services collected the data I wanted (often by paying people to watch C-SPAN), but they sell access to it. Government data should be free! And if they weren't going to share it, I was going to build the best darn database of congressional information I could and make it available to all—undercutting commercial services and outdoing the government if I could.

Congressional Mashups

A number of other websites now reuse GovTrack's open legislative database. One of the most notable of these is MAPLight.org. MAPLight draws on congressional voting data from GovTrack and campaign contribution data from the Center for Responsive Politics (OpenSecrets.org) to identify correlations between money and votes in Congress. OpenCongress.org is a more social version of GovTrack based on GovTrack data. Almost half of the entries to Sunlight Foundation's 2009 Apps for America contest (*http://www.sunlightlabs.com/contests/appsforamerica/*) drew on data from GovTrack. The winner, Filibusted.us, uses data from GovTrack to highlight the senators who most often voted against *cloture*—that is, which senator most often derails progress in the Senate through a form of filibuster; see Figure 18-4. (Most of the websites reusing GovTrack data, including MAPLight and OpenCongress, have something or other to do with Sunlight Foundation, a new leader in developing and funding projects along these lines.)

> **NOTE**
>
> **Other sites that reuse GovTrack's district maps widget include 50 Congress members' websites, the National Institutes of Health (NIH) recovery spending website, and My.BarackObama.com.**

MAPLight.org is a particularly important example (see Chapter 20). Many uses of government data, including GovTrack, are attempts to provide something that some might say the government ought to be providing itself. But MAPLight.org is different because it does something we definitely wouldn't want the government to do: be its own watchdog.

There is no doubt that legislative data has uses and is of value to society in ways that we have not discovered yet. Each of these other sites contributes to getting the public more engaged in government and each educates the public in a unique way. The sites would be sorely missed if legislative data was not open: available online, in formats suitable for analysis and reuse, and free to be shared.

Changing Policy from the Outside

For the LOC to run its THOMAS website, it put together an XML database of legislative information. House and Senate clerks dutifully enter each day's proceedings into a computer, and this is what the public sees on THOMAS generally the next day. Not to diminish the great benefit to the public of THOMAS itself, but is that good enough? Given that the LOC is already putting together a legislative database, something that we know now can be the basis of many innovative and useful tools, what is their reason for not sharing it? If they shared that database in raw form with the public, building websites such as GovTrack would be much easier because screen scraping would no longer be necessary. Managers at the LOC have told me that they

On Tuesday, September 8, 2009, 19 Senators attempted to filibuster an amendment to S. 1023 and failed.

19 Republicans tried to stall legislation they didn't like.

Senate Roll Call #271:
On the Cloture Motion (Upon Reconsideration Motion to Invoke Cloture on the Dorgan Amdt. No. 1347).

Vote passed, 80-19.

What does this mean?

It takes **51** votes to pass a bill in the Senate. But it takes **60** votes to end debate. These days it's quite common for the minority party to threaten to *filibuster* (to debate indefinitely) in order to prevent action on a measure.

A *cloture vote* is the Senate's way of asking **"Can we move on, please?"** It needs 60 votes to pass. There are 100 senators. As a result, as few as **41** senators can, as a bloc, bring the U.S. Senate to a standstill.

Still confused?

Why this bill?

Good question. Read more about this bill and **decide for yourself** if it was worth holding up the business of the U.S. Senate.

- Amendment: **Of a perfecting nature.**
- Bill: **Travel Promotion Act of 2009**

Why Republicans?

In the 111th Congress, Republicans tend to vote against cloture because they're in the minority. Historically, the party that is outnumbered wields the filibuster — but they've done so **more and more often** in recent years.

24 Votes

7.59% Gridlocked

Scoreboard

This was the **22nd** cloture vote of the 111th Congress.

So far there have been **24** cloture votes out of **316** roll call votes — a percentage of **7.59%**.

The 110th Congress (2007-2008) set a crazy record: **112** cloture votes out of **657** roll call votes. That's a percentage of **17.0%**! When it

Who voted against cloture?

Is one of your senators in this list? Get in touch and ask what's up.

AL Jeff Sessions
AZ Jon Kyl, John McCain
ID Mike Crapo, Jim Risch
IA Chuck Grassley
KS Sam Brownback, Pat Roberts

FIGURE 18-4. Filibusted.us, created by Andrew Dupont for Sunlight Foundation's Apps for America contest, reuses GovTrack's legislative data to highlight the filibuster

have to balance sharing data against their responsibility to provide accurate information. And although this is a fair concern, it's not a difficult one to overcome.

Not only does the government not always share, as in the case of THOMAS, but sometimes they charge for data. The Government Printing Office (GPO) has had the audacity to sell some of its legislative and law data to the public at ridiculous prices (starting at $8,000 per year per database), which is quite contrary to its mission, as given in law, to provide documents of value to the public at only the "marginal" cost of distributing them, meaning the cost of one additional copy. Today, the marginal cost of distributing most data on the Internet is $0.00 (that's a tad less than $8,000).

The GPO is an unusual case, however. The United States is generally a leader when it comes to not selling government information back to its citizens. The European model is cost-recovery plus *crown-copyright*. Citizens are charged a fee intended to let the government agency recoup costs (beyond the marginal cost), and the government asserts copyright over government publications to prevent citizens from redistributing them at a lower price. In the United States, distributing information at no more than the marginal cost is certainly the norm and government works are generally not subject to copyright, which means that if you can afford to buy the documents from the GPO, you can give them away for free. Which I've tried to do.

What data the government should share and how it shares it is a policy question. However, policy can change. An active government transparency community, as well as interested congressional staff members (as part of Sunlight Foundation's Open House and Open Senate projects), are working toward changing policies that restrict open data. In September 2008, a number of us, including Carl Malamud of Public.Resource.Org, bought the Code of Federal Regulations (CFR; one of the components of U.S. law) from the GPO for $17,325 with the intention to make it easier for other civic hackers to access the law of the land. Even though you can read the CFR on the GPO website, we wanted the underlying datafiles so that anyone can freely read and use the CFR as he likes. In 2009, under pressure from Malamud, congressional offices, and the White House's open government directive, the GPO finally begin to acknowledge the value to the public of free access to raw materials. The CFR will likely be freely available by the time you read this.

Like the LOC, the Senate has an XML database of its roll call vote records. An XML database of roll call votes makes it easier to build visualizations of voting records like GovTrack and the *New York Times* do, for instance. I didn't know this for sure at the start, but it was a reasonable bet that any website with a lot of records stores its information in a database, and other pages on the Senate website about Senate committees had mistakes in the HTML (non-HTML XML tags showing through) that suggested that the information came from an XML database. (I had to look closely at the HTML to screen scrape it to form my own XML database.) Unlike the House, which has made roll call vote records available in XML since 2003, the Senate actually had a policy forbidding its webmaster from doing the same (something about senators reserving the right to inform their constituents as they saw fit). When I spoke with the director of law library services at the LOC about THOMAS and the Senate's webmaster about roll call votes, I didn't get the impression at all that either actually thought sharing their legislative databases with the public was a bad idea.

However, when I started GovTrack, neither the LOC nor the Senate webmaster had the appropriate mandate from Congress to share data, which was the biggest hurdle. In 2009, the Senate Rules Committee, which governs the Senate website, changed its policy on XML roll call votes (see Figure 18-5). This happened only after some prodding by myself, others inside and outside Congress, and finally, Senator Jim DeMint.

Another win for open data came in the Omnibus Appropriations Act of 2009. This bill directed the LOC to assess providing bulk, raw access to its legislative data. The provision was the result of The Open House Project Report (*http://www.theopenhouseproject.com*), which provided the House of Representatives guidelines on how to use technology better in the interests of transparency. Luckily, Rep. Mike Honda (D-Calif.) took an interest in this and had a bulk-data paragraph inserted into the legislative language. The LOC has not followed through yet, however.

```
- <roll_call_vote>
    <congress>111</congress>
    <session>1</session>
    <congress_year>2009</congress_year>
    <vote_number>319</vote_number>
    <vote_date>October 8, 2009, 04:26 PM</vote_date>
    <modify_date>October 8, 2009, 04:51 PM</modify_date>
    <vote_question_text>On the Motion to Recommit H.R. 2847</vote_question_text>
  - <vote_document_text>
        A bill making appropriations for the Departments of Commerce and Justice, and S
        the fiscal year ending September 30, 2010, and for other purposes.
    </vote_document_text>
    <vote_result_text>Motion to Recommit Rejected (33-65)</vote_result_text>
    <question>On the Motion to Recommit</question>
  - <vote_title>
        Ensign Motion to Recommit to H.R. 2847 to the Committee of Appropriations
    </vote_title>
    <majority_requirement>1/2</majority_requirement>
    <vote_result>Motion to Recommit Rejected</vote_result>
  - <document>
        <document_congress>111</document_congress>
        <document_type>H.R.</document_type>
        <document_number>2847</document_number>
        <document_name>H.R. 2847</document_name>
      - <document_title>
            A bill making appropriations for the Departments of Commerce and Justice, and
            for the fiscal year ending September 30, 2010, and for other purposes.
        </document_title>
```

FIGURE 18-5. The Senate began publishing voting records in XML format in 2009, which helps sites such as GovTrack display the information in new ways

The what and how of open government data is increasingly becoming a mainstream policy question. Government transparency groups are suggesting open government data principles to guide policy (*http://razor.occams.info/pubdocs/opendataciviccapital.html*), but policymakers are taking the movement more seriously as well.

Engaging the GovTrack Community

The focus of GovTrack so far has been on providing comprehensive no-nonsense reference and tracking for legislative information. One of my long-term goals has been to build a community. Last year a GovTrack user asked me a procedural question about how Congress works: *can members of Congress change their vote*? (In the Senate, yes, with some restrictions.) It made me realize that there are many simple questions that people would like to ask about Congress or bills in Congress but have no one to turn to. Crowdsourcing could solve this problem. GovTrack users could gain from the wisdom of the crowd by having other users answer their questions. A user in the community might be an expert on a subject or be willing to do some legwork to find out the answers, such as reading the text of a bill.

And crowdsourcing worked. No sooner did I add question-and-answer boxes to pages for bills that visitors started asking questions and answering them. A visitor can post a question without logging in, as well as answer already posted questions. More than 7,500 substantive questions and answers have been posted over the past year (that's about one interaction for every 1,000 visits to the site). The Q&A submissions are moderated to ensure that users stay on topic. One of the most-answered questions has been "How will this bill impact day traders who may trade dozens to hundreds of trades per day?"

WHAT'S NEXT FOR GOVTRACK

I'm launching a Citizen Reporters experiment. The goal is to open the proceedings of congressional committees to the public. Committees are most visible when they hold hearings, which, when widely televised, are often a stage for posturing, but committee meetings are actually the locus of much of the legislating in the Capitol. Bills live or die at the mercy of committee chairs, and they also can be radically altered by committee member negotiations. The Citizen Reporters will go to public committee markup meetings and write up the proceedings of these meetings on GovTrack.

Other community tools exist on the sites reusing GovTrack's data. OpenCongress.org adds basic social networking, discussion forums, and a wiki. *Represented By* and *Laws I Like* are Facebook applications based on GovTrack data that let users track representatives and bills from within the social networking site.

Conclusion

The new guiding direction of GovTrack is to use technology to subtly change the dynamics of the system by helping the public to get a deeper understanding of how their government works. Congress will make better decisions when the public is more engaged, and the public can be more engaged if they better understand how Congress works. It's not about accountability so much as it is about education.

This is a learning process, though. The technologists have to figure out how Congress works before we can help others appreciate how complex it is. And we're just getting started.

About the Author

 **JOSHUA TAUBERER** began GovTrack.us in his spare time in 2001 and is the director of Civic Impulse, LLC, a company he started in 2009. He is a software developer and is also finishing a Ph.D. in linguistics at the University of Pennsylvania. He holds a B.A. from Princeton University and an M.A. from the University of Pennsylvania.

CHAPTER NINETEEN

Case Study: FollowTheMoney.org

Edwin Bender

Transparency surrounding state-level campaign-donor information has improved greatly in the past decade, largely due to significant improvements to the Internet and the demand it has created for access to all types of government information. But for all the good that technology has made possible, the age-old lack of political will has stymied efforts to significantly advance transparency in many states.

Accessing Political Donor Data Fraught with Problems

Government at all levels has yet to realize the efficiencies and cost benefits that transparency has to offer—whether political donor data, lobbyist information, contracts and vendors, or legislation. Agency directors must guide reluctant lawmakers to the table with concrete examples of reduced duplication, more competitive contracting, and due diligence where candidates and political favors are concerned. The potential is staggering, for taxpayers and voters, and for our democracy in general. But we have a long way to go.

The good news about political disclosure is that ethics commissions or campaign finance disclosure agencies in all 50 states have a web presence, which shows they understand that the public now expects political donor information to be available online.

The bad news is that agencies in 35 states think "electronic data" means online PDF images of reports for some, not necessarily all, of the candidates. For four other states, the online databases created by disclosure agencies are of such poor quality that the data itself must be reentered from paper reports originally filed by committees.

One dramatic shift toward transparency took place when Wyoming passed legislation in 2008 requiring full electronic filing and disclosure beginning in 2010—a far departure from the infrequent and paper-only filings required up through the 2008 elections that had for years earned that state failing grades in national state-of-disclosure reports.

The National Institute on Money in State Politics' Role in the Fight for Greater Transparency

The National Institute on Money in State Politics (*http://www.followthemoney.org/*) is the only nonpartisan, nonprofit organization revealing the influence of campaign money on state-level elections and public policy in all 50 states.

In 2009, the Institute itself launched three significant projects:

- The Lobbyist Link mashup of lobbyists registered in 2006 and 2007 in the 50 states (adding 2008 and 2009 now), their clients, and the donations made by both (see Figure 19-1). So, in a couple of clicks on a map, users can see a list of lobbyists active in a state, their clients, and, most important, to whom those clients gave campaign donations. Search for, say, *Verizon* and see that in 2006 the company hired lobbyists in 47 states and gave more than $3.4 million in donations in 35 states.

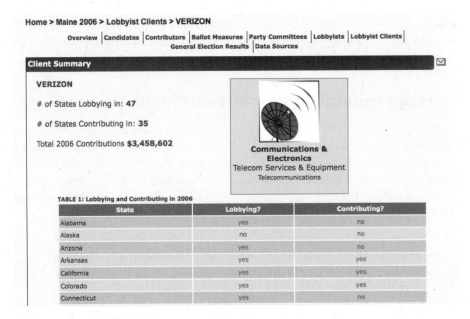

FIGURE 19-1. Lobbyist Link mashup example

- The Legislative Committee Analysis Tool uses application programming interface (API) data calls to Project Vote Smart's database so that political donors can be grouped by legislative committee assignments—where the most important legislative activities occur (see Figure 19-2). By selecting a state and a House, Senate, or Joint Committee, a user can see a list of committee members and how much they raised in their campaigns. The true power of this tool comes with the next step, when the user filters by the economic interest of donors to committee members. For example, selecting Illinois and its House Insurance Committee shows the 23 members, their parties and districts, and totals raised. Then, filtering by donors from the finance, insurance, and real estate industries, the user sees how much each member received from those donors, as well as a list of those donors, how many committee members they gave to, and how much they gave in total. This way, users can see which donors with an economic interest targeted their donations to members of committees with specific interests. The PVS icon next to the member's name takes the user to biographical information compiled by Project Vote Smart for each member.

Home > Explore > Tools and Features > Legislative Committee Analysis Tool (L-CAT)

See for yourself where the public interest and special interests collide.

The L-CAT is a mashup of state legislative committee rosters and campaign donor data. It illustrates the intersection of campaign money with the laws that affect everyday life.

The following lists of legislative committee members are researched and provided by Project Vote Smart and updated simultaneously on our Web site.

The committees listed here are from **2008** sessions. Start a search now!

Please select a state: [Illinois] [House Committees]

House committees from Illinois: [Insurance]

See contributions by Sector: [Finance, Insurance & Real Estate] What is a Sector?

TABLE 1: Illinois Insurance Committee Members

	Candidate	Party	Office/District	Sector $	Total $
PVS	DAVIS, MONIQUE D **(Chair)**	DEMOCRAT	HOUSE DISTRICT 027	$4,250	$145,646
PVS	YARBROUGH, KAREN A **(Vice Chair)**	DEMOCRAT	HOUSE DISTRICT 007	$45,124	$191,274
PVS	BEAUBIEN JR, MARK H	REPUBLICAN	HOUSE DISTRICT 052	$40,800	$232,987

FIGURE 19-2. Legislative Committee Analysis Tool example

- Just one year earlier, the Institute and Project Vote Smart (*http://www.votesmart.org/*) first used APIs to combine candidate biographies and voting information with donor lists. More than 300 individuals and organizations have now signed up for the Institute's APIs, which can automatically feed and update donor information to outside websites. Project Vote Smart and the Center for Responsive Politics (CRP; *http://www.opensecrets.org/*) also now make their data available via APIs. Sunlight Foundation (*http://www.sunlightfoundation .com*) is advancing transparency via grant-making and innovative projects.

Additional data visualization tools at FollowTheMoney.org let users see when a company's or industry's donations were made in a two-year timeline that corresponds to an election cycle with the Timeline tool, see a specific industry's donation totals over several election cycles with the Industry Influence tool, or look at how competitive legislative races are in their state with the (m)c50 tool.

Bolstering the Spirit of Public Disclosure Laws

Any researcher or reporter knows that if this type of information isn't in a complete, accurate, searchable database, the relationships between politicians and donors can't be revealed in a meaningful way. So, while lawmakers and disclosure agencies are complying with political donor reporting requirements by making paper or PDF copies available to the public, they are ignoring the spirit of the public disclosure laws.

The Institute compiles state-level donor information from all 50 states, filling the huge void between important public information and the public's ability to access that information. To do so, it has to build a database of all 16,000-plus state candidates and committees that register each two-year election cycle. These candidates file upward of 100,000 campaign finance reports, which result in a database of more than 3 million records that total more than $3 billion. Most of this donor information is reported in the couple of months preceding and just after the elections, but untimely filings and amendments complicate the work.

Like other nonprofits involved in government oversight and transparency, the Institute strives to show agency officials and staff members that people *want* the public information they compile, and that this lack of political will is a barrier whose days are numbered. Most agency staff members are eager to see the fruits of their efforts elevated to twenty-first-century standards.

In 2008, the public was offered an excellent example of what is possible if elected officials and disclosure staff members work together. The Illinois State Comptroller's office launched its Open Book (*http://www.openbook.illinoiscomptroller.com/*) mashup of state contracts and political donors. Thus, for the first time, Illinois voters had information that lets them ask whether political donations result in favoritism in state contracting. In contrast, more than 20 states offer search functions for vendor or contract information on their websites, but only a handful offer downloadable databases. As of May 2009, Alaska, Kansas, Missouri, and Texas had launched sites that show detailed fiscal information, such as revenue, expenditure, program, and vendor payments.

State-Level Transparency Faces Serious Challenges

The fledgling transparency movement is quickly moving from childhood to adolescence. The sobering developments around the economy, economic stimulus spending, and corresponding accountability efforts have elevated the public's desire for more digital information and spurred organizations to develop evidence-based visual analyses. As the federal government ramps up Recovery.gov, designed to track stimulus spending, the transparency movement will mature further. But the infrastructure of democracy will increase in efficiency only if and when the collective political will catches up with the potential of technology.

Defining "a lack of political will" is difficult. But it is easy to recognize when you experience it. Perhaps the best example of a lack of political will for transparency is at the federal level, where the U.S. Senate refuses to move its campaign finance disclosure to an electronic format—despite the millions spent on sophisticated campaigns. At the state level, it manifests in different and often subtler ways. Missouri disclosure officials insist that the jumbled, undelimited electronic data they provide in a single field is the best they can offer. That strains credulity. When, years ago, Utah's new campaign finance website went offline for the duration of the legislative session, that, too, strained credulity.

More commonly, disclosure agencies and staff members get caught in the "two bosses" trap, where they must pay attention to the desires of elected lawmakers who control the agency's budget, and the public, which is genuinely hungry for information about political donors, lobbyists, and their relationships to legislation and contracts. Montana is a good example of this. During the tenure of at least four political practices commissioners, the campaign disclosure agency has hired vendors to help implement an online filing and disclosure system, purchased several software packages, and input donor data and campaign expenditures in different formats and programs. Now, more than seven years later, electronic disclosure in Montana has improved to include PDF images of contribution and expenditure reports online, but still no database.

South Carolina has long been judged one of the most fragmented and unavailable states for public disclosure of campaign finances. Statewide candidates and political party committees filed reports with the State Ethics Commission, Senate candidates with the Senate Ethics Committee, and House candidates with the House Ethics Committee. None of this information was available online for viewing. It was available to the public only after the Institute obtained paper copies of filed reports and manually input the data to its online database. In 2003, South Carolina legislators passed legislation requiring online filing of campaign finance reports. Sounds good, right? Nothing changed—due to a failure to include any funding to develop an electronic filing system. In 2006, statewide candidates were supposed to begin filing online reports; the first reports for these candidates were not filed until January 15, 2008, even though none of those candidates were up for office again until 2010. In April 2008, some Senate and House candidates began filing their reports online. However, large campaign war chests raised during 2007 for these elections are not disclosed on the state website. It remains to be seen how the online filing actually works during the 2010 election cycle, but the current data is not easily searchable and it can be downloaded in only bits and pieces from individual pages of each report. While this would be a marked improvement over the previous processes, it underscores the type of foot-dragging encountered on the long and tortuous trail toward real transparency in South Carolina state politics.

Connecticut is another example. It has had an electronic reporting system for campaign contributions for a few years. However, at first the online data was not downloadable and the private contractor operating this database quoted the Institute a price of $10,000 for each download of data. Therefore, Institute staff members had to print the reports, then input, audit, standardize, and upload this data to provide free public access. With a change in administrations in 2006, the state began implementing a new electronic filing system. However, current election-cycle reports are not searchable or downloadable during the cycle; one is only able to view individual reports in PDF format. To provide a transparent, searchable database, the Institute still must print individual reports, then input, audit, standardize, and upload the data.

MEANINGFUL DISCLOSURE OF DATA WITH MACHINE-READABLE FORMATS

PDFs are not ideal formats for distributing lists of political donors or lobbyists. They are digital images, or pictures, of paper reports. But because of lower costs, among other factors, they are often used to fulfill "electronic filing" requirements. For disclosure to be meaningful, donor information must be accurately entered into a spreadsheet or database program by the campaign committee itself. (States that enter data from paper reports often have very poor accuracy rates and do not audit their input.) Once entered in a database, the data can be sifted and sorted to show patterns, such as a donor who gave to many candidates, a candidate who received donations from many donors at a single business address, or large donations to many candidates from a single donor on a specific date. These are the types of analyses that lead researchers to the conclusion that incumbent candidates are reelected so often because they raise the most money the earliest in a campaign. Ideally, the public would have access to a database of donors for deep analyses and be able to see PDF versions to verify the accuracy of the input.

Arkansas makes available online images of candidate and political party committee reports. But when it comes to reporting donors to ballot measures, the reports are sporadically posted for select ballot measure committees. In fact, the online listing of the registered committees—needed to expedite requests to the state for reports—is incomplete, so the public has no way of knowing if a committee was formed officially or if it filed reports.

Many states that do offer electronic filing, and databases for download or purchase, do not provide complete information in their databases. For example, Texas, New Jersey, Colorado,

Iowa, and California do not require all candidates to file electronically, so the Institute must manually enter paper reports into a searchable database. Other states, such as Indiana, Kentucky, Colorado, and Michigan, do not include data for small contributions reported as lump sums, loans, and returned contributions in their electronic data—again requiring manually input data to complete the stories.

While Missouri has an online searchable database, the contributor data provided to anyone ordering a copy of the data is sent all in one field. Parsing the contributor data into separate fields to make the data useful is a more egregious task than reentering all the data from scratch from printed copies of the reports.

Finally, as the public begins to look at and download data from disclosure agencies, they must keep a critical eye out for clues about the completeness of the data. In Utah, the Institute has requested electronic data time and again, only to find on closer inspection that large chunks of the database are missing. Successive requests have resulted in no satisfaction, so the Institute simply prints off the paper reports and enters the data manually.

California offers yet a different example of issues facing public disclosure in the states. While it probably has the most complete and easily searchable database of campaign contributions at the state level, the system is in peril of crashing due to its aging information and hardware architecture. When coupled with ongoing budget shortfalls that preclude spending funds to revamp this massive database, one major glitch could cause the whole system to become ineffective.

In an Ideal World: Recommendations for Open Data

While it's easy to point out the flaws with disclosure of political and other types of public information at the state level, offering concrete, implementable solutions is more difficult, given the nature of the information being requested and the potential political pitfalls that cause elected politicians to balk at approving solutions.

In the perfect world envisioned by staff members at the National Institute on Money in State Politics:

- Disclosure, enforcement, and ethics agencies would be independent of elected offices and, as much as possible, of elected officials themselves. Political donor and lobbyist disclosure in many states is housed in the office of the governor, secretary of state, or lieutenant governor, who often don't see that the advantages of robust disclosure far outweigh any political liabilities.

- Budgets for independent disclosure agencies would be set at realistic levels and protected from the whims of political retribution. For instance, ethics commissions in both Alaska and Washington have seen their budgets cut as a result of enforcement actions against politicians, even when further review found those actions to be warranted. Staff members need to be free to perform professionally without fear of retribution, and have the technology and equipment to do their jobs properly.

- Electronic filing of candidate personal disclosure, campaign donor, lobbyist, and client as well as legislative committee and legislation information would be required of all who use computers. Staff members would input all information or would offer computer access for those who don't have computers. The data input by state staff members would be audited for accuracy. (Exemptions from donor filing requirements are reasonable for candidates who raise less than, say, $2,500.)

- A unique ID would be assigned to any candidate or lobbyist and would follow that person through his career, providing easy access to personal disclosure and donor information, committee assignment, legislation, and voting records.

- Databases and information filed by candidates and lobbyists would have to adhere to standard database protocols, including delimitation of fields, and be downloadable in Excel and basic text formats.

- Donor and lobbyist information would include full addresses, and occupation and employer information, to aid in accurate identification of individuals and the analysis of relationships.

- RSS and API methods would be established so that groups as well as individuals would be able to easily track information and the activities of their elected officials.

On the larger stage, this level of transparency would enable deeper integration with state contracting/vendor information, thus allowing the public the opportunity to judge whether policy and spending decisions are based on political influence and friends of politicians, or on the weight of their value.

Conclusion

Data wonks understand that if you put all the candidate information, the political donor information, the lobbyist information, and legislation, fiscal impact, contract, and vendor information into one database and perform basic businesslike analytics on that data, you would discover tremendous duplication of services at different costs, low-value program cost-benefit relationships, and even the appearance of influence peddling, which could be used to establish new due diligence protocols for policymakers and politicians. The public is quickly learning how to do such analyses themselves, through new social networks developed on the Internet.

Our democracy, already a powerful and vibrant method of organizing activities and resources for the common good, can become even more effective by applying simple cost-benefit measures at the policy implementation level, and placing a broad understanding of the players and their motivations at the forefront of the debates.

If we let it, the Internet will ensure that many eyes are on the lookout for bugs in the policy/fiscal soup.

Institute Deputy Director of Operations Linda King contributed to this chapter.

About the Author

 **EDWIN BENDER** is executive director of the National Institute on Money in State Politics. Edwin was named executive director in August 2003 after serving as the Institute's research director since its creation in 1999. In that role, he led the research functions of the Institute, directing both the development of campaign finance databases and analyses of those databases. A former journalist, Edwin also worked for seven years as research director for the Money in Western Politics Project of the Western States Center. While there, he helped develop many techniques for researching state campaign-finance data.

CHAPTER TWENTY

Case Study: MAPLight.org

Daniel Newman

In 2005, California legislators passed California Fresh Start, an $18 million pilot program intended to help schools pay for fresh fruit in students' breakfasts. But there was a voice of opposition: the food processing industry, which makes money from the sale of processed fruit, not fresh fruit. Between 2001 and 2006, the food processing and sales industry contributed $2.3 million to 189 different candidates.*

Acting at the behest of the food processing industry, a Central Valley lawmaker deleted the word *fresh* from the proposed program in 12 places, replacing it with the word *nutritious*.†

The bill was signed into law. Schools used millions of dollars, originally intended for fresh fruit, to serve canned fruit in sugar syrup.

In 2003, Assembly Bill 83 (A.B. 83) was introduced in the California legislature. Had it passed, this bill would have imposed the same safety standards on bottled water as those applied to public water systems. A broad array of consumer and environmental groups ranging from Physicians for Social Responsibility to the state attorney general came out in favor of its passage.

After flying through the Assembly, A.B. 83 was killed in the Senate Appropriations Committee by a single vote. It never became law.

---

* National Institute on Money in State Politics (*http://www.followthemoney.org*).

† *San Francisco Chronicle*, September 16, 2005 (*http://www.sfgate.com/cgi-bin/article.cgi?f=/c/a/2005/09/17/MNGU6EPFB51.DTL*) and March 7, 2006 (*http://www.sfgate.com/cgi-bin/article.cgi?f=/c/a/2006/03/07/MNG9OHJT1F1.DTL*).

The beverage industry, which opposed A.B. 83, gave an average of $1,833 to each of the five Senate Appropriations Committee members who voted "no" on the bill—more than seven times as much money as they gave to the four committee members who voted for its passage. In an earlier vote in the Assembly, Assemblyman Alan Nakanishi accepted $1,000 from the California/Nevada Soft Drink Association and voted against the bill the very next day.[‡]

Why We Founded MAPLight.org

Our politicians make decisions about the water we drink and the sugar syrup our children eat with a bias toward the bottled water firms and fruit-canning firms that hand them campaign cash. After all, elected officials must collect vast sums of money to run their campaigns, and the best sources of that money are companies and organizations with a vested interest in how these officials vote.[§] Our system is designed with corrupting influence built-in.

Profit-driven companies wouldn't be making campaign contributions if doing so didn't buy them influence or access. In many cases—such as California Fresh Start and the bottled water bill—targeted campaign contributions now can generate a sky-high return on investment down the road in the form of favorable laws and looser regulations. Although money doesn't carry the day on every bill or in every vote, in the aggregate it is striking how strongly the money tends to correlate with the votes on issue after issue.

Why, then, isn't there the same kind of public anger and organized advocacy around campaign contributions as there is around health care, education, the environment, taxes, and the host of other issues that ignite public controversy and activism? In a 2000 Gallup poll asking a national sample of Americans to rank the relative importance of 25 different policy issues, campaign finance came in second to last.[‖]

It certainly isn't because people lack a broad understanding of the money–politics connection—ask around and you'll notice a widespread cynicism about the cozy relationship between politicians and special interests. Rare is the idealist who believes that the river of money flowing through Congress leaves politicians utterly untainted.

Perhaps it is because, cynicism aside, the tangible consequences of this system remain largely invisible. People care more about bottled water and fresh fruit than they do about the abstract issue of money and politics, even though the river of money that underlies our politics critically affects what we eat and drink.

[‡] Contributions from 2001 to 2004: *http://maplight.org/map/ca/bill/5577/default/votes/vote-58113*. Nakanishi: *http://maplight.org/map/ca/bill/5577/default/timeline/93*.

[§] For the 2008 election, the average winning U.S. House candidate spent $1,372,539. That requires raising $1,880 every day—including weekends and holidays—for an entire two-year term. The average winning Senate candidate in 2008 spent $8,531,267. That's $3,896 raised every day—for six years. Source: Center for Responsive Politics (*http://www.opensecrets.org/bigpicture/elec_stats.php?cycle=2008*).

[‖] *A User's Guide to Campaign Finance Reform*, Gerald C. Lubenow, Rowman & Littlefield Publishers, 2001.

I came to politics as a volunteer and observer. As a political volunteer, I was frustrated with the uphill battle that issue-oriented nonprofits and community groups fight against big-money special interests. I saw that activists trying to change the system have the deck stacked against them. When I tried to explain these money-influence connections to others who did not yet see them, however, my examples were not good enough. It took too much hand waving to explain to people what money and politics had to do with the issues they cared about. The complex relationships between legislators, their donors, and the votes that resulted were too complicated to explain using the tools available. So, I and other like-minded folks decided to build a new tool: a website that would show the specifics. And thus MAPLight.org was born.

We created MAPLight.org to make these money-issue connections transparent—to connect the abstract topic of campaign money to the specific issues that affect people's lives. The "MAP" in "MAPLight.org" stands for Money And Politics. MAPLight.org is a groundbreaking public database that illuminates the connection between money and politics in unprecedented ways.

The MAPLight.org website allows citizens and journalists to answer questions such as:

- How did a legislator vote on a particular bill, and who are the top contributors to that legislator?
- When did legislators vote to support bills their top contributors supported?
- When did special interests (such as insurance companies or drug companies) succeed in blocking bills that did not serve their interests?

We give citizens the tools to find out for themselves how campaign contributions affect the issues they care about. We make the abstract connection between campaign donations and legislative votes visible and concrete. Connections that once would have taken days or weeks to uncover are now available at the click of a mouse. In the past year and a half alone, we have reached more than 12 million people with our groundbreaking money and politics data—on our website and through news stories on television and radio and in newspapers and blogs. By making money–vote correlations transparent, easily researched, and publicly accessible, we finally stand a chance at holding legislators accountable.

MAPLight.org's Unique Contribution

MAPLight.org is a Web 2.0 transparency mashup that puts together three data sets that have never before been combined: campaign money, votes, and special interest positions on bills. We combine campaign contribution data from the Center for Responsive Politics (OpenSecrets.org; see Chapter 21) and the National Institute on Money in State Politics (FollowTheMoney.org; see Chapter 19); legislative voting records and bill information from GovTrack.us (see Chapter 18); and special interest support and opposition data gathered by MAPLight.org's in-house research team.

For each bill, our research team uses public-record sources such as congressional hearing testimony and news databases to determine:

Organizations in support or opposition
> For example, ExxonMobil or American Bankers Association

Industries in support or opposition
> Industry categories, such as multinational oil companies or commercial banks

For example, we found that the Credit Cardholders' Bill of Rights of 2009 was supported and opposed by the organizations and industries listed in Table 20-1.

TABLE 20-1. Organizations and industries that support and oppose the Credit Cardholders' Bill of Rights of 2009

Organizations that support	Organizations that oppose
Americans for Fairness in Lending	Association of Community Organizations for Reform Now
Center for Responsible Lending	Consumer Action
Consumer Federation of America	Consumers Union
Demos	National Association of Consumer Advocates
National Consumer Law Center	National Small Business Association
National Training and Information Center	Public Citizen
U.S. Public Interest Research Groups	American Bankers Association
Credit Union National Association	Independent Community Bankers of America
Industries that support	**Industries that oppose**
Small business associations	Consumer groups
Commercial banks and bank holding companies	Credit unions

Our research team has gathered support/opposition data for more than 3,000 bills to date.

By itself, our support and opposition information gives immediate insight into what is really at stake for bills in Congress, quickly orienting readers to the interest groups behind legislation. It is often difficult to understand the true intent and beneficiaries of congressional legislation. MAPLight.org's unique data provides valuable signposts, showing who is on which side.

Even more significantly, our data provides the "glue" to connect political inputs (such as campaign contributions and lobbying) to political outputs (such as contracts and legislation). A vital part of making the transparency movement useful to ordinary people is connecting government information with the specific issues that people care about. MAPLight.org's data links campaign dollars to relevant issues with everyday impact—prescription drugs, gas prices, credit cards, and more.

Nuts and Bolts: Using MAPLight.org

With campaign contributions, politicians' votes, and interest group positions all loaded into our website, MAPLight.org's "transparency tools" allow users to go in and find data by bill, legislator, or interest group. The data can then be "sliced and diced" in myriad ways to drill down to specifics.

Votes

For example, if you were to search our site for A.B. 83, the bottled water bill, you could see the imbalance in campaign donations by opposing/supporting interests and to legislators voting yes/no (see Figure 20-1).

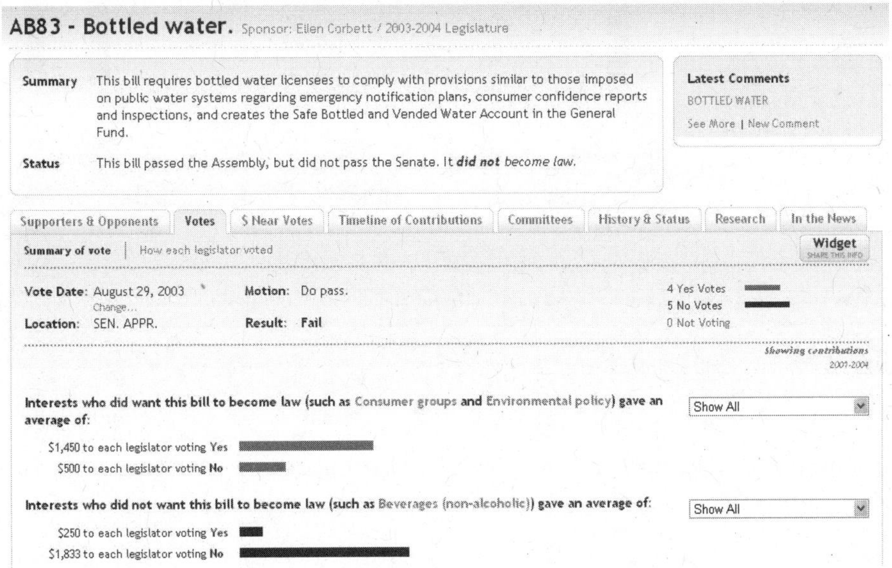

AB83 - Bottled water. Sponsor: Ellen Corbett / 2003-2004 Legislature

Summary	This bill requires bottled water licensees to comply with provisions similar to those imposed on public water systems regarding emergency notification plans, consumer confidence reports and inspections, and creates the Safe Bottled and Vended Water Account in the General Fund.
Status	This bill passed the Assembly, but did not pass the Senate. It **did not** become law.

Latest Comments
BOTTLED WATER
See More | New Comment

Supporters & Opponents | Votes | $ Near Votes | Timeline of Contributions | Committees | History & Status | Research | In the News

Summary of vote | How each legislator voted

Widget SHARE THIS INFO

Vote Date: August 29, 2003
Change...
Location: SEN. APPR.

Motion: Do pass.
Result: Fail

4 Yes Votes
5 No Votes
0 Not Voting

showing contributions
2001-2004

Interests who did want this bill to become law (such as Consumer groups and Environmental policy) gave an average of:

Show All

$1,450 to each legislator voting **Yes**
$500 to each legislator voting **No**

Interests who did not want this bill to become law (such as Beverages (non-alcoholic)) gave an average of:

Show All

$250 to each legislator voting **Yes**
$1,833 to each legislator voting **No**

FIGURE 20-1. Bottled water bill and campaign donations

Overviews such as this reveal the big picture—the broad correlations between money and votes.

Timeline

MAPLight.org's timeline feature allows users to see both overall and individual legislators' contributions over time, with dates of votes marked. For A.B. 83, the bottled water bill, Alan Nakanishi's timeline looks like Figure 20-2.

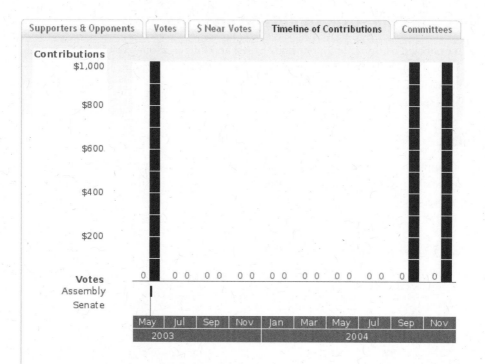

Contributions

This chart shows contributions and votes for **Alan Nakanishi**.

Quarterly   **Bi-monthly**   Monthly

FIGURE 20-2. Alan Nakanishi's contributions

Nakanishi voted "no" on this bill on June 4, one day after he accepted $1,000 from the bottled water trade association.

Committees

MAPLight.org's committee tool allows users to drill deeper, uncovering the money behind a bill even before a vote has occurred.

For example, in 2009, Representative John Conyers, D-Mich., introduced H.R. 801, the Fair Copyright in Research Works Act. The bill would reverse the National Institutes of Health's Public Access Policy and limit public access to peer-reviewed journal articles produced by scientists receiving taxpayer funding for their research.

Figure 20-3 shows the MAPLight.org committee data on H.R. 801, showing campaign dollars given to each House Judiciary Committee member by publishers and other interests who supported and opposed this bill.

H.R.801 - Fair Copyright in Research Works Act Sponsor: John Conyers / 111th Congress

Title	111th Congress - To amend title 17, United States Code, with respect to works connected to certain funding agreements. *Other titles*
Summary	HR 801 is a bill attempting to reverse the Public Access Policy of the National Institutes of Health that allows NIH to make freely available online peer-reviewed manuscripts within 12 months of their publication. *(by MAPLight.org)*
Status	The bill has been introduced.

Latest Comments

Who does HR 801 really help? Public Access vs. Market Research

See More | New Comment

Supporters & Opponents | Votes | $ Near Votes | Timeline of Contributions | **Committees** | History & Status | Research | In the News

This bill was referred to these committees:

House Committee on the Judiciary

House Committee on the Judiciary
Contributions received from interests who:

Showing contributions
Jan 2003–Jan 2009

Legislator ▲	Party	State	Did want this law	Did not want this law	
			• Book, newspaper & periodical publishing	• Education	
			• Psychiatrists & psychologists	• Schools & colleges	
			• Other physician specialists	• Museums, art galleries, libraries, etc.	
			• Health & welfare policy		
			• Chemicals		
Conyers (Chair)	D	(MI-14)	$39,168	$5,725	(details...)
Smith (Ranking Member)	R	(TX-21)	$90,450	$8,200	(details...)
Baldwin	D	(WI-2)	$92,500	$67,650	(details...)
Berman	D	(CA-28)	$70,650	$7,050	(details...)
Boucher	D	(VA-9)	$140,500	$17,250	(details...)
Chaffetz	R	(UT-3)	$8,950	$7,300	(details...)
Coble	R	(NC-6)	$29,250		(details...)
Cohen	D	(TN-9)	$27,550	$22,033	(details...)
Delahunt	D	(MA-10)	$9,750	$11,500	(details...)
Forbes	R	(VA-4)	$48,975	$1,485	(details...)
Franks	R	(AZ-2)	$9,150	$7,956	(details...)
Gallegly	R	(CA-24)	$10,548	$3,800	(details...)
Gohmert	R	(TX-1)	$137,925	$26,400	(details...)

FIGURE 20-3. MAPLight.org committee data on H.R. 801

On March 2, 2009, law professor (and MAPLight.org board member) Lawrence Lessig published an article on the Huffington Post website regarding this copyright-related bill.[#] The article criticized Conyers' role as the bill's sponsor, claiming his position on the issue was influenced by the publishing industry, and cited MAPLight.org's figures on publishing-industry contributions to Conyers and other bill sponsors.

The article set off a wave of critical blog posts and phone calls to Conyers' office. Conyers posted a response on the Huffington Post website defending his position, and readers added more than 100 comments, most of them taking issue with his position. By March 15, the story had generated more than 100 blog posts that cited MAPLight.org's report. Likely as a result of this public outcry, the bill has stalled and seems unlikely to make it out of committee.

[#] *http://www.huffingtonpost.com/lawrence-lessig-and-michael-eisen/isjohn-conyers-shilling_b_171189.html*

This public outcry was spurred in part by people's ability to learn about the campaign money behind the bill in time to influence the legislative outcome. In this case, our money/votes data was used to bring public attention to an issue early in the legislative process, before a final vote, when public opinion could still sway the result. Instead of money-influenced results being presented as an entrenched fact of life, inviting cynicism, MAPLight.org's new, quick-response tools allowed this money–politics connection to be presented as an actionable incident—and it got results.

How Each Legislator Voted

MAPLight.org also allows visitors to see the detailed contribution and vote data for individual legislators. For example, S. 3044, the Consumer-First Energy Act of 2008, was supported by consumer groups, among others, and was opposed by industries including independent oil and gas producers.

If a constituent of a particular legislator wants to see exactly how much money that legislator received, and from whom, he can see the contributions broken down by category on MAPLight.org's site. For example, Senator John Thune voted "no" on this energy bill. Figure 20-4 shows his contributions from industries supporting and opposing the bill.

John Thune (R-SD) Voted No

*Showing contributions
Jan 2003-Jun 2009*

Contributions he received from groups who:

Did want this law		Did not want this law	
Elderly issues/Social Security	$300	Independent oil & gas producers	$72,104
Environmental policy	$0	Commodity brokers/dealers	$20,000
Consumer groups	$0	Manufacturing	$18,900
Teamsters union	$0	Chambers of commerce	$6,700
Labor Unions	$0	Fiscal & tax policy	$100
TOTAL	$300	TOTAL	$117,804

FIGURE 20-4. How each legislator voted

Other Tools

Other tools at the MAPLight.org site allow users to explore money–politics connections through other views—who a particular legislator's main funders are, or who the biggest recipients of a particular industry's contributions are. Data can be screened by state or by political party.

Our customization tools even allow users to combine our tools with their own outside knowledge. For example, if you happen to know about a group that supports or opposes a bill that isn't listed in our database, you can customize your data view to incorporate that knowledge. That data won't be added to our database until it's verified by our researchers, but in the meantime you can analyze the data based on the knowledge you bring.

MAPLight.org's data currently covers the U.S. Congress, the California State Legislature, and Los Angeles elected officials, with more states and cities to come. We aim to create transparency sites tracking money and politics in all 50 state legislatures.

The MAPLight.org organization, based in Berkeley, California, is lean and efficient. We use open source software to keep our costs low and our software development flexible, and we've created the technological infrastructure to build sites for all 50 states using the same software platform and visualization tools. Our financial support comes from foundations and individuals who see that a small investment in transparency yields big returns in accountability and reform.

Barriers to Transparency

It is an extraordinarily exciting time for the transparency movement. Advances in information technology have created the potential for citizens to hold legislators accountable with an immediacy that has never before been available. Yet the burgeoning transparency movement is fighting against government resistance every step of the way.

In California, for example, the state refused public access to its extensive database of how state lawmakers vote, instead opting to publish voting records one cumbersome page at a time. With our partner, the First Amendment Coalition, we sued the state of California and won public access to this database, which we will combine with campaign contributions to illuminate money's effect on politicians' votes in California.

It shouldn't take a lawsuit for the government to realize its data belongs to the people. In this new era of open government and transparency, we hope our legal settlement serves as an example to city and state governments across the country to provide public access to public information.

In the U.S. Senate, senators (as of this writing) prepare their campaign contribution records on computers but then print them out and file them on thousands of pages of paper, which the government then keys in to a computer in a slow, error-prone, expensive process that obscures who contributes to Senate campaigns until after an election. House members and U.S. presidential candidates must file electronically. It takes public organizing and outcry to get senators, states, and towns to open up and share the key information citizens need.

Conclusion

Transparency is of great value in informing citizens and helping them hold legislators accountable. But transparency isn't enough. Citizens shouldn't *have* to play watchdog for their legislators. We might hope that with more transparent data we might curb the most blatant problems, but we still have a corrupted system.

MAPLight.org's research department reveals how contributions correlate with legislation so that citizens have key information needed to draw their own conclusions about how campaign contributions affect policy. The correlations we highlight between industry and union giving and legislative outcomes do not show that one caused the other, and we do not make this claim. We do make the claim, however, that campaign contributions bias our legislative system.

In the worst case scenario, special interests buy votes. In the best case scenario, candidates who are favorable to industry interests have more money to run and win office, while candidates who take positions contrary to industry interests are unlikely to receive industry funds and thus have fewer resources for their election campaigns. Either way, Congress as a whole (and state legislatures) is biased in favor of special interests, even if no legislators change their views or votes. Campaign donations are not the only factor that influences how lawmakers vote, but with politicians continually dependent on corrupting dollars from industries seeking special access, our country will never get the solutions we need.

To solve the problems our country faces, transparency alone is not enough. Citizens need to take action. Groups such as Public Campaign (*http://publicampaign.org*), Change Congress (*http://change-congress.org*), and many others are seeking to change our corrupt system of money-dominated politics. Transparency by itself won't solve the problem, but it can highlight the problem. With the transparency work of MAPLight.org, citizens now know where to focus their efforts for change.

About the Author

 **DANIEL NEWMAN** is cofounder and executive director of MAPLight.org, a nonpartisan nonprofit illuminating the connection between money and politics in unprecedented ways. An entrepreneur and political organizer, Dan is the author of three books on speech recognition software and is the founder of Say I Can, a speech recognition firm. Dan cofounded the Berkeley Fair Elections Coalition and has served as a consultant to various political and nonprofit groups, including the Center for Voting and Democracy, the Israel Venture Network, and the Mental Health Association of San Francisco. He received an M.A. in psychology from the University of California at Berkeley, where he attended on a National Science Foundation Fellowship, and a B.A. in biomedical ethics from Brown University. He lives in Berkeley, California.

CHAPTER TWENTY-ONE

Going 2.0: Why OpenSecrets.org Opted for Full Frontal Data Sharing

Sheila Krumholz

The day arrived, rife with anticipation—and laced with trepidation. It was April 14, 2009 when the Center for Responsive Politics (CRP; *http://www.opensecrets.org/*) made our value-added campaign finance, lobbying, and other political finance data (coded by industry, standardized by organization and individual) fully "open" for the first time in our 26-year history. We had been guarding the "crown jewels"—the detailed transaction-level data that are the building blocks for everything we do—and here we were, financially strapped ourselves, but giving away what we considered precious gems. As an NGO that tracks money in politics, we are passionate about our data and particularly convinced of the need for unbiased, unassailable data of the kind CRP produces. And this data is unique at the federal level. There's nothing comparable to what we produce, in part because we pour our passion into creating and maintaining this trusted resource. CRP's data and nonpartisan analysis provide the public with the information they need to hold their government accountable while also educating the public about how money and elite influence so often control who wins political office and what laws get passed.

The Decision to Let Go of the Data

CRP has already had its own share of seriously useful research tools, beginning with our creation of a now well-tested system for categorizing contributions, a creation of former CRP

Executive Director Larry Makinson. Larry had actually created this system for state-level contributions in Alaska and came to CRP suggesting that the same system could be applied, and tailored, to federal politicians. This was really the first chapter in CRP's history. The second chapter began with the launch of our site (then called CRP.org) in 1996, which included political action committee (PAC) profiles, an individual donor search feature, and the essential elements of funding for every member of Congress, including total funding by industry and top organizations. Sections for presidential candidates, congressional committees, and national parties, among others, followed. Then, in 2000 we published online profiles of all political money by industry—including not only totals back to 1989, but also summary highlights such as top contributors and top recipients. Even back then, there were misgivings about "putting it all out there" and how no one would ever call or cite us again because the information is free. Anyone can *just take it*! Which was, of course, precisely the idea. Nine years later, lo and behold, we're still standing.

Incorporating data on lobbying—the other side of the coin to campaign contributions—in 1997 was another leap forward in covering the major ways that elite influence can skew our nation's politics and priorities. The "revolving door," a companion database covering the traffic between government and "K Street" (shorthand for the lobbying industry), came online in 2006. Keying data from politicians' convoluted personal financial disclosure reports was another big boon to the study of influence, allowing anyone to more effectively monitor potential conflicts of interest, to instantaneously find those who have both jurisdiction over an industry or company and substantial holdings in it. All three of these data sets were funded substantially by Sunlight Foundation. And since 2003, CRP has offered up in-depth analyses of "heavy hitters," detailing the biggest firms and specific organizations bankrolling U.S. politics.

And we had already dipped our toe in the "open data" water. First, we had often waived fees for people and projects that had no funding themselves. Even when we did charge—unless the requester was well funded—our fee was usually nominal. But more importantly, in 2007 we began to create customized, private application programming interfaces (APIs), and in the summer of 2008 we published our first public APIs and widgets. (*APIs* allow users to get a data feed directly into their own sites, providing continually updated, "streaming" data for display on their own sites. *Widgets* are small graphical presentations of CRP data—and are now available for users to plug into their own sites or blogs.) Users can also "embed this chart" for even easier use of our analyses.

It's Not Easy Being Open

In fact, during the 2008 presidential election cycle, our team was literally working around the clock to post the latest data following first quarterly—and then monthly—reports. It was insane! As soon as a filing appeared on the Federal Election Commission (FEC) website (see Figure 21-1), we had to gather, process, code, standardize, proof, publish, analyze, and report on these massive sets of contribution data beginning within hours of their being filed.

FEC FORM 1

STATEMENT OF ORGANIZATION

FILING FEC-440891

1. Obama for America

PO Box 8102
Chicago, IL 60680
Email: ageitner@barackobama.com

NOTE: Email address is different than previously reported

FIGURE 21-1. Example of an FEC filing

We could achieve this *only* because our staff was so dedicated to getting it done (and, let it be said, by occasionally roping in the dean of this research, Larry Makinson). After all of that effort, the last thing we wanted to do was shackle it with subscription fees or further restrict access. We wanted to make it available as quickly as possible to the millions of people who visited our site last year—and the reporters, bloggers, and activists who were waiting to use this information in analyses geared for their audiences.

It also proved a relief, to be honest, to be able to simply put our data out there and say "Come and get it." This seemed preferable to wasting time creating little data sets here and there for folks who could do it themselves—if only they had access to what we had internally. We were wasting time invoicing and collecting payment. Or trying. (We found we aren't a very good collection agency.) For years we had tried to scrape together pennies by charging not just for research, but also for the data itself. We almost reached the point of launching a subscription-only website to make transaction-level detail accessible to what we assumed would be "advanced users"—journalists, mostly, and maybe some new media types and for-profit corporations. But it was not a satisfying feeling to cater to these few, relatively well-off interests when people have grown to expect online data to be open and free. It was especially frustrating because our very mission, our core raison d'être, is to disseminate our information to the *public*, to educate voters, to encourage average Americans to take our research and *do something* with it.

So, we did it. We chucked the subscription model and instead listened to the steady drumbeat coming from open data devotees (notably CRP board member Ellen Miller, who as cofounder and executive director of Sunlight Foundation has been a major funder of CRP, and Sunlight Labs' former chief data architect and open data evangelist, Greg Elin), and threw wide the doors. The obvious rationale, as championed for years by our many users—especially journalists, academics, activists, and data geeks—was that our research would be disseminated far more widely if we offered it up freely, rather than selling it by the record. We knew this instinctively; it was never in question. The *only* question? Cost recovery. And our funders were encouraging us to generate income. For 20 years, we split the difference by charging less than we thought it was worth—and frequently reducing fees, or waiving them altogether.

Finally, though, the positive aspects of open data won over CRP's board and staff. First, it would reduce those financial and technical barriers that then prevented many organizations from using CRP data to tell the stories of particular relevance to their audiences. So, we were tempted to see what might happen if we expanded our audience to include everybody else's audience. We were confident we had the best data and we were contextualizing it well, but we wanted to see what others could add to it. We were tired of the administrative aspect of charging—and spending so much time creating custom data sets on demand. Furthermore, in the "age of transparency," it seemed important to us that we live up to our own standards of disclosure. Sure, we felt justified in retaining control of the value we added to the data, in part because we were funded by private sources, not taxpayers. And those sources were telling us to generate income to diversify our funding, to become more self-reliant. Still, that didn't appear to make a difference to most of the open data community. And—importantly—those carrots didn't serve as the only motivators. A stick also appeared: Sunlight Foundation announced that it would only fund projects that made its data wholly and freely available to the public. Losing the support of Sunlight could have been disastrous for the Center.

So, with all of these obvious, even critical, benefits, one might think the choice was a no-brainer. But it wasn't. At least not from our vantage point.

Creating a New Model for Transparency

In 2008, CRP stood at a crossroads; one we felt might well turn out to be a choice between the yellow brick road and a long walk off a short plank. Our stalwart supporters in the foundation world agreed that our research was as essential as ever—but funding began to contract. The same was true for other organizations in our field, so we didn't take it personally. "(Foundation) boards get bored," as one foundation officer—who had funded us for nearly 20 years—put it to me. So, it seemed clear to us that the time for fresh thinking and a new approach was never better. We needed to find a way to attract new attention—and new funding—to sustain the organization and the important research we've been conducting for the past 20 years. Like news media, we endeavored to recognize the changing environment in which we're operating, and then adjust.

Of course, some of this is semantics. While *campaign finance* may sound like a dated term and has clearly lost some sheen as an issue for foundations, government transparency and accountability has never been hotter. It's not that the funders thought our work was any less relevant; we just couldn't call it campaign finance. And it *was* more than that: lobbyists became the bogeymen of the 2008 presidential campaign, yet perhaps surprisingly, their place in Washington remains salient. Earmarks, both the nutty and those nakedly used as trading chits by members of Congress, still merit front-page treatment—and FBI investigations. Powerful special interests have continued to reap both riches and resentment when energy or health care costs soar, but now they are also standing in line for the Troubled Assets Relief Program (TARP) Recovery Act, and any other public handout they can justify. Since transparency—and tracking elite influence—has been CRP's essence since day one, this is our sweet spot, and it should be our heyday.

But ironically, despite being a major player in the transparency field since even before the field had a name, that wasn't our image. We needed to redefine ourselves. As is so often the case in life, image, language, and shameless self-promotion really do make a difference, perhaps nowhere more so than in Washington. Instead of promoting our work, we were slogging it out in the trenches, doing what we do best. We primarily relied on the mainstream press to cite us in their stories for our outreach and promotion strategy. But we slowly began to recognize that this wasn't leveraging the variety of new methods for disseminating information that had appeared online since the late 1990s. Part of this reality is the nature of our research. As an organization, CRP historically wasn't looking to be first, necessarily. We were striving to be comprehensive—and right.

To take advantage of the new forms of communicating with the world, we needed to return to our core mission. We generally felt successful in helping to reshape the American public's distilled understanding of how policy is made (adding an important footnote—"*aided by money for campaign contributions and lobbying"—to that *Schoolhouse Rock* jingle about how a bill gets signed into law). The next step: continue connecting the dots, telling the stories behind the numbers, and crucially, helping *others* to tell the stories to *their* audiences using solid, reliable, CRP-branded data. CRP may or may not get the media citation in the future. (In fact, ironically, if our strategy succeeds we'll probably get less and less.) But we do hope to be a partner on some groundbreaking investigations by (what's left of) traditional media, new media, and a whole host of individuals brought in through technology and open data communities. And we hope that all of us, whether together or apart, can create interesting new lines of inquiry and graphical visualizations using this research. Finally, we aim to be the "Intel Inside" for political stories that incorporate facts about how money greases the skids in Washington.

The Future Is Now

So, what's next? We know what we *hope* will happen. But really, who knows? It's an experiment, a leap of faith, perhaps. However, a few things are certain. Data enthusiasts are already happy—and busy—grabbing, mining, and mashing up our data with their own. (Some of them are perhaps happier than they deserve to be—ahem, *data brokers*. It *is* a noncommercial license, after all.) Journalists now have an easier time getting the nuggets of information they are looking for—whether simple stats or complicated analyses—without having to call us and explain what they want (previously requiring much back and forth) to put their request "in the queue." Furthermore, as seasoned journalists take buyouts, our work serving up reliable, value-added data will help fill the growing hole in investigative journalism. We will also provide useful tools at "very affordable rates" (i.e., free) for new journalistic enterprises struggling to compensate for a traditional media in decline.

Activist and nonprofit groups such as Common Cause (*http://www.commoncause.org*) and LittleSis (*http://littlesis.org/*) (a project of the Public Accountability Initiative) are finally able to use our data without worry about cost or delay. And academics may finally obtain *all* the data, to do the kinds of analyses that only sizable data sets allow without swallowing up meager grant funding. Most importantly, academics will produce scholarly work that never fell within CRP's mandate or capacity to create, but will expand our knowledge about how money truly influences politics and policy.

Perhaps most exciting is the ideal timing for going open with regard to empowering citizen watchdogs. After the intense interest Americans displayed in the 2008 presidential election and the degree to which people of all partisan stripes now participate and engage in the process and debate, feeding CRP data into the centrifuge of citizen analysis makes perfect sense. We're confident that data developers and web developers will incorporate CRP information to create new tools for democracy activists, build and empower new communities, and—ultimately—educate and engage more voters. It's already happening. MAPLight.org is a perfect example, taking CRP data on contributions to members of Congress and mashing it up with voting records. OpenCongress.org uses CRP's API to stream data into its profiles of bills pending in Congress. Sunlight Foundation will incorporate CRP data into a future "data commons," which will connect volumes of distinct but related data sets. And new sites are cropping up all the time using clever and useful visualizations, distributed initiatives, and interesting new combinations—usually on low or no budget.

Conclusion

Open data, we believe, will enhance CRP's reach and utility. Not only will distribution of our research be more efficient and widespread, but we may also focus more of our attention on the critical work of showing the links between money and influence. CRP's Capital Eye blog (*http://www.opensecrets.org/news/*) and e-newsletter are critical to making these connections for people. But more is needed to explain to a general audience how a tiny elite uses its political influence to shape everything from gas prices to our health care options. And of course, CRP will continue to maintain up-to-date data on OpenSecrets.org because, although bulk data is a huge boon to tech-savvy users, a reporter or blogger looking for one figure does not want to download literally millions of records. Furthermore, most users probably do not need (or possess) the skills or comfort level to accurately process and use massive data sets.

OpenSecrets.org continues to evolve. Concurrent with the "OpenData" release, we expanded our "Member Profiles" to the top 100 organizations and *all* industries, and simultaneously made these tables downloadable in various formats. We'll expand these further so that users may ask what should be a simple question: did Congressman A get money from Organization B? Getting that answer is still not as easy as it should be, but it will be much easier once we add all of our standardized employer information (instead of just raw FEC data) to the individual donor search section. This is among the most valuable—and unique—tools that nobody other than CRP offers, yet we hadn't allowed access to that data on OpenSecrets, even though the donor lookup feature is one of the most popular on the entire website! Therefore, very soon we will reprogram the donor lookup to deliver our clean, uniquely CRP data, instead of holding it back.

CRP is poised to add new features to OpenSecrets.org that maximize user flexibility and to connect the dots more effectively—linking individual and organizational donor dossiers to lobbyists, their clients, and politicians' personal financial holdings. These will be integrated, and then presented with interactive options, not presented as static add-ons. And they need to pull from useful, related troves of data that other organizations publish and maintain, while also enabling new features on their sites that speak to their audiences. One such CRP mashup compares campaign contributions to earmarks, incorporating data from Taxpayers for Common Sense. And FedSpending.org (and now the government's own USASpending.gov) makes it easy for us to incorporate government contracts that those earmarks subsidize. Especially as the Obama administration and Congress tackle wide-ranging policy debates such as health care, energy policy, and the re-regulation of Wall Street, these dossiers of leading Washington players could emerge as vital tools to clarify and inform the debate—on our site and, now, on many, many other sites too.

About the Author

SHEILA KRUMHOLZ is the Center for Responsive Politics's executive director, serving as the organization's chief administrator, the liaison to its board and major funders, and its primary spokesperson. Sheila became executive director in December 2006, having served for eight years as CRP's research director, supervising data analysis for OpenSecrets.org and CRP's clients. She first joined the CRP staff in 1989 and was assistant editor of the very first edition of Open Secrets, the Center's flagship publication.

CHAPTER TWENTY-TWO

All Your Data Are Belong to Us: Liberating Government Data

Jerry Brito

When government refuses to make itself transparent and open and fails to make public information meaningfully available, hackers will liberate the data. It has happened many times over, and it will doubtlessly happen again. Each time government data is freed, citizens gain useful access to valuable information that rightly belongs to them. But perhaps more importantly, government is forced to deal with the new reality of a networked world in which the people demand free online access to public information.

Data is liberated by hacking government. Because of how the popular press has used it, the word *hack* is often misunderstood to mean only illicit access to computer networks. In fact, to techies that is only one possible meaning. According to Wikipedia, the term usually means "a clever or quick fix to a computer program problem" or "a modification of a program or device to give the user access to features that were otherwise unavailable to them."

Liberating Government Data: Carl Malamud Versus the Man

Carl Malamud is probably the original government hacker. A technologist, activist, and entrepreneur, Malamud is well known for having forced the U.S. Securities and Exchange Commission (SEC) to make much of its public data available to the public over the Internet in 1995. At that time, the SEC did not provide free access to the corporate filings it collected. Instead, the SEC's database, the Electronic Data Gathering Analysis and Retrieval system

(EDGAR), was operated under contract with information wholesaler Mead Data, which provided data feeds to data retailers who in turn sold access to the public. According to John Markoff, author of the *New York Times* article "Plan Opens More Data to Public" (*http://www .nytimes.com/1993/10/22/business/plan-opens-more-data-to-public.html*), "Under this system, a retail information provider, like Mead Data's own Nexis service, charge[d] about $15 for each S.E.C. document, plus a connection charge of $39 an hour and a printing charge of about $1 a page." One can imagine customers were largely limited to firms on Wall Street.

After first trying and failing to convince the SEC that it should make its database available on the Internet, Malamud began to purchase the SEC's wholesale data and made it available on his own website free of charge to anyone. The service included corporate annual reports, 10-K filings, proxy statements, and other data valuable to investors, journalists, and others. In December of that year, Malamud expanded his free offerings by adding large portions of the U.S. Patent and Trademark Office's (PTO) patent and trademark database, including full text of all patents, and text and images from the trademark database.

Malamud, however, always believed that it was government's responsibility to provide its data for free to the public, especially since the then-recently enacted Paperwork Reduction Act mandated that agencies make public information available electronically. On August 11, 1995, Malamud announced on his website that it would discontinue its free access to government data on October 1. As Malamud later recounted (*http://www.mundi.net/cartography/EDGAR*):

> Our goal, however, wasn't to be in the database business. Our goal was to have the SEC serve their own data on the Internet. After we built up our user base, I decided it was time to force the issue. That's when the fireworks began. When users visited our EDGAR system in August 1995, they got an interesting message:
>
> This Service Will Terminate in 60 Days Click Here For More Information
>
> Click here they did! One of the lessons I've learned from building Internet services is that when people get something for free, they want their money's worth.

The message informed users that under no circumstances would the unofficial service be continued, and suggested that it was "time for the stakeholders in this data to step up to the plate and forge a solution." It also asked users to write to Congress and the administration, which they did.

The SEC at first resisted. Eventually, however, it relented and the agency took over Malamud's service as the core of a new online EDGAR system. The public uproar apparently caught SEC commissioners off guard and they took on the responsibility of making data available before Malamud's October deadline. According to Malamud, "The commissioners of the SEC had clearly not been aware of the issue, but there is nothing like pieces in the *Wall Street Journal* and 15,000 messages to the Chairman to raise the profile of an issue" (*http://www.mundi.net/ cartography/EDGAR*).

Malamud had similar plans for his patent and trademark database. In 1998, he wrote to Vice President Al Gore and Commerce Secretary William Daley (who oversaw the PTO), announcing that unless the PTO began offering its databases on the Internet, he would create a free and robust online alternative. In the years since Malamud first put a patent database online in 1994, the PTO had not been as accommodating as the SEC. The agency was self-financed by user fees, a large portion of which came from requests for paper copies of patent and trademark information. As the commissioner for patents told the *New York Times* (*http://www.nytimes.com/1998/05/04/business/us-is-urged-to-offer-more-data-on-line.html*), "If he can [put the patent and trademark database online] we'd be out all $20 million we now receive in fees.... Why would anyone want paper?"

Malamud's strategy to overcome government's resistance was a familiar one. "I'm going to buy the trademark data and will build the user base as big as I can in a year," Malamud said at the time. "At the end of the year, I'll pull the rug out from the users and give them Al Gore's E-mail address" (*http://www.nytimes.com/1998/05/04/business/us-is-urged-to-offer-more-data-on-line.html*). The gambit worked, and less than two months later the Clinton administration announced that it would put the full patent database online. In each instance, by forcefully but legally releasing online data that the government had either not disclosed on the Internet or not made easily accessible, Malamud was able to effect a change in policy that led to a more open and transparent government (see Chapter 14).

Disclosing Government Data: Paper Versus the Internet

The United States is one of the most open and transparent countries in the world. Citizens generally have the right to inspect the records, minutes, balance sheets, and votes of almost all public bodies.

Laws encouraging government transparency and accountability have been a feature of the U.S. system of government since the founding of the Republic. The Constitution, for example, requires that each house of Congress "keep a Journal of its Proceedings, and from time to time publish the same, excepting such Parts as may in their Judgment require Secrecy." Today, the Congressional Record satisfies this requirement.

Unfortunately, many of the statutory requirements for disclosure do not take Internet technology into account. For example, the 1978 Ethics in Government Act requires the disclosure of financial information—including the source, type, and amount of income—by many federal employees, elected officials, and candidates for office, including the president and vice president, and members of Congress. The act further requires that all filings be available to the public, subject to certain limited exceptions. One might imagine, then, that every representative's or senator's information would be just a web search away, but one would be wrong.

Members of the House of Representatives must file their disclosures with the clerk of the House of Representatives, while senators must do the same with the secretary of the Senate. Each of these offices maintains a searchable electronic database of the filings. However, until very recently, to access these databases citizens had to go to Washington, D.C., and visit those Capitol Hill offices during business hours. There were no other means of searching the databases, something that presented a major barrier to the widespread dissemination of nominally publicly available information. Even today, the disclosure forms offered are scanned images that are not easily searched or parsed.

The result is that to make the information available online, third parties such as transparency website LegiStorm (*http://www.legistorm.com/*) must acquire paper copies of the forms and manually scan and parse them. In contrast, the clerk of the House and the secretary of the Senate could likely make their existing databases available online at little extra cost. LegiStorm also offers something the official sites still won't: financial disclosure forms for congressional staffers, not just members.

So, why would government fail to take advantage of the benefits of online disclosure? Not only would using standard Internet technologies make it easier for citizens to find and access government information, but it would probably also present efficiencies and cost savings to government itself. In most cases, the obstacle is likely bureaucratic inertia. In other cases, however, government will have little incentive, and often a disincentive, to make public information easily accessible.

Sometimes, as we saw with the PTO, government agencies make data freely available, but collect user fees for easy access to that data. This can create an incentive to protect the revenue stream at the expense of wider public access to government information. In other instances, government reticence to make data easily accessible can have political motivations.

Accessing Government Data: Open Distribution Versus Jealous Control

Much like Josh Tauberer's GovTrack.us, the *Washington Post*'s Congress Votes database allows users to easily search and sort through a database of congressional bills and votes. When the *Post* was building its site, the House offered its roll call votes in XML, a standard machine-readable format, while the Senate did not. This forced the *Post*, like GovTrack, to rely on cumbersome "screen scraping" of Senate web pages to make their roll call votes usable (see Chapter 18).

In 2007, however, co-creator Derek Willis was poking around the Senate website when he discovered a directory of XML files of vote data for past sessions. This demonstrated that the Senate had the ability to make its votes available online in a structured format. Willis was elated at the thought that perhaps there was easy access to Senate vote data after all. He wrote to the Senate webmaster asking whether structured voting data was available for the current session and, if so, whether this data would be made public. The telling response read, in part, as follows:

A few representative votes (only a few from the early congresses) were published out to the active site during some testing periods. I really need to remove them from the site.

We are not authorized to publish the XML structured vote information. The Committee on Rules and Administration has authorized us to publish vote tally information in HTML format [not a structured format]. Senators prefer to be the ones to publish their own voting records. As you know, looking at a series of vote results by Senator or by subject does not tell the whole story. Senators have a right to present and comment on their votes to their constituents in the manner they prefer. This issue was reviewed again recently and the policy did not change.

Senators doubtlessly would "prefer to be the ones to publish their own voting records." But jealous control over information by government is anathema to democracy. Looking at a series of votes by a senator does in fact tell the "whole story" of that senator's voting record, and despite what the webmaster said, senators do not have a "right" to present their votes to the public "in the manner they prefer." Of course, this only motivated hackers such as Willis and Tauberer further.

When third parties make government data available, it demonstrates that it is possible to do so cheaply and efficiently. In some cases, officials can be unaware of what is technically possible, or they may believe that state-of-the-art technology is prohibitively expensive. Freeing information can also generate an awareness and demand for the newly accessible data among citizens. This can lead to embarrassing questions for government: why isn't it making the data available itself? Why are citizens forced to hack the data in order to access it? Also, hacking government data can demonstrate to cautious officials that when information is made accessible and useful, the world does not end.

In fact, since GovTrack.us and the *Washington Post* Congress Votes database (*http://projects .washingtonpost.com/congress/*) brought attention to the issue, the Senate Rules Committee finally relented and has recently begun to make roll call votes available in XML. Two years after Derek Willis was rebuffed by the Senate webmaster, a group of seemingly embarrassed senators wrote to Committee Chairman Chuck Schumer demanding a repeal of the prohibition on XML.

"This policy has created a situation where outside groups are forced to create databases that are more likely to contain errors and omissions," they wrote. "The suggestion that the Senate would intentionally hamstring the distribution of roll call votes so Senators could put a better spin on them is concerning. The public is capable of interpreting our votes on its own."

Demanding Government Data: Public Money Versus Private Research

The release of Congressional Research Service (CRS) reports is another example of hacking that is slowly leading to change. CRS is a think tank for Congress that is funded by U.S. taxpayers to the tune of $100 million per year. It produces objective in-depth briefings and high-quality research papers on topical public policy issues. The studies it produces are widely well regarded, and members of Congress and their staffs rely on them as they legislate.

By law, however, CRS can make its reports available only to members of Congress. There are several oft-cited rationales for this policy. First is the idea that by releasing reports directly to the public, CRS would come between lawmakers and their constituents. There is also the concern that if CRS reports were widely disseminated, they would come to be written with a public audience in mind, rather than focusing on congressional needs. Finally, some fear a burden on CRS and congressional staff members who might have to respond to questions and comments generated by publicly available reports. Not surprisingly, several third parties who are not persuaded by these rationales have taken it upon themselves to collect and make the reports available on the Web.

Members of Congress are free to release copies of the reports to citizens if they wish, and they often do so at the request of a constituent. Unfortunately, constituents must first know of a report's existence before they can request it. There is no public listing of all the available titles, so the fear is that embarrassing reports are never released. Once a report is released, however, one is free to copy and disseminate it because works of the U.S. government are not protected by copyright.

For several years, many organizations, including the Federation of American Scientists and the National Council for Science and the Environment, have published on their websites hundreds of CRS reports related to their research areas that they have collected over the years. In 2005, the Center for Democracy and Technology (CDT), a nonprofit dedicated to Internet public policy issues, brought the different CRS collections under one roof at OpenCRS.com. There, users can search the combined collections of CDT and partner groups, which total more than 8,000 CRS reports.

More importantly, the site invites users to upload to the online library reports that they have acquired. It also provides a list of CRS reports that are missing from the library and instructions on how citizens can request them from their representatives. CDT acquires this list from a sympathetic but anonymous member of Congress who provides it on a regular basis. Further compromising the secrecy surrounding CRS reports, in February 2009 whistleblower site WikiLeaks.org released 6,780 CRS reports, which it said "represents the total output of the Congressional Research Service electronically available to Congressional offices" (*http:// wikileaks.org/wiki/Change_you_can_download:_a_billion_in_secret_Congressional_reports*).

For more than a decade, lawmakers sympathetic to open government have perennially introduced bills or resolutions to make CRS reports public. While these efforts have so far failed, the vast number of CRS reports now available to the public on third-party sites undercut the rationales for a policy of selective release. Citizens have access to a wide array of CRS reports, yet the quality of those reports has not suffered, CRS's institutional character has not been diminished, and constituent relationships with representatives remain intact. As unofficial collections of CRS reports continue to grow, not only will citizens benefit from access to this information, but the selective release policy will become increasingly untenable and ripe for change.

RECAP: Freeing PACER Documents for Public Use

As long as some public documents are out of reach online, third parties will be motivated to free them. Carl Malamud's most recent intellectual descendants may be a team of hacker scholars dedicated to liberating the millions of pages of public records now locked behind a paywall on the federal court's online database. Stephen Schultze, Tim Lee, and Harlan Yu of the Center for Information Technology Policy at Princeton developed a web browser plug-in—RECAP (*https://www.recapthelaw.org/*)—that distributes the hacking of the court database among many users.

Each day, federal courts around the country generate thousands of pages of court filings, transcripts, judgments, and opinions—all of public interest. Free access to these documents is guaranteed to all citizens, so long as you visit the courthouse in question during business hours. The Public Access to Court Electronic Records (PACER) system was created in 1988 as a dial-up service that charged by the minute and afforded attorneys convenient remote access to court dockets and filings. In 1998, the system was migrated to the Web, and the per minute charge was replaced by a charge per page downloaded.

Today, PACER charges 8 cents per page accessed, which doesn't sound like much. However, the charge is completely out of proportion with how much it costs the court system to make the data available. As a result, the court system has found its IT budget with a substantial surplus. Some estimate that in 2006, the cost to maintain PACER was about $27 million, yet the system brought in $62 million in revenue.

This is not a concern for lawyers, who pass their costs on to clients, or to commercial data retailers, such as Westlaw and LexisNexis, that purchase their data in bulk and benefit from the lack of convenient free access to court records. However, scholars, journalists, and average citizens are left without free online access to court records.

Schultze, Lee, and Yu's scheme to free the documents on PACER is an ingenious one. They have built a Firefox plug-in called RECAP that attorneys, librarians, and other regular users of PACER can install on their computers. When a user downloads a document from PACER, the plug-in sends a copy to RECAP's server, where it is made publicly available. If enough PACER users install RECAP, it will only be a matter of time before the entire database is liberated.

This is a brilliant system, but it raises the obvious question: altruistic motives aside, why would attorneys or other PACER users install the RECAP plug-in? The answer is just as brilliant. When a user clicks to download a document from PACER, the RECAP plug-in first searches its own server to see whether that document has already been made publicly available. If it has, then it is served to the user, who avoids PACER's download charges. Additionally, the RECAP plug-in adds some nice touches, including reformatting the document filename and adding useful metadata.

Although it is a shot across the bow of PACER's revenue stream, RECAP is entirely legal. The court documents that RECAP shares, like CRS reports, are not subject to copyright and can be freely distributed by citizens. By creating a public repository of these documents, the RECAP team is forcing the issue and making the court system implement legal or technical countermeasures, or seek a new business model that includes public access to its documents.

Conclusion

This tough-love approach is a necessary counterpart to a public education and advocacy strategy for realizing a more open government. While we must convince citizens and government officials of the merits of transparency, talented hackers can often simply show them. When this happens the burden of proof is shifted to government. And, in turn, it's difficult to make the case that more, better, and easier access to public data isn't a good thing.

About the Author

JERRY BRITO is a senior research fellow at the Mercatus Center at George Mason University, and is director of its Technology Policy Program. He also serves as adjunct professor of law at George Mason University. His research focuses on technology and telecommunications policy, government transparency and accountability, and the regulatory process. Jerry is the creator of OpenRegs.com, an alternative interface to the federal government's regulatory docketing system, and the cocreator of the accountability website Stimulus Watch.

CHAPTER TWENTY-THREE

Case Study: Many Eyes

Fernanda Viégas
Martin Wattenberg

Crime rates in local communities. Campaign donations. Testimony before Congress. Open government connotes open data. The Obama administration has acted on this premise and produced a series of websites that will function as repositories for government data, at both national and state levels. The next step for public engagement will be to make sense of this data. Visualization can help.

Visualization is a key medium for communication in a data-rich world. It can have a catalytic effect on data "storytelling" and collective analysis. We have seen examples of that power in Many Eyes (*http://www.many-eyes.com*), a public website we launched where anyone can upload and visualize data. The site fosters a social style of data analysis that empowers users to engage with public data through discussion and collaboration. Political debate, citizen activism, religious conversations, game playing, and educational exchanges are all happening on Many Eyes. The public nature of these visualizations provides users with a transformative path to information literacy.

Policy

Citizens are starting to realize the power of interactive visualization to help make sense of the political world around them at both the national and local levels. In this section, we will illustrate how people have been using visualization to think and talk about policy, the economy, the health of their communities, and their expectations for government.

Looking closely at one's own backyard can be quite revealing. This is what Jon Udell, a prominent blogger, did when he created a series of Many Eyes visualizations of crime statistics in his hometown of Keene, New Hampshire. Udell wanted to understand whether the facts supported rumors of a crime wave in the area. After looking at the graphs and comparing historical, national, and local trends, Jon concluded that the perception of a local crime surge was not warranted. He then created a screencast documenting his motivating questions, the data collection process, the visualizations he created, and how playing with the visualizations helped him deduce that perception was harsher than reality. His blog post on this screencast generated a healthy number of comments, some of them from people who were hoping to do the same kind of analysis in their own communities.

In addition to individual citizens, institutions have also been making use of Many Eyes visualizations to monitor the economic and political world around them. ProPublica, a nonprofit newsroom for investigative journalism, has used Many Eyes to cover a range of issues from unemployment insurance to weatherization projects in the United States. One of the most popular visualizations ProPublica created is a *treemap* of the February 2009 federal stimulus bill (see Figure 23-1). The interactive visualization was embedded on the ProPublica website and became one of a series of charts created to follow the bill as it passed both the House and Congress deliberations.

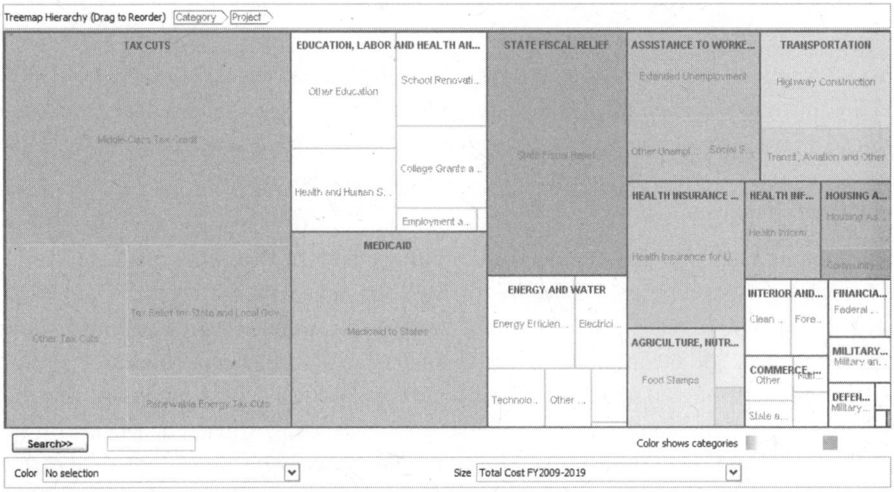

FIGURE 23-1. Visualizing the federal stimulus bill of February 2009; rectangle size corresponds to amount of money allocated (Many Eyes treemap created by ProPublica)

Another example shows both the power of visualization to make an argument engaging, and the potential for web-based visualizations to spread to new sites and audiences. Sunlight Foundation used data on congressional "earmarks" to create Many Eyes *bubble charts* (a new visualization technique that represents a set of numbers by circles whose areas are proportional to the underlying numbers); see Figure 23-2. A number of blogs picked up the visually striking results. We then saw one of these charts appear in a video created by law professor and reformer Lawrence Lessig, who used it as evidence of the favoritism that permeates the lawmaking process.

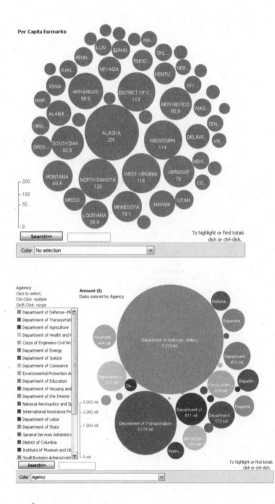

FIGURE 23-2. Earmark bubble charts created by Sunlight Foundation; the visualization on the top shows the amount of money per state in 2005, and the visualization on the bottom shows the amount of money per government agency in 2005

Visualization can function as an accessible way to engage with intimidating amounts of textual data as well as numeric data. In March 2009, President Obama invited citizens to ask him questions about the economy in the first-ever online town hall meeting. More than 71,000 people submitted questions to the White House website. Such a collection can be hard to parse, and the Obama team combed the collection to select the questions that the president should address. But what about the entire collection of questions? As a whole, they could represent the concerns of a nation. The collection was publicly available, but vast, unstructured, and unwieldy. Shortly after the question-and-answer session, Many Eyes users busily began visualizing the entire set of submitted questions. One *phrase net* (a visualization technique introduced on the Many Eyes site; see Figure 23-3) mapped all the questions on education, revealing islands of subjects: "schools and teachers," "science and math," and "college tuition."

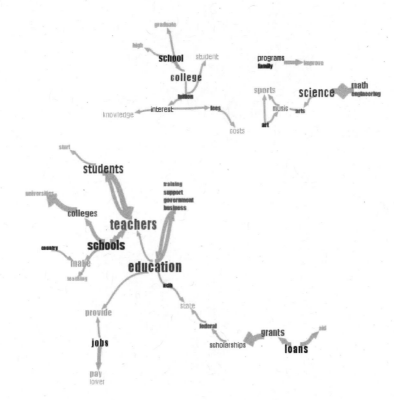

FIGURE 23-3. Visualizing questions on education that were submitted to the online town hall meeting in March 2009

From Policy to Politicians

On September 3, 2008, Alaska Governor Sarah Palin gave a speech accepting the Republican nomination for the vice president of the United States. Within 24 hours, more than a dozen visualizations of her words appeared on Many Eyes. These visualizations (including tag clouds or "wordles") were accompanied by others that sought clues to her personality and perspective, among them an Alaska State of the Union speech and an adoring column by William Kristol (see Figure 23-4).

FIGURE 23-4. Wordle of Sarah Palin's acceptance speech of September 2008

These colorful visualizations are a far cry from the numerically intensive crime visualizations described earlier. Yet they serve a clear purpose. In our representative democracy, it's not the citizens who will change policy, but the politicians they elect. Getting to know these people—their personalities, values, and motivations—is just as important as understanding the issues of the day.

Of course, politicians have always been willing to introduce themselves. (Palin's speech was a masterpiece of the art of introduction, giving the Republican ticket an instant boost in the polls.) But citizens have always treated politicians' words with a healthy dose of skepticism. It's assumed that before a speech is uploaded to a teleprompter, sent to the Associated Press, or posted to a blog, it has been dutifully vetted to remove anything that might be too revealing.

One of the most interesting uses of text visualization is to find a new perspective on carefully manicured words. With the right tools, it might be possible to uncover a perspective that a politician's handlers did not plan for. We saw examples of this search for meanings on Many Eyes. One user, for instance, created a *comparison tag cloud* showing John McCain's blog contrasted with the blog of his 23-year-old daughter Meghan, who was appearing with him on the campaign trail (see Figure 23-5).

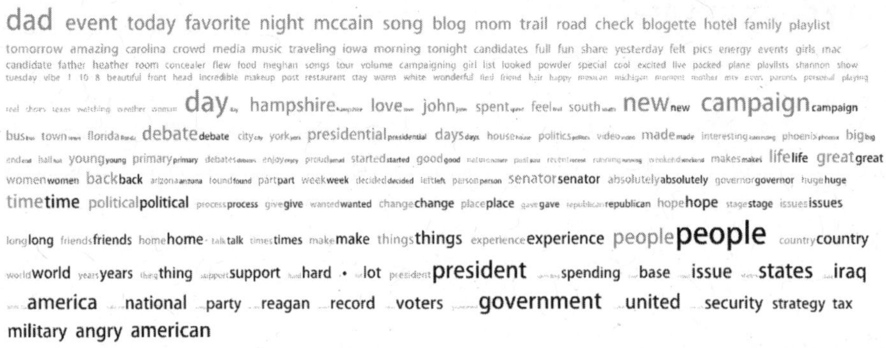

FIGURE 23-5. Comparative tag cloud of two McCain blogs: John's (in dark text) and Meghan's (in light text)

In this visualization, the words in orange are taken from Meghan's blog, while the words in blue are from John's. The size of each word tells how frequently it occurs, and the words are sorted from more frequent use in Meghan's blog (top) to more frequent use in John's (bottom). The comparison ends up being a kind of filter, with common and clichéd words in the center (*time*, *things*, *senator*). At the bottom, however, we see the three words *military*, *angry*, and *American*. At a time when McCain's campaign was trying to project a softer image, it is interesting to see *anger* take a prominent place.

In some cases, a politician may not be merely spinning but actively evading an issue. A recent notorious case was the 2007 testimony of then–Attorney General Alberto Gonzales, regarding the firing of U.S. lawyers. After one of the Many Eyes team members put up a *word tree visualization* of his testimony, showing the prevalence of the phrase "I don't recall" (see Figure 23-6), another user on the site quickly followed with an analogous visualization of Bill Clinton's words in another famous piece of testimony (see Figure 23-7). In this case, the creation of the visualization may be seen as a kind of debate statement in itself—not about policy, but about making the point that evasive testimony crosses party lines.

Visual Literacy

How broadly accessible are these sometimes esoteric visualizations? There's no doubt that some of the visualization activity on Many Eyes (and other sites) is created by, and plays to, an early-adopter audience that enjoys engaging with data for its own sake. But at the same time there is evidence that both creators and viewers of the visualizations are a diverse group. In interviews with Many Eyes users, we learned that some of the most active users had never worked with data before—and in at least one case, had never used a spreadsheet. We have also seen more than a dozen different classes use Many Eyes for class assignments, indicating that some teachers are putting an emphasis on teaching visual literacy.

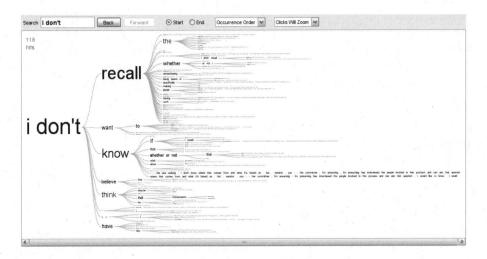

FIGURE 23-6. Word tree of Alberto Gonzales's 2007 testimony before Congress

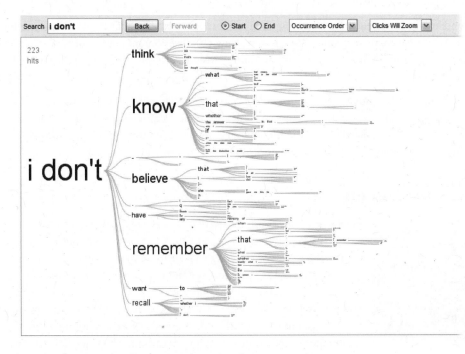

FIGURE 23-7. Word tree of Bill Clinton's 1998 grand jury testimony

Indeed, new and unusual visualization types seem to have the power to pique readers' interests. Part of what drew bloggers to the earmark bubble chart, for instance, may have been its striking appearance. We certainly see this happening elsewhere as well. Alluring charts and graphs from the *New York Times* and CNN, for instance, have become national conversation pieces. CNN launched an interactive wall that visualized the evolution of voting patterns during the last presidential election. The *New York Times* has used interactive visualizations to cover a variety of subjects, ranging from the war in Iraq to how Congress questions Supreme Court nominees.

Conclusion

Our experiences with Many Eyes suggest three principles for how visualization can help with open government.

First, statistical graphics ground debate in reality. For readers, they are effective at communicating basic aspects of an issue. But just as important is the fact that graphs and charts impose a kind of discipline on authors. To create an illuminating visualization, a writer must gather a complete data set, which usually means finding and checking original sources. As we saw with the example of crime in Keene, this process may cause an author to rethink his original point and a healthy debate to ensue.

Second, text is data. People have become used to showing numbers in bar charts or line graphs, but the ability to create diagrams of text is new. New visualizations aimed at words rather than numbers hold out the hope of providing unfiltered insight into the minds of politicians and citizens alike.

Finally, readers today are becoming visually literate. We've seen broad uptake and popularity of visualizations that are complex, sophisticated, and often unfamiliar. As far as we can tell, readers are good at understanding the message of complex visualizations, and an unusual diagram is often an active draw for audiences rather than a turnoff.

About the Authors

 **FERNANDA VIÉGAS** and **MARTIN WATTENBERG** are research scientists in IBM's Visual Communication Lab. Viégas is known for her pioneering work on depicting chat histories and email. Wattenberg's visualizations of the stock market and baby names are considered Internet classics. Both Viégas and Wattenberg are also known for their visualization-based artwork, which has been exhibited in venues such as the Museum of Modern Art in New York, the London Institute of Contemporary Arts, and the Whitney Museum of American Art. The two became a team in 2003 when they decided to visualize Wikipedia, leading to the "history flow" project that revealed the self-healing nature of the online encyclopedia. They are currently exploring the power of web-based visualization and the social forms of data analysis it enables.

CHAPTER TWENTY-FOUR

My Data Can't Tell You That

Bill Allison

In April 2009, the Bureau of Labor Statistics, in its monthly Employment Situation update, reported that some 539,000 Americans lost their jobs, pushing the total number of job losses since the recession began to more than 5.7 million. Job losses were widespread across all economic sectors; the unemployment rate rose to 8.9%.*

The worsening employment picture contradicted projections made by a pair of advisors to the incoming administration of President Barack Obama. On January 10, 2009, in a report titled "The Job Impact of the American Recovery and Reinvestment Plan," Christina Romer and Jared Bernstein suggested that, with a $775 million stimulus bill, unemployment would peak at around 7%—in the fourth quarter of 2009. In fairness to Romer and Bernstein, they also cautioned that their estimates were just that—estimates. Nevertheless, actual job losses, which occurred even though Congress passed a slightly heftier $787 billion American Recovery and Reinvestment Act, galloped along much faster than the pair of advisors said would occur if Congress had done nothing. Absent a stimulus, they warned, the unemployment rate could hit 9% sometime in late 2009. In reality, the U.S. unemployment rate reached 9.4% in May.

Around the time these job loss numbers were coming out, I started looking into the Obama administration's efforts to make stimulus spending as transparent as possible. I began with the idea of doing a quick review of the website, Recovery.gov, which was supposed to be the place to "follow every penny." However, as often happens to investigative reporters, it wasn't long before I had wandered far afield and started asking what was going on, not with Recovery.gov

---

* *http://www.bls.gov/opub/ted/2009/may/wk2/art02.htm*

but with the Recovery Act itself. How much money had actually gotten out to states and local communities?

It didn't take long to track down examples of projects in the works. A press release from a member of Congress boasted about dozens of local housing authorities receiving funding, including one in Mercer County, Pennsylvania, for new construction projects.

A quick review of the data available on Recovery.gov showed no record of the project. *USASpending.gov*, the federal government's one-stop shopping site for information on grants and contracts, did list the $1.7 million grant, but did not show how much, if any of it, had been spent. Looking back at previous grants, one quickly finds that while USASpending.gov lists the amount of grant money awarded to all kinds of things—thousands of public housing authorities each year—it doesn't track when spending occurs, or when it concludes. Does that mean every single federal grant spent down to the penny, in exactly the period of time for which it's given? Do grantees never spend less than they're awarded? Do they ever run out of money much sooner than expected? Do they ever have to return to the federal government for additional funds? One would never know from looking at USASpending.gov. How quickly government money actually gets to the economy—of particular interest when looking at the effectiveness of the American Recovery and Reinvestment Act—isn't something they track; their data can't tell you that.

The How and Why of Data Collection

In this brave new era of transparent government, more and more departments and agencies are publishing more and more of the data they collect online. Yet we are finding that, for this information to be useful, it requires a great deal of analysis and explication, and that *how* and *why* the data is gathered sometimes tells us as much about government as the information itself. And sadly, one of the things we'll also hear when we have vital questions to answer about the economy, health care, national defense, energy policy, the environment, and education is a response I've heard, in various forms, when I've asked government officials specific questions about the numbers they collect, record, analyze, summarize, correlate, and disseminate to the public: "My data can't tell you that."

This isn't a particularly original insight: investigative reporters, economists, academics, and others have long found fault with the accuracy of government data. I've spent most of my professional life as a researcher, reporter, and editor working with government data in one form or another, from agencies ranging from the Federal Aviation Administration to the Agriculture Department's Food Safety Inspection Service, from the Internal Revenue Service to the Defense Advanced Research Projects Agency. I've found that government officials keep track of all sorts of incredibly valuable minutiae.

Years before US Airways Flight 1549 lost engine power after hitting some birds and subsequently made an unscheduled landing in the Hudson River, civil servants were collecting from pilots and airports around the country information on incidents in which birds had interfered with the operation of aircraft. (It happens, on average, 20 times per day.) Sadly, the FAA kept that data under wraps for years. Had they made it public, perhaps biologists, pilots, statisticians, naturalists, or people who just like puzzles could have put the data to good use. Perhaps someone would have come up with countermeasures that might have kept the passengers of Flight 1549 from their wet landing.

But to do that, the data has to be reasonably accurate. And federal data can be inaccurate, misleading, or downright wrong—sometimes impossibly so. One absolute certainty we've been living with since the advent of commercial nuclear power is that the number of spent fuel assemblies—the highly radioactive metal rods that power nuclear plants—can, for practical purposes, only increase. They are lethal, and will remain so for thousands of years. They are mostly stored in cooling tanks at the nuclear power plants where they were used. Federal efforts to come up with a permanent solution for spent nuclear fuel—a process that began with the first atomic energy projects in the 1950s—have hit another dead end with the cancellation of the Yucca Mountain project.

Even if government can't find a final destination for the nation's nuclear waste, one would imagine that at least it could keep track of where it is. But that's not the case. When examining records maintained on the buildup of spent fuel assemblies at power plants across the United States for their 1985 book, *Forevermore: Nuclear Waste in America* (W.W. Norton & Company), Donald L. Barlett and James B. Steele looked at the monthly reports that the Nuclear Regulatory Commission issued on the inventories of spent fuel assemblies in nuclear plants. A nuclear-generating station in Dresden, Illinois, owned at the time by the Commonwealth Edison Company of Chicago (now called ComEd, a subsidiary of the Exelon Corporation), reported having 3,512 stored assemblies in December 1982, then 1,873 in February 1983, then 2,880 in March, then 2,054 in May. Numbers which a Commonwealth Edison representative said should "constantly be going up" were bouncing both ways.

This is especially troubling when one considers that the NRC and the nuclear industry had developed an elaborate system, one in which each fuel assembly was assigned its own serial number, to make certain that the nation's deadliest industrial waste was accurately accounted for. "When the conflicting figures…were called to the commission's attention, a spokesman said the NRC had no explanation," Barlett and Steele reported in their book. They added, "Because the federal government issues precise numbers on nuclear energy and waste production, we have used those figures. But they should be viewed, in every case, as nothing more than approximations."

Federal Data: Approximations Galore

That sort of caution is a prerequisite when approaching federal data. OMB Watch, a Washington, D.C.-based nonprofit group, keeps a close eye on federal contract and grant data. They built, with a grant from Sunlight Foundation, a database called FedSpending.org—which became the model for the government's primary site for publishing information on contracts and grants, USASpending.gov. The folks at OMB Watch noticed an anomaly in how their official government counterpart was handling companies that, through mergers, sales of business units, or spinoffs, acquire new parent companies. Halliburton, which spun off its Kellogg, Brown and Root subsidiary in 2007, was no longer listed as KBR's parent in any of the years preceding the breakup. The government in essence backdated KBR's emergence as a separate business, so anyone searching for Halliburton's government contracts would find no references to those of its controversial subsidiary.

Exactly how that problem came about is unclear—it may be a programming error, or it might be a methodological problem. Data can also go awry due to its source. In 1973, journalist Jessica Mitford noted in her seminal book *Kind & Usual Punishment: The Prison Business* (Knopf) the impact that local officials can have on the FBI's Uniform Crime Reports. These statistics, currently compiled from reports sent in from some 17,000 jurisdictions that include big-city police forces, state law enforcement agencies, university public safety offices, and small-town sheriffs, are used to justify tougher federal crime laws and larger budgets for law enforcement at the federal, state, and local levels. Yet the numbers are subject to wild fluctuations based on who collects them. "Much depends on the local police chief," Mitford wrote, "thus there was an 83 percent increase in 'major crimes known to the police' in Chicago between 1960 and 1961 when a zealous new chief revised reporting procedures."

Such difficulties persist to the present. Consider an August 8, 2008 article by Ryan Gabrielson of *The Easy Valley Tribune* that informed readers of a dispute between the mayor of Phoenix and a local law enforcement official.† Mayor Phil Gordon cited the FBI Uniform Crime Reports, which showed that violent crime rates had increased from 2006 to 2007 in Maricopa County, to criticize the county's sheriff, Joe Arpaio, a controversial figure who, among other things, once marched prisoners from one county jail to another wearing nothing but underwear and flip-flops. Gordon was less concerned about underwear than he was about a policy Arpaio adopted in 2006, when the sheriff told his deputies to detain illegal immigrants after the Arizona state legislature passed a law authorizing local police to do so. Gordon claimed that FBI statistics showed Arpaio's immigration enforcement diverted resources from the first duty of the sheriff's office: protecting Maricopa County's citizens.

Arpaio, who styles himself the "toughest sheriff in America," quickly fired back. His office said that, in the first seven months of 2008, violent crime had fallen 10% compared to the same period from the previous year. Lisa Allen, a spokesperson for the sheriff's office, dismissed Gordon's claims by saying, "I don't know where that man gets his information." The mayor responded by evoking the prestige and authority of the nation's top law enforcement agency: "I will rely on the FBI numbers, and not any other numbers, to judge," he told *The Easy Valley Tribune*.

In fact, Gordon was relying on Arpaio. The ultimate sources of the FBI's numbers are local law enforcement agencies, including the Maricopa County sheriff's office. For the record, doubts

† *http://www.eastvalleytribune.com/story/122571*

about Arpaio's priorities were the subject of a series of articles by *Tribune* reporters Ryan Gabrielson and Paul Giblin, who won a Pulitzer Prize for their investigations into the Maricopa County sheriff's office.‡ In a series of articles published in July 2008, they found that the office was overwhelmed with increasing numbers of unsolved crimes and exploding budgets for overtime pay for immigration enforcement duties while citizens endured longer response times for emergency calls. But questioning Arpaio's numbers—those that showed his performance had improved—would be difficult. As *The Easy Valley Tribune* noted, "In fact, there is no way to independently verify the sheriff's office numbers. The county also does not audit or attempt to verify the statistics."

Unaudited, unverified statistics abound in government data, particularly when outside parties—local government agencies, federal lobbyists, campaign committees—collect the data and turn it over to the government. Here is the opening paragraph of a story based on data currently available on a government website that you'll never read, and for a very good reason:

> Edward Newberry, a registered lobbyist with the powerhouse firm of Patton Boggs, violated campaign finance laws by personally contributing more than $11 million to the campaigns of a half dozen members of Congress and the presidential campaign of Sen. John McCain. Newberry, whose clients include universities, municipal governments and private companies doing business with the government, wrote checks ranging from $1 million to $2.3 million—some one thousand times more than the legal limit of $2,300 for an individual contribution—in the first five months of the 2008 election cycle.

Now, let's profusely apologize to Mr. Newberry, who violated no law. His contributions actually ranged between $1,000 and $2,300—absolutely legal in the 2008 cycle. But when he or someone at his firm submitted to the Senate Office of Public Records his form LD-203—a relatively new report that lobbyists must file listing their campaign contributions—somehow those $1,000 and $2,300 contributions ended up with an extra "000" tacked on to the end. A corrected form was filed within a week, but the Senate database to this day contains both the original, faulty filing showing millions in contributions as well as the corrected one showing thousands—with no indication of which set of contributions is the proper one. On the plus side, the data is available in XML format, so at least all the errors are easily read by machines—anyone pulling down the raw Senate feed would get both Mr. Newberry's actual contributions and the inflated ones. Sadly, the only way to extract meaningful information from those records is to go through them, line by line, and eyeball each entry.

That's something the Center for Responsive Politics (CRP) has been doing for decades now with the campaign finance disclosure data published by the Federal Election Commission. Over the years, CRP has raised millions of dollars to hire dozens of researchers to literally eyeball record after record, standardizing the names of donors and their employers, matching subsidiaries to parents, and coding by industry, so that journalists and the public can make

‡ *http://www.eastvalleytribune.com/page/reasonable_doubt*

some sense of what little information federal election law requires campaigns to disclose about those who fund them (see Chapter 20).

Good Data Doesn't Mean Good Results

But even meticulously going through line after line of government data can't guarantee that one will end up with good results. Sunlight Foundation undertook a project awhile back called Fortune 535. Our goal was pretty simple: we wanted to see whether some members of Congress had gotten rich during their years of public service. To do so, we tried to use the personal financial disclosure forms that members of Congress file each year. Since 1978, members have had to list each individual asset they and their spouses own, the debts they've incurred, their sources of outside income, and other financial information on a form that's publicly available (one major asset is excluded: homes). By comparing each member's first filing with the most recent filing, we reasoned, we should be able to show whose pockets had gotten deeper while in office.

We knew at the outset we'd have to consider all kinds of variables, everything from the rate of inflation and the average return on investments to whether a member's spouse had inherited money. But what we hadn't counted on was that the way Congress has required members to disclose their information makes it virtually impossible to answer the question we wanted to answer.

Personal financial disclosure forms have always required members to value their assets within broad ranges—say, between $1 and $1,000, $1,001 and $15,000, $15,001 and $50,000, and so on. Thus, a member won't report 500 shares of Ford Motor Company stock, but rather Ford Motor Company stock worth somewhere between $1,001 and $15,000. In theory, one should be able to calculate lower and higher end ranges for the assets over time—a member may have been worth between $265,005 and $450,000 in 1978 and between $13,500,048 and $45,500,000 in 2007. The first problem we encountered: Congress changed those ranges several times, so forms filed before 1995 couldn't be compared with later forms.

Let's say a member had an asset worth $10 million in 1978. He would have reported it on his personal financial disclosure form as being worth more than $250,000. In 1995, let's say the asset had appreciated to $19 million. It would be reported as being worth more than $5 million. Let's say the asset depreciated—maybe it was stock in an auto company or a newspaper chain. By 2007—the year we did our Fortune 535 research—the asset is worth a little more than half of what it was in 1978; say, a little more than $5 million. While in reality the member had lost much more than half his investment (we're not even adjusting for inflation yet), it would be reported as an asset that was worth more than $250,000 in 1978 and now is worth more than $5 million—a great return on investment if you can get it, but one that doesn't reflect reality.

There were other problems as well. Members report the value of their assets as of a date of their choosing in the month of December. They report their debts as well, but at the high point of their liability. A member who borrows $2 million in January and pays it all off by July will still report that she had a liability of between $1 million and $5 million. Consider the example of Nancy Pelosi, the Speaker of the House and third in line for the presidency. According to her 2007 personal financial disclosure form, she and her husband are either tottering on the brink of bankruptcy with a net worth of *negative* $9 million, or they enjoy a robust fortune of $86 million.

The House Ethics Manual tells us that financial disclosure is "the preferred method of regulating possible conflicts of interest" for members of Congress, but when the information disclosed is so vague that one can't tell whether it's indicating rags or riches, it's of little utility. And trying to compare disclosures year to year to track changes in net worth—to see whether a member's official actions might have benefited his bottom line (the whole point of the system)—is a bit like trying to compare apples to oranges to glockenspiels. The data can't tell you whether a member of the House is rich or broke, or whether a senator made or lost millions. It sometimes seems that the more reasonable the question is, the more likely it is for government data to be unable to answer it.

This brings us back to the American Recovery and Reinvestment Act and its hundreds of billions of stimulating dollars ready to reinvigorate our ailing economy—and a very simple question. As unemployment continued to rise during the first half of 2009, past 8%, past 9%, more and more people began asking, "Where is the money?"

Back in early May, when the April jobs report put the unemployment rate at 8.9%, Recovery.gov, the website that was supposed to answer that question—"every American will be able to see how and where we spend taxpayer dollars," President Obama said when it was launched—proclaimed that $55 billion in stimulus funds had already been spent. While the site didn't list any of the recipients of these funds, it did break it down by program. Additional Medicaid funding for states—some $29 billion worth—received the lion's share of the early stimulus dollars. USASpending.gov, another site that tracks government spending and tracks recipients, listed the California Department of Health and Human Services, which administers the state's Medi-Cal program, as the top recipient of health care stimulus funding through April, with just less than $3.3 billion spent…well, not really spent.

Tony Cava, a spokesperson at the Department of Health and Human Services, said that the money had been "obligated," which means the federal government has promised to pay it out when the state asks for it. In other words, the money is sitting in an account in Washington, not in the coffers of the state—or in the accounts receivable of hospitals, the checking accounts of doctors and nurses and orderlies who treat Medi-Cal patients, or the cash registers of the businesses they patronize. When they bill for their services, the state will pass on to the federal government a bill for the federal share. "It's not like we're getting a check for $8 billion," Cava explained.§

§ Author interview.

The picture is just as murky when it comes to shovel-ready projects. Search USASpending.gov for Recovery funds going to the Mercer County Housing Authority in Pennsylvania, and you'll find an award for $1,703,727 from the Department of Housing and Urban Development's Capital Fund Program. On March 18, 2009, local housing authorities across the country started receiving letters from HUD, informing them of the stimulus money they'd receive from the Capital Fund Program, which pays for development and modernization of public housing.

That still leaves the question of when the money will actually be spent. Jim Cassidy, director of the HUD Office of Public Housing in Pittsburgh, says the timeline goes like this: by March 17, 2010 (a year after the initial award), Mercer County Housing Authority, and the rest of the recipients of stimulus funds, are required to have legally binding contracts signed to do the work. By March 17, 2011, they must have paid out 60% of the funds, and one year later, 100%.

So, how is this playing out on the ground? Beth Burkhart, the administrative director of the Mercer County Housing Authority, said they decided pretty quickly how to spend their stimulus funds—converting efficiency units in the county's Vermeire Manor retirement homes to one-bedroom apartments. They have some firms lined up to do some of the project, but they were still accepting bids for plumbing, electrical, HVAC, and general contracting work through July 14, 2009. That means that almost none of that $1.7 million had reached the guys with the shovels, wire strippers, duct tape, and hammers.

That kind of information isn't what government provides on USASpending.gov—instead, it tracks the amount of money awarded by government to contractors and grantees. One can find tons of data about how much stimulus money government has decided to give out, but very little on how much of it has actually been spent.

When Vice President Joe Biden released his report on the first 100 days of the stimulus program, called "100 Days, 100 Projects," he noted in the introduction that "we have obligated more than $112 billion." He went on to describe some of the good works that the stimulus funds had launched—the New Hampshire company hiring back workers to take on a road project, the Florida school districts hiring back teachers, the first road project in Illinois to cause new hires. Not once in his report did Biden cite Recovery.gov as a source of his information.

Conclusion

No citizen should have to rely on the word of Joe Biden (or any other politician) to judge the efficacy of government programs. Being able to see for oneself with a few clicks of the mouse—to know, for example, whether there's a Superfund site near the home one is thinking of buying—is the great promise of online, transparent government. But if half the Superfund sites aren't listed in the data, or are in the wrong place because of transposed digits in the zip codes (a common federal data problem), one might end up owning a dream home next to a toxic sludge hole.

That means that auditing government data—determining what's collected, how it's collected, what it's used for, and how accurate it is—should be a priority. Certainly, government should take up the lion's share of this work, but the public, the press, and academics also have a crucial role to play in finding bad data.

So, while it's unlikely to top a list of voter concerns in any poll, the quality of federal data—what they get wrong and what they leave out—is rapidly becoming a critical issue for the country. We can't create data-driven decision-making processes when the data itself is unreliable. Whether it's bad data on crime rates, spending programs, or the disposition of nuclear waste, it's awfully hard to make decisions when you're basing them on faulty information.

About the Author

 **BILL ALLISON** is the editorial director at the Sunlight Foundation. A veteran investigative journalist and editor for nonprofit media, Bill worked for the Center for Public Integrity for nine years, where he coauthored *The Cheating of America* with Charles Lewis (Harper Perennial), was senior editor of *The Buying of the President 2000* (Harper Perennial), and was coeditor of the *New York Times* bestseller *The Buying of the President 2004* (Harper Paperbacks).

CHAPTER TWENTY-FIVE

When Is Transparency Useful?

Aaron Swartz

Transparency is a slippery word; the kind of word that, like *reform*, sounds good and so ends up getting attached to any random political thing that someone wants to promote. But just as it's silly to talk about whether "reform" is useful (it depends on the reform), talking about transparency in general won't get us very far. Everything from holding public hearings to requiring police to videotape interrogations can be called "transparency"—there's not much that's useful to say about such a large category.

In general, you should be skeptical whenever someone tries to sell you on something like "reform" or "transparency." In general, you should be skeptical. But in particular, reactionary political movements have long had a history of cloaking themselves in nice words. Take the Good Government (goo-goo) movement early in the twentieth century. Funded by prominent major foundations, it claimed that it was going to clean up the corruption and political machines that were hindering city democracy. Instead, the reforms ended up choking democracy itself, a response to the left-wing candidates who were starting to get elected.

The goo-goo reformers moved elections to off-years. They claimed this was to keep city politics distinct from national politics, but the real effect was just to reduce turnout. They stopped paying politicians a salary. This was supposed to reduce corruption, but it just made sure that only the wealthy could run for office. They made the elections nonpartisan. Supposedly this was because city elections were about local issues, not national politics, but the effect was to increase the power of name recognition and make it harder for voters to tell which candidate was on their side. And they replaced mayors with unelected city managers, so winning elections was no longer enough to effect change.*

Of course, the modern transparency movement is very different from the Good Government movement of old. But the story illustrates that we should be wary of kind nonprofits promising to help. I want to focus on one particular strain of transparency thinking and show how it can go awry. It starts with something that's hard to disagree with.

Sharing Documents with the Public

Modern society is made of bureaucracies and modern bureaucracies run on paper: memos, reports, forms, filings. Sharing these internal documents with the public seems obviously good, and indeed, much good has come out of publishing these documents, whether it's the National Security Archive (*http://www.gwu.edu/~nsarchiv/*), whose Freedom of Information Act (FOIA) requests have revealed decades of government wrongdoing around the globe, or the indefatigable Carl Malamud and his scanning (*http://public.resource.org/*), which has put terabytes of useful government documents, from laws to movies, online for everyone to access freely.

I suspect few people would put "publishing government documents on the Web" high on their list of political priorities, but it's a fairly cheap project (just throw piles of stuff into scanners) and doesn't seem to have much downside. The biggest concern—privacy—seems mostly taken care of. In the United States, FOIA and the Privacy Act (PA) provide fairly clear guidelines for how to ensure disclosure while protecting people's privacy.

Perhaps even more useful than putting government documents online would be providing access to corporate and nonprofit records. A lot of political action takes place outside the formal government, and thus outside the scope of the existing FOIA laws. But such things seem totally off the radar of most transparency activists; instead, giant corporations that receive billions of dollars from the government are kept impenetrably secret.

Generating Databases for the Public

Many policy questions are a battle of competing interests—drivers don't want cars that roll over and kill them when they make a turn, but car companies want to keep selling such cars. If you're a member of Congress, choosing between them is difficult. On the one hand are your constituents, who vote for you. But on the other hand are big corporations, which fund your reelection campaigns. You really can't afford to offend either one too badly.

So, there's a tendency for Congress to try a compromise. That's what happened with, for example, the Transportation Recall Enhancement, Accountability, and Documentation

* For more, see *http://sociology.ucsc.edu/whorulesamerica/power/local.html*.

(TREAD) Act. Instead of requiring safer cars, Congress simply required car companies to report how likely their cars were to roll over. Transparency wins again!

Or, for a more famous example: after Watergate, people were upset about politicians receiving millions of dollars from large corporations. But, on the other hand, corporations seem to like paying off politicians. So instead of banning the practice, Congress simply required that politicians keep track of everyone who gives them money and file a report on it for public inspection.

I find such practices ridiculous. When you create a regulatory agency, you put together a group of people whose job is to solve some problem. They're given the power to investigate who's breaking the law and the authority to punish them. Transparency, on the other hand, simply shifts the work from the government to the average citizen, who has neither the time nor the ability to investigate these questions in any detail, let alone do anything about it. It's a farce: a way for Congress to look like it has done something on some pressing issue without actually endangering its corporate sponsors.

Interpreting Databases for the Public

Here's where the technologists step in. "Something is too hard for people?" they hear. "We know how to fix that." So they download a copy of the database and pretty it up for public consumption—generating summary statistics, putting nice pictures around it, and giving it a snazzy search feature and some visualizations. Now inquiring citizen can find out who's funding their politicians and how dangerous their cars are just by going online.

The wonks love this. Still stinging from recent bouts of deregulation and antigovernment zealotry, many are now skeptical about government. "We can't trust the regulators," they say. "We need to be able to investigate the data for ourselves." Technology seems to provide the perfect solution. Just put it all online—people can go through the data while trusting no one.

There's just one problem: if you can't trust the regulators, what makes you think you can trust the data?

The problem with generating databases isn't that they're too hard to read; it's the lack of investigation and enforcement power, and websites do nothing to help with that. Since no one's in charge of verifying them, most of the things reported in transparency databases are simply lies. Sometimes they're blatant lies, like how some factories keep two sets of books on workplace injuries: one accurate one, reporting every injury, and one to show the government, reporting just 10% of them.[†] But they can easily be subtler: forms are misfiled or filled with typos, or the malfeasance is changed in such a way that it no longer appears on the form. Making these databases easier to read results only in easier-to-read lies.

Three examples:

† *Fast Food Nation*, Eric Schlosser, Houghton Mifflin, 2001.

- Congress's operations are supposedly open to the public, but if you visit the House floor (or if you follow what they're up to on one of these transparency sites) you find that they appear to spend all their time naming post offices. All the real work is passed using emergency provisions and is tucked into subsections of innocuous bills. (The bank bailouts were put in the Paul Wellstone Mental Health Act.) Matt Taibbi's *The Great Derangement* (Spiegel & Grau) tells the story.

- Many of these sites tell you who your elected official is, but what impact does your elected official really have? For 40 years, people in New York thought they were governed by their elected officials—their city council, their mayor, their governor. But as Robert Caro revealed in *The Power Broker* (Vintage), they were all wrong. Power in New York was controlled by one man, a man who had consistently lost every time he'd tried to run for office, a man nobody thought of as being in charge at all: Parks Commissioner Robert Moses.

- Plenty of sites on the Internet will tell you who your representative receives money from, but disclosed contributions are just the tip of the iceberg. As Ken Silverstein points out in his series of pieces for *Harper's* (some of which he covers in his book *Turkmeniscam* [Random House]), being a member of Congress provides for endless ways to get perks and cash while hiding where it comes from.

Fans of transparency try to skirt around this. "OK," they say, "but surely *some* of the data will be accurate. And even if it isn't, won't we learn something from how people lie?" Perhaps that's true, although it's hard to think of any good examples. (In fact, it's hard to think of any good examples of transparency work accomplishing *anything*, except perhaps for more transparency.) But everything has a cost.

Hundreds of millions of dollars have been spent funding transparency projects around the globe. That money doesn't come from the sky. The question isn't whether some transparency is better than none; it's whether transparency is really the best way to spend these resources, whether they would have a bigger impact if spent someplace else.

I tend to think they would. All this money has been spent with the goal of getting a straight answer, not of doing anything about it. Without enforcement power, the most readable database in the world won't accomplish much—even if it's perfectly accurate. So people go online and see that all cars are dangerous and that all politicians are corrupt. What are they supposed to do then?

Sure, perhaps they can make small changes—this politician gets slightly less oil money than that one, so I'll vote for her (on the other hand, maybe she's just a better liar and gets her oil money funneled through PACs or foundations or lobbyists)—but unlike the government, they can't solve the bigger issue: a bunch of people reading a website can't force car companies to make a safe car. You've done nothing to solve the real problem; you've only made it seem more hopeless: all politicians are corrupt, all cars are dangerous. What can you do?

An Alternative

What's ironic is that the Internet does provide something you can do. It has made it vastly easier, easier than ever before, to form groups with people and work together on common tasks. And it's through people coming together—not websites analyzing data—that real political progress can be made.

So far we've seen baby steps—people copying what they see elsewhere and trying to apply it to politics. Wikis seem to work well, so you build a political wiki. Everyone loves social networks, so you build a political social network. But these tools worked in their original setting because they were trying to solve particular problems, not because they're magic. To make progress in politics, we need to think best about how to solve its problems, not simply copy technologies that have worked in other fields.

Data analysis can be part of it, but it's part of a bigger picture. Imagine a team of people coming together to tackle some issue they care about—food safety, say. You can have technologists poring through safety records, investigative reporters making phone calls and sneaking into buildings, lawyers subpoenaing documents and filing lawsuits, political organizers building support for the project and coordinating volunteers, members of Congress pushing for hearings on your issues and passing laws to address the problems you uncover, and, of course, bloggers and writers to tell your stories as they unfold.

Imagine it: an investigative strike team, taking on an issue, uncovering the truth, and pushing for reform. They'd use technology, of course, but also politics and the law. At best, a transparency law gets you one more database you can look at. But a lawsuit (or congressional investigation)? You get to subpoena all the databases, as well as the source records behind them, then interview people under oath about what it all means. You get to ask for what you need, instead of trying to predict what you may someday want.

This is where data analysis can be really useful. Not in providing definitive answers over the Web to random surfers, but in finding anomalies and patterns and questions that can be seized upon and investigated by others. Not in building finished products, but by engaging in a process of discovery.

But this can be done only when members of this investigative strike team work in association with others. They would do what it takes to accomplish their goals, not be hamstrung by arbitrary divisions between "technology" and "journalism" and "politics."

Right now, technologists insist that they're building neutral platforms for anyone to find data on any issue. Journalists insist that they're objective observers of the facts. And political types assume they already know the answers and don't need to investigate further questions. They're each in their own silo, unable to see the bigger picture.

I certainly was. I care passionately about these issues—I don't want politicians to be corrupt; I don't want cars to kill people—and as a technologist I'd love to be able to solve them. That's why I got swept up in the promise of transparency. It seemed like just by doing the things I knew how to do best—write code, sift through databases—I could change the world.

But it just doesn't work. Putting databases online isn't a silver bullet, as nice as the word *transparency* may sound. But it was easy to delude myself. All I had to do was keep putting things online and someone somewhere would find a use for them. After all, that's what technologists do, right? The World Wide Web wasn't designed for publishing the news—it was designed as a neutral platform that could support anything from scientific publications to pornography.

Politics doesn't work like that. Perhaps at some point putting things on the front page of the *New York Times* guaranteed that they would be fixed, but that day is long past. The pipeline of leak to investigation to revelation to report to reform has broken down. Technologists can't depend on journalists to use their stuff; journalists can't depend on political activists to fix the problems they uncover. Change doesn't come from thousands of people, all going their separate ways. Change requires bringing people together to work on a common goal. That's hard for technologists to do by themselves.

But if they do take that as their goal, they can apply all their talent and ingenuity to the problem. They can measure their success by the number of lives that have been improved by the changes they fought for, rather than the number of people who have visited their website. They can learn which technologies actually make a difference and which ones are merely indulgences. And they can iterate, improve, and scale.

Transparency can be a powerful thing, but not in isolation. So, let's stop passing the buck by saying our job is just to get the data out there and it's other people's job to figure out how to use it. Let's decide that our job is to fight for good in the world. I'd love to see all these amazing resources go to work on *that*.

About the Author

AARON SWARTZ is the cofounder of reddit.com, OpenLibrary.org, and Watchdog.net. He is a coauthor of the RSS 1.0 specification and is on the board of Change Congress. He currently codirects the Progressive Change Campaign Committee (*http://boldprogressives.org*).

CHAPTER TWENTY-SIX

Transparency Inside Out

Tim Koelkebeck

A surprisingly regular experience in the Pentagon is what I call the boomerang email. You email a question to a colleague. Not knowing the answer, he forwards the email on to someone else, restating the question in his own words. Through subsequent forwarding, the email passes through government offices and military bases across the country, and the question is rewritten several times over. Days later, someone forwards you an email with a question similar to yours, asking if you have any insights. The sender never scrolled to the bottom of the long thread to see that you were the original person to ask the question.

While the Pentagon is notorious for its opacity to the public, one would assume we are transparent to ourselves. Yet an insider, not knowing where to find necessary information, can email an inquiry to a colleague and a few days and dozens of people later get nothing in return but an echo. I've spent three years at the Pentagon as an on-site contractor in an organization that oversees the acquisition of all major military systems, including ships, planes, tanks, and satellites. We don't have a secret dashboard with all key information ready for analysis. We certainly collect data and generate a lot of reports, but too often the information is either out of date, incomplete, scattered across dozens of databases, or all of the above. In some cases, the desired information is simply never captured. In my world, it's implicitly understood that the only reliable way to follow the week-to-week evolution of an issue is to participate directly in the discussion or talk to someone who has.

In his Transparency and Open Government memo, President Barack Obama declared that "executive departments and agencies should harness new technologies to put information about their operations and decisions online and readily available to the public" (see the

Appendix). To the average citizen this may sound like simply uploading existing government information to a web portal. The difficult reality is that the departments and agencies *themselves* do not have easy access to information about their operations and decisions. For government to be appropriately transparent to the public, it must figure out how to be more transparent to itself.

I've recently begun to focus on how to foster internal transparency within my organization. My leadership wants more visibility into a host of operational information, including all relevant tasks, meetings, events, and formal staff opinions about proposed decisions. As it stands, most of this operational information is either recorded without structure (emails, documents) or not recorded at all (meetings, phone calls). In other words, it's not usefully visible. I am one of many focused on laying the groundwork for a migration of these invisible operations into online applications that will automatically capture the underlying data in a structured, analyzable format—for example, an online task manager, public calendar, and opinion coordination system.

Face-to-face meetings, phone calls, and emails are indispensable, but to answer the current call for transparency we need nothing short of an e-government that formally recognizes a vote, decision, or any piece of information only once it is properly captured. This is not simply a matter of training federal employees to use existing Web 2.0 applications. Undoubtedly some consumer application concepts can and should be incorporated into government, but few organizations have figured out how to facilitate staff operations with services like Facebook and Twitter. This is also not simply a matter of duplicating enterprise information technology (IT) practices. Government can learn valuable lessons from companies like Amazon, Walmart, and Google about integrating IT into operations, but given its enormity, special constraints, and wide range of responsibilities, government faces different and tougher management challenges than any commercial business. Achieving e-government requires a 233-year-old behemoth to leapfrog most of the enterprise world and pioneer new IT management approaches.

As I've begun to experiment with e-government within a single organization in the Office of the Secretary of Defense (OSD),* I've had the privilege (or misfortune) of experiencing many of the obstacles firsthand. In the upcoming sections of this chapter, I briefly cover a few of these obstacles to provide needed context for the dialogue about government transparency. I then offer several guiding principles for overcoming them.

Please keep in mind that it's impossible to generalize about the many disparate organizations that make up the federal government. My experience working on collaboration and knowledge management tools within an OSD bureaucracy probably best compares to similar efforts within other large bureaucracies in the Department of Defense (DoD), State Department, and

---

* OSD is composed of the civilian staff organizations that work for the Secretary of Defense. It is distinct from the military departments like the Army, Navy, Air Force, and Joint Staff that report to the Secretary. All of these departments and organizations are collectively the DoD.

Department of Homeland Security, and likely overlaps somewhat with efforts in other major federal agencies. But I have little to no idea, for instance, how the Federal Reserve, Department of Agriculture, or FBI operates. Even the military organizations within the DoD are notably different from OSD. (Rather than introduce confusion about the distinctions between OSD and DoD, however, I will stick with the familiar "DoD" acronym.) My experience is far from the entire story, but I believe it still offers important lessons for the general discussion.

As a final caveat, I will intentionally avoid the issue of what information should and should not be available to the public. My efforts are focused on creating the window, not deciding who gets to see through it.

Complexity Creates Opacity

Complex systems are fundamentally difficult to render transparent, and the U.S. federal government is arguably the most complex institution ever known to man. It is a massive, constantly evolving, highly interconnected bureaucracy. Winston Churchill said it best: the worst form of government, except all the others.

Our federal government employs roughly 1.9 million civil servants.[†] If all of them retired tomorrow, Uncle Sam would have to hire every U.S. college graduate for the next two years to be fully staffed again. This army of civil servants is augmented by more than 7 million contractors like me whose day-to-day responsibilities are often indistinguishable from their government counterparts. Add them to the count and the executive branch is more populous than Sweden, Austria, or Israel. There are also roughly 1.5 million people in the military, nearly 3 million workers funded by federal grants, and around 750,000 employed by the postal service.

This nation-size institution is made up of a labyrinth of organizations and processes that are continually reshuffled by competing and changing powers. DoD leadership often addresses a major challenge by shaking up existing offices and processes, and even in times of relative stability the gray area between organizational lines of responsibility is the source of constant debate driven by internal politics. Congress also has the power to modify operations through DoD-specific legislation. The DoD gets some interpretive wiggle room when it decides how to translate law into practice, until Congress decides to again intervene. The back and forth can be unending. If the dust ever settles, the next president is sure to kick it up again by demanding dramatic changes within the bureaucracy. It can take months, if not years, to translate a president's vision into concrete changes within the executive agencies. Toward the end of George W. Bush's second term of office, DoD leadership hastily finalized a flurry of overdue policy and process changes that were years in the making. And just a few short months later, the Obama administration promptly began to revisit many of them.

---

† All figures are from Paul C. Light's research at NYU in 2005, which the *Washington Post* nicely profiled at *http://www.washingtonpost.com/wp-dyn/content/article/2006/10/05/AR2006100501782.html*.

This constant churn combined with the vast size of government introduces uncertainty about who does what, which is a frequent problem in an institution that operates via consensus. For example, a Pentagon analyst may need up to two dozen organizations from various agencies to concur with a draft decision memorandum before getting it approved, and it's next to impossible for her to know which specific person in each organization is qualified to review the memo on its behalf. So, the analyst sends it to the organizations' central administrative offices, which reroute it to suboffices, which reroute it again, and so on, until the memo reaches someone willing to review it. Ambiguities surrounding who should review a memo can introduce substantial delay in the form of increased processing time, routing errors, or political infighting. I've received memos for review that were originally distributed weeks ago by someone whose office is a minute away from mine.

In the age of Amazon and Twitter, OSD's memo routing process feels a lot like early twentieth-century telephony, when human operators routed calls. It's unfair, however, to compare government to businesses and consumer web products. The DoD is not simply an online bookseller that can focus on optimizing and organizing a well-defined, recurring transaction. Its issues won't reach a conclusion through haphazard, open communication (much less in 140 characters). It must manage a bewildering array of nuanced issues in an evolving political, legal, and diplomatic landscape; balance the competing demands of saving money and saving lives; and make long-term preparations for an uncertain future. This complexity has frustrated countless efforts to develop simplified, optimized work processes. To simplify the DoD's byzantine memo-routing process might sacrifice thoroughness for efficiency, which can be an inappropriate trade-off given the gravity of the department's sphere of operations and decisions.

Transparency thrives on simplicity. Our steady march toward larger, more complex government means that transparency will be an ongoing challenge. Consider the "Transparency and Open Government" memo itself: six months after President Obama signed it I conducted an informal poll within a DoD office. No one had heard of it.

Transparency, Meet Institutional Inertia

Establishing e-government requires recognizing IT as an enabler of operations and decision making. Fascinating examples can be found in companies like Walmart, which uses IT to automatically manage store inventories in response to sales data. When you check out with your cereal, toothpaste, and flat-screen TV at any Walmart store, headquarters instantly adjusts its distribution of those products accordingly. The company also knows to overstock stores on beer and strawberry Pop-Tarts before a hurricane, for instance, since pre-storm sales of those items tend to skyrocket.‡ Through information technology, Walmart makes customers implicit company managers. Your purchases determine its operations.

‡ *http://www.nytimes.com/2004/11/14/business/yourmoney/14wal.html*

My organization, on the other hand, treats IT like an administrative assistant: it stores information, maintains calendars, and creates handy presentations. While the help is greatly appreciated, it is not considered integral to operations and decision making. This mentality is a vestige of the pre-Internet era when the computer was a miscellaneous toolbox that patiently stood by on your desk. Many people in government began their careers during this era, if not before it. The average age among civil servants is just over 46,§ and about half of them are now eligible for retirement. The organizations at the top of the food chain, which set policy and operational procedures, are nearly exclusively composed of senior staff members. In my organization, which sits on top of all military acquisition, 46 is relatively young.

But this mentality is less a function of the individual employees as it is institutional inertia. Some of my colleagues demonstrate a formidable grasp of the power and future of IT. Formal organizations, however, tend to evolve more slowly than individuals. While many of us use Facebook and Flickr at home, the established standards at work are Microsoft Office, Web 1.0, and the C drive. People are willing to try something new independently and in their free time, but group work habits are hard to break, especially when they're reinforced by legacy management processes.

And it's not just about work habits. The administrative image of IT means senior analysts and their bosses simply don't believe they should have to bother with it. They involve themselves only in important discussions and decision making, all of which occurs in the real world of face-to-face meetings and phone calls. Most of us are stuck with email, but if you're important enough, even that becomes an afterthought. One of the first pronouncements of a newly appointed leader in my department was that he would not be personally checking his email.

People sometimes actually refuse to use helpful software on the grounds that it is beneath them. My organization, for instance, maintains an online calendar that displays meetings of general interest. In the past, anyone holding a meeting emailed or called the calendar's administrator with the details. Because she was generally busy, she became a bottleneck to announcing meetings on the calendar. To remove this delay, the calendar was redesigned with universal access. The analysts calling the meetings, however, continued to contact the administrator directly. Though still frustrated by the lag time, they preferred not to bother with inputting the data themselves. Calendars are for secretaries.

Because we value IT but cannot commit to it as a medium of operations and decision making, we end up hedging—doing official business on paper while maintaining digital records online. The memorandum, the classic vehicle of decision making, is a prime example. A proposed memo is presented to the decision maker with a standard set of explanatory materials that are assembled according to strict protocols, from the ordering of documents down to the size and content of their footers and margins. This highly organized package is essentially the decision memo's metadata, albeit on paper. The executive summary defines the purpose and context and highlights the key issues. The background materials include previous decisions, law, budget

§ *http://www.washingtonpost.com/wp-dyn/content/article/2009/01/12/AR2009011202572.html*

documents, and other official information that supports the proposed decision, as well as a list of the opinions of relevant government authorities: whether they agree, partially agree, or disagree, any comments they had, and whether those comments were incorporated or ignored.

After a paper package is dutifully assembled, it is archived online by scanning it in PDF format. If you're a data geek, you winced already. If you're not, put it this way: from a machine's point of view, this PDF copy could be anything from a presidential memo issuing a nuclear attack to a Dr. Seuss excerpt. To find an issue of interest among these documents without making a bunch of phone calls you would have to individually read every memorandum rather than perform a five-second search within machine-readable text. All of the formatting, tagging, and text searchability of the information is lost in a scanned document. A scanned document can be translated back into machine-readable text, but the process is error-prone and often skipped. And our online archive does have a very basic tagging feature, but generally speaking, no one uses it. All eyes are on the paper package, as that's what the boss will see. After the boss signs, the scanned memo is distributed and the rest of the package, with all of its carefully composed metadata, is never looked at again.

Storing structured information via structureless scanning is the e-government equivalent of burning the files. If the boss were to review the decision-making information online, his meticulous staff would ensure that all content was properly formatted, linked, and tagged for his benefit. This digitally structured package would then be archived online and, unlike a scanned copy, be amenable to search, mashups, data mining, and so forth. Something as simple as switching from paper to electronic signatures could yield dramatically more transparent operations and decision making.

But while the technology of electronic signatures and packages is simple, convincing and training thousands of legacy organizations to use the technology is not. The DoD CIO is actually planning to pilot an application that would manage the assembly of a decision document online, including collecting input from multiple organizations. This is a laudable step in the right direction, though it remains to be seen whether the pilot organization fully adopts the virtual document management approach or simply incorporates it as another layer that shadows the tried and true paper process.

In a similar situation, my organization has taken the latter route. The staff is so busy handling day-to-day issues that it never seems to have time to completely reboot its work processes. And given the comfort level with the established way of doing things, many simply don't want change. Among those who do want change, there is disagreement about which change is the right change. Despite my leadership's desire for increased transparency, institutional inertia holds us back.

Kaleidoscope IT: One-Off Apps Obscure Information

Imagine yourself as a senior official within one of the dozens of departments in the DoD. You care deeply about your organization's mission, and you're always looking for ways to improve its performance. One day, you're told that a web application custom-built for your organization runs on outdated technology and will be obsolete in two years. You request funding to rebuild the application with newer technology, the funding is approved, and the 18-month development project begins. A few months later, someone approaches you from a different organization about building an application similar to yours. Because your organizations work with overlapping information, this person suggests that you collaborate on building a single application that serves both, thus expanding the information-sharing community and increasing internal transparency.

It sounds like a nice idea, but it would delay your progress while the requirements are developed for the new, combined application. Even worse, replacing your current effort to collaborate on another means you would lose your current funding, as it was specifically approved for the project in its original form. You would be forced to reapply for funding for the new, combined project and risk being declined. Your dilemma: continue on your path, guaranteeing your organization continued access to the application it knows, or agree to collaborate with another organization, incur delays, and risk your funding for the sake of experimenting with the idea of a larger information-sharing community. What would you do?

The Pentagon official who is the basis for this story very quickly opted to stick with his original plan. I approached him about combining efforts. He was committed in the abstract to exploring "synergies," but outright merging our efforts would have been too costly and risky for him. This kind of tragedy of the anticommons happens everywhere, all the time. While it's ideal for everyone to adopt a common framework that ensures shared standards, it's usually too difficult and costly for any one group in an organization to take on the challenge of creating it. On the occasion when one tries, the minor network effects of an infant framework are typically not compelling enough for other organizations to be willing to make the necessary changes and sacrifices to join. It's difficult, then, for a standard to ever take off.

The core problem is the fact that DoD organizations are responsible for their own IT solutions. Many of them have their own, internal IT teams. When authority is fragmented, solutions are fragmented. Most organizational decision makers don't even think to consider a solution that could expand its reach beyond their niche. It's beyond their scope. They're not IT product managers looking to increase market share. They fund IT projects that support their particular mission.

As a result, the DoD is riddled with one-off applications. It's analogous to commerce before mass production. If every county designed and manufactured its own brand of vehicle we'd have a lot of trouble driving between counties: some places would put the driver on the right, others on the left; city cars would be go-carts that top out at 40 mph; rural vehicles wouldn't bother with turn signals or door locks.

In the same vein, government's custom applications cannot communicate with one another, making them counterproductive information silos that reduce transparency. I might research the test plan for a helicopter prototype within one application and never know about additional information within another application. On the other hand, many applications store copies of the same underlying data, but these copies are not linked. When the helicopter's cost estimate changes, for instance, each application's data set must be independently updated. Inevitably, some data sets are not updated, meaning that an analyst will run into different cost figures for the same helicopter within different applications. Sometimes meetings devolve into determining whose data is correct rather than discussing the significance of the data.

The variety of unique needs among the DoD's many organizations makes any standardization effort fundamentally difficult, but in some cases even easy opportunities for consolidation are lost. My organization developed its own collaborative calendar even though many other DoD organizations already use some form of public calendar. Multiple instances of meetings are passed back and forth across one or more systems, some up-to-date and others not. A meeting might have only a partial attendee list in one system and simply not exist in another. This fragmentation makes meeting management more tiresome and opaque than it should be. A universal calendar framework would enable consistent transparency into what meetings are being held and who's attending them.

The lack of IT standards is a recognized problem in DoD and throughout government. Countless consolidation efforts have been unraveled by institutional inertia, the politics of agreeing on a standard, and the inherent difficulty of standardizing complex data sets. As a result, my experience with government IT has been a bit like looking through a kaleidoscope, where each organization has added its own, uniquely colored shard. Through this kind of lens, a piece of information may be inaccurate, lack context, or simply be invisible. It's an unreliable kind of transparency.

A Market Focused on Proposals, Not Products

While some DoD applications are handicapped from the beginning by a needlessly niche mission, many are in fact designed to achieve some level of cross-organizational transparency. The Pentagon manages a web-accessible central repository of cost data, for instance, with the stated purpose of providing government analysts with complete, timely, and accurate information about the costs of major military acquisitions. It sounds like a perfect example of a web service providing internal transparency. Unfortunately, the user interface is so clunky and the data so poorly structured that no one uses it. Even the analysts in the office that manage the repository don't use it. When they need cost data, they ask the people who input the data into the system to email it to them directly, sometimes only days after the very same data was submitted to the repository.

Many of the one-off apps we create are not used enough to justify their existence. This in itself should not be blameworthy. Most commercial software products are flops too. In a free market, however, flops die. In my area of the DoD, flops are sometimes ignored or even expanded, because decision makers often do not have the right type of information to judge the success of an application. Understanding why requires understanding how the government IT market works.

When a government organization needs an IT solution, it will usually release to the public a document called a Request for Proposals (RFP) that outlines its specific needs. Companies respond to this solicitation with write-ups of their proposed solutions and costs. The organization evaluates all proposals and picks a winner. The idea is that when companies compete for the government's business, the government gets the best value. The process is also meant to reduce the chance of corruption, as government officials cannot simply pick any company to do a particular job. Instead, they must choose the winning proposal based on predefined cost, performance, and schedule criteria. It's a good model, in theory.

There are, however, a number of well-known problems with the way this model plays out in practice. First and foremost, it puts the government organization in charge of identifying its own technical needs and, often, specifying high-level solutions. But an organization with a nontechnical mission like policy-making or contract oversight is not especially qualified for this role. And though the IT companies that develop software for the government may themselves be qualified, the RFP process rewards those who provide what the government client requests, not businesses looking to solve unidentified root problems.

A nontechnical government colleague of mine recognized a few years ago that his organization did not manage meeting notifications well and wanted a new system built. Because the organization's in-house development team was occupied with an ongoing effort, he contracted an outside IT company. Unfortunately, given his lack of technical expertise, he did not know to specify that the system should interact with existing applications that manage related information. The system's resultant isolation meant that its data quickly became out of sync with those more established applications. Lacking any user interface design experience, my colleague also did not recognize problems with the interface that inevitably frustrated early users. Today the application is replete with out-of-date information and usage has tapered off. My colleague cannot be blamed for his lack of technical or design knowledge, and the IT company cannot be blamed for developing the product as requested and approved by the client. The failure lies with the RFP process, which puts a nontechnical user in charge of requirements. If the consumer world worked that way, you'd be expected to dream up Google or Facebook yourself.

Another problem with the RFP process is its complexity. Much like tax law, the legal requirements of writing and responding to proposals have evolved over the years to close loopholes, meet quotas, and stay consistent with laws enacted by Congress in its fervor to improve the system. As an IT company, participating requires substantial time and specialized knowledge. This effectively shuts out both small companies who can't afford the overhead of writing the proposals and highly tech-oriented companies that don't specialize in paperwork.‖ The companies that do participate typically have built their business model around writing winning proposals, which has little to do with creating worthwhile applications.

In my experience, the company that wins the contract often has an existing relationship with the organization that released the RFP, which also has little to do with an ability to create worthwhile applications. Naturally, a company with experience supporting the government organization will have a better sense of the type of proposal the organization is looking for than will an outside company that knows nothing more than the high-level description of technical requirements in the RFP. The inside company knows how the organization thinks and works and the nuances of its needs. After winning the contract, this inside company expands its IT services within the organization and becomes further entrenched. Over time, the government organization and its entrenched supporting company might form a nearly inseparable bond. The dividing line gets blurry when onsite company personnel actually influence how future government RFPs are written.

Companies like this are called "government contractors" because they specialize in supporting the government. They hire government retirees, attend government meetings, and have staff members on-site in government offices. In some cases, there is little actual difference between them and the government. These contractors' strong incumbent advantage and experience with the complex RFP process virtually guarantees that they will continue to win government IT contracts, making the government market a poor choice for innovative startups. While young companies like Google, Facebook, and Twitter dominate the Web, only one of the top 10 government IT contractors# was founded after the 1960s:* Dell, where we buy our computers, not our software. Despite the government's wide variety of IT needs, half of all spending in the civilian technology sector finds its way to one of these 10 companies. It's a market dominated by long-standing government–contractor relationships, not IT products that speak for themselves.

It's also a market not driven by user-level supply and demand. On the general Web, we gauge the value of an app through the feedback of others and direct experience. Since proposals are often not tied to existing products, however, the government must commit to paying the costs of building a solution (plus profit) before anyone can see or use it. Trying to gauge the value of an app from a paper proposal is a bit like trying to guess how good an apple pie will taste from a recipe.

As a result, the government is often more or less blind in determining how useful and user-friendly an application will be. And rather than "take a peek" with a pared-down beta version, my organization tends to initiate multimillion-dollar development efforts based on the paper proposal alone.

‖ Government does set aside a small percentage of contracts for small businesses and other under-represented companies. These quotas introduce their own problems.

In terms of civilian, not defense, revenue.

* *http://washingtontechnology.com/toplists/top-100-lists/2008.aspx?Sort=Top-100-Civilian-Revenue*

Once an app is launched, the blindness is often maintained by failing to collect rigorous usage metrics. The company that manages one of my organization's primary web applications only records the number of people that log in. It's a motley app with tools for everything from document preparation to cost analysis. People in my office regularly use one small feature buried within the app, a simple form that we fill in, print out, and incorporate in the memo packages discussed earlier. Most of the more sophisticated and costly tools within the app are poorly designed and left untouched. Our use of the form helps validate the entire app, however, since a login is a login.

Many apps I work with do not seem to collect any usage metrics at all. If they do, they're not discussed. Because decision makers generally do not use the applications themselves, with little to no usage data they tend to believe the new app is a success. After all, they chose the solution in the first place. As new IT needs arise, they naturally look to leverage previous investments by modifying an existing app, regardless of whether anyone is actually using it.

This lack of emphasis on user adoption, combined with the fact that the government RFP defines both the problem to be solved as well as the desired solution, drives IT contractors to be more service-oriented than product-oriented. A product-oriented company focuses on end-user value. A service-oriented contractor, on the other hand, is incentivized to simply find work. It doesn't matter if that work produces an application that gets used or collects dust; the company gets paid either way, as long as the app meets the spec defined by the government. Outright creating *additional* work is profitable too. A close friend works for a company that intentionally develops a government application to require dedicated, company software administrators to keep it operational. The yearly profit on charging the government for these staff hours is a lucrative part of their business model. Making a simple, standalone product would mean less profit. To a certain extent, it makes good business sense to develop a solution that is *not* user-friendly.

The government IT market too often rewards *incumbent contractors* with paper proposals that check the requirements boxes rather than *applications* that employees want to use to get the job done. In the general consumer world, where companies fully understand that software lives or dies based on its usability, the number of failed products clearly demonstrates that usability is difficult to achieve. Naturally, when usability is not properly incentivized, the resultant apps are frequently clunky and unhelpful. If managing many social networking and web accounts seems annoying, try working regularly with dozens of apps that are so confusing you feel like you have to relearn them on every visit. People tend to give up. When a new government app is launched that promises to make our work lives easier, my office doesn't applaud, it groans. Rather than even bother figuring out the clunky app, they stick with what works: email, Microsoft Office, a few helpful websites, and the C drive. Without new IT solutions that are both pleasant to use and helpful for government workers, these workers will continue to operate as they always have, and transparency will be just as difficult tomorrow as it is today.

Framing the Window

Each of these challenges reinforces the others. The pre-Internet mentality of the computer as administrative toolbox underlies the pursuit of one-off IT solutions, and the one-off solutions reinforce the toolbox mentality. The size and complexity of government creates a disparate, complex web of authority, making it difficult and somewhat unnatural to seek out government or even department-wide solutions. The lack of standards, in turn, drives complexity in government. Because one-off solutions are rarely optimized for usability, people tend to avoid them and fall back on older, more reliable methods, like emailing files back and forth, which maintains the pre-Internet mentality regarding IT. And when the dysfunctional IT market promises helpful tools but never delivers, that mentality seems justified.

These challenges, then, cannot be addressed in isolation. And they are not the only ones. I didn't even discuss the wide variety of regulations, for instance, covering everything from security to the environment to equal opportunity, which constrict a problem solver's range of motion, sometimes rightly and other times in silly ways. There are no easy answers or step-by-step processes to addressing all of these challenges. There are, however, a number of principles that can and should guide our e-government and transparency efforts. Here are a few to consider.

Downsize or Eliminate Organizational IT Development Teams

Many federal organizations, including mine, have in-house IT development teams for smaller projects that aren't contracted out via an RFP. This leads us down the path of custom, one-off solutions, both because we have the dedicated resources to build a custom application and because those resources are focused only on our specific requirements. My organization's IT development office should be replaced by a smaller corps of in-house technologists who have intimate knowledge of and experience with the organization's goals and needs. These technologists should focus on finding existing solutions and interoperating with partner organizations, not on building organization-specific tools. Keeping internal technologists is vital, as too often the process of nontechnological clients defining the problem for contracted technology providers to solve ends up producing short-sighted solutions.

User Analytics

The Federal Chief Information Officer (CIO) should create a standard usage analytics kit that must be installed on all federal web applications. The kit would collect standard app usage metrics like number of daily and monthly users, user loyalty, and view counts for all pages, and would also offer users a standard method for providing feedback on an app. Though there are a wide variety of federal apps with user bases of different sizes and different intended usage patterns, these metrics would provide some basis for comparing apps across government agencies. The metrics could serve as a basis for eliminating or expanding existing solutions that are clearly behind or ahead of others in their respective categories. The CIO might also pilot an IT procurement process that ties compensation to these metrics rather than development cost, which would incentivize companies to produce apps that employees will actually use.

IT Transparency

In June 2009, the government launched an IT Dashboard on *http://www.usaspending.gov* that makes available a variety of information about government IT investments, including a description of the investment, the prime contractors and monthly updates on cost, schedule, and performance figures, and agency CIO ratings. This is a great example of holding the government accountable to the public through greater transparency. I would like to see it expanded, where prudent, to include things like subcontractors, user analytics, underlying technologies, informational and operational interdependencies, reused code components, and even demos. This would afford greater transparency into how the government is using technology, allowing technologists, whether for profit or simply for the public good, to identify redundancies across government applications, opportunities for adoption of existing enterprise solutions, or just plain inefficient or poorly designed solutions. The government would be wise to both invite and capture this kind of feedback so that the collective dialogue builds upon itself.

IT Products, Not Projects

This dashboard could help the government initiate fewer one-off IT projects and begin reusing existing solutions. As government, industry, and citizens tag, group, and comment on government's IT investments, the dashboard could evolve into a Federal App Catalog. Aided by a growing body of helpful metadata, government organizations could browse the catalog for existing solutions that partially or fully meet their needs. The federal CIO could facilitate this process by identifying its "best-of-breed" picks within functional categories like public calendars, workflow tools, and document management systems. Eventually, shopping the catalog could become a formalized, mandatory step in pursuing a solution before an organization decides to initiate a new IT project. The organization could include the public in this step by sharing its requirements—not just through an opaque, formal document, but also by having government officials and staff members explain their needs in plain English via videos and open discussions—and soliciting shopping recommendations. Ideally, the CIO's best-of-breed picks would evolve into a suite of standard federal applications. This would greatly simplify government's information management and, in turn, increase operational and decision-making transparency.

Set the Tone at the Top

The federal government is too large and varied to be changed all at once. In this situation, it makes sense to initiate change at the top to serve as an example for the rest of government. The federal CIO could focus resources on integrating IT into White House operations and decision making. Even something as simple as having President Obama electronically sign laws, budgets, and executive orders would be substantial. Any e-government measure adopted by the White House would be a forcing function as well as an example for the rest of the executive branch. If the White House reviews packages exclusively online, for instance, then the executive agencies will have to prepare those packages online, in which case they might as well adopt online package processes.

Bottom-Up Change Through Young Technologists

While top-down change sets an example, it's generally more effective at adopting existing innovations than driving innovation itself. Innovation tends to be bottom-up and fueled by fresh minds. Government needs to recruit young, talented technologists to begin and later lead the transition to e-government and greater transparency. Many young people, however, are turned off by the lack of responsibility in most entry-level government positions. One notable exception is the prestigious Presidential Management Fellows (PMF) Program. Graduate students interested in civil service apply to the competitive PMF Program to spend two years working in challenging developmental roles across multiple federal agencies in four 6-month rotations. Many go on to lead distinguished careers in public service. It's a fast-moving career track with the cachet to attract top-notch graduates. A similarly prestigious program for technologists interested in transparency would instantly create a fresh cadre of on-the-ground eyes and ears to both report back to leadership as well as play roles in transparency initiatives and pilot applications. It would also plant the seed for tomorrow's technology and transparency leadership in government.

Conclusion

While transparency clearly requires operational changes within government, the system does not need to be completely reinvented. I opened with the boomerang email as an example of the lack of internal transparency. Yet the fact that my question can pass through dozens of relevant people in different parts of the country and, not finding an answer, naturally make its way back to me without any top-down control is also a remarkable testament to the inherent order within government. E-government will sometimes require brand-new, web-inspired approaches, but many other times it will be a matter of transitioning existing, well-ordered "analog" processes to a new medium. These processes were engineered before the web medium introduced an entirely new notion of transparency, where information is expected to be instantaneous, granular, accurate, complete, and universally accessible. Government's current lack of transparency by this standard is not necessarily an explicit choice. In many cases, it simply has not yet had a chance to catch up with the new definition.

Figuring out how to "catch up" an enormous, complex, legacy institution and make it transparent to 300 million citizens will be an ongoing effort. The call for a more transparent government has no final solution, only a general direction against which incremental improvements can be measured. Fortunately, the pace of these improvements should accelerate, as transparency efforts benefit from a powerful positive feedback loop. When government becomes more transparent, more people have a greater understanding of its operations and the challenges it faces, including the obstacles on the path to greater transparency. These additional, diverse minds are then primed to help clarify and overcome these challenges. Transparency is more than a vehicle of accountability. It is a platform that educates and empowers citizens and businesses to offer better solutions for government. Better solutions lead to greater transparency, which further empowers those outside government. The natural conclusion of transparency is a blurring of the line between government and the governed, when the window becomes so clear that it's difficult to tell who is outside and who is in.

About the Author

 Since February 2009, **TIM KOELKEBECK** has focused on facilitating collaboration and increasing transparency within his department at the Pentagon by transitioning its analog work processes to web applications. During the preceding two and a half years, he was a senior analyst fully immersed in the day-to-day operations of the department, which oversees the acquisition of major military systems. Tim was introduced to the Government 2.0 community in November 2008, when he and two friends won the first Apps for Democracy contest hosted by Vivek Kundra, then the Chief Technology Officer of Washington, D.C. Tim received an Honors B.A. in computer science from Harvard, where he focused on the intersection of computation and neuroscience. He reengaged this line of thought in 2008 by launching MyType, a web app experimenting with personality-driven recommendation technology.

CHAPTER TWENTY-SEVEN

Bringing the Web 2.0 Revolution to Government

Gary D. Bass
Sean Moulton

President Barack Obama has promised the most open and transparent government in the history of the United States. Sounds like great news. However, we know from experience that he will run into many barriers. In this chapter, we identify three such barriers, provide suggested solutions, and conclude with an example using federal spending to show how to move transparency into the twenty-first century.

Government Transparency: Three Hurdles

President Obama, on his first full day in office, sent a memo to agency heads saying that his administration will be guided by transparency, increased participation, and improved collaboration. The memo stated that the administration is "committed to creating an unprecedented level of openness in government," adding that greater openness "will strengthen our democracy and promote efficiency and effectiveness in government."* (See the Appendix.) Of course, saying this is much easier than achieving it.

---

* "Transparency and Open Government," President Barack Obama, Memorandum for the Heads of Executive Departments and Agencies, January 21, 2009 (*http://www.whitehouse.gov/the_press_office/ Transparency_and_Open_Government/*).

Six months into the Obama administration, Maura Reynolds wrote in *Congressional Quarterly* that, "In practice, the new president's record on government secrecy and transparency has turned out to be decidedly mixed, with his administration seeming to take as many steps toward shielding government information as it has toward exposing it to the sunshine."[†] She described one example of the Obama administration refusing to disclose records about coal company executives' visits to the White House. Since that article was published, the White House has also refused to disclose logs about White House meetings on health care policy.[‡] A similar concern has been raised about the Obama administration's decision to withhold photos of suspected terrorists being interrogated by the U.S. government. In each of these cases, the administration has taken a position that is virtually identical to that of the Bush administration.

Yet by September, after a little more than seven months in office, the Obama administration began to make meaningful changes in transparency policy. On the White House visitor logs, it reversed course and announced that, starting in 2010, the names of nearly all visitors, when they visited, and who they visited will be posted to a website, starting with people who visit the White House complex as of September 15, 2009.[§] No other president has ever agreed to such disclosure. Additionally, in September, the president announced a new policy on state secrets after having been widely criticized as continuing the Bush administration's policy of claiming a privilege to withhold information from the courts, making it impossible to challenge the government on various actions.[‖] The new policy establishes procedures within the administration for providing evidentiary information on the need for the privilege and extensive reviews. According to Attorney General Eric Holder, the new procedures "ensure the state secrets privilege is invoked only when necessary and in the narrowest way possible."

Even as the Obama administration develops new policies that make the White House more transparent and accountable, the actions are not all that the transparency community has hoped for. The procedures under the state secrets policy have been criticized as a "trust us" approach and as lacking meaningful oversight and judicial review. Some have argued that the disclosure of White House visitor logs should be retroactive and applied to all agencies, not just the White House. While it may be challenging for the Obama administration's actions to fully satisfy transparency advocates, any significant progress will require overcoming three difficult and intertwining barriers:

- Current laws and policies on public access are inadequate for today's 24-hour-per-day, seven-day-per-week Internet-enabled world. Too often, the burden falls on the public to

---

† "Open Government – Or 'Transparency Theater'?", Maura Reynolds, *CQ Online News*, July 24, 2009 (*http://www.cqpolitics.com/wmspage.cfm?docID=news-000003175686*).

‡ See *Citizens for Responsibility and Ethics in Washington v. U.S. Department of Homeland Security* (*http://www.citizensforethics.org/node/41934*).

§ See *http://www.whitehouse.gov/VoluntaryDisclosure/*.

‖ See *http://www.usdoj.gov/opa/pr/2009/September/09-ag-1013.html* for the Department of Justice press statement and *http://www.usdoj.gov/opa/documents/state-secret-privilieges.pdf* for the policies and procedures.

request information, and there are far too many loopholes that allow agencies to withhold information. These policies need radical overhaul.

- The federal government's use of interactive technology is largely grounded in the twentieth century. The use of Web 2.0 technology and thinking is only starting to make its way into government via the Obama administration, but the hardware, software, and capacity of public employees need significant upgrades.[#]

- Even with the best technology and policies, an underlying culture of secrecy pervades government. No civil servant gets rewarded for improving public access, but they do get attention if they give out information that could be misused. Disincentives for openness are built into the way agencies and the whole of government operate. Civil servants need to be given the freedom to disclose information, and they need to be rewarded for doing so.

Changing Policies

When it comes to transparency, many important policy areas need overhaul: the Freedom of Information Act (FOIA), whistleblower protections, handling of security-related materials, access to presidential records, and more.

FOIA, which is the backbone of public access today, provides a good example of the importance of each administration's policy. Memos in 2001 and 2002 from Attorney General John Ashcroft and White House Chief of Staff Andrew Card encouraged agencies to aggressively use various FOIA exemptions to withhold information. For example, in handling "sensitive" information, the memos instructed agencies to liberally use FOIA Exemption 2 (Internal Agency Rules), Exemption 4 (Proprietary Information, Trade Secrets), and Exemption 5 (Interagency Memoranda) to withhold information from the public.

The data (see Figure 27-1[*]) shows that these types of policy memos make a big difference in government. Comparing the five years after the Bush administration memos were issued with the previous five years, the number of times Exemption 2 was used to withhold records went up 239%; Exemption 4 went up 46%; and Exemption 5 jumped 72%.

The Obama administration moved quickly to improve FOIA policy (see also Chapter 30). On his first full day in office, the president signed a memo instructing his attorney general to develop new guidelines that put a premium on disclosure. According to the president, "In the face of doubt, openness prevails.... The presumption of disclosure also means that agencies

---

[#] For example, on July 31, 2009, the Department of Defense launched the Web 2.0 Guidance Forum (*http://web20guidanceforum.dodlive.mil/*) to discuss use of new media. Another example is that the Obama administration launched a Federal Web Sites Cookie Policy Forum (*http://blog.ostp.gov/category/cookie-policy/*) that closed on August 10, 2009.

[*] Source: OMB Watch analysis of data from Coalition of Journalists for Open Government, "An Opportunity Lost: An in-depth analysis of FOIA performance from 1998 to 2007," July 3, 2008 (*http://www.cjog.net/documents/Part_1_2007_FOIA_Report.pdf*).

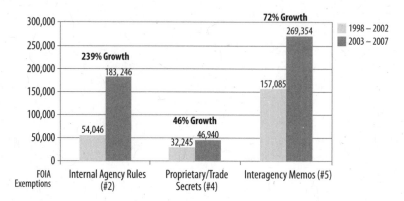

FIGURE 27-1. Use of FOIA exemptions in denying requests

should take affirmative steps to make information public. They should not wait for specific requests from the public."[†]

Attorney General Eric Holder followed suit and published guidelines on March 19 that emphasize the new presumption of disclosure.[‡] Among other things, Holder's memo promises to defend agency decisions to withhold information only if the agency demonstrates a reasonably foreseeable risk of harm to an interest protected by FOIA exemptions or statutory law. This represents a 180-degree shift from the Bush administration's position that the Justice Department would defend agency decisions to withhold information so long as they were made on a sound legal basis.[§]

The Obama administration's Department of Justice provided additional guidance in a FOIA Post that describes Holder's guidelines as "a sea change in the way transparency is viewed across government."[||] The FOIA Post gives agencies specific frameworks within which to interpret FOIA exemptions, with a bias toward disclosure. It also places new emphasis on agency requirements, recognizing that transparency and accountability are inherently linked.

It should be noted that for all of its importance and usefulness, FOIA contains serious flaws and inherent limitations. David Vladeck, an expert on these matters, has noted that "FOIA's

---

† "Freedom of Information Act," President Barack Obama, Memorandum for the Heads of Executive Departments and Agencies, January 21, 2009 (*http://www.whitehouse.gov/the_press_office/ FreedomofInformationAct/*).

‡ "The Freedom of Information Act (FOIA)," Eric Holder, Memorandum for the Heads of Executive Departments and Agencies, March 19, 2009 (*http://www.usdoj.gov/ag/foia-memo-march2009.pdf*).

§ "The Freedom of Information Act," John Ashcroft, Memorandum for Heads of All Federal Departments and Agencies, October 12, 2001 (*http://www.justice.gov/archive/oip/011012.htm*).

|| "Creating a 'New Era of Open Government'," Office of Information Policy, Department of Justice, FOIA Post, April 17, 2009 (*http://www.usdoj.gov/oip/foiapost/2009foiapost8.htm*).

file-a-request-and-wait-for-a-response approach is also an anachronism."[#] FOIA is a law designed for the paper world functioning in an electronic era. It's also a requestor-driven law: an individual must file a request for records from the government, and the government, after review, takes action to give or not give the requestor the records. The government's responsibility under FOIA is to *respond* to requests for information, not to *initiate* the publication or dissemination of information. Thus, while improvements in the FOIA policy are essential, much more is needed to alter the fundamental principles under which the government operates.

We need to institute an affirmative obligation on federal agencies to disclose information, what we will call the Right to Know (RTK). Instead of government *responding* to requests for information, it must *initiate* the disclosure. In this RTK model, FOIA becomes the vehicle of last resort, not the first tool citizens turn to. It is still an essential tool in promoting transparency, but it becomes part of the safety net of public access. The RTK affirmative disclosure model would create a more open and transparent government in pursuit of a free, permanent public access strategy. While some information would not be disclosed under RTK, the burden to justify withholding information should be a government responsibility, should be set at a high standard, and should be fully disclosed and explained in terms all Americans can understand.

So, how might this new model work? Anytime the government proceeds to collect information, it should presume that the information will be disclosed in a timely and searchable manner. When information is collected, the agency must get approval from the Office of Management and Budget (OMB). These requests, required under the Paperwork Reduction Act, should contain a plan for dissemination of the information being collected or an explanation for why the information cannot be disclosed.

There should be three levels of review for information that agencies seek to withhold. First, the OMB should review these items when it does the paperwork review. Second, the Government Accountability Office, the investigative arm of Congress, should also review these decisions to inform Congress about public disclosure in the executive branch. Finally, there should be a citizens' panel that reviews the actions taken by agencies and the OMB with regard to RTK decisions.

At a minimum, in addition to the affirmative disclosure of all information collection activities, each agency should be required to make basic information publicly available. This includes:

- A directory of all government employees, job titles, and contact information.
- A calendar for top-level agency officials (e.g., the secretary, deputy secretary, and assistant secretary).
- Correspondence logs of top-level agency officials.
- An index of all information holdings, including those that are not disclosed.

[#] "Information Access—Surveying the Current Legal Landscape of Federal Right-to-Know Laws," David C. Vladeck, 86 *Texas Law Review*, 1787, June 2008.

- A list of all FOIA requests. Any documents released as a result of a FOIA request must automatically be posted to the Web, starting with electronic records.

- A list of records that will be declassified and the timetable for such action.

- A list of all Requests for Proposals and a copy of all contracts.

- A plan for digitizing nonelectronic information (including archival information) and making it publicly accessible.

Deploying Twenty-First-Century Technology

It isn't enough to fix policy. We also need a Web 2.0 Revolution in government, which includes new thinking and new tools for openness.* As the amount and complexity of information increase, it becomes the responsibility of government to not only allow access to information, but also provide tools that enable the public to effectively search, analyze, and understand the information.

This is not an argument for simply throwing open the doors on new media tools. We all know there is a big difference between answering questions in an online town hall and delivering transparency via meaningful government data on the Internet. We are striving for the latter.

In today's Internet age, agencies must be able to flexibly use web technology and web design that aim to enhance creativity, information sharing, and collaboration among users. Building the government's capacity to construct, modify, and maintain websites should be a priority for the Obama administration—it will certainly save money even as it gives agencies more flexibility to quickly respond to events.

Another priority for the Obama administration should be to make databases more publicly accessible. Federal agencies should allow commercial search engines to index all government information, whether in databases or not. Government must provide the open programming interfaces to data that allow the public to build upon government information in ways the government cannot do. The information that is provided must also be authoritative and authentic, and the government must vastly improve on the metadata associated with all databases.

Online access is vitiated if the public cannot be assured that the information on the website is equal in authority to the information in an official reading room with hard-copy documents. This is the case with online access to agency regulatory activity, such as is now provided through Regulations.gov. If it is not authoritative—in this case, meaning the complete rule-making document is available—then it will never be useful no matter how wonderful the technology tools may be. Additionally, the public must be assured that the information that is

---

* While we use the term Web 2.0 throughout this paper, we use the term loosely. For example, when using the term we also mean to include Web 3.0, sometimes called the Semantic Web. If Web 2.0 can transform the way people network and interact with their government, Web 3.0 can revolutionize the way government data is handled and presented to the public.

provided is authentic, including that it really was provided by the individual whose name appears on the document.

Appointing the first federal CIO

The new Federal Chief Information Officer, Vivek Kundra, has made improving the public's access to and ability to use government data a top priority. For example, Kundra launched Data.gov in 2009 as a new and positive effort to make databases more available to the public. The public can search for data in various ways and obtain access through three "tabs": a data catalog, which provides access to the raw data in whatever format the agency makes available (e.g., XML, CSV, SHP, and KML); a tools catalog, which provides hyperlinks to the database; and a geodata catalog, which provides access to boundaries and other mapped characteristics.

Kundra promised that the website would include more than 100,000 data feeds on a variety of topics by the summer of 2009, and, depending on how *data feed* is defined, he can argue that has been achieved. (There are more than 100,000 boundary and geocoded files on Data.gov, but few government databases on the website. Moreover, one database, the Toxics Release Inventory, is counted many times, as the database is subdivided into downloads for each state.) But almost all of the databases available on Data.gov were already publicly available through the various agencies, such as the Census. Moreover, some of the larger databases, such as the data housed on USASpending.gov, and older data, such as information from the Toxics Release Inventory before 2005, are not available through Data.gov. Freeing up more databases from the agencies and making the information easily digestible is sure to prove a challenge.

Kundra also played a lead role in the quick establishment of an innovative new transparency tool, the IT Dashboard (*http://it.usaspending.gov/*), that lets users access data on every federal information technology project. It also provides the tools to easily analyze performance of agencies in staying on schedule and on budget, as well as trends in spending over time. The dashboard, which is modeled on a similar project Kundra implemented during his tenure as CIO of Washington, D.C., is part of a redesigned USASpending.gov. The site also allows third parties to download XML versions of the data and potentially develop their own tools for presenting the information or linking it up with other data. The IT Dashboard is a building block for demonstrating how government spending and performance data can be linked together to help the public and government focus on improving performance and wisely spending taxpayer dollars.

Encouraging data mashups

One often overlooked but vital issue in moving government to a Web 2.0 mindset is providing key identifiers that allow accurate data mashups. Without reliable identifiers across databases, outside groups and programmers will not be able to develop their own IT dashboards or other tools to allow easier review and analysis of government information. For instance, the government has data on federal contractors—who gets how much money—but it is nearly impossible to combine and analyze that data with regulatory data from the agencies to assess whether the contractors are complying with federal laws and regulations. The reason it is so hard is that the government does not provide a corporate identifier that the public can use. This means that there will be uncertainty about whether the Acme, Inc., that received a $100 million contract from the federal government is the same Acme, Inc., that violated Occupational Safety and Health Administration (OSHA) and Equal Employment Opportunity Commission (EEOC) rules. Even with the growing use of semantic technologies, there is a need for government to provide common identifiers.

Changing the Culture Within Government

Even if the policies change to expand the presumption of openness, and even if newer interactive technologies are deployed throughout government, there will still be a need to change the culture of secrecy prevailing in most federal agencies. In his 1997 book covering the results of the Commission on Protecting and Reducing Government Secrecy, former Sen. Daniel Patrick Moynihan wrote, "Departments and agencies hoard information, and the government becomes a kind of market. Secrets become organizational assets, never to be shared save in exchange for another organization's assets.... The system costs can be enormous. In the void created by absent or withheld information, decisions are either made poorly or not at all."[†] While Moynihan was discussing national security information, he could easily have been talking about almost any type of agency information. Agencies approach public access in an elegantly insouciant manner; with few incentives to advocate or promote openness, the path of least resistance is to let information sit behind closed doors. From an agency perspective, who would want to work in a fishbowl of transparency?

Unlike policy or technology changes, assessing a new culture of transparency, or a spirit of government openness, will be difficult to do. As such, the administration should be judged on whether it has established the mindset that makes public access a priority within government. Are there incentives to encourage agency personnel to promote the public's right to know in their daily work? It will also be important to create mechanisms that deliver the benefits of transparency to government officials and reinforce the new mindset.

Here are several ideas for encouraging civil servants to make transparency an important part of what they do:

- Create new review processes that deliver feedback on transparency to government officials. This includes making public access and other government openness issues part of formal government employee reviews. If it is clear that promotions and bonuses derive from actively disseminating information to the public, that behavior will be reinforced.

- Create a review and reporting process in which agencies annually evaluate their performance on transparency, a sort of transparency report card that all agencies fill out.

[†] *Secrecy: The American Experience*, Daniel Patrick Moynihan, Yale University Press, 1999.

- Establish mechanisms for the public to provide better feedback about government actions based on the information being disclosed. For instance, if an online tool such as the Amazon.com five-star rating system allowed the public to indicate their approval or disapproval of programs or spending decisions, then officials would actually benefit from the disclosure. This public assessment should be linked to the agency report card and employee reviews.

- Building on the report cards and public input, the government could grant awards, given by the White House, for the best agency efforts on transparency. Awards from the White House are coveted, pushing agency staff members to be recognized for good work. This might be done like the Annual Golden Hammer Award, which is a peer-recognition award identifying elite suppliers who support retailer sales, marketing, and partnership efforts. Groups outside government could also provide best *and* worst awards—sometimes shame works wonders.

There are other ideas for changing the climate within agencies. For example, why not require agencies to announce the public's transparency rights at the start of public meetings and conferences, on websites, in reading rooms, in libraries, and in other forums? This would be like a Right-to-Know Miranda warning, letting everyone know that they have access to information and that they have certain rights when disclosure failures occur. To complement the RTK Miranda warning, Congress should grant new rights for citizen suits against agencies that fail to comply with basic RTK requirements.

Agency staff members should also be required to attend periodic trainings on RTK issues so that they are familiar with the public's right to know, as well as the tools they can use to carry out transparency efforts. The mandatory trainings could also result in a certification that signifies a level of understanding in how to disseminate government information.

Putting It All Together: Disclosure of Federal Spending

One key test of the Obama administration's success in bringing government transparency into the twenty-first century will be how the White House and agencies handle the disclosure of government spending. The emphasis on government spending was elevated by passage of the $787 billion American Recovery and Reinvestment Act, commonly called the Recovery Act. Of Recovery Act spending, Obama promised "…every American will be able to go online and see where and how we're spending every dime."‡ The Recovery Act's website, Recovery.gov, will be the test case for the administration's approach to achieving government transparency online.

The administration may be underestimating the challenge before it in this test case. USASpending.gov, a searchable website of nearly all government spending required by the

‡ President Obama's first prime time news conference, February 9, 2009.

Federal Funding Accountability and Transparency Act of 2006,§ may offer some insight into the awaiting difficulties. The law, which was cosponsored by Sens. Barack Obama and Tom Coburn, was hailed by conservatives, libertarians, and progressives as revolutionary in vision and for breaking out of the antiquated FOIA file-a-request approach by requiring affirmative dissemination of nearly all government spending on an ongoing basis. But while USASpending.gov delivered on better and faster access to information regarding who gets how much money from the government, the project revealed several glaring weaknesses. Chief among those weaknesses was data quality, including accuracy and timeliness of the information. The site also failed to deliver on a requirement to post information about subawards by January 1, 2009. Given USASpending.gov has been unable to report on subcontracts and subgrants, it seems dubious that the president's promise regarding the Recovery Act can be fulfilled without a radical overhaul in how reporting and disclosure is done.

In order to ensure that Recovery Act spending is fully transparent, the government and the public should have access not only to data about who is getting money, but also to data about what they are doing with those funds—and the public should also be able to easily access and understand that information. It is quite likely that there will be bumps in the road with Recovery Act transparency, lots of frustration with implementation, and problems with data quality. Some will criticize Recovery.gov either for its cost or for services (or both), and some will knock the administration for not having the data to demonstrate how Recovery Act funds have helped to spark economic recovery and investment in a sustainable future. Yet the efforts that are being undertaken to build Recovery.gov can serve as important building blocks for a new paradigm in reporting and disclosure for annual federal spending initiatives.

Building on the policies, technologies, and cultural changes we talked about earlier in this chapter, there are three factors to consider for effective spending transparency. We will use the context of the Recovery Act, but the ideas can and should also be applied to annual government spending activities through USASpending.gov.

Policy Changes to Get Deeper Information on Recipients

Americans have a right to know how and where public dollars are being spent, but the information on USASpending.gov takes you only so far because of limitations in reporting requirements. Significant policy changes are needed for the reporting and oversight of the use of public funds. Without sufficient transparency, pay-to-play scandals and corruption are endemic to large federal expenditures. Proper choices in transparency policy will help mitigate this by tracking the money further and making it more difficult for less scrupulous operators to abuse the system.

---

§ Federal Funding Accountability and Transparency Act of 2006 (Public Law 109-282) (*http://frwebgate .access.gpo.gov/cgi-bin/getdoc.cgi?dbname=109_cong_public_laws&docid=f:publ282.109.pdf*).

The good news is that for the first time, the federal government is instituting a policy that requires those receiving financial assistance (e.g., grants, loans, insurance) and contracts under the Recovery Act to report directly on the use of those funds. The bad news is that the new policy requires only prime recipients and one level of subrecipients to report (see Figure 27-2). This means that if a grant is made to a state, and the state provides a subaward to a city, the public will know about the activities of each party. However, if the city subcontracts the money to several companies to carry out the work—a likely scenario—the public will not know who received the money or what they did with it.‖ Thus, the public will not know whether the money went to a mayor's brother-in-law as a special favor or to a company that won it through a competitive bidding process. For those interested in improving the quality of government programs, there won't be data to show who the service provider was or what the provider did with the funds.

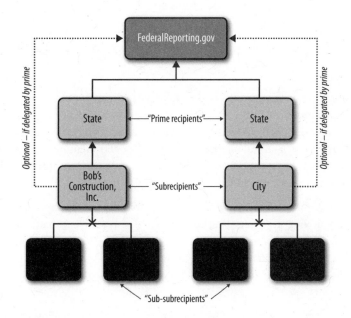

FIGURE 27-2. Who will be reporting? New Recovery Act guidance

Recipients of Recovery Act funds are required to report on the spending through a new website called FederalReporting.gov, but three policy mistakes have created significant weaknesses in the process.

First, prime recipients are allowed to delegate reporting on FederalReporting.gov to subrecipients, but this is not required. (The prime recipient cannot, however, delegate

‖ The public will know the identity of subrecipient vendors that receive more than $25,000, but not those entities that receive subawards from the subrecipient; that is, the ultimate recipient.

reporting on estimating the number of jobs created.) The policy should require each recipient and subrecipient, regardless of tier, to report directly to the federal government—and there should be a clear system to identify the original source of the funds to avoid confusion and double-counting.

Second, the Recovery Accountability and Transparency Board—also known as the Recovery Board—which oversees Recovery Act implementation is not responsible for making certain that the recipient data is accurate. Instead, the law requires a 20-day error correction window for reporters and federal agencies. Twenty days is simply not enough time for improving data quality. Moreover, there are no penalties for errors or for nonreporting.

Third, there should be clear, concise definitions for each reporting field. Unfortunately, when it comes to the fields dealing with jobs, the government punted. It told recipients to estimate the number of full-time equivalent jobs created, but left it to each recipient to define what a full-time equivalent is.

Using Technology to Make Recovery Act Data Accessible, Understandable, and Usable

Information submitted to government should take place through publicly visible channels, as should information produced by federal agencies. Agencies that withhold information—either intentionally or unintentionally—feed a perception that government is hiding something. In some cases, this requires a radical overhaul in the way government perceives its role; call it a Web 2.0 Revolution. It is not simply about employing twenty-first-century technology tools; it is also about embracing a distributed, open standards mindset.

For the Recovery Act, this means government must not only provide a robust, searchable website, but also provide the underlying data in machine-readable formats that allow developers to create their own websites and uses of the data. This data cannot be provided in aggregated form; instead, the data must provide information about each grant and contract, as well as information about the flow of federal funds from these grants and contracts to various tiers of subrecipients.

From a user perspective, there should be a simple user interface that allows people to search, filter, and download data. There should be data visualization tools that allow users to not only map information, but also conduct analyses. An essential element to designing the website is to get viewpoints of different types of users and to design it with both the novice and professional in mind.

From a developer's perspective, there should be an open architecture that allows people to design their own applications. Developers should be able to access source feeds via download, via RESTful web service discovery, via Atom or RSS feeds, or via an open reporting language (e.g., XBRL). This capability will allow other government agencies or nongovernmental organizations to create mashups using authoritative Recovery.gov data. As the government provides data through machine-readable feeds and through its own website, it also needs to synchronize the underlying data so that the public does not become confused.

Designing the website and other tools from these perspectives will reflect the Obama administration's mantra of transparency and openness. It uses technology to foster a sense of community while not escaping responsibility. It also greatly enhances the potential of any government site. Instead of limiting the site's development to a small set of contracted professionals, it opens it up to a new realm of solutions and creative insights.

As described earlier, all recipients and subrecipients of federal funds should report directly to a website on spending and performance. Additionally, all entities that will spend federal funds should be required to register in a federal registry that provides common information about the entity, including entity and parent identifiers. Figure 27-3 presents the model as applied to annual spending beyond Recovery Act funds.

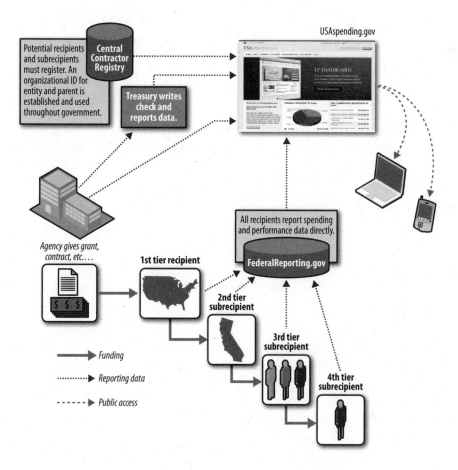

FIGURE 27-3. Building on the Recovery Act: a new reporting and transparency system

Changing the Culture to Emphasize Effectiveness, Performance, and Equity

The long-standing practice in reporting on government spending has been to present an accurate spreadsheet about who got the money, what it was for, and when it was spent. While these are certainly important facts about spending, government must go further and start connecting the spending to other data to answer more difficult questions about effectiveness, performance, and equity.

The federal government must begin to think about spending in a broader context and link spending data with four types of content:

Needs data

> Is the money going where the need is? For example, if money was supposed to go to rural areas, did it? If it was to be used for low-income populations or to address equity issues, was it?

Jobs data

> Estimates should be provided by all reporting recipients on the number of jobs created, saved, or lost. There should be uniform definitions and actual numbers, not estimates, where possible. There should also be related data, including wages, benefits, and demographics.

Performance data

> Performance data should allow the public to see agreed-upon benchmarks and whether the recipient of the funds is reaching those benchmarks. The issue is not simply who is getting how much money, but whether the money is being used effectively. Having this data leads to a discussion about how to improve the quality of government services and activities. Also, equity issues need to be addressed, including race, class, gender, and disability.

Requests for proposals and contracts

> Regardless of whether a federal contract was given by the federal, state, or local government (through a subcontract), there should be a copy of the request for proposal, information on whether the contract was awarded through open competition, and a copy of the actual contract.

Carefully tracking expenditures will allow the public to judge the effectiveness of public investments only if data on the performance of entities that undertake Recovery Act projects is included alongside basic spending data. This would help to answer the fundamental question of what we got for our money. Linking performance data with spending information creates new opportunities for dialogue about improving the quality of government programs and eliminating programs that continue to fail.

Including performance data would be a change from simply tracking expenditures, but we need an even greater shift in how the government conceives of effective spending. All too often, key equity metrics—such as race, gender, economic status, age, and disability—are overlooked when measuring against benchmarks. In the case of the Recovery Act, equity metrics are essential to measuring success and need to be given greater prominence.

Unfortunately, there is no mechanism for collecting performance information from those who receive federal funds. Under the Recovery Act, the prime recipient is required to provide estimates of jobs saved or created, including estimates for its subrecipients one tier below. There is no definition of a job (e.g., 30 hours or 40 hours per week), and there is no supplemental information such as the level of wages paid, whether benefits are provided, or who got the jobs. Regarding program implementation, there is no information about performance that is to be collected.

Conclusion

There is great reason to be optimistic about improving government transparency. President Obama strongly supports openness and accountability in government and has said that he wants government to be more transparent, participatory, and collaborative. The growth of Web 2.0 and 3.0 tools and ideas is advancing rapidly, making the vision for openness more of a reality than the promises of vaporware.

Creating an affirmative obligation to make government information available to the public should not be considered as the ultimate endgame, however. Rather, it is a means for empowering the public to become more engaged in government, to rekindle the spirit of "We the people." Fulfilling the public's right to know is about government accountability, improving the quality of government programs, and creating an informed citizenry.

Even though the cards seem stacked in favor of greater government transparency, achieving this goal will not be easy. This chapter described some challenges, if not barriers, to success. This is precisely why now is the time to work hand in hand—conservatives, libertarians, and progressives—to forcefully advocate for change. We have a window of opportunity, and we need to seize the moment.

About the Authors

GARY D. BASS is the founder and executive director of OMB Watch, a nonprofit research and advocacy organization that promotes greater government accountability and transparency and increased citizen participation in public policy decisions. He is well known for assisting nonprofit organizations in better understanding federal rules affecting their groups and constituencies, and in 2003 he created NPAction.org as a one-stop website on building nonprofit advocacy. He is also a coauthor of the 2007 book *Seen but not Heard: Strengthening Nonprofit Advocacy*, published by the Aspen Institute.

SEAN MOULTON has served OMB Watch since early 2002, as director of federal information policy with special attention on environmental information and right-to-know issues. Interestingly, one of Sean's first jobs was environmental researcher and data manager for the Council on Economic Priorities (CEP), manipulating and analyzing the information that is disseminated under the policies he now advocates. Sean's work at CEP focused on evaluating and reporting on individual corporate environmental policies and performance.

CHAPTER TWENTY-EIGHT

Toads on the Road to Open Government Data

Bill Schrier

One of the latest trends in governing is exposing many of the records and much of the data collected by governments for public viewing, analysis, scrutiny, and use. This trend started a number of years ago, with the federal Freedom of Information Act (FOIA) and local government equivalents such as Washington state's Public Disclosure Act. The trend has recently accelerated with the election of President Barack Obama, who has promised an "open and accountable" government.

While open government advocates applaud this movement, and it has many notable benefits, there are also noticeable "toads" obstructing the road to an open government future. Some of these toads are implicit in the nature and culture of government. Others represent simple resistance to change. Still others present troubling ethical issues.

What Is Government?

Government is about services and geography and information. Governments should provide services which are difficult or impossible for the public to provide for themselves, or which are hard to purchase from private businesses. It is difficult, or at least troubling, to envision a police force or fire department operating as a for-profit business. Regulatory agencies such as those issuing building permits or enforcing food safety codes also are a natural fit for government. Of course, one can envision—or experience—a private water company, ambulance company, or even for-profit parks department. Still, those are natural monopolies best served at least by a nonprofit model, and probably by government.

Government is also about geography. Cities and counties and states define themselves by their geographic boundaries. Sometimes this geography gives rise to odd anomalies. You can be in a town where the prices of most goods are 9% higher than the sticker, and travel a few hundred feet away where you pay no sales tax or need to have someone else pump your gasoline for you. But such is the nature of city limits and county boundaries and state lines. Complicated technology systems are built (e.g., 911) to guarantee that the proper service is dispatched from the proper government—for example, city police versus county sheriff's deputies versus the state highway patrol.

All of this is based on the geographical nature of governments. Technology—specifically, the Internet and the World Wide Web—is making boundaries less important. Do you care whether the recycling (or dumping) of your TV is handled by your city or your county or your state? No, but that difference is a major issue for the governments involved. Meanwhile, you simply want to go to a website and find out how to recycle.

In this way, government is also about information, because not only do governments need data to provide services, but they also thrive on data about services and about their constituents, and on turning that data into more or less usable information.

Data Collection

Most cities collect data in a variety of ways, and the most fundamental way is the phone call. A requestor (citizen, customer, constituent, member of the public, complainant) calls 911 for emergencies or calls 311 (in some more enlightened communities) for anything else. This starts the massive engine of data collection about the call and service. A simple call about a microwave oven left in the street can generate a huge amount of data collection. Is it in the street or on the curb? Is it a traffic hazard or, indeed, has it caused a collision? Who should pick it up and dispose of it—the streets department, solid waste department, or police department? Who left it there? Did they break a law? Should they be fined?

Usually, the person requesting a service must, at a minimum, provide his name, his phone number, and a detailed description of the request, including a specific geographic location. Often, she will need to provide a lot more information, such as her date of birth or Social Security number or home address to get a license or permit or piece of identification.

Beyond service calls, governments collect or generate a wide variety of data from a whole host of other sources. For example:

- Detailed financial information about payments received from companies and people.
- Business location, nature of business, ownership, business income, payroll, and a wide variety of other information about each business operating within the particular government's grasp.

- Statistics such as the number of cars passing through a particular intersection or the number of people living in a given census tract. Indeed, the amount of statistical information collected about economic, personal, and governmental activity probably far exceeds the data collected about individual complaints or requests for service.

Exposing the Soul of Government

The information in government databases is vast and, indeed, is probably the "soul" of government. Certainly, in a democracy all of this information is owned in common by the governed. And most of it should be freely turned over to anyone who asks. So, what's the problem? Why isn't all the data collected by government freely available and posted on websites for anyone to take and use?

I believe there are probably seven general reasons most data owned by governments is still locked in our virtual vaults:

- Privacy and legal restrictions
- The culture of bureaucracies and homeland security
- Ancient media
- Proprietary and medieval databases
- Ethically questionable (privacy)
- Ethically questionable (sharing)
- Cost

Privacy and Legal Restrictions

This restriction is the easiest to understand, although not necessarily to interpret or put into action.

Clearly, we do not want to "make open" any information restricted by law or prone to criminal use. Health records are certainly private, for example, as is personal information such as date of birth and Social Security number in combination with legal name and residence. This latter combination can be used to obtain credit and steal identities. The names of victims and often the names of accused are private, as are active criminal investigation files. Conversations between attorneys and clients, including between an assistant city attorney and clients such as department directors who are conducting personnel investigations or hiring/disciplining employees, are private.

The difficulties with releasing information and records are primarily the myriad laws and rules which protect privacy. There are federal, state, and local laws. There is case law. There are special laws such as the Health Insurance Portability and Accountability Act of 1996 (HIPAA). Interpreting which laws apply often requires legal opinions from a government-employed attorney. Then, redacting or removing protected information from records requires considerable time, effort, and expense by government workers.

There are amazing sets of twists and turns and incongruities.

For one example, investigations of misconduct or discrimination are generally and amazingly in the public record. In the Seattle Transportation Department in 2008, for instance, certain employees claimed discrimination in job promotions and other personnel actions. The department hired an outside law firm and spent $800,000 investigating the issues. The entire file was opened as a public record, although the names of individual employees were redacted. One twist in this case is that employees who were interviewed as part of the investigation were notified prior to the release of the record—they could have hired a personal attorney to sue the city to block the release of the records.

In another situation, the city of Seattle has an ordinance, dating from the 1970s, restricting the police from collecting information about the activities of people other than for criminal investigations. This ordinance was enacted partially as a reaction to the FBI activities of 1975 and earlier, where that agency, under J. Edgar Hoover, collected vast files on the private lives of the people of the United States, both prominent and unknown. One twist in this Seattle ordinance is that the Seattle police not only are restricted from collecting such information, but also are restricted from obtaining it (via, say, an automated link) if it was collected by another agency.

In still another situation, an employee requested all records referencing her name, including performance evaluations, emails about her, and notes in supervisors' files (files kept by supervisors about an employee's performance). This single request resulted in a search or scan of files and email messages held on desktop, server, and mainframe computers, plus a physical search of paper files to find all the relevant material. Then it all had to be redacted to remove the names of other employees or other protected information before it was released.

In the end, simply determining which laws might protect data and information held by the government is a daunting task. Often, it is easier to let information sit rather than make this determination and open the information to public scrutiny.

The Culture of Bureaucracies and Homeland Security

Information is power. It is in the nature of bureaucracies to be both protective of their information and fearful of its release. This fear gained new legal and emotional standing after the terrorist attacks on September 11, 2001, laws resulting from those attacks, and the creation of giant federal bureaucracies such as the U.S. Department of Homeland Security. A whole new class of restrictions on sharing of information was enacted for fear that certain kinds of information might be an aid to future terrorists.

Specific examples of such information include:

- Plans for buildings on file in building departments.

- Locations of public communications infrastructure such as fiber optic cable for phones and data systems. There have been "terrorist" incidents in both Bellingham, Washington, and Santa Clara County, California, where cables have been intentionally cut and 911 service interrupted.

- Plans for and even the location of other infrastructure such as water pipelines, electrical lines, highway bridges, and microwave and radio towers (their locations are obvious, but what services are provided on any particular tower are not obvious).

- Government plans for protecting such infrastructure or responding to emergencies.

While this set of restrictions generally seems to make sense, the climate of fear gripping the nation after September 11 added a whole other set of issues. For example, the city of Seattle had published, on its website, the location and nature of all calls to which the fire department and its medical service were dispatched. After September 11, that information was curtailed, probably without specific legal authority, but because of Seattle's home city security concerns.

Many cities do restrict making public the locations and nature of 911 calls—police or fire. A domestic violence call to a specific address could, if revealed, fuel additional attacks on the victim. But is there a good reason to withhold information about thefts or barking dogs or even assaults? Shouldn't people know what is going on in their neighborhoods? On the other hand, what if releasing that information depresses housing values or sales in that neighborhood, or causes discriminatory lending practices?

Many officials inside government also fear misinterpretation of data, and crime data specifically. If the geographic location of all crimes is made public in a data feed, it certainly would be possible to draw lines around certain locations and declare that crime is increasing (or decreasing) in those locations. People outside government might draw erroneous correlations from the data, especially when compared with other information such as census data or anecdotal information, e.g., "This is a high crime neighborhood because many legal and illegal immigrants live here."

NOTE

The book *Inside Bureaucracy* by Anthony Downs (Waveland Press, 1993) contains further reading on the culture of government—or indeed, the culture of any large bureaucracy, public or private.

Ancient Media

Large quantities of government information are still stored on ancient media. In many cases, these are maps with locations of infrastructure or photographs. There are also filing cards or paper files with building permits and other permitting activity, criminal case files, legal opinions, and a variety of other data. In some cases, the older paper media have been moved to "newer" microfilm or microfiche, which—in these days of fully electronic and digital records—makes them even harder to access! In a few cases, data might be stored on magnetic tape, audio tape, or floppy disks, although those media are too short-lived to really be repositories for significant amounts of information.

In most cases, I think, the information held on ancient media which is most needed for current government operations has already been digitized. Over time, this sort of information will become less and less relevant and important.

Perhaps we need a "Google Books" project for government!

Proprietary and Medieval Databases

A related issue is data which is presently in electronic format but which is held in proprietary and ancient databases. In some cases, the *schemas* (designs or plans) for those databases never existed or have been lost. In other cases, the vendor that sold the database considered its format to be proprietary, usually to guarantee the vendor's income stream in consulting fees to create reports to pull data from the databases. I refer to such vendor behavior as "medieval" because most software companies today freely give schemas and database structures to the governments that pay for the software.

Here are a few examples of this problem:

Electronic mail archives

Many different email systems have come and gone over the years. Today, just a few systems are in common use, such as Microsoft's Exchange/Outlook and IBM's Domino. But email archives stored in older and less common systems (e.g., Novell's GroupWise) may not convert to a newer format, or may continue to be held in the older format even when an organization converts to a newer email system. Even with newer email systems, the email message stores and archive stores may be scattered around on desktop and server computers throughout the enterprise, making it difficult to collect and expose the messages.

Older versions

In many cases, governments installed computer systems for specific tasks, such as records management for a police department or customer billing for a water department. In the (seemingly) never-ending economic and budget cycles, it is often tempting for a government to stop paying maintenance to the software vendor on such systems. As the vendor comes out with newer versions of the system, the government doesn't have license to the new version, and doesn't upgrade. So, the software continues to work, spitting out reports and bills. But the government can't take advantage of features in the new versions which allow greater portability and exposure of the data.

Custom software applications

Before 2000, it was very common for all enterprises to write custom software applications for particular business problems. In other words, rather than buy commercial off-the-shelf (COTS) software, an enterprise would do custom programming of a system in COBOL or another software language. These systems often were not well documented, and are hard to modify and very hard to "open up" for a public data feed.

Proliferation of databases

Another problem is the sheer proliferation of databases in government. This is especially a problem in that some software became "too" easy to use. Individual employees, with minimal training, could create databases from FoxPro or Microsoft Access and use them for specific purposes. In 2008, the city of Seattle planned to upgrade the entire city government to Microsoft Office 2007. One component of Office 2007 is Access 2007. But Access 2007 formats are quite different from previous Access versions. We did a scan for older Access databases to determine the magnitude of the effort to do the conversion. In one single city department alone we found more than 25,000 Access databases, 15 times the number of employees in that department! Now, most of those databases were undoubtedly old or out of use, but this does illustrate the proliferation problem.

Ethically Questionable Information (Privacy)

Legal restrictions notwithstanding, whole sets of information are ethically troubling to expose. Here are some examples:

- In the city of Seattle, a local radio/TV station (KIRO) requested the full name, employment date, and date of birth of every city employee. KIRO was trying to determine how many employees might retire from city service, and when. But full legal name and date of birth are two of the three pieces of information (the third is Social Security number) that are necessary to steal employee identities. After considering legal action to prevent the release, the city determined that it had to release the information to KIRO.

- Most elected officials and city departments maintain lists and databases of email addresses for use in contacting constituents. This is public information and is a common target for public disclosure requests. While requestors are not supposed to use such information for commercial purposes (e.g., sending penis- or breast-enlargement emails to those constituents), that's hard to prevent. Typically, I advise departments to turn such information over as a paper record so that at least the requestor needs to manually enter all the addresses!

- Employees have a right to file grievances or complaints of harassment or discrimination. Usually, governments hire outside private companies to investigate such complaints, and then render a report. But as I mentioned earlier, such investigations are public records and are open to disclosure after redaction. This is ethically troubling, at least. Employees are much less likely to discuss the details of issues if they know their identities could be inferred or revealed after the investigation ends. Public disclosure, in this case, could have a chilling effect on the investigation of harassment and discrimination. Often, governments will try to protect employees by having the private investigatory agency keep all the original source material (i.e., interview notes) and turn over only a summary report to the government, thereby preventing its release.

- Voicemail messages are held electronically. Most governments do not, I believe, keep such messages for any length of time. But such messages could well be considered public record and made public upon request.

Ethically Questionable Information (Sharing)

More and more government data is collected and held in "open" formats—ones which are easily shared. Certainly, that data could be shared publicly on websites such as Data.gov. But the data could also be shared among government agencies, and even correlated among agencies. This leads to the possibility of creating large databases of information about individuals. If you just think about the number of interactions you have with governments, this becomes a staggering amount of information: your driver's license, moving violations, parking tickets, pet licenses, building permits, electricity usage and bill, water usage and bill, license plate number, car make and model, property taxes, and so forth.

We've certainly thought about creating customizable web portals for the city government, where individuals could sign in and be presented with news from their neighborhood, for example, or an opportunity to pay their electric bill. Would we also want to give them the option to pay their parking ticket or renew their pet license? Would we want to correlate this information so that an animal control officer could be dispatched to the address on a cat owner's electrical bill and arrest her because Fluffy is unlicensed?

Laurence Millar, former CIO of New Zealand, had one interesting and partial solution to this issue: allow sharing among agencies only when explicitly authorized by the individual. This would certainly suit my taste, as I don't want my speeding tickets with the Washington State Patrol cross-correlated with those of the Seattle police and other agencies!

This sort of information sharing is, of course, not unique to government. There are recent reports that social networking sites (MySpace, Facebook) might "leak" information to web search engine sites (Google, Yahoo!) so that the web browsing habits of consumers can be cross-correlated with their personal information and used for a variety of purposes, such as targeted advertising, I presume.

An interesting (or terrifying) marriage of these two data sources is public information about individuals from governments on an open data feed used by the same companies that track social networking and web browsing or online purchasing habits. "Ethically troubling," to say the least.

Cost

In some cases, the cost to keep and expose government data is just too high to make it practical. The best example of this is email. The city of Seattle has an active email store of about 5 terabytes. That's 5,000,000,000,000 bytes. (The contents of the printed matter of the entire Library of Congress are estimated to be 10 terabytes.) We have a rule that all email is deleted after 45 days unless the individual user explicitly archives it as being a public record or otherwise valuable. We've been criticized that 45 days is just too short a time—the records should be kept longer. We've estimated that keeping email for a year would require a message store of about 30 terabytes, and an additional initial cost of $1.8 million in storage. Furthermore, it would take at least two days just to back up a message store of this size.

Clearly, there are limits on how much data should be kept and exposed in terms of the cost to taxpayers.

Conclusion

I'm an open government advocate. I believe most of the data held by government should be freely available on the Internet for use by the public who paid for its collection and storage. I list the "toads in the road" of open government in this chapter simply to demonstrate that this is not a trivial or inexpensive task. It will take some effort (and perhaps a bulldozer) to get past some of the reasons not to share data. I do believe that, over time, as systems are upgraded and replaced, most of this data will become exposed.

We also need better systems for document management, content management, and searching. Some of those systems exist (e.g., Microsoft's SharePoint and Oracle's Stellent). But again, they are relatively expensive and not trivial to implement.

Finally, exposing this data does have its ethical consequences, especially if all government data is open. Data collected by private companies—for example, telecommunications companies, web e-tailers, and search companies—can be cross-correlated with the government data by those companies or others for purposes of marketing, advertising, and even criminal activity.

Yes, the road to open government data is pockmarked with many toads and bumps. Yes, most of them can eventually be overcome. But do we really want to make it that easy for everyone to obtain and use that data?

About the Author

 **BILL SCHRIER** is the chief technology officer (CTO) for the City of Seattle and director of the city's Department of Information Technology (DoIT), reporting directly to Mayor Greg Nickels. Seattle has a population of about 600,000 residents and a city government of about 11,000 employees. DoIT has 215 full-time employees and a budget of $59 million. Approximately 600 employees work in information technology units throughout city government. Bill writes a blog (*http://www.digitalcommunitiesblogs.com/CCIO*) about the intersection of information technology and government, how they sometimes collide but often influence and change each other. He tweets at *http://www.twitter.com/billschrier*.

CHAPTER TWENTY-NINE

Open Government: The Privacy Imperative

Jeff Jonas
Jim Harper

When President Obama issued his open government directive on his first full day in office, he signaled in dramatic style that his administration would be more committed to collaboration, transparency, and participation than any prior administration (see the Appendix). With an administration committed to openness and with continuing advances in information technology, the stars are aligning for major changes in the way government operates. But implementing open government will produce new challenges. One significant challenge will be the protection of privacy.

As with all other digital interaction, online democracy that is collaborative and participatory will require U.S. citizens to reveal more personal information to government than they have before. Participating in online communities can produce deep reservoirs of information, raising acute sensitivities in the governmental context. Data collection can chill free speech or threaten legal rights and entitlements, undermining the valuable potential of open government if online privacy issues are not handled well.

If participatory government is to have the confidence of citizens, it must be very sensitive to individual privacy and related values. Open government will not truly succeed if it is not welcoming to everyone. The most credible and successful open government systems must have the trust of all potential users, not only that of technophiles and the web generation. Open government systems must garner the trust of people who disagree with administration policies, people who distrust government generally, and people who are leery of the Internet.

As governments enter the 2.0 era, they must examine what information they collect from citizens and the rules governing how these data collections are used and controlled. A variety of techniques can protect privacy and foster the sense among all citizens that interacting with government will not expose them to adverse consequences, retribution, or negative repercussions. New and improved privacy practices can help fulfill the promise of open government.

Privacy-Enhancing Practices

As strongly as many people feel about privacy, it is not a simple concept. Privacy and privacy-related values have many dimensions that must be balanced and calibrated to achieve the goals of open government. A number of practices can enhance privacy, encourage participation, and build the credibility of open government.

Data Minimization

By default, most information technology systems are built to retain data. This is the reverse of the human experience, in which most data is never recorded—indeed, it is often not even thought of as data. What is recorded is captured imperfectly, and most of the information collected is later forgotten or kept practically obscure. For open government systems to be human-friendly, they should generally act more like the organic human environment.

One buzzword that describes how data collection can be made more human is *data minimization*. People should not face unnecessary data collection when they open a channel to their government. Open government systems must collect data that is necessary for interaction, of course, but they should otherwise be tactfully calibrated and tailored to each interaction.

A starting point for minimizing data is to define the goals of any open government system. Is the goal of the system to provide the public an outlet for complaints or compliments? Is it for constituents to request services? Is it for communicating political information to supporters or opponents? Is it for communicating legal and regulatory information to regulated parties? Is it for gathering data about technical or regulatory problems? Is it a collaborative tool for designing new government programs? Is it for gauging public interest in a specific issue? Each goal warrants a particular level of data collection.

If, for example, the system is responsible for providing a service, such as resolving a complaint about a passport application, the system will need to collect contact information and other personal data. To protect privacy, data minimization might call for using a *problem ticket* or *incident log* format, in which all data is associated and held with the ticket. When the service has been rendered, it may be appropriate to keep and disseminate statistical information, such as the type of service, response time, and outcome. Specific information about the service and details about the beneficiary might be warehoused once the service is complete, then outright deleted as soon as possible.

If the goal is to gather data about a specific technical or regulatory problem, on the other hand, data minimization may call for eliminating the collection of personal identifiers entirely. Say, for example, that a traffic safety agency wants to collect information about road conditions, lighting, and hazards—"crowdsourcing" information that was previously compiled by its own crews. The system that gathers this information could decline to record any identifying data about people submitting information to a wiki or via phone, email, or web-based submission form. The incentive to "spoof" data in this example would be low, and falsified data would have little, if any, cost.

If the goal is to gather public opinion data, a system likewise need not record opinions tied to identifiers of each person submitting a view. Rather, opinions can be collected in generic form, ranked as to level of intensity, and so on, without creating records of the political opinions of specific individuals. As long as the system can count unique respondents in some way, and measure demographics if need be, there is likely no need for the retention of personally identifiable data. Privacy considerations must be carefully weighed against the demand for detail.

These are examples of data minimization options that can be put into practice because the discrete goals of a system are clear. There are many data minimization strategies, such as anonymous access, controlled backups, data destruction/decommissioning, and minimal disclosure.

Anonymous Access

In many cases, people should be able to interact with policymaking anonymously so that they can share insights that they otherwise would not. Consider the example of an immigrant who suspects that an error in her documentation might not allow her to gain permanent residency, and might even be grounds for deportation. She wants to learn the rules from the Department of Homeland Security, share her story with congressional representatives, and share the source of her confusion with policymakers in the White House.

She should be able to create a stable identity for conducting these interactions, but deny immigration law enforcement the ability to track her down. If she cannot communicate this information anonymously, she almost certainly will not ask questions or volunteer information, denying herself help she might deserve while denying policymakers relevant information.

Anonymity will always be a moving target. Stripping away name, address, and email address does not make data anonymous. As data analytics improve and as data stores grow and become more interoperable, it will be easier to piece together identity from seemingly nonidentifying information. Combinations of data elements, such as date of birth, gender, and zip code,* can

---

* "k-anonymity: a model for protecting privacy," L. Sweeney, *International Journal on Uncertainty, Fuzziness and Knowledge-based Systems*, Vol. 10, Issue 5, October 2002; pp. 557–570.

be used to hone in on specific individuals. Being aware of this and minimizing data that is likely to facilitate reidentification will protect privacy.

Controlled Backups

Another difference between the digital environment and the human experience is the way data tends to replicate. The good practice of backing up digital data creates many more copies of information than there are in the "real world." Copies of data create the risk of unintended disclosure, theft, or future repurposing of the data.

As important as good backup practices are, restraint in backup policy is worth considering. Open government systems must account for where backed-up data is stored, who handles it, and how many copies are truly necessary. Similarly, stale backups should be destroyed.[†]

Special consideration will be necessary as the government looks to *cloud computing*. Cloud computing is the use of distant servers for applications, analytics, data storage, and management. Most users of publicly available cloud computing services today have no idea how many copies of their data exist, much less exactly who controls each copy and who may have access to it. People who are skeptical about sharing data with a government agency or entity may be wary of "the cloud." Cloud computing can be demystified and secured with careful policy; controls on data access, storage, and replication; and strong penalties for data theft or data misuse.

Data collected in support of collaborative, participatory government systems must be managed and controlled in such a manner as to reduce the risk of inadvertent disclosure and undesirable reuse. This risk can be minimized in part by reducing the number of times data is copied.

Data Retention and Decommissioning

Similarly, open government systems must give careful consideration to data destruction. Data stores are perfectly secure only when they no longer exist.

As with other data minimization practices there are balances to be struck. For good reason, laws such as the Presidential Records Act[‡] require retention of materials that have administrative, historical, informational, or evidentiary value. Presidential records contain important insights that can benefit society, and it is appropriate to retain them whether it is political scientists or law enforcement officials that later discover the actions, thinking, or motivations of government officials.

The Presidential Records Act is meant to open a window into the government for the benefit of the people, of course, not a window into the people for the benefit of the government. And

---

† Often, the destruction process is actually achieved by overwriting or cycling a backup; that is, reusing the backup media.

‡ Presidential Records Act (PRA) of 1978, 44 U.S.C. § 2201.

the spirit of this law should shape policies about retention or destruction of information about citizens.

For example, the IP addresses of the computers people use to interact with the White House are almost certainly never used or considered by decision-making officials. In most cases, there is little reason to retain this data for very long. For the security of the president and the White House, of course, immediate destruction is not advisable, but retention of this data has privacy costs that can threaten participation and collaboration.

The treatment of White House records under the Presidential Records Act is just one example of where trade-offs among privacy and data retention are in play. There will be thousands of others where the law, a program's or a policy's goals, and U.S. citizens' privacy interests must be balanced.

The options are not constrained to just retention or destruction, of course. Archived data can be deoptimized for information retrieval, rendering it available only for infrequent, forensic inspection. Low-tech solutions such as microfiche or paper storage can still be used to maintain accountability while minimizing the risk of unintended disclosure, misuse, and repurposing.

After data has outlived its relevance for explicitly stated purposes, though, policy should mandate wholesale data destruction. Clear language must govern storage, retrieval, archiving, and deletion processes.

Minimal Disclosure

When information will be transferred from one project, program, or agency to another, it should be transferred in the most limited form that still serves the purpose for which it is being transferred. As discussed earlier, the initial design of an open government system should minimize data collection. Being precise about purposes is key to protecting privacy. This applies to transferring data after it has been collected as well.

Consider a simple example: say a social network for patent lawyers offers its members the opportunity to join a Patent Office project for advising the public on the patent process. The transfer of data to the new project might include the individuals' names, firm names, and contact information, but there is no need to transfer the social network's data reflecting which lawyers are connected to whom.

For more complex situations, there are methods that can mask data such as identity information while retaining the ability to match it with other data. Running a *one-way hash* (an algorithm that transforms data into a non-human-readable and irreversible form) on data in two data sets allows the discovery of common items without wholesale sharing of the information. This protects privacy relatively well while still allowing useful analytics to be run. There are methods to attack this form of protection.

NOTE

Simple hashing techniques are at risk from a number of attacks, such as one party hashing all known values (a *dictionary attack*). This necessitates careful implementation, including such things as using third parties who do not have the ability to similarly hash the data.

Consider a situation in which two separate agencies would like to compare user demographics to see whether their educational and community awareness programs are reaching distinct populations or the same people. They are not legally allowed to copy or swap each other's data.

A Social Security Administration program could take its private list of citizen email addresses from which its system has been accessed and anonymize it by scrambling it with a one-way hashing algorithm. A Medicare agency operating a wiki dealing with benefit administration can take its list of citizen email addresses and one-way-hash it the same way. These two deidentified data sets can then be evaluated for matches—finding common identities without revealing specific identities. If more demographic information is required for analysis, such as state of residence, such values can be associated with the hash values, though this can increase the risk of reidentification.

There are a variety of ways to configure anonymized matching systems that serve different purposes and protect against different attacks. Such systems must be well designed and carefully operated to reduce the risk of reidentification and other unintended disclosures. One example of good design might be automatic destruction of irrelevant data immediately after the comparison process. One-way hashing and other more sophisticated cryptographic means reduce the risk of unintended disclosure while revealing useful information.

There are also methods that obscure data while maintaining its statistical relevance. This involves changing or scrambling confidential values—such as identity, income, or race information—so that it reveals aggregate information, averages, or trends.

Minimal disclosure—sharing only the necessary and directly relevant information—protects privacy even in the context of limited information sharing. This and most of the privacy protective techniques discussed earlier are aimed at reducing the collection of information and the use of what is collected. This is so that the public can engage with government while giving up the least possible control of personal information.

Sometimes, of course, collection of personal information is necessary and appropriate, and data sharing is called for. In these cases, other privacy values are at stake. Methods are available for protecting the public's interests here, too.

Data-Sharing Integrity: Data Tethering

There are times when it is entirely appropriate for governments to collect and use personal information. Individuals' interests do not disappear when this happens, of course, but the values at stake shift.

More and more, federal, state, and local government entities will use digital data to make many decisions that affect people's lives. Such decisions may govern their ability to access open government and their role in collaborative government. Such decisions may affect whether individuals are deemed suspects of crime, whether they receive licenses, benefits, or entitlements, and so on. Even when people have given up control of information, they want government decisions to be intelligent and fair.

To deliver on this expectation, personal data should be kept current and accurate, and only relevant data should be used in government decision making. Data integrity helps provide important elements of fairness and due process, treatment that the Constitution requires in many cases and that the public demands of government. The Privacy Act requires agencies to "collect information to the greatest extent practicable directly from the subject individual when the information may result in adverse determinations about an individual's rights, benefits, and privileges."[§] This is intended to foster accuracy.

Another technique to ensure data integrity is noting the source of the data. Knowing where data came from gives the recipient entity some sense of its quality and it allows the data to be validated or updated if needed. But without additional checking, simply knowing the source of the data does not reveal when the data has changed in the originating system. Data may grow stale or be eclipsed by new information when this model is the only protection for data integrity. The greater the window between database refreshes, the greater the error rate. Especially in national security and law enforcement settings, source attribution alone can be problematic, as real privacy and civil liberties consequences can result from using stale data.

If data accuracy is important, *data tethering* should be employed. Data tethering means that when data changes at its source, the change is mirrored wherever it has been copied.[‖] Every copied piece of data is virtually "tethered" to its master copy. Unlike source attribution, in which the recipient of shared information looks after its pedigree, data tethering involves outbound record-level accountability[#] on the part of the organization that originally disseminated the information. Data tethering is an important protection for data integrity and good government decision making.

---

§ 5 U.S.C. § 552a(e)(2).

‖ Exceptions would include backups and static snapshots used for time-series analysis.

The sharing party tracks what records were sent to whom, when, and so on.

Government systems engaged in transferring personally identifiable information are candidates for outbound record-level accountability and data tethering. Without well-synchronized data, open government systems will become mired in errors.

Accountability

All government systems should prevent intentional data misuse. Active audit systems and immutable audit logs are important tools for watching the watchers.

An active audit system watches what users are doing and either prevents them from violating policy or exposes them to oversight mechanisms. It can detect certain kinds of legal or policy misuse, such as an insider using a system in a way that is inconsistent with her job, as it is happening.

Immutable audit logs are tamper-resistant recordings of how a system has been used—everything from when data arrives, changes, or departs to how users interacted with the system.* Each event is recorded in an indelible manner. Even the database administrator with the highest level of system privileges is unable to alter the log without leaving evidence of her alteration.

These systems help to create needed accountability. Their existence will also, of course, deter infringement of data use policies. It is important to recognize, however, that audit logs are copies of data that bring with them the risk of unintended disclosure, misuse, and repurposing.

Transparent Transparency

The mantra inspired by President Obama's open government directive—collaboration, transparency, and participation—refers to government itself: collaborative public policy development, transparency in government decision making and outcomes, and participation by the widest possible cross section of the public. For open government to maximize its successes, the technical systems that produce these good things must be transparent as well, revealing the collection and movement of personal data.

A major challenge to privacy is the fact that average consumers, citizens, and even savvy computer users are not aware of what they reveal when they enter digital environments. Amazing insights can be gleaned about people using sophisticated analytics on enormous data sets in large computing facilities. Uses of data that may seem standard to technology sophisticates today may be regarded as threatening privacy violations to the many less-well-informed citizens whom the government serves.

* See "Implementing a Trusted Information Sharing Environment: Using Immutable Audit Logs to Increase Security, Trust, and Accountability," Jeff Jonas and Peter Swire, February 2006 (*http://www.markle.org/ downloadable_assets/nstf_IAL_020906.pdf*).

The solution is transparency in the technical systems that underlie open government, but it is also much more than that. Every significant organization on the Internet and every actor in the digital revolution has some responsibility to educate the public about the information age, the economics of data, and how systems work. Without this education—without transparency about the whole information ecosystem—members of the public may fail to seek privacy protection, revealing sensitive information that cannot be concealed again. And they may fail to place blame in the appropriate place when they lose privacy or suffer ill treatment.

Average people need to better understand the importance of valuing their personal data. They need to know what types of data are collected and stored, and for what purpose. Consumers and citizens should know what data analytics can produce from their data—what information can be learned or inferred about them.

Privacy notices have been a focus over the past decade, but "notice" is only a small part of what it takes to educate the public and energize people about their privacy. Users of open government systems should be directly assured by notice that the Privacy Act, the Freedom of Information Act,[†] and other laws, when they apply, are being observed by open government systems.

Improved public awareness can result from demonstrations of how information is being used. Open government projects should make publicly available the statistics they gather from open government systems including wikis, cloud-based services, web portals, and so on. Increasing transparency of open government systems can both educate the public and deter excess data gathering.

To further educate and empower, perhaps data transfers should be traceable by individual citizens themselves. Presenting data transfer information to citizens in an easy-to-understand format can increase their awareness, as they are able to see each instance when their data is shared, and with whom.

A model of sorts for this is the Fair Credit Reporting Act,[‡] which requires credit bureaus to document every time a third party has accessed consumers' credit files. This audit trail of "inquiries" allows consumers to understand who has been looking. The government could improve on this early attempt at data transparency by applying such obligations to itself. It is a good example of how data about data could be shared, giving the consumer real insight into how information about her is being used.

Providing individuals access to data about them raises security issues, of course. Individual privacy could be degraded by attempts to educate the public that reveal sensitive information to fraudsters or other snoops.

† 5 U.S.C. § 552.

‡ 15 U.S.C. § 1681 et seq.

Open government will fall short if the public cannot be educated enough to benefit from systems while understanding their rights and how data can be crunched to reveal things they have regarded as private or unknown. If users are caught by surprise due to a lack of transparency around where their data travels, if and how it is aggregated, how they are observed through data, and so on, they will shun open government systems.

Conclusion

The advance of more collaborative, transparent, and participatory government must embrace all of society's values, including privacy. Open government will succeed only if it appeals to the widest possible audience, including skeptics of government, opponents of any given administration, and people who do not trust technology.

The heart of privacy protection in open government is data minimization, requiring citizens to reveal the least amount of information required for any given transaction or relationship. Open government systems should be designed with their precise goals in mind. Under these circumstances, they can minimize the data they collect.

Permitting citizens to deal with the government anonymously will foster participation. Carefully planning backup strategies and establishing thoughtful data retention and decommissioning policies can reduce the risk of unintended disclosure and misuse of personal data.

When it is appropriate to share information, minimal disclosure techniques can minimize the loss of privacy even in that context. And, of course, when it is appropriate to share personal information, there are techniques to ensure that this does not degrade data quality and cause errant decisions that could deny people rights or benefits.

Accountability can be enhanced by active audit and immutable audit systems that deter and expose wrongdoing. And transparency in open government data systems can educate and empower a public that too often today remains indifferent to how data is used by the government and throughout society.

For all of the promise of open government to come to fruition, systems must be designed with basic values such as privacy in mind.§ With luck and lots of hard work, open government systems can fulfill the privacy imperative.

§ See "Privacy by Design," by Ann Cavoukian (*http://www.ipc.on.ca/images/Resources/privacybydesign.pdf*).

About the Authors

JEFF JONAS is chief scientist of the IBM Entity Analytics group and an IBM Distinguished Engineer. The IBM Entity Analytics group was formed based on technologies developed by Systems Research & Development (SRD), founded by Jonas in 1984 and acquired by IBM in January 2005. Prior to IBM's acquisition of SRD, Jeff led it through the design and development of a number of extraordinary systems, including technology used by the surveillance intelligence arm of the gaming industry. Leveraging facial recognition, this technology enabled the gaming industry to protect itself from aggressive card count teams, the most notable being the MIT Blackjack Team, which was the subject of the book *Bringing Down the House* (Free Press) as well as the recent movie *21*. Today, Jonas designs next-generation "sensemaking" systems that fundamentally improve enterprise intelligence, making organizations smarter, more efficient, and highly competitive.

JIM HARPER is the director of information policy studies at the Cato Insititute and focuses on the difficult problems of adapting law and policy to the unique problems of the information age. Jim is a member of the Department of Homeland Security's Data Privacy and Integrity Advisory Committee. His work has been cited by *USA Today*, the Associated Press, and Reuters. He has appeared on the Fox News Channel, CBS, MSNBC, and other media. His scholarly articles have appeared in the *Administrative Law Review*, the *Minnesota Law Review*, and the *Hastings Constitutional Law Quarterly*. Recently, Harper wrote the book *Identity Crisis: How Identification Is Overused and Misunderstood* (Cato Institute). Jim is the editor of Privacilla.org, a Web-based think tank devoted exclusively to privacy, and he maintains online federal spending resource WashingtonWatch.com. He holds a J.D. from UC Hastings College of Law.

CHAPTER THIRTY

Freedom of Information Acts: Promises and Realities

Brant Houston

The U.S. Freedom of Information Act (FOIA) is fraught with paradoxes.

It's good in theory, but difficult in practice. It has produced the disclosure of illuminating, shocking, and invaluable information, but requests under the act can entail months or years of waiting. And though writing a request letter for public records under the act is relatively simple to do, relatively few citizens do so.

In fact, after the act's nearly half-century of existence, surveys have shown that corporations and paid researchers are among the heaviest users. In 2005, the Coalition of Journalists for Open Government said it analyzed 6,439 FOIA requests to 11 Cabinet-level departments and six large agencies. The report, which echoed previous surveys, said the following:

> The review found that more than 60 percent of the requests came from commercial interests, with one-fourth of those filed by professional data brokers working on behalf of clients who wanted such information as the asbestos level on old Navy ships, cockpit recordings from crashed airliners and background data on prospective employees.

> The second-largest group of requesters—categorized as "other" and consisting mostly of private citizens—comprised a third of the total. These were individuals from a wide swath of society: a movie producer doing research for *The Road to Guantanamo*, a divorcee searching for hidden assets and UFO enthusiasts seeking evidence of other worldly visitations.

There were also requests from a local police department mining for information on federal grants, a whistleblower trying to shore up a claim of government wrongdoing, historians digging into original source material, a cryptologist trying to recover a Navy intelligence report he had worked on years earlier, and a lawyer in the Texas Attorney General's office trying to locate parents overdue on child support payments.

"Media" requests accounted for 6 percent of the total. Many reporters say it takes too long to get information through FOIA to make it a meaningful tool for newsgathering. It is used more frequently by journalists working on longer, investigative projects.

The Act and Amendments

The federal Freedom of Information Act was created in 1966. Thirty years later Congress added an amendment to include electronic records to make it clear that the medium did not matter: databases and other repositories of digital government information are just like paper records and also are public. In general, the 50 states have followed the federal government's lead, enacting similar laws, including those concerning electronic records. Those laws are helpfully indexed at the Reporters Committee for Freedom of the Press website (*http://www.rcfp.org*), among other websites.

> **NOTE**
> **The FOIA does not apply to the judicial or legislative branches, which have their own disclosure guidelines, or to parts of the president's office.**

The act was strengthened again in 2008, when then-President Bush signed a bill that bolstered the act by closing some loopholes, limiting fees, and demanding more accountability from federal agencies in how they handled requests. The bill, called The Open Government Act, created phone service for federal agencies to deal with FOIA problems and called for a chief FOI officer at agencies who would monitor compliance. The act also said each agency shall have a "FOIA Public Liaison, who shall assist in the resolution of any disputes between the requester and the agency." And the act allowed the public and news media to keep better track of the status of their requests.

But the FOI laws still contain many exemptions. Other laws also have been passed concerning the privacy of health records, among them the Health Insurance Portability and Accountability Act of 1996 (HIPAA); and the Critical Infrastructure Information Act of 2002 allows government officials to close off for security reasons records which used to be public on potentially vulnerable facilities.

Nevertheless, every year organizations and individuals do succeed in obtaining or prying information from agencies—information that serves the public good or brings to light issues otherwise hidden. The National Security Archive, which specializes in using FOIA, notes 40

stories over a four-year period that could not have been done without the act (see *http://www2*
.gwu.edu/~nsarchiv/nsa/foia/stories.htm), and journalism organizations such as Investigative
Reporters and Editors (*http://www.ire.org*) and the Society of Professional Journalists (*http://*
www.spj.org) recognize inspirational and effective use of the act for news stories.

Open to All

Any citizen, whether a U.S. resident or from another country, can request information under
the act. All that is required is the ability to write a letter, which often can be faxed or emailed,
to the government agency that has the records containing that information.

While filing a "FOIA" request may seem daunting at first, many organizations offer advice on
how to do so and offer samples of FOIA letters.

For example, the Reporters Committee for Freedom of the Press has letter "generators" on its
site that provide an electronic template for making requests (see *http://www.rcfp.org/foialetter/*
index.php). The form includes the necessary important legal language, and you can fill in details
about the agency and the documents you want.

The National Security Archive also offers a wealth of information on filing requests (*http://*
www2.gwu.edu/~nsarchiv/nsa/foia.html), and the National Freedom of Information Coalition has
many helpful links at *http://www.nfoic.org/states* on filing both federal and state requests.

In addition, many organizations offer practical advice about the FOIA process—both its formal
and its informal etiquette. The FOIA process has many twists and turns that occasionally can
resemble the ordeal of buying a car.

Often, the first piece of advice experienced users of FOIA will give is surprising: don't use FOIA.
Instead, they suggest that you simply ask an agency for the records you want. There are many
records, especially online, that agencies make available without requiring a FOIA request.

That is followed by the second piece of advice by experienced users: do a thorough search of
an agency's website and of the entire Web for the information before requesting the
government records you want. The information may be sitting out in the open and ready for
easy downloading. If it is not at the agency's site, the information might have been released
already and posted by a citizen, journalist, or blogger.

Research and Prepare

If a citizen is going to file a request under FOIA laws, he needs to do some thinking, research,
and preparation beyond just seeing whether the records are already on the Web. It helps
immensely to know what question is to be answered and what agency might have the records
that will answer that question.

One way to think about who to ask is to match the topic with the agency. If the topic concerns
the environment, you likely would contact the U.S. Environmental Protection Agency (EPA).

If it concerns housing, you likely would contact the U.S. Department of Housing and Urban Development (HUD). Another way is to search the site of the Government Accountability Office (*http://www.gao.gov*) for reports and audits on agencies. Frequently, the reports and audits cite agency records the GAO looked at during the audit.

Once the agency has been determined, obtain the blank forms that someone or some entity would have to fill out if it comes under an agency's jurisdiction or does business with the agency. Those blank forms will show what records the agency collects and stores, and this will help a requester narrow the specifics of the request or go to another agency. (After all, if the agency doesn't collect the information [even if it should], then it doesn't have it.)

Once a requester has pinpointed the agency that has the records, it is important to obtain the name of the person who handles requests. Nearly every federal agency has a FOIA officer, and the federal agencies (and most state agencies) have become very adept at making sure every request ends up with the officer no matter who a requester starts with. It usually helps to place a phone call to that officer (the contact information is usually on a website) to let him know a request is coming and that you will follow up on the request.

NEED FOR CHANGES

FOIA will be improved by the electronic tracking of the status of files, but the act can be improved further in several ways.

First, the restrictions on critical infrastructure information must be reviewed and a more reasonable balance struck between the public's need to know and national security.

For example, the U.S. Army Corps of Engineers still has not reopened data on the condition of dams across the nation after promising to do so. The National Dam Inventory, which gives the age, location, inspection history, and other information about dams, was made secret after the 9/11 terrorist attacks in the United States. Then it was made public in 2002 and then promptly closed again.

When satellite photos are available and a large amount of the data is still on the Web, this secrecy makes little sense. And of course, previous data is archived on many computers and, since dams don't move (unless they collapse, or are torn down as happens occasionally) the data set from 2001 can still be used. But without updates, the public cannot keep current on inspections and repairs.

Furthermore, the data serves a public interest because the public and the media have used the inventory to identify potentially dangerous dams that are old, have not been inspected, and would cause serious injuries or deaths downstream if they collapsed.

This is just one of many other instances where the government overreacted after 9/11 and made information and data secret.

Second, the ridiculously high fees sometimes levied by agencies must be policed by an independent monitor, and governments need to give specific guidelines for fair and reasonable costs for information and data as well as give agencies specific examples of how to use those guidelines.

For example, the U.S. Department of Justice told the National Institute for Computer-Assisted Reporting that a database that the organization's data library sought would cost more than $2 billion. The Department of Justice said it intended to print out tens of thousands of electronic records, black out parts that needed to be redacted, and then scan the records back into an electronic database. This came from the department that is supposed to audit and police FOIA practices.

Third, to ease access to electronic information, governments should make the data available in an open format by the Open Source Initiative. This would speed up the release of government data and save both government officials and requesters countless hours of negotiations and dealing with technical issues. In addition, the government should reveal in general what categories of information are being disclosed when it releases information and data.

Exemptions, Denials, and Delays

Before beginning the process, a requester should also be familiar with exemptions to the act so that he doesn't waste his time or so that he knows how to recognize an incorrect denial to a request. Here are the exemptions straight from the law:

1. Specifically authorized under criteria established by an Executive order to be kept secret in the interest of national defense or foreign policy and (B) are in fact properly classified pursuant to such Executive order;

2. Related solely to the internal personnel rules and practices of an agency;

3. Specifically exempted from disclosure by statute (other than section 552b of this title), provided that such statute (A) requires that the matters be withheld from the public in such a manner as to leave no discretion on the issue, or (B) establishes particular criteria for withholding or refers to particular types of matters to be withheld;

4. Trade secrets and commercial or financial information obtained from a person and privileged or confidential;

5. Inter-agency or intra-agency memorandums or letters which would not be available by law to a party other than an agency in litigation with the agency;

6. Personnel and medical files and similar files the disclosure of which would constitute a clearly unwarranted invasion of personal privacy;

7. Records or information compiled for law enforcement purposes, but only to the extent that the production of such law enforcement records or information (A) could reasonably be expected to interfere with enforcement proceedings, (B) would deprive a person of a right to a fair trial or an impartial adjudication, (C) could reasonably be expected to constitute an unwarranted invasion of personal privacy, (D) could reasonably be expected to disclose the identity of a confidential source, including a State, local, or foreign agency or authority or any private institution which furnished information on a confidential basis, and, in the case of a

record or information compiled by a criminal law enforcement authority in the course of a criminal investigation or by an agency conducting a lawful national security intelligence investigation, information furnished by a confidential source, (E) would disclose techniques and procedures for law enforcement investigations or prosecutions, or would disclose guidelines for law enforcement investigations or prosecutions if such disclosure could reasonably be expected to risk circumvention of the law, or (F) could reasonably be expected to endanger the life or physical safety of any individual;

8. Contained in or related to examination, operating, or condition reports prepared by, on behalf of, or for the use of an agency responsible for the regulation or supervision of financial institutions; or

9. Geological and geophysical information and data, including maps, concerning wells.

It quickly becomes apparent that the potential is there for agencies to misinterpret or stretch the law to close off records, and some agencies do. For example, the U.S. Small Business Administration over the years has routinely cited the exemption on trade secrets and private commercial information as a reason not to disclose whether businesses that had received government-backed loans were delinquent in their loan payments. Yet a review of bankruptcy court records would show that some businesses were not only delinquent, but actually defunct, and had been out of business for some time.

Furthermore, security concerns increased exponentially after the 9/11 terrorist attacks on the World Trade Center in New York City. Not only did denials increase under that exemption, but databases and electronic information were erased from government websites.

Even before the Critical Infrastructure Information Act, then–Attorney General John Ashcroft issued the infamous "just say no" memorandum in 2001 to federal agencies in which agencies were told that when in doubt they should deny records to the public and that the Department of Justice would support them. That memo effectively turned FOIA's presumption of openness upside down, and denials and delays in responses to requests soared.

Since then, Congress has pushed through a bill requiring agencies to reduce backlogs and the administration of President Obama has proclaimed its support of transparency, with Attorney General Eric Holder issuing a memo that reversed the Ashcroft memo. Nonetheless, many denials are still under the umbrella of the national security exemption.

There are always denials, too, based on weak excuses and/or just a plain reluctance by officials to release information. Although federal agencies have only 20 business days to respond to a request, that often is only the beginning to a back and forth that can go way beyond 20 days. Both federal and state agencies use those strategies, particularly when electronic information is requested.

Among the common denials are:

- The agency can't quickly find the records and it would be expensive to do an extensive search.

- The electronic records are kept in proprietary software that can't be disclosed or kept by a contractor working for the agency who can't be reached quickly.

- Parts of the records need to redacted (blacked out or deleted), and that will take too much time.

- The request is too broad or they don't understand the request.

- They lack the staff to make copies of the records.

There are answers to all of these denials, but it can be time-consuming and agencies know that many requesters will give up or just have to wait—and that wait can be long.

The National Security Archive reported that in 2007 it had:

> ...filed FOIA requests with the 87 leading federal agencies and components for copies of their "ten oldest open or pending" FOIA requests. The Department of State, responding to an Archive "ten oldest" request for the first time, reported ten pending requests older than 15 years—the majority of the oldest requests in the entire federal government. Other agencies with the oldest requests include the Air Force, CIA, and two components of the Justice Department, the Criminal Division and the FBI.

One of the most serious challenges to getting records, however, is the cost of producing a copy of the records to give to the requester. Although costs are supposed to be fair and reasonable, the cost factor—or the pay-to-play situation—leaves citizens knocking at a closed door because they don't have the money to pay the agency for the records. Often, requests for fee waivers under a provision of the law are denied. And indeed, some state legislatures have passed laws specifically making certain public records a revenue source by setting high copying fees.

FOIA Strategies That Work

After reviewing all the exemptions and common denials, a potential user of FOIA could be easily discouraged. But there are many counterstrategies that work to get government records and to keep government as open as possible, whether it's federal, state, or local government.

One strategy is to remember that the complexity and fragmentation of government bureaucracy can play in a requester's favor. The bureaucracy often does not communicate well within itself and has contradictory guidelines and policies that can result in records being released by one agency while another is still denying them.

For example, when seeking government records it can be helpful to think about how the records are shared. Records might be shared vertically—that is, a smaller agency in a state might have to share a set of records with a larger federal agency, or the federal agency might share information with the state agency.

If a requester files a state FOIA request for the records with a state agency and a federal FOIA request for the same records with a federal agency, one of the agencies might disclose the records while the other agency maintains the records are exempt from FOIA.

Or a requester can think "horizontally." A set of records may be shared among agencies that are on the same level within a federal department, or state agencies also may share information laterally. Again, requests to multiple agencies or bureaus could result in the release of documents. This happened when *Washington Post* reporters were seeking records from the U.S. Food and Drug Administration (FDA) on a story on prescription drugs and FDA bureaus gave out the records while the home office did not.

There are many basic tips for making FOIA work. Many of them come from journalists and nonprofit organizations that serve the public.

Among the tips:

- Check with an agency's own FOIA logs to see whether the record has previously been released.

- Make your request broad enough to ensure that you get the records you need, but be ready to narrow the request to get it expedited, to lower costs, or to just be reasonable.

- If there are any charges, ask for a breakdown of costs and check to see whether they are allowable under the law. If they are allowable, ask to "inspect"—look at—the records first at no charge and then decide what you want copied.

- Be prepared to negotiate over redacted information. Many times it is wise to ask for a bit more than you want. Somehow, agency officials seem satisfied if they can deny at least a part of the record.

- If it is a database, ask for a record layout of the categories (columns) of information so that you know whether the agency is supposed to collect the information you are requesting. And make sure that the agency is filling in those columns of information and not leaving them blank before requesting the entire database.

- Follow up on your request. Confirm that the request was received by the agency whether it's snail-mailed, faxed, or emailed. If it is hand-delivered, get a receipt. Also, let the agency know that you are willing to answer its questions about your request and possibly narrow your search. Continue to follow up and let the agency know you are prepared to appeal denials.

And file your request early. There often is a direct correlation between successful requests and the time allowed by the requester for responses. FOIA requests generally fail on a quick turnaround deadline, and this is why citizens and journalists in a rush don't think FOIA is useful and they stop filing requests.

There also can be a correlation between the cost of records and how much time a requester has. The longer you can wait for a request to be fulfilled, the greater the chance you can negotiate a lower price. In Connecticut, the cost of one database dropped from $3 million to $1 after lengthy negotiations. Of course, it took several years to get there, but the reporters were persistent.

Most of all, when it comes to FOIA persistence pays off.

Conclusion

Despite their limitations, FOIA laws, at both the federal and state levels, are crucial devices to keeping government open and accountable. But the public needs to use the laws frequently by making requests for important information. Such requests keep the laws up-to-date and relevant, help identify changes that need to be made, and keep officials respectful of the laws and the public.

Furthermore, a citizen can monitor the use of and changes in FOIA through numerous websites and can join some of those groups. Here is a partial list of the relevant websites:

- ACLU Freedom Network (*http://archive.aclu.org/library/foia.html*)
- American Society of Access Professionals (*http://www.accesspro.org/*)
- The Brechner Center for Freedom of Information (*http://brechner.org/resources.asp*)
- A Citizen's Guide to Using the Freedom of Information Act (*http://www.fas.org/sgp/foia/citizen.html*)
- Electronic Privacy Information Center (*http://epic.org/*)
- Federation of American Scientists (*http://www.fas.org/index.html*)
- Freedom of Information Center, University of Missouri (*http://foi.missouri.edu/*)
- Investigative Reporters and Editors (*http://www.ire.org*)
- National Freedom of Information Coalition (*http://www.nfoic.org*)
- The National Security Archive (*http://www.gwu.edu/~nsarchiv/nsa/foia/foia_guide.html*)
- Open the Government (*http://www.openthegovernment.org/*)
- Public Citizen (*http://www.citizen.org/litigation/free_info/*)
- The Reporters Committee for Freedom of the Press (*http://www.rcfp.org*)
- Society of Environmental Journalists (*http://www.sej.org/initiatives/foia/overview*)
- SPJ Open Doors (*http://www.spj.org/foi.asp*)
- The Sunshine in Government Initiative (*http://www.sunshineingovernment.org/index.php*)

These websites also offer guides and tips on how to most effectively request government records and how to appeal denials. In addition, the Department of Justice has a presence on the Internet to oversee FOIA (*http://www.usdoj.gov/04foia/*), and most government agencies post their FOIA handbooks.

About the Author

BRANT HOUSTON is a professor and the Knight Chair in Investigative and Enterprise Reporting at the University of Illinois in Urbana-Champaign, where he teaches investigative and advanced reporting. He is the coauthor of *The Investigative Reporter's Handbook* (Bedford/St. Martin's) and author of *Computer-Assisted Reporting: A Practical Guide* (St. Martin's Press). Houston is deeply involved in the creation of investigative journalism centers in the U.S. and internationally, and serves as chair of the steering committee of the new Investigative News Network. He is working on projects that demonstrate the use of the latest digital tools to collect and analyze information, including helping to coordinate a community news project on poverty issues, and developing a new website for investigative reporters world-wide. For more than a decade, Houston was executive director of Investigative Reporters and Editors (IRE), a nonprofit group of 4,000 members. He was also a professor of journalism at the University of Missouri, where IRE is located. For 17 years before joining IRE, Houston was a daily journalist. He was an award-winning investigative reporter at the *Hartford Courant* and at the *Kansas City Star*, where he was a member of the newsroom staff that won the Pulitzer Prize for its coverage of a hotel building collapse that killed 114 people.

CHAPTER THIRTY-ONE

Gov→Media→People

Dan Gillmor

In the old days of the twentieth century, journalists imagined that information about government activities moved this way: government→news media→people. Journalists selected from the torrent of government activities—including the day-to-day doings of legislators, executive branches, and bureaucrats; press releases and other documents; and so on—and decided what was important enough to tell readers. Imagine a one-way hourglass with the bulb at the top called Government, the slender neck in the middle called Media, and the immense container at the bottom called the People, namely the rest of us. That description was always too simplistic, of course. But now it's downright quaint. The system has evolved, largely due to the democratization of media. When anyone can publish, and when anyone else can read (listen to, watch, work with, etc.) what's been published, roles shift—and blur—in dramatic ways.

To understand how thoroughly things have changed, consider what happened when I posted the following on Twitter a day before leading a session at Transparency Camp West—a Silicon Valley "unconference" (attendees controlled the agenda) held in August 2009, of open-government advocates—on evolving media and government roles. I said (editing slightly to correct the grammar in this greater-than-140-character medium): "I'm asking what replaces gov→media→people in a more open world."

A few minutes after my posting, I got a reply from a Twitter user named Tara Haelle, a student who was working during the summer on a project at Northwestern University's journalism school. She offered the following construction:

gov't→ppl→blogs/Tw/FB/etc→media coverage→ppl→comments on media; alongside gov't
WhtHs PresCor→media→ppl→ppl commentary

Let's translate Haelle's rejoinder. The flow she suggested went like this: government information becomes available to the people. Via blogs, Twitter, Facebook, and other mechanisms, the people (including journalists) look at and analyze the information. This leads to some media coverage, which some people see. The media audience comments on the journalism, both directly to the journalists and in the people's own media (blogs, etc.). Meanwhile, a parallel process occurs: government and journalists do their traditional dance, and tell the people what they consider important via the traditional press, and the people comment in traditional ways, such as op eds and letters to the editor.

We know which is better, don't we?

That Haelle's quick response had come from the Net was instructive in its own way, of course; a demonstration of how we communicate. And it helped to frame the conversation the next day. Her mini flowchart brought a more nuanced view of the way information will move among those who govern and those who are governed, and she correctly envisioned the traditional press playing a still-important but dramatically evolving role.

If this is obvious to many people, it seems less so to the traditional journalists themselves, by all appearances. Many, if not most, still cling to their self-appointed old role: as intermediaries. They need to get over it, not just because in an era of democratized media they can't possibly be the sole or even main funnel, but also because new media tools will give them better ways to do their jobs.

Whatever they do (or don't do) to improve their craft, journalists will be obliged to understand that roles in the emerging mediasphere are complex, and blurred. At the Transparency Camp session, John Wonderlich, Sunlight Foundation's policy director, and other participants came up with a long list of roles. These included (in the order I wrote them down on a whiteboard): validator, provocateur, analyst, storyteller, fact checker, collector, curator, distributor, and amplifier.

The terms overlap, and some are plainly more, well, journalistic than others, at least in any modern notion of the craft. More important, everyone in the flow of information can play one or more of these roles at different points in the conversation. That includes people in government.

The word *conversation* is key, moreover. Governments, like all other enterprises, have a variety of constituencies. These include citizens, taxpayers, employees, suppliers, media, and others. (Note that media isn't near the top of that list.) Governments don't tend to converse with constituencies, but over time they'll understand why this is better than current practice; more liberal data policies are a solid first step in the right direction, however.

Journalism organizations will, if they grasp the possibilities, become more than simple reporters of (some of) what government does. One key method will be to leverage application programming interfaces (APIs) that connect all kinds of web-enabled data and services.

Another will be to bring citizens into the journalism process itself. Both will boost the most essential role the journalists have performed in the past: that of watchdogs. Governments, at least honest ones, will have an incentive to help.

How might this work? We've already seen some glimmerings of the possibilities:

- Journalists have been doing what's been called *computer-assisted reporting* for several decades now. In most cases, this means using databases to better understand trends and issues. These databases can be created internally or, increasingly, are obtained from government agencies. They include census and other demographic information; environmental data; worker injury records; and many other kinds of things. When translated into charts, maps, and other visually understandable formats these data sources are useful elements of modern journalism.

  What journalists rarely do, however, is to open up the latter data type—government information—to their audiences. Rather, journalists pluck what they consider important from the information and present it. If they instead made the data available to the wider public, and with interfaces that gave nontechnical people easy ways to play with the data, everyone would be better off. Making the data available is a form of journalism, after all. Members of the audience would surely find things the journalists had missed, and with the help of the news organization, that new information could make its way to the rest of the community.

- Several years ago *The Bakersfield Californian* created what has become a signature feature on its website: a pothole map, a mashup of Google Maps and people power. Residents of Bakersfield, a small inland city north of Los Angeles, were encouraged to put virtual pins in the map showing which streets had potholes in them. The newspaper doesn't begin to have enough staff members to do this itself, but the people of Bakersfield are more than capable of telling each other where the potholes are on their own streets.

  The *Californian* didn't leave it there. The paper gave residents an easy way to contact the city government with their reports, and asked them to post back to the site when the potholes had been repaired. (Still better would be direct links via APIs, should they exist, to the city's own street-repairs database.)

  There's rich potential for follow-up journalism in this project. For example, what neighborhoods get the most and fewest potholes per capita? And in which parts of the city are potholes repaired most quickly, and slowly, when they do appear? One would guess that residents in richer parts of Bakersfield might fare better on both of these questions.

The Bakersfield project isn't the only one of this kind. In the United Kingdom, FixMyStreet asks people to report potholes and other urban-infrastructure issues and then transmits those reports to the local government agencies tasked with fixing the problems. FixMyStreet is a project of mySociety, an activist organization, not a journalistic one. mySociety holds a number of innovative projects in this arena, including PlanningAlerts.com, which lets residents of neighborhoods know about urban-planning applications, such as for construction permits, in their vicinity. These projects serve vital community information purposes no matter what we call them. Why journalism organizations themselves don't do these things or, for the most part, license them for their audiences is a mystery.

Tom Carden, interaction designer and engineer at Stamen Design, a small San Francisco company that does brilliant visualizations of data, explains some of the possibilities: "Perhaps," he says, "the future of journalism involves the finding and maintaining of effective feedback loops between throwaway (zero effort) problem ticketing applications and the people who can actually follow through and fix the problem." Just as the pothole maps need to connect directly with municipal databases, Carden suggests that crime mapping sites could track solved crimes as well as incident reports.

Government taxation and spending are among the equally obvious places where journalism organizations could add great value on behalf of their communities. Again, rather than think of themselves as filters, the journalists will need to be connectors in ways they haven't done before to any great extent. Specifically, they'll need to:

- Learn the language and techniques of programmers who create APIs to government data.
- Create APIs to their own journalistic work.
- Find ways to connect those APIs.
- Help their audiences understand how to use the result, often to go even further.

The connections media organizations create don't have to be technical, though they'll always involve technology. Some of the best examples are already in use, though not to the degree they could be. *Crowdsourcing*, gathering knowledge in an organized way from an audience, is an almost ideal way for smart journalists to help get the news to the most people in the best way.

Crowdsourcing in Action

One of crowdsourcing's most ardent practitioners is Joshua Micah Marshall, founder and editor of the Talking Points Memo (TPM) family of sites. The work by Marshall and his team on the Bush administration's politically charged firings of many U.S. attorneys during the second Bush term relied, in part, on smart collaboration with the audience—and it won a major journalism award. What TPM did was simple: every time the Justice Department dumped a pile of documents into the public record, as it did repeatedly during the prosecutors episode, Marshall and his team asked their readers to help vet the documents and pull out the nuggets that might otherwise have gone unnoticed for some time.

A potentially brilliant variation on that theme is ShovelWatch (*http://shovelwatch.org*), a joint project of several journalism organizations including ProPublica, WNYC radio, and The Takeaway news program. The project aims to track the federal government's fiscal stimulus package "from bill to building" and is "organizing citizens nationwide to watchdog local stimulus projects."

What gives these ideas special power is the opportunity to help people who've been passive consumers of media to better understand some essential journalism principles. When people help with the reporting—that is, the gathering of information—they may appreciate what it takes to create high-quality journalism.

That was one motivation behind a suggestion I made after the *Wall Street Journal* exposed the apparently widespread backdating of executive stock options at public companies. I say "apparently" because even the talented staff at the *Journal* could analyze only a relatively small number of the 5,000-odd public companies to come up with its analysis. The newspaper used a formula, created with the help of a Yale professor, to calculate the odds that the options grant dates were a coincidence or a deliberate occurrence.

The *Journal* could have then embarked on a national effort, effectively deputizing shareholders and other interested readers to help finish the research. The paper might have created an online tool into which any self-appointed citizen journalist could, with detailed guidance from the newspaper, do the following:

1. Look up the relevant data for a given company, using the U.S. Securities and Exchange Commission's (SEC) database of corporate filings and other public data sources.

2. Plug the correct numbers, along with the URLs of the SEC filings from which the data came, into an online calculator that determines, based on the researchers' methodology, whether the odds suggest backdating chicanery.

3. And finally, upload the results to a public database for use by journalists, prosecutors, other shareholders, and anyone else who might find it interesting.

As noted, this web-based tool set would include some serious teaching materials, such as an easy-to-understand explanation of how to find the data, likely to be buried deep in a corporate report or even a footnote. I remain convinced that the educational value alone would make this worth the effort—though the collaborative work on this or any number of similar projects could yield stunning results in the old-fashioned notion of watchdog journalism and citizenship.

Even if today's pro journalists fail to grasp the possibilities, a new generation of media creators will certainly take advantage of them, and they are endless. So is the available talent.

In early 2009, Stanford University students showed up at a public forum featuring former Secretary of State Condoleezza Rice, with their mobile phone video cameras. They respectfully but insistently asked Rice about her role in our nation's torture of prisoners in recent years. To call her response inept is an understatement, as many have explained; she fumbled around, yet all but implicated herself in war crimes even while trying to deny the obvious truth. The students' video became a widely seen sensation on YouTube.

The Nation magazine's Ari Melber understood the larger import of the students' action. "(T)his incident also shows the prospects for what we might call a substantive Macaca Moment—using YouTube and citizen media to scrutinize our leaders on the issues, not gaffes," he wrote.

Macaca refers, of course, to former U.S. Sen. George Allen's racially tinged slur of a volunteer for his opponent, made in a public place, caught on video, and also posted to wide notoriety on YouTube in 2006. Allen, a Virginia Republican who turned out to have a history of making odd racial remarks, lost his bid for reelection in part because of this incident.

Allen's self-inflicted wound was one of many such milestones. Public figures are learning that when they say something stupid, ugly, or just plain wrong, someone with a video camera may well capture it and make it widely available. The fact that politicians haven't wholly absorbed this lesson even now is astonishing, but they will.

Rice's well-earned predicament had a more directly relevant antecedent. That was when former President Bill Clinton, prompted by a question from a citizen journalist for *The Huffington Post*'s Off the Bus project, furiously denounced a magazine article about him and the then-fading presidential campaign of his wife, Hillary. He did himself and his wife no favors.

We need to take the best lessons from the Clinton and Rice meltdowns and find a way to re-create such confrontations, again and again: we need to organize to ensure that public figures—especially politicians and business leaders—are asked key questions, and not let them off the hook the way the traditional media tend to do.

We know that the political press corps and business journalists often avoid asking hard questions, or fail to follow up on each other's good questions when the politicians and businesspeople duck honest answers. This has many causes, including the worry of losing access to the rich and powerful people they count on to supply quotes for their too-often stenographic reporting. Rice's years in Washington surely taught her, as Scott Horton noted in a blog posting, that journalists were all like the "Beltway punditry and the access-craving White House press corps."

Not the Stanford students. And not the rest of us, who don't especially care if we occasionally make the rich and powerful uncomfortable.

Slowly, the traditional media have been inviting the rest of us to come up with questions for the people they cover. NBC played at this a bit in 2009 by inviting audience questions that might or might not be asked at an Obama press conference. Other news organizations did similar things.

Meanwhile, the savvy Obama media team has created an "Open For Questions" area (*http://www.whitehouse.gov/Openforquestions*) on the White House website. It conducted an Online Town Hall experiment, drawing from citizens' questions, that was modestly successful.

The Nation, for which Melber is Net movement correspondent and blogger, joined with *The Washington Times* and the Personal Democracy Forum on a project they've called "Ask the President"—creating what Melber called a "people's press conference" of sorts. Again, a positive step forward, in particular because it uses online community tools to (attempt to) figure out what the best questions may be.

But the press conference metaphor misses the wide potential, which the Stanford students so neatly captured. While a traditional press conference consists of a person in a room answering questions from the people assembled there—picking the questioners (and, in Obama's case, most of the actual questions)—we can use the growing ubiquity of digital recording devices to turn the world into the pressroom.

How? By leveraging all of these devices, and the people willing to use them, in a wider and much more organized way—insisting, respectfully, that public figures answer the questions that matter.

The key would be to use technology—and public-spirited people's willingness to participate—to aggregate unanswered questions, select ones that are most important, and get participants to ask these questions of public figures when they appear in public.

A simple example: congressional Democrats have been largely unwilling to confront President Obama on his endorsement of Bush-era presidential-power claims. Unfortunately, the Washington press corps and journalists in their districts have not bothered to inquire whether these representatives are as bothered by these claims as many said they were during the Bush years. Our team might agree to find members back in the district at small public events and insist on individual answers that would add up to some clarity on whether we'll get any pushback against Obama's own power grab.

Keeping in mind that I haven't begun to think this all the way through, here's an initial cut at how we might do it. I'd include the following criteria:

- Questions would be submitted by anyone—journalists, users, experts, whoever.

- We would collectively vote on the most important questions. (This is tricky, subject to gaming.) Alternatively, but not my favored method, we might ask a team of unquestioned experts to choose. (This is not very democratic or webby.) Whatever the method, we'd end up with some question(s) to ask.

- We'd gather and publish information, submitted by users or gleaned from calendars, about public and semipublic appearances of those we want to approach. An example of a semipublic appearance is a corporate annual meeting where only shareholders are permitted to ask questions.

- Vitally, we'd require that the questions be asked in a respectful way, and that we capture the exchanges on video if at all possible, but on audio at the very least.

- Answers would be posted immediately, to avoid repetitive questions that have already been answered.

In the end, this isn't about creating a global, distributed press conference (which isn't a bad idea in itself). It's about accountability.

And accountability is at the core of public knowledge and understanding government processes and results. Transparency is insufficient unless citizens can act effectively if they disapprove of what they've learned.

Journalists have spent decades framing their role in the context of being the lynchpins of accountability. Sometimes they've succeeded, but their larger failure has stemmed from their inability to imagine themselves in the less powerful (in a centralized way) but ultimately more influential place they'll have in the emerging world.

Conclusion

For any or all of this to succeed, of course, the former audience—people who've been mere consumers of media—will need to become active users. We'll have to learn, or relearn, key principles including the necessity to be skeptical of everything we see from media of all kinds, but not equally skeptical of everything. We'll need to do more of our own homework when confronting issues. We'll need to listen to others whose views make our blood boil. And we'll need to learn media techniques, especially the ways media can be used to manipulate public opinion.

Moreover, in the new ecosystem of media that includes the people as participants, we'll have to learn what amounts to Journalism 101: principles of thoroughness, accuracy, fairness, independence, and transparency. The more we expect of others, the more we should demand of ourselves.

We can get this right. We won't get it right quickly, however. This is a multiyear, multidecade, and maybe even multigenerational process. But in the end, when we have a media ecosystem that is more diverse and robust than the one we've had, we'll be better off individually and as citizens. A lot rides on whether we want to make the effort.

About the Author

Dan Gillmor is the director of the Knight Center for Digital Media Entrepreneurship at Arizona State University's Walter Cronkite School of Journalism and Mass Communication. The Center, funded by the Knight Foundation and the Kauffman Foundation, is working to help create a culture of innovation and risk-taking in journalism education, and in the wider media world. He remains director of the Center for Citizen Media, originally a joint project of the University of California-Berkeley School of Journalism and the Harvard Berkman Center for Internet & Society. He was a fellow at Berkman from 2006–2009 and is now a faculty associate.

CHAPTER THIRTY-TWO

Open Source Software for Open Government Agencies

Carlo Daffara
Jesus M. Gonzalez-Barahona

The theme of open government that pervades this volume depends on drawing participation from as wide a swath of the public as possible, and this goal in turn calls for the use of software that is universally available, easy to use, easy to adapt to specific needs, and easy to modify to match evolving requirements. Free and open source software meets these goals more consistently than any alternative.

In this chapter, we use the term *FLOSS* for this type of software: free/libre/open source software. Although it's usually distributed free of charge, its distinguishing trait is a license that allows anyone to change the code and redistribute the changes. This keeps FLOSS from being dominated by one set of developers, and therefore from being burdened with restrictions that users may reject and that even may violate government policies (e.g., terms of service that let the developers collect personal information from users). The alternatives are usually called "proprietary software" because they are often free of charge but are still under the control of the organization that created them.

FLOSS is already in widespread use within government agencies, and will have an even greater role to play in open government technologies that can be really useful for public administrations. However, adopting or migrating to FLOSS is a complex, multidisciplinary effort involving several areas of expertise. It requires taking a hard look at current workflows in the organization, as well as how people interact with information technology (IT) systems day to day. The unique complexities found in each public agency add more difficulties.

So, FLOSS migration is a major endeavor, and as any migration, it can easily go wrong. All too often, agencies are discouraged by one failure from pursuing other opportunities, and may even blame the software or the community that supports it instead of the logistics of the migration. This chapter will hopefully persuade you that adopting FLOSS is crucial and will additionally give you guidelines to avoiding mistakes during its adoption.

The common hurdles in adopting FLOSS fall into three major categories:

Management
> Understanding the procedures that agency heads need to put in place, and how staff members must be coordinated

Technical
> Choosing software appropriate for the job, and interacting with the community that developed the software in a productive manner

Social
> Presenting change to staff members in a positive manner and handling the various forms of resistance they will put up

Before introducing guidelines based on experience, we'll lay out some of the specific advantages of FLOSS for public agencies. Then we'll present a set of best practices obtained through research by European projects that have analyzed adoption and migration experiences.

Advantages of FLOSS for Government and Public Agencies

Government agencies, and public institutions to which they contract out services, are large software users with special characteristics derived from their obligations toward citizens and their unique legal status. For example, most agencies are expected, or even required by law, to provide services accessible to all residents of their regions, including those who are disabled, who lack education, or who are geographically isolated. Agencies must also be neutral in their relationships with manufacturers, and must often guarantee the integrity, privacy, and security of the data they handle over long periods of time.

All these needs play into their considerations when adopting software, beyond the cost/functionality evaluation that businesses and individuals perform. An analysis of these common requirements shows a clear advantage to FLOSS solutions where they exist.

Independence from Suppliers

Any institution values the advantages of keeping open options for different vendors, because it tends to lower costs and leave an escape path when a chosen vendor leaves the business or fails to provide up-to-date features. But for public agencies, a competitive market is usually more than a preference—it's a legislative requirement. The legislation enjoins them to initiate procurement by issuing calls for tenders that don't favor a single vendor. Any interested company that fulfills reasonable criteria can produce a bid that competes on its own merits with everyone else.

But this critical adherence to disinterested policy is violated in the case of proprietary software. Each product is available from only one supplier (even if it uses a number of intermediaries). If a particular product is specified in a call for tenders, the administration has predetermined the supplier that gets the contract. In the case of computer applications, it is virtually impossible to avoid specifying a particular product because the agency needs compatibility with products that are already deployed, savings in training and maintenance, or other reasons.

Requiring a proprietary format (such as the ability to deal with certain kinds of spreadsheets) is a looser limitation but still a means of lock-in, because the vendor that defined the format and continues to update the format over time is the only one the agency can rely on to handle the format in all its subtleties.

FLOSS offers a way out of this situation. If the specified functionality is delivered by FLOSS, any interested company can offer the product and any service based on it, subject only to the capabilities and knowledge of the company. In addition, agencies that enter contracts this way can easily switch to another supplier without needing to switch to a new product.

Fulfillment of Specific Requirements

Public agencies, like other organizations, benefit from using software they can adapt to specific requirements. When they license a proprietary product, modifying it normally involves reaching an agreement with the producer, the only party that can legally (and often technically) make modifications. Under these circumstances, getting the company to agree to and deliver the desired changes is hard to achieve.

In the case of FLOSS, software can be adapted either by its copyright owners or by any third party, which means that instead of negotiating with a single company, the service can be purchased in a competitive market. Some companies that deliver FLOSS will stop support if the software is altered by the customer—but support for these products is also available on an open market.

Adoption of Open Standards

FLOSS commonly follows open, published standards. In addition, because the source code is available, any format and protocol the standards implement can be reimplemented by other software developers, effectively turning the format or protocol into a standard. The advantages of this neutrality are especially significant for public agencies, particularly in their interactions with citizens, who should not be forced to purchase a product from a particular company just because it is the only one that implements a proprietary protocol the agency is using.

Public Scrutiny

Public agencies have become increasingly committed to transparency. The public rightfully demands not only to be kept apprised of each stage of decision making—such as in urban planning—but to see the data behind the planning, the steps made in taking the decision, and the reasons for the decision. Being able to let citizens inspect the agency's software extends this public scrutiny to the field of IT. In addition, agencies need to guarantee that their computer systems do what they are intended to do (in many countries, by legal requirement). Many systems manage data with privacy restrictions (tax data, criminal records, health information, etc.), which must be kept out of the malicious grasp of unauthorized third parties. Ironically, experience has taught that systems tasked with keeping secrets are more secure and more likely to fulfill their requirements if the source code is open to examination; only encryption keys should be secret.

Proprietary applications without source code are difficult to evaluate rigorously to guarantee that the application will process the data in the way that it should, with no leaks or back doors. Even if a vendor does provide a customer with its source code, the possibilities of a public institution ensuring that it is free of malicious or insecure elements are very limited. Remember that every major software product contains security flaws that are routinely reported and fixed only after the product has been in the field for months, or even years. Only if software inspection can be routinely done by third parties, including any citizen who may want to do it, can the agency be sure that it is taking all reasonable measures to comply with this fundamental duty.

Long-Term Availability

Much of the data processed and stored by agencies, and the programs used to manage this data, have mandatory availability requirements measured in decades. Proprietary software, being subject to the commercial strategy of the company producing it, cannot be guaranteed to be available in the platforms of the far future. It is quite possible that the producer will lose interest in the product, or in the data format used to store the information. Since only the producer can port the software to new platforms, negotiation will be difficult. A producer can go out of business or be purchased by another company that decides to leave the current business. Producers have even been known to deliberately change software so as to make it incompatible with earlier data formats, leaving all documents in those formats unreadable unless the agency can maintain an old computer system running old software.

In the case of FLOSS, however, the source code of the application is certainly available and the vendor has given permission for its modification. Therefore, many companies can compete to provide the porting service when the agency decides to contract it. Documents in old formats can also be recovered because the programs can be revived or reverse-engineered.

Impact in the Society at Large

Many applications used by public agencies are useful to other sectors of society as well. That means that investments in software can have an impact on those sectors, well beyond their use by the administration itself. Common examples involve sophisticated new technologies developed for military use, which often prove valuable later in civilian aviation, communications, or even consumer products.

If the government's investment is devoted to proprietary software licenses, the impact does not reach outside the administration. But if it is devoted to FLOSS, the improvements, adaptations, or new software that results from the investment is also available for the rest of the public.

A specific example case concerns localization of FLOSS. When a public agency localizes a product, that localization is almost automatically available to citizens. In the case of small linguistic communities, this can be the only way to have localized software available.

Impact on Local Industry

FLOSS can help to develop or support a local IT industry, which in some cases is a secondary mission for the investment of public agencies in software. In the case of proprietary software, the expenditure in licenses usually goes directly to the producer, generating little technological activity in the region.

But in the case of FLOSS, local companies will compete to provide software and services to the administration. FLOSS therefore levels the playing field, making it easier for anyone to compete. Companies with a strong local presence will usually have a competitive advantage, all other factors being equal.

Staff Empowerment

Although some FLOSS developers provide excellent support, formally or informally, both the developers and the larger community surrounding the software tend to expect a user to take some responsibility for understanding the software and investigating a problem before asking for help. Whether the user is reporting a bug or merely trying to get information about confusing product behavior, the request should show care, thought, and research; failure to do so in a free-support forum may be received with negative messages that may be perplexing for the user. The availability of source code, while usually not of interest to end users, guarantees that an internal support staff can, eventually, reach an arbitrarily high degree of expertise on the software being employed, and at the same time it provides for the opportunity of creating local modifications that in some instances may provide a significant added value.

These expectations place more of a burden on the agency's IT staff, but the long-term effects can benefit the agency. Staff morale may be improved because these professionals feel they have more control over the resources they're working with, and they have more scope to learn skills they find both interesting and valuable for career advancement.

Best Practices: Management

The advantages introduced in the previous section are, however, not guaranteed. To really benefit from FLOSS, adoption and deployment have to be successful. Fortunately, after many case studies of transitions to FLOSS in public administration, there is some evidence of good practices that can be considered in new cases.

Good project planning and management are the main prerequisites for a successful migration to FLOSS. Agency leaders must start by understanding the environment in which the software has been developed, as well as have a clear vision of what the agency wants to achieve and the support required to succeed. The differences between FLOSS and proprietary products in development and support require a significant change in procurement and accounting practices. Finally, the use of FLOSS often entails a shift of responsibility from outside contractors to in-house personnel.

Consider All the Factors, Both Technical and Contextual

Before deciding which products to deploy, and before defining specific implementation or migration plans, it is important to consider all the factors involved. In addition to the usual technical aspects (such as functionality and reliability), decision makers also have to examine factors that could have an impact on future phases of the project, such as licensing (e.g., compatibility with other OSS or proprietary software products), community (the strength of the community surrounding the product), and business (such as the availability of support, or even the level of competitiveness between the companies that provide it).

Some approaches for evaluating OSS projects have been explored as part of the QSOS and FLOSSMETRICS projects, along with examples and tools for facilitating the estimation of parameters such as stability and community liveness.

Pure cost/functionality evaluations usually show only a part of the story, and decisions based only on these factors can lead to problems in the future. A consideration of the software's context can provide a more three-dimensional view that is likely to lead to better strategic decisions.

> **WARNING**
> If the evaluation is based only in functionality and cost aspects, project management is probably missing many important issues that could lead to problems in the deployment phases.

Be Sure of Management's Commitment to the Transition

Management support and commitment have been repeatedly found to be one of the most important factors for the success of complex IT efforts, and FLOSS migrations are no exception. This commitment must be guaranteed for a time period sufficient to cover the complete migration. In organizations where IT directors change frequently, or where management changes at fixed periods of time (such as electoral terms), a process must be in place to hand over an understanding of the migration to the new management. The commitment should also extend to funding (as transitions and training will require resources, both monetary and in-house).

Be particularly alert to the involvement of nontechnical managers. The best way to ensure continued coordination is to appoint a team with mixed experience (management and technical) to provide continuous feedback and day-to-day management.

WARNING

If the only people planning the migration are from IT/MIS, there may be insufficient information in upper management and financial planning to continue the migration after the initial step.

Prepare a Clear View of What's Expected, Including Measurable Benchmarks

A transition can be started for several reasons, including better control over IT costs, independence from suppliers, more flexibility, or support for open data standards. To be sure that the migration is effectively producing benefits and is going according to plan, you have to know beforehand what indicators will be used to evaluate the progress. Those requirements must be scrutinized to ensure that they are realistic. In particular, expectations of TCO (Total Cost of Ownership) reductions must be compared to publicly available data for other projects.

WARNING

If the only advantage promulgated within the agency for the change is that "the software comes from the Net for free," managers will misunderstand both the reasons and the pitfalls of migration and will probably end up with a negative final judgment about the project.

Make Sure the Timetable Is Realistic

The introduction of a new IT platform always requires a significant amount of time. As a rule of thumb, the time to perform a full transition to FLOSS is comparable to that of introducing a new agency-wide enterprise resource planning application. The time you expect to perform a less comprehensive change can be scaled accordingly.

WARNING

When migration time is measured in days, and no postmigration effort is planned, the process may be forced to a stop after the allocated resources are exhausted.

Review the Current Software/IT Procurement and Development Procedure

As adoption procedures are shifted from proprietary software to FLOSS, the procurement and development process needs to be updated accordingly. In particular, the focus may change from acquisition to services, as less software is bought "shrink-wrapped" (commercially licensed). This change may require further changes in the allocation of the internal IT budget. The plan should take into account a port or transition for internally developed software to multiplatform standards or interfaces that support more standard access methods (e.g., web applications).

WARNING

When no change in procurement and development is planned, management may not have understood the scope of change required for the adoption of FLOSS.

Seek Out Advice or Search for Information on Similar Transitions

A considerable number of companies and public agencies have already performed migrations to FLOSS by now, so it is easy to find information about what to expect and how to proceed. A mainly European-based project called the Consortium for Open Source Software in the Public Administration (COSPA) has developed an online knowledge base concerning such migrations (*http://www.cospa-project.org*). Some countries also have FLOSS Competence Centers that provide information and support for the migration process to local agencies.

WARNING

When no previous cases are mentioned, or no study on similar transitions is performed, there is a high risk of missing valuable information about past experiences that could help to avoid known problems and follow known good practices.

Avoid "Big Switch" Transition, and Favor Incremental Migrations

Most large-scale migrations that are performed in a single, large step (involving the abrupt change from one IT environment to the other) are usually marred by extremely high support and technical costs. While the need to support more than one environment also increases support and management cost, "gentle" or incremental migrations usually bring a better overall experience for the users and result in minimal disruption of business processes.

An example of gentle migration can begin with the migration of server-side applications, which are usually standards-based or network-based and thus easier to replace, leaving desktop and user-facing applications last. Figure 32-1 depicts such a scheme.

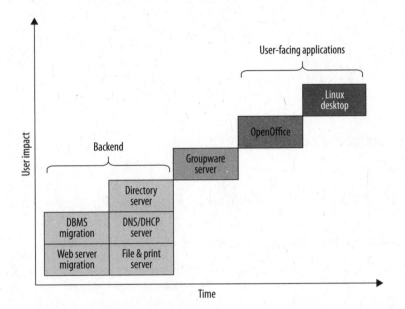

FIGURE 32-1. Phased migration to FLOSS

A significant advantage of FLOSS is the availability of free online resources, in the form of knowledge bases, mailing lists, and wikis, that often provide support comparable to commercial offerings. The biggest problem is finding such knowledge sources. The IT team should assign at least one person to interact with the FLOSS community or the FLOSS vendor; in the long run, this time commitment can reduce the cost of support. A common way to provide a unified source of information within an organization is to set up a small intranet web page with links to online resources.

WARNING

When no one knows where to find information on the tools that are in use, or when everyone has to conduct web searches on their own for usage tips, the agency is failing to take advantage of online resources, one of the most compelling advantages offered by most FLOSS.

Promote Collaboration and Pooling of Resources

Once your management has decided to adopt a FLOSS solution, one way to multiply the advantages of the choice is to coordinate with other agencies using similar solutions. In fact,

FLOSS may become a model for collaboration between public bodies, leading to new and productive forms of working together.

One simple form of collaboration, of course, is to pool resources for improving specific packages, or adapting them to local agency needs. But FLOSS allows for more agile forms of collaboration, often not needing any formal agreement between agencies. A significant example of such cooperation is the distributed improvement of the VistA hospital management system, one of the largest OSS packages in existence;* many other examples are published through the EU Open Source Observatory (*http://www.osor.eu/*), which provides best practices and case studies on the adoption of OSS in European Public Administrations.

Best Practices: Technical

A significant difference between proprietary and FLOSS adoption is the different development model adopted by most open source projects, including differences in the delivery of updates and support. This requires a change in how the agency handles adoption and updates.

Understand the Way FLOSS Is Developed

Most FLOSS projects are based on a cooperative development model, with a core set of developers providing most of the code (usually working for a commercial firm) and a large number of noncore contributors. This development model can provide excellent code quality and a fast development cycle, but requires a significant effort to track changes and updates. The adoption of a FLOSS package should be suggested when:

- The project itself is "alive"; that is, it has an active development community as evidenced by source code contributions and participation in online forums.

- There is a clear distinction between "stable" and "unstable" software. Many projects maintain two distinct and concurrent development branches, one devoted to integrating new features and another focused on improving stability and bug fixes. Periodically, developers will "freeze" development to turn the former, unstable version into a new release of the stable one. After that, they will create a new development, bleeding-edge version.

The second practice just described allows developers to satisfy both the users willing to experiment with the latest functionality, and those using the software for day-to-day operations. But the process complicates agency tasks in collecting information and new versions. Agencies may find it easier to ask for a commercially supported version of the

---

* VistA is an enterprise-grade health care information system developed by the U.S. Department of Veterans Affairs (VA) and deployed at nearly 1,500 facilities worldwide. It was open-sourced through the Freedom of Information Act (FOIA) that allowed for the source to be publicly available in the public domain. After publication, several groups used the source code as a basis for further improvement, giving back the results.

software. In many cases, the commercial vendor also contributes new source code and financial backing to the FLOSS project.

> **WARNING**
> When the IT manager or the developers think that FLOSS is some kind of commercial software that someone is offering for free on the Net, they will become ineffective when they find that it doesn't "just work" and that updates take special effort.

Survey the Agency's Software, Hardware, and Required Functionality

Migration of an unknown environment cannot succeed. But unfortunately, most companies and agencies have no process for auditing software and hardware platforms, and thus are unable to quantify the number of tools and software that need to be replaced or integrated in a FLOSS migration. A survey process must also take into account the number of concurrent users, average use across the organization, and whether the software uses open or closed communication protocols and data formats. The survey will be the basis for deciding which users to migrate first, and the cost of software redevelopment or migration to a different data format. Automated software inventory tools are available to perform these sorts of surveys. The tools may reduce the cost of the inventory and allow stricter control over installed software (thus reducing the maintenance cost).

Some of the aspects that should be surveyed are:

- Data formats in use at all levels: document exchange, database, and network protocol
- Applications in use, including standalone programs that are internally developed, macros, and active documents
- Available functionality
- Shortcomings and problems in the current infrastructure

To justify a migration, management usually has to anticipate that the new software can improve on the current IT infrastructure, either functionally or in aspects of quality (availability, reliability, performance, etc.). But at the very least, it is essential to make sure the new software can fulfill existing functional requirements, which a conscientious survey can do.

Use the Flexibility of FLOSS to Create Local Adaptations

The differentiating characteristic of FLOSS is the flexibility and freedom that it gives to users and developers in creating new or adapted versions. This flexibility can greatly enhance the perceived value of FLOSS. For example, it is possible to create customized packages that contain local configurations, special fonts, and other supplemental material such as preset macros and templates in use throughout the organization. Also, a custom look and feel may significantly improve chances that users will accept the software, both by presenting a nicer-looking desktop and by maintaining familiar links and menu entries.

Many users of FLOSS packages have created customizations and integrated them in popular Linux distributions so that other users can select the customizations easily without further coding.

Much More Software Is Available Than What Is Installed by Default

Licensing or design issues limit substantially the amount of software that is usually included in the default installation of the most used Linux distributions. For example, only a few include playback capability for the most common audio and video formats, due to licensing and patent issues. For the same reasons, the distributions leave out some packages that are of interest to only a minority of users.

For this reason, it is important to research and add to the default distributions additional packages that may be valuable in your organization. Such packages include the aforementioned multimedia support, additional fonts, and specialized plug-ins.

Always Favor Stability over Functionality

In the desire to be inclusive and reward participation, FLOSS tends to include optional packages that don't meet the same standards of quality and stability as the core software. Often, many packages provide similar functionality, but some are much more stable and reliable. In general, you should give preference to the one that is most stable. Stable packages have racked up longer experience in the field (and thus more information is available for the administrator) and should suffer from less variability between releases.

> **WARNING**
> When the IT administrator wants the latest version of everything on a user's desktop, bugs could not only frustrate the user but also cause unexpected failures in more stable components that eventually lead to rejection of the entire project.

Design the Workflow Support Infrastructure to Reduce "Impedance Mismatches"

Every transition from one IT infrastructure to another leads to some *impedance mismatches*, small differences and incompatibilities that keep a process from moving smoothly. This can be observed, for example, when documents travel from one data format to another. The overall infrastructure should reduce the number of such transition points—for example, by redesigning the document templates in the ODT (OpenDocument) open format instead of reusing previously developed versions made using proprietary tools. This reduces greatly the formatting and style differences that arise when one format is translated into another.

Introduce a Trouble Ticket System

IT staff members can find it hard to assess the degree of difficulty users have in adopting new solutions, as well as general user satisfaction and degree of acceptance. The difficulty increases with the size of the organization. An online trouble ticket system may provide an easy way to collect weak points in the deployment, and can help identify users who need additional training by analyzing per-user submission statistics. The system may also bring weaknesses in the deployment to the surface, such as by highlighting several trouble tickets related to a specific area.

> **WARNING**
>
> When it is difficult or impossible to track the problems and issues perceived during the transition, and how they were addressed, the adoption process is uncontrolled and may be mishandled for lack of information.

Compile and Update a Detailed Migration Workbook

A large-scale migration effort requires coordinated action and clear, up-to-date information. The best way to provide this information is through a *migration workbook*, a single point where project members can find the documentation prepared for the migration (including the rationale, the detailed plan, and the technical documentation) and the timetable, updated as the project progresses. This also simplifies project management when there is a change in the team performing the migration.

> **WARNING**
>
> Lacking documentation about the transition process makes it more difficult to overcome problems or to provide to users a clear view of the transition process.

Best Practices: Social

Although everyone places lip service nowadays to the organizational and psychological pressures users feel during a migration, all too often the IT staff remains blind to these aspects of change or lacks the tools and training to collect information and deal with problems. If left to fester, problems in the social environment for a migration can derail the project.

Provide Training and Communication About the FLOSS Model

A significant obstacle to FLOSS adoption is acceptance by the users, who usually have a very limited knowledge of FLOSS and open data standards. In many cases, FLOSS is perceived as lower quality because it is freely downloadable from the Internet, and users may have had negative experiences with shareware packages or amateur projects. It is important to cancel this perception, and to provide information about how FLOSS is developed, its rationale, and the business models behind it.

In particular, specific training on legal, economic, and sociotechnical aspects should be provided to the different actors involved in FLOSS adoption. This training has to be adapted to their roles and needs, ranging from a strategic vision for decision makers to basic, close-to-the-ground concepts for end users. As an example, for IT managers and decision makers, the following issues should be clearly addressed:

Legal implications
> How to choose licenses for code distribution, and what obligations are enforced by the licenses of the FLOSS programs used

Economic implications
> How sustainable FLOSS ecosystems are formed and maintained, how to work with them to take into account specific agency needs, and the role of public agencies in these areas

Sociotechnical implications
> How FLOSS communities work, including the role of companies and volunteers, and the processes they use to improve quality and respond to the needs of users

This kind of training will ensure that agencies take full advantage of the FLOSS model instead of just grasping its surface. In addition, it will help all actors involved understand the big picture, and how the move to FLOSS is much more than a mere change in technology. Providing factual, unbiased information will also help to mitigate false expectations, while at the same time spreading the word about FLOSS's potential.

Training and communication should not be improvised. On the contrary, one of the first tasks in any move to FLOSS should be the design of a detailed training and communication plan.

> **WARNING**
> When a training or communication plan is not a fundamental part of the transition preparation, there may be a lack of coherent information transferred to the users, leading to confusion and unsatisfactory perception of the adoption process.

Don't Force the Change on Users; Provide Explanations Instead

A change in IT infrastructure will force a significant change in how users work and use internal resources, and therefore is likely to arouse their resistance. This natural resistance may be lessened by explaining clearly why and how the change will happen, and the long-term benefits in both internal factors (such as lower cost, better flexibility, and stronger security) and external factors (openness, adherence to international standards, and less burden on external users).

It is important to provide enough information and support to be able to skip the "opposition gulf" that typically accompanies radical changes.

Use the Migration As an Opportunity to Improve Users' Skills

Because any new infrastructure calls for training, it may be used as an opening to improve overall IT skills. Historically, public agencies have offered little formal training to their staff members. A conscious allocation of time and funds to training will help not only to improve productivity, but also to increase user confidence and harmonize skills among groups.

The migration may arouse some resistance from the so-called "local gurus" who could perceive this overall improvement as diminishing their social role as technical leaders. The best way to counter such resistance is to identify those users and offer them higher-level training material. Finally, it's useful to identify local "champions"—local FLOSS enthusiasts, who, surprisingly, often exist in the agency—who can provide peer support to other users. Management can offer these champions additional training opportunities or recognition.

It's useful to create an internal, intranet-accessible page that provides links to all the different training packages. Both local gurus and champions will take advantage of the resource.

Make It Easy to Experiment and Learn

The licensing freedom that is the main point of FLOSS allows for free redistribution of software and in many cases of training material as well. Management can increase staff members' expertise and overall project acceptance by taking advantage of this openness, providing users with Linux Live CDs or live USB sticks (which require no hard disk installation) as well as printed material. Users can be encouraged to take them home and play with them to increase their comfort with FLOSS.

Setting up comprehensive information repositories, probably in coordination with other public agencies with the same interests, will also help users probe further. In particular, documents that explain not only the main characteristics of the FLOSS solutions used, but also their limitations and advantages, will help motivated users. FAQs, success stories, and links to websites will show users that their deployment is not an island, but is related to other similar projects worldwide.

Establish Meeting Points and Repositories

One of the problems to avoid, when asking for a wrenching change in behavior and attitudes, is the perception of isolation. Luckily, one of the main strengths of FLOSS is how it facilitates the replication of solutions and the spread of good practices. Therefore, it is important to establish meeting points, both physical and virtual, where people with responsibility for FLOSS deployments can meet and share experiences.

These points can be used not only by public agency employees, but also by companies providing them with FLOSS-based solutions, thus helping to cancel the impression that there is no support for those solutions. Having a place that developers from the FLOSS community can visit will enable them to understand the specific requirements of public agencies.

Those meeting points should also include repositories, both of software solutions and of case studies. These can spread the benefits of experience and propel the reuse of solutions.

Conclusion

The adoption of FLOSS can have a significant positive impact on the IT infrastructure of a public agency. The unique needs and scope of modern agencies, however, require specific attention to the management, technical, and social aspects of adoption to make sure that it is effective and brings the promised advantages. The list of best practices in this chapter will hopefully improve the migration or adoption effort of FLOSS, and provide guidelines to assess the overall process.

References

1. Applied Research and Innovation Fund, InnovationBG 2007 report.
2. "Living with open source: The new rules for IT vendors and consumers," L. Augustin, OSBC 2004 conference.
3. "Open Source Software for the Development of the Spanish Public Administration," CENATIC, Reports CENATIC 01, National Observatory of Open Source Software, Almendralejo, Spain, 2008.
4. CIOINSIGHT OSS survey, CIOInsight, 2007.
5. "D6.1 Report evaluating the costs/benefits of a transition towards ODS/OS," EU COSPA project.
6. "Free Software/Open Source: Information Society Opportunities for Europe?" working paper, C. Daffara and J. M. Barahona (*http://eu.conecta.it*).
7. "Business models in OSS-based companies," C. Daffara, accepted paper, OSSEMP workshop, Third International Conference on Open Source, Limerick, Ireland, 2007.
8. "Open source going mainstream," Gartner Group, Gartner report, 2006.

9. "Introduction to Free Software, Second Edition," Jesus M. Gonzalez-Barahona et al., Fundació per a la Universitat Oberta de Catalunya, Barcelona, Spain, 2008 (*http://ocw.uoc.edu/computer-science-technology-and-multimedia/introduction-to-free-software*).

10. "Free/Libre/Open Source Software Worldwide impact study: FLOSSWorld," Gosh, et al., FLOSSWorld project presentation (*http://www.flossproject.org/papers/20051217/flossworld-intro3.pdf*).

11. "Economic impact of FLOSS on innovation and competitiveness of the EU ICT sector," Gosh, et al., November 2006.

12. *Government Policy Towards Open Source Software*, W.R. Hahn (ed.), AEI-Brookings, 2002.

13. "Linux Client Migration Cookbook, Version 2: A Practical Planning and Implementation Guide for Migrating to Desktop Linux," IBM, October 2006 (*http://www.redbooks.ibm.com/abstracts/sg246380.html?Open*).

14. "Open Source in Global Software: Market Impact, Disruption, and Business Models," IDC, IDC report, 2006.

15. Germany: KBSt migration guide (*http://www.cio.bund.de/DE/IT-Methoden/Migrationsleitfaden/migrationsleitfaden_node.html*).

16. *Democratizing Innovation*, Eric Von Hippel, MIT Press, 2005.

About the Authors

CARLO DAFFARA is head of research at Conecta, an open source consulting company based in Italy. He is the Italian member of the European working group on libre software, and chairs several other working groups, such as the open source middleware group of the IEEE technical committee on scalable computing and the SME working group of the EU competitiveness task force. His current research activity is centered on the sustainability of OSS-based business models.

JESUS M. GONZALEZ-BARAHONA teaches and researches at Universidad Rey Juan Carlos, Mostoles (Spain). He first got involved in libre software in 1991. Since then, he has collaborated on several working groups, developed research lines, and initiated training programs. He also collaborates on several libre software projects and associations, writes in various media about topics related to libre software, and consults for companies and public administrations on issues related to their strategies, in the framework of the GSyC/LibreSoft research group (*http://libresoft.es*).

CHAPTER THIRTY-THREE

Why Open Digital Standards Matter in Government

Marco Fioretti

Although we are rarely aware of the standards that are the foundation for our everyday activities, a host of such standards facilitate these activities and protect us from dangerous consequences.

Let's start our look at standards with three little questions:

- How did standards enrich or limit President Barack Obama's activities during his first day in office?

- How could standards have saved the twin children of movie actor Dennis Quaid from serious injury?

- Why is a lack of standards making it hard to repair the U.S. Navy's much-heralded Nimitz nuclear aircraft carrier?

The answers will show why standards are relevant in many situations, and demonstrate the importance of the government using truly open standards in its digital media and processes.

Let's start with Barack Obama. On his first day in office, he issued two memoranda, one about transparency and open government (*http://www.whitehouse.gov/the_press_office/ TransparencyandOpenGovernment*) (see the Appendix) and another about the Freedom of Information Act (FOIA) (*http://www.whitehouse.gov/the_press_office/FreedomofInformationAct*). Despite the historic importance of these documents, almost nobody would be able to answer a simple question: what brand and model of pen did the president use to sign those memoranda?

Of course, almost nobody knows the answer to this question because nobody cares or needs to care. This brings us to the two really important questions: what conditions make it irrelevant which pen the president uses? And crucially, what conditions could change the situation so that the tools he uses to write or sign a document suddenly matter?

Before answering these questions, let's look at what happened to actor Dennis Quaid's children. In November 2007, his two-week-old twins nearly died after being given a drug at 1,000 times the recommended dose for newborns (*http://www.foxnews.com/story/0,2933,312357,00.html*). Later, Quaid asked for "a technological way to track the life-and-death decision making in medicine" since "100,000 people are killed every year because of medical mistakes," and created the Quaid Foundation to tackle the answer. In another recent story, while being cured of cancer, former U.S. Rep. Billy Tauzin had a very similar problem: he had to fill out the same forms for six months—every time he went to a new hospital or test center—and also had an unnecessary operation because the surgeons didn't know about earlier operations.

As for the U.S.S. Nimitz, launched in 1972 and considered a hallmark of American military excellence, she's still in pretty good shape. Which is lucky because some of the technical diagrams that explain how to fix the reactors and other critical systems are blurry when viewed on computer monitors (*http://www.popularmechanics.com/technology/industry/4201645.html*). It turns out that the diagrams were stored in a file format that today's computer programs do not completely understand. Reassuring, isn't it?

Badly Used Technology Hinders Progress

These examples may seem totally unrelated, but they contain a common link. Every aspect of our existence is managed and mediated by data, documents, and communications that are increasingly digital: your civil rights and the quality of your own life heavily depend on how software is used *around* you. This data includes almost everything informational, from the critically important (databases, government reports, regulations, TV broadcasts, blueprints, maps, and contracts) to the casual (blog entries, home movies, and music).

Unfortunately, although the technology to handle these documents has made huge advances in the past 100 years, we often use software, or let it be used, in the wrong way. The software we use to manage government documents, the treatment plans of the Quaid children and Rep. Tauzin, and the design specifications of the Nimitz carrier is much less reliable and, in some ways, much less technically sophisticated than the old-fashioned pen Obama used to sign the memoranda.

The Digital Age Explained

To really understand the nature of the problem, we need to step back and establish a few simple definitions. All the forms of data I mentioned earlier—which I'll just refer to as "documents" for the sake of simplicity—are increasingly being created, processed, distributed, and read digitally—but just what is a digit?

A *digit* is a single character in a numbering system (*http://mason.gmu.edu/~montecin/digits.htm*). Internally, computers can generate, recognize, and store only two states: the presence or absence of a small electric charge, called a *bit*. Consequently, they can represent only two digits, 1 or 0, just like we'd be forced to do if we had only one hand with only one finger. Commands, signals, and data are called digital when they are translated into series of ones and zeros. Normally, the bits are bundled in groups of eight called *bytes*.

When done right, digitization is good. It reduces every kind of data management to operations on bit sequences, which in turn are easy to manage with computers. If all conceivable kinds of documents (from texts to music, maps, images, and 3D models) can be represented as series of bits, we need only one class of generic, completely interchangeable devices to store them. Back in the twentieth century, we couldn't save love letters or movies on an LP album, nor could we preserve live music on sheets of paper. Today, instead, flash cards made for digital cameras will store PhD theses, songs, or tax forms without ever noticing that they aren't photographs. For the same reason, if everything is digital we can get rid of the telephone systems, the TV and radio broadcasting systems, the telegraph, and so forth and employ just one (very large) class of telecom networks to act as bit transporters. The cost and time savings enabled by this approach to information management are so big that the trend toward digitization is unstoppable.

However, digitization has several traps.

Everything we do to make meaning out of bits—to turn a VoIP transmission into our child's beloved voice, to display a legal document for editing, to check Google Maps for a location—involves a specification that says what each group of bits means and how they should follow one another. Digital documents require complete format specifications to remain usable, now and in the future. For the same reasons, clearly defined rules known as *protocols* are necessary when bits travel between systems, whether as email or as computer animation.

Theoretically, agreement on file formats and protocols is all that is needed for different computers and software programs to work together, no matter how the data is generated, stored, or transmitted: programs on one remote computer could automatically retrieve data from other computers, process the data in real time, and send the result—for example, the best deal on an airplane ticket—directly to your home computer.

In the real world, legal restrictions and implementation issues impair the value of file formats and communication protocols. Companies can change them unexpectedly and prevent anybody they choose from using their formats by legal means. Where good will prevail, ambiguities can lead to incompatible products. Thus, format and protocol specifications have real value for users only when ratified as official standards which everybody can reuse without legal restriction or paying any fees. When they choose to, governments can mandate standards of this kind as compatibility requirements in public requests for proposals, and can have confidence that such standards provide high-quality features, reliability, and real interoperability both now and in the future.

Standards and the Problems with Digital Technology

The switch to digital documents entails two separate problems: obsolescent media and unreadable software formats.

The obsolescent media problem is hardware-related. Digital storage media are much more fragile than nondigital ones: parchment lasts millennia when handled well, hard drives just a few years. Furthermore, digital media go out of date as new and better ones are invented—for instance, lots of people stored documents on floppy disks in the 1980s and 1990s, but hardly any computer systems can be found now with floppy disk drives.

The second problem is much more serious. Even when the container works perfectly, bit sequences are absolutely useless if you don't know what they mean, and if the instructions you need to read or translate them are lost or too expensive to buy.

These aren't hypotheses. Almost all the files created by public and private businesses around the world are already encoded in a way that only one suite of programs, from one single, for-profit company, can read without compatibility problems. What if that company went belly up? Think it's too big to fail? Isn't this what everybody would have said in 2008 about Lehman Brothers, General Motors, or Chrysler?

According to Jerome P. McDonough, assistant professor in the Graduate School of Library and Information Science at the University of Illinois at Urbana-Champaign, the total amount of data in the files of all types, from "government records to tax files, email, music, and photos" that could be lost due to "ever-shifting platforms and file formats" is about 369 billions of billions of bytes (*http://news.illinois.edu/news/08/1027data.html*). (As a reference, the size of this chapter is less than 30,000 bytes.)

The Nimitz diagrams are locked inside files whose format, being unknown, can't be decoded with modern software. This is not an isolated example; all over the world, billions of designs, from furniture to water purification systems, bridges and buildings, plane and car parts, are stored in a format that only the few developers of one program ever knew how to read without errors.

We can't go back to the predigital era. It would be stupid to do so. But if we don't start managing digital data and communications the right way—with a view toward both real interoperability and future readability—both private and public life will become harder to manage.

Luckily, many governments are aware of these hardware and software problems, but the only recourse they've found is precisely the one I just derided: sticking to nondigital media. Most national archives, and many other public and private organizations around the world, still waste a lot of money and resources because they don't feel safe depending only on digital documents for long-term storage. For example, the Virginia State library *"cannot accept records for permanent storage on digital media at this time due to the lack of hardware and software standards."* Consequently, *"Electronic records identified as permanent...must be converted to archival quality microfilm or alkaline paper before being transferred to the Library"* (*http://www.archiveindex.com/laws/ law-va.htm*). What if, 20, 30, or 40 years from now, the digital records of your pension payments were unreadable? What is the benefit of digital documents for a small business, if it must continuously update software and hardware without any need except to maintain archives, or continue to (re)enter data by hand in incompatible systems?

The health care system experiences the worst of the situation, suffering from both high costs and subpar care. For example, Rep. Tauzin explicitly complained that none of the hospitals he visited were able to share digital records with one another.

Many governments worldwide are fighting the same battle, on a much bigger scale. In the United States, the George W. Bush administration left behind 100 trillion bytes of electronic records (*http://www.nytimes.com/2008/12/27/washington/27archives.html?_r=1*). That's 50 times as much as President Clinton left in 2001, but surely much less than what the Obama administration will produce. Already, the Bush archives, which include historical documents such as top-secret email tracing plans for the Iraq war, contain data in "formats not previously dealt with" by the U.S. National Archives.

So, to come full circle, if Obama's pen was like digital media, anyone wanting to read the memoranda would have to buy the same kind of pen. Not much openness or freedom of information in that!

Why Has Digital Gone Bad So Often?

There are several reasons for this mess, but a particularly important one is our ignorance as a society. Software is still so new in our culture that most of us (including many people who consider themselves "experts" because they spend lots of time using office suites, computer games, or social networks) haven't actually realized yet the roles played by formats and protocols, and how they can run against our interests.

Consider how people refer to office files. Nobody would talk about a handwritten letter by mentioning the name of the pen used to write it; saying "I sent you a Bic letter" or a "Mont-Blanc letter" would be a sure way to have everyone laugh at you. Yet most people regularly say "I'll send you a PowerPoint" or "I need to check the figures in that Excel file," which is the same thing, but with no embarrassment.

Such phrases would trigger concern if the public knew why and how software is different from Obama's pen. Not only do people use the software without regard for compatibility and future access, but worse still, they make schoolchildren addicts to that software because "everybody else does it," or to learn what advertising says to be the best the industry offers, or to "have more opportunities." This is at least counterproductive, if not actually dangerous.

In every generation, automobile companies go out of business. It becomes difficult to buy spare parts for existing cars, but at least the disappearance of the product line has no effect on your ability to buy and drive cars in the future. You don't lose all your memories of trips made with the old car, or have more trouble dealing with the businesses you drove to. And your new car need not be "compatible" with any other, old or new.

But when a software company goes out of business, or simply discontinues a product, all the documents you created with it could go out of your reach for good. All it takes is a switch to a new computer. (Modern proprietary software licenses make it hard to run an old program on a new computer even if they're technically compatible.) The software is similar to a nuclear plant without any waste management policy, or to depleted uranium weapons: they hurt people who weren't there when they were used, for a long time afterward. A company or government agency that uses software in nonstandard formats constrains without any real reason not only its own choices, but those of everybody who interacts with it for all of history.

Software developers have two ways to make their users come back for a new version of their programs. One is to keep writing software that's actually better than the previous version: faster, easier to use, more flexible, and with support for new contexts such as the Web. The other way is not to struggle for improved quality, but to create secret file formats or protocols and change them without a really valid reason every year. People who stick to the old versions of the software find they can't do business with people who bought the new version, so everyone is forced to upgrade.

Once a movie, contract, or business report has been saved in a format that can be read by only one software program, you can forget copyright. That document now belongs to the developer or company that developed that program. If you still want it, you must accept their conditions. That's how Word/Excel/PowerPoint and AutoCAD became de facto monopolists in their respective markets: their file formats, not the software itself, are secret. People who were already using those programs could not get rid of them without losing the files they had already created and distributed to other people, who, in turn, were forced to buy the same programs to open them, and so on. Had the file formats been really usable with other programs, no one would have cared about those programs being secret.

Which is why I declared at the beginning of this chapter that software is less sophisticated than pens, because pens create none of these problems. What they produce is 100% guaranteed compatible with all other pens and sheets of paper in the world. You don't need to own the same pens as Obama to read what he writes, or to write a letter to him. There are two foundations for this openness: first, pens are tools that are completely independent from the document format, which in their case is the alphabet, that is the shape and meaning of the characters in which languages are written. Second, alphabets are not secret and no one needs permission to use them. Software should work in the same open way.

Standards are meant to ensure that data can be accessed in a variety of ways so that no single program or software vendor is indispensable. There's an art and a science to writing standards, of course. If they're ambiguous, incomplete, or poorly written, they won't do their job. That's why standards committees sign up a wide variety of experts to write standards, and it takes years to do.

Formats and protocols are often more important than software, because most programs are worthless without other programs to talk to (imagine if you were the only person in the world with an email program) or without data to process (like if you had a word processor that couldn't open or save a file). We run software to manage data, not the other way around. The only way to guarantee that our data remains ours, and always immediately available, is to store it in file formats which are really independent from any single software product.

The Huge Positive Potential of Digital Technologies

Democracy implies accountability, efficiency, optimal usage of public money, and transparency in all public operations and services, regardless of whether they are managed by the private or public sector: in a word, *openness*. Software and digital data can help tremendously to achieve these and other crucial goals.

For example, according to "Standards and the Smart Grid: The U.S. Experience," "increased use of digital information" is one of the essential prerequisites for building the smart energy grid that will help to decrease U.S. dependence on foreign energy and fuel job creation (*http://www.consortiuminfo.org/bulletins/apr09.php#feature*). Getting hundreds of companies around the continent to share this information requires open, standard formats.

There are huge efforts these days to digitize individual medical histories, drug records, test results, and surgeries all in one big file for each individual, called an electronic health record (EHR). Personal EHRs could help to greatly reduce paperwork, treatment costs, and time spent in hospitals and labs, and will facilitate people moving from one city, health insurance company, or service provider to another. In contrast to the ordeals of Quaid's children and Rep. Tauzin, doctors could always make the best decisions for your health in the safest, fastest, and cheapest way possible. As long as their computers can read your EHR, of course.

Publishing online without legal restrictions raw data such as maps, census records, weather surveys, agricultural statistics, court rulings, and agency budgets (while protecting citizens' privacy, of course) makes two wonderful things possible. One is the generation of new wealth: if both public agencies and private businesses can freely use all that data to make better decisions and offer new services, they'll minimize their expenses and make more money. This will both stimulate the economy and increase the tax base. The other advantage of correctly publishing public raw data online is much more control by private citizens over their governments, as well as closer cooperation with them.

Having such data online makes it possible for civic-minded programmers to finally build and use "follow the money" search engines. Everybody could use or develop interfaces such as Google Squared (*http://squared.google.com*) to display, all in one table, things such as who got money from a public contract, who approved it, all the present and past relationships among those people (such as sitting on the boards of the same companies), the percentage of contracts assigned to some firm from each public officer, and so on. It would be much easier for everybody to visualize how numbers, decisions, and physical places are related. You could generate on-the-spot maps that show how tax money moves from one county to another and why, and how it varies over time with the party in power. Residents of each town could see without intermediaries how demographics and pollution sources in any given area increase the occurrence of some specific illness. It would also become much easier to contribute data into these systems, which makes them more useful to public administrators.

Demanding that all public administrations and schools, at all levels, accept and store office files only in nonproprietary standard formats such as OpenDocument (the only viable alternative today to the forced upgrades caused by the continuous changes in *.doc*, *.xls*, and *.ppt* file formats) would leave all their partners free to use whatever office software they like best. At the same time, it would protect the pockets and freedom of choice of millions of small businesses, schools, and students who can't afford the licensing costs of "industry-standard" word processors.

In principle, the current U.S. administration is in favor of going digital this way. The Obama stimulus package signed in February 2009 provided $19 billion to bring hospitals the benefits of digital technology (*http://www.healthcareitnews.com/news/congress-passes-stimulus-package-19b -healthcare-it*). The "Transparency and Open Government" memo includes statements such as the following:

> Government should be transparent. Transparency promotes accountability and provides information for citizens about what their Government is doing. Information maintained by the Federal Government is a national asset. My Administration will take appropriate action, consistent with law and policy, to disclose information rapidly in forms that the public can readily find and use. Government should be collaborative. Collaboration actively engages Americans in the work of their Government. Executive departments and agencies should use innovative tools, methods, and systems to cooperate among themselves, across all levels of Government, and with nonprofit organizations, businesses, and individuals in the private sector.

The truth, however, is that these and many other things, including FOIA, will be technically possible only if by mandating the use of open, standard formats.

Free and Open Standards and Software: The Digital Basis of Open Government

To enshrine open standards in government and make sure they are robustly implemented, governments should lean whenever possible toward free/libre/open source software (FLOSS). As described in Chapter 32, FLOSS code is available to everybody without any royalty or legal restriction. Everybody can install as many copies of the program as they wish, or create and redistribute, under the same conditions, custom copies of that program starting from the source code.

Still, FLOSS is not enough to guarantee that owners of documents will always be able to read them, because the original source code might be lost or fail to work on newer computer systems. In such cases, files become unreadable not because of software licenses, but simply because their authors never bothered to demand that the programmers use fully documented file formats. That's why it's important to stick to really open standards that exist and are defined regardless of any specific software program, regardless of its license.

So, FLOSS is an important step toward open government, but truly open formats and protocols are often even more important, because most programs are worthless without other programs with which to talk, or without data to process. We run software to manage data, not the other way around. Open formats and protocols are standards whose complete specification is published in enough detail that any programmer can, without royalties or other conditions, write new software fully compatible with that format or protocol. Such standards don't rely on any proprietary subcomponents, are developed through consensus and experimentation, and are maintained by a recognized international, nonprofit community. Only standards such as these give real guarantees that our data remains ours and that its formats will remain readable, while no one can exploit them to lock in users and exclude competition.

So-called de facto or industry standards often aren't open. They often belong to one (usually for-profit) company. Even when they are entirely published, their owners can change them at will, whenever they feel like it, and without informing everybody else of which changes were made. In other cases, you need explicit permissions to use the standard. Such standards may even be created just to stifle competition: a company may create a specification that describes the file format incompletely and with proprietary features that only it can provide, and then lobby to have it recognized as a standard. This is a mock standard, because no one else can develop software that really works with the format.

This is relevant because conformance to some standard is often (rightly!) a mandatory requirement in contracts for information and computer technology products and services paid with your tax money.

There is another reason why relying only on adoption of FLOSS to keep everything open, instead of starting from truly open standards as defined earlier, is not the optimal solution. File formats should be as few as possible and as stable as possible. FLOSS makes it always possible to convert data from one format to another, but why create the need for conversion if it isn't absolutely necessary? Think of software as pens, and formats as alphabets. We went from quills to email in just a few centuries exactly because the alphabets remained practically unchanged, allowing each generation to learn and build on what already existed rather than rewrite every manuscript in a different way every few years. Innovation whose impact is limited to internal software features is less of a problem, as it leaves documents readable by everybody. An insistence on open formats and protocols (which can be used also by proprietary software) will actually stimulate developers to improve the user experience and other aspects of their software (aspects that are independent of the standards) rather than try to dominate the market through their control over formats.

In other words, insistence on open standards for file formats and protocols will also make it much easier to evaluate software programs according to their actual merits: performance, flexibility, ease of use and customization, documentation quality, and so forth. Think again to pens and alphabets. There is nothing wrong in selling luxury pens made with secret or patented technology, as long as cheap pens can also exist. But the whole thing is contingent on everybody using the same alphabet, without needing to pay fees or learn special secrets.

Conclusion

Digitization is good, but only when it's open in the ways described in these pages. Governments must lead the way in this goal, both by example and by enforcing interoperability through really open digital standards, for several reasons:

- Without exploiting all the potential of open standards and FLOSS, there can be no open government, no FOIA, no smart energy grids, and no efficient services. Open data and file formats are mandatory to guarantee that all citizens can analyze raw public data or submit their own information, or that data can be retrieved 20, 50, or 100 years later. The first, nonnegotiable step toward any open government policy is therefore to demand that only really open formats and protocols be used for public data and digital interaction with any public administration.

- In the modern world, technology (especially digital technology) is legislation. A government that insists on using, or tolerating, closed, secret formats and protocols has abdicated part of its duty to protect individual freedom and equal opportunities, both in business and in education, as well as the hope of reducing costs.

- To emphasize the preceding point, open formats save money. Only if there is no vendor lock-in can public agencies, businesses, and individuals get really competitive offers from many providers.

- Open formats and protocols are both an extremely profitable investment and an enabler. Compared to reforming pension systems, health care, transportation, energy, pollution, or public education, open formats, protocols, and FLOSS are much quicker and cheaper to adopt. Therefore, since software is so ubiquitous, the adoption of open formats has a positive impact on all those other fields. There is probably no other way to save so much money in so many different places and free vital resources with so (comparatively) little effort than through these technologies—as long as that effort is coordinated, of course. That's why it must be governments that set the example and constitute the critical mass that makes open standards and FLOSS accessible to everybody.

About the Author

 **MARCO FIORETTI** is a freelance writer, an activist, a popularizer, a teacher, and a speaker about open digital standards, Free Software, and digital technologies and their relation to and impact on education, ethics, civil rights, and environmental issues. Marco is the webmaster of Stop/Zona-M (*http://stop.zona-m.net/*), a website designed to help all normal people stop and learn the essentials of, and think about, the things that matter to them. Marco is the author of *Family Guide to Digital Freedom (http://digifreedom.net)* and a regular contributor to several print and online ICT magazines. His website is *http://mfioretti.com*.

CHAPTER THIRTY-FOUR

Case Study: Utah.gov

David Fletcher

A Historical Perspective

Fifteen years ago, a group of Utah government leaders met in the basement of the state office building to listen to a presentation on how to use the Netscape browser. At that time, they had no idea that this new tool would completely change the nature of their work and in many cases even eliminate much of what they did and replace it with something dramatically different.

In 1993, Governor Mike Leavitt talked to state workers about an information highway. He stated, "I believe we are entering an exciting new era in society…our world is becoming an information ecosystem, and the ramifications are monumental. Futurists believe there will be a massive shift in the nature of work and that the impact of the information age may be as great as the societal changes that occurred during the industrial revolution" (*http://www .governor.state.ut.us/governor/elhighwy.htm*). He followed up on that vision with a challenge that included five basic parts:

- In government, we must change the way we think. We must think of technology, think of new applications, and think of new ways of doing things.

- We must use existing resources and find ways to reallocate them, rather than raise taxes.

- We must "put the state of Utah at citizens' fingertips." (He issued the first call to deliver specific services, including driver's license renewals, tax payments, and fishing license purchases, electronically.)

- Agencies must make "enormous amounts" of information and data available to the public electronically.

- Leaders must encourage a strong competitive environment among infrastructure providers.

Sixteen years later, this vision has been replaced with reality. Because of the confidence in a 24/7 government service infrastructure, Governor Jon Huntsman made a bold decision to move forward in testing a statewide four-day work week in August 2008. Seventeen thousand employees made this change basically overnight. Utah leads the nation in terms of online services and e-government adoption. In 2008, the state was recognized by the Center for Digital Government as the top digital state in the nation. Following dramatic revisions to the state's website in 2009, Utah.gov was recognized as the best state portal by the Center as well (see Figure 34-1).

The Utah.gov portal, updated in June 2009, includes Web 2.0 services integration along with new functionality such as GeoIP/location-based services, multimedia, and a statewide data portal.

With millions of online transactions and hundreds of unique communications channels that extend Utah government into the public arena, the online channel is now the predominant channel. For many government workers, it is tightly integrated into every aspect of their daily regimen. Many are quickly evolving from communications that consisted primarily of telephone calls and email to a multifaceted and more interactive communication structure that includes text and instant messaging, online chat, Twitter, and other social media channels.

What Today's Landscape Looks Like

Utah now provides more than 870 online services to citizens and businesses. Many of these are common services such as renewing driver's licenses, purchasing a fishing license, and paying taxes. Over the years, the state has learned how to improve online service through citizen interaction. In 2003, it became the first state to implement a 24/7 online chat service, allowing citizens direct contact with service personnel when they have questions. The state also includes an optional feedback channel with most services and has received thousands of responses that have been useful in improving the quality of service.

This new era of openness did not come easy. In 1995, there was still a lot of concern about how the Internet would be used. Leaders in every branch of Utah government worried about how their employees would utilize this new phenomenon and how it would affect their productivity. Some agencies banned use of the Internet while they worked to understand how to use it.

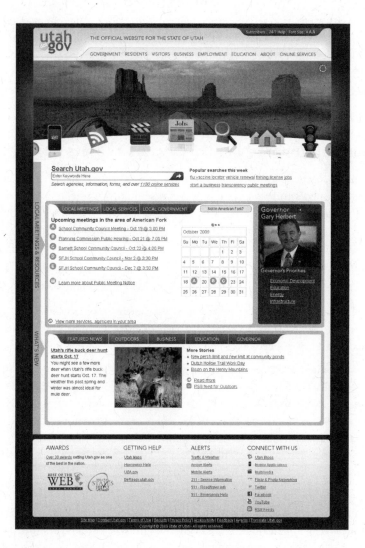

FIGURE 34-1. Utah.gov portal

When streaming media first became available, there were debates about how much access the public should have to legislative hearings and meetings and how it would affect open discussion among legislators. Today, that same legislature pushes for more openness each year. In 2007, it passed a new law creating a public meeting notice system that required information regarding all state and local government meetings to be posted in a statewide system where anyone could find it. A year later, it passed a bill requiring that all state financial records be made available online and then extended that requirement to local government (*http://transparent.utah.gov*). "Government transparency has become a reality in Utah," said Lt. Governor Gary Herbert. "This site allows everyone to see where and how their tax dollars are being spent. This commitment to openness and transparency will strengthen our state management." News media and others interested in government spending no longer need to make special requests to agencies; they can find every expenditure online. Utah's cities, counties, school districts, transit districts, and so forth will be providing their finances online within the next two years, since the state legislature expanded the bill creating the system to all local governments within Utah.

Champions Discovered in All Branches of State Government

The movement to create a more open and responsive government using the Internet as a medium has been successful to a large degree because there have been champions in all branches of the state government that have supported it. Legislative leaders such as Steve Urquhart and John Dougall started blogging as a way to share their thoughts with constituents and receive valuable feedback.

In 2007, Rep. Urquhart launched Politicopia, a wiki with the goal of increasing citizen involvement in the political process. Into the second week, he announced:

> One week into the experiment, Politicopia is working. Citizens are participating and citizens are being heard. Legislators are talking to me about things they've read on Politicopia. Because of input I received, I have changed a position I've held for years.

The Utah State Senate has also been very progressive in its adoption of new methods for involving the public. The Senate Majority introduced SenateSite.com, which leverages YouTube, Twitter, Facebook, Gcast, and blogging in various experiments to involve the public. The Senate has held online town hall meetings where citizens can interact with and ask questions of the senators in real time. These experiences have resulted in a continually evolving and increasingly open setting where the business of government is conducted (see Figure 34-2).

The Utah State Legislature meets in open session for six weeks each year beginning in January. During this short period, more than 600 bills are considered, many of which make significant changes to state law. At the same time, the Legislature must review and approve a multibillion-dollar budget that covers state government as well as public and higher education. The tools of Web 2.0 now make this process much more understandable and open to all interested parties and the public at large. These users can subscribe to custom RSS feeds of any bill and get notified in real time anytime there is a change in content or process. This capability along with the ability to provide direct feedback through multiple channels is a huge change to the entire scene.

Utah bloggers have been participating in the Utah openness debate. In the last legislative session (February 2009), Rep. Urquhart held a press conference specifically for bloggers where he introduced a new bill. We have also witnessed significant growth in blogger participation in traditional press conferences which has added to a diversity of coverage and opinion on

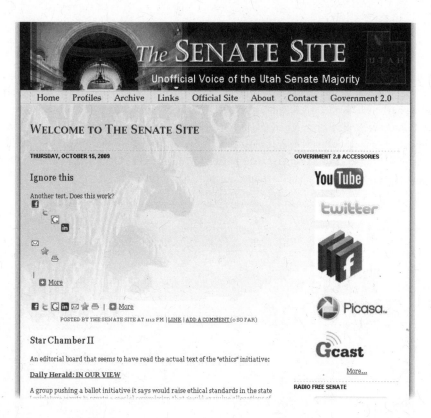

FIGURE 34-2. The Utah State Senate website

public issues. The bloggers have brought a new perspective to the debate that is different and unique from the traditional media. Often they are more intent on expressing an opinion or viewpoint that is frequently representative of a community within the state.

The Utah judiciary has also been involved in accepting new media tools for sharing information. The Utah Supreme Court has sought ways to make the courts more efficient by adding online services, self-help resources, and multimedia to their website. Citizens and attorneys are able to subscribe to the latest court opinions with a simple-to-use RSS feed. Citizens can prepare for jury service by accessing the online Jury Room. Utah state courts even facilitate access to these services by providing free wireless access in many Utah courthouses.

To a significant degree, the growth in the number of Government 2.0 advocates within an organization correlates to the amount of success generated in areas related to the goals of digital government, social networking, and open government. As successful initiatives are completed, promoted, and recognized, others within the organization will see that success and naturally want to replicate it (see Figure 34-3).

THE BLOGGING EXPERIMENT

In 2002, when blogging was still in its infancy, former Utah CIO Phil Windley announced an initiative to pay for blogs for the first 100 state government bloggers on Radio Userland. Employees from various agencies enlisted in the experiment and began to share their ideas about government and how to improve it. Although only a couple of employees remain from this early experiment in social media, it was enough to create a sense of what might happen as state workers began to understand concepts such as RSS and why interchangeable formats might be important to the state's ability to share and publish information to the public.

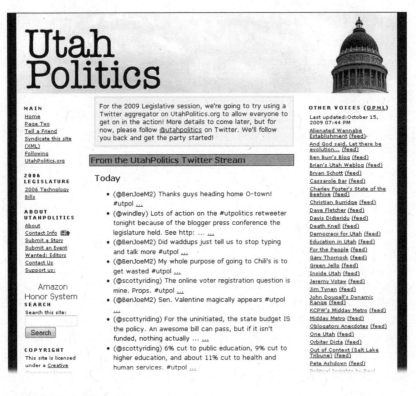

FIGURE 34-3. Utah Politics Twitter stream

Former Utah CIO Phil Windley now runs Utah Politics, a private sector site that aggregates blogs and microblogs discussing the Utah political scene.

The Dramatic Shift to Web 2.0 Principles and Tools

In Utah, the transition to a new level of openness embracing those concepts and tools identified as Web 2.0 has been about as dramatic as the initial move to embrace digital government in the 1990s. Many new relationships among government agencies and personnel begin on the Web as government workers identify new ways of getting work done and servicing constituents. For example, a recent statewide health conference session was successfully arranged entirely on Twitter by parties that had never met prior to the event. The collaboration involved five separate agencies and quickly came together in just a few hours.

In 2002, the state began managing its online presence as a product and e-government product managers were assigned in each agency. These managers, often high-level officials within the agency, were tasked with coordinating their efforts through a statewide "product management council." Over the years, this council has become a think tank where the best ideas are shared and filtered to the top. New websites and concepts are shared every month in this statewide forum and the product managers return to their agencies with ideas about how to improve what they are doing online.

Many government events are streamed live, such as Governor Gary Herbert's inauguration on U-Stream (see Figure 34-4).

FIGURE 34-4. Governor Herbert's U-Stream channel

As information technology (IT) assets were moved into a single organization in 2005, CIO Stephen Fletcher challenged that organization to become world-class in everything it did. To meet that challenge required an understanding of best practices, not just in government but also in business, and caused many employees to stretch as they sought to reach their potential. The Department of Technology Services is now the home agency for all of the state's technology workers and has been consolidating data centers and other platforms while developing statewide standards to make IT more efficient. Through all of this transition, the number one priority has still been to ensure that agency business needs are met.

External Users Dictated Technology Course

Although Utah had developed a state IT plan for many years, this plan often tended to focus on traditional solutions and infrastructure. At the end of 2006, an e-government plan was created for the 2007–2009 period which emphasized specifically the goals and initiatives that would focus on delivering services and information to citizens and business. IT leaders regularly measured the growing trend in the use of online services and the website in general. During the two years from 2007 to 2008, average monthly use of the Utah.gov domain increased from about 700,000 unique visitors to more than 1 million. The demographics and technical capabilities of these users had also changed significantly from the early part of the decade, and by 2008, more than 95% of incoming users had access to broadband service. Utah's web audience is also younger and more tech-savvy than what has been measured by some other government websites. These users were now expecting to find government services online as a matter of course, rather than as the exception. And they expected those services to be easy to use and more interactive. Utah's efforts to create dynamic and visually appealing services also paid dividends, resulting in some of the highest adoption rates for online government services anywhere in the country (see Figure 34-5).

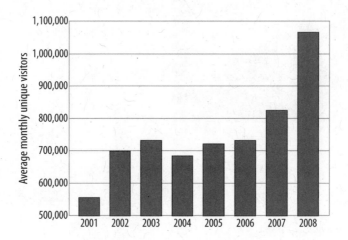

FIGURE 34-5. Unique visitors to the Utah.gov domain

Web 2.0 Becomes Part of the Technical Architecture

The initial e-government plan included an entire section on government collaboration.

In June 2008, Utah Governor Jon Huntsman announced a new initiative which he called Working 4 Utah. More than 17,000 Utah government employees would move to a four-day work week, and the state planned to close about 400 government office buildings for the entire three-day weekend. The move was facilitated by the fact that a large number of critical services were now online. The change meant that citizens would have access to traditional services for an extended business day (7:00 a.m. to 6:00 p.m.) from Monday through Thursday, but would need to rely entirely on digital services on Friday. The transition to a 4/10 work week that occurred in 2008 was easier as a result of agencies' efforts to put more services online. Utah had already evolved to a model where numerous services were provided on a 24/7 basis, and many citizens were already accustomed to receiving their services through the online channel. Many citizens became advocates of the new initiative in the social media debates that ensued following the decision, even to the extent of promoting the use of the state's online services in the online chats and forums. Although the standard work week is still 40 hours long, more than 80% of employees prefer it to the previous model. When customers have questions about how to get something done on Fridays, more often than not the agency can refer them to online information and services. After an initial review, it was noted that lines at the DMV actually got shorter as people continued to migrate to the online service.

The Utah Architecture Review Board (ARB) approves technical standards that apply to all of the state's executive branch agencies. Many agencies have been uncertain about how to utilize new social networking and other Web 2.0 tools and have been reluctant to move forward. The ARB passed a standard that identified best practice tools, reassuring agencies that these tools would not be blocked by state filters. This resulted in increased use by the agencies of tools such as Twitter and YouTube. Once agencies recognized that social media outreach and interactive online customer service using popular social media channels was officially sanctioned as a standard, the reluctance by employees to use these tools decreased.

Utah's Multimedia Portal Leverages Web 2.0 Services

Today, because of their extensive use throughout Utah government, open environments have actually been incorporated into the Utah.gov portal with pages such as the Utah Multimedia portal (*http://www.utah.gov/multimedia/*) and the Utah Connect page (*http://connect.utah.gov*). The increased collaboration through Twitter has been phenomenal, evidenced through the Utah Twitter page (*http://www.utah.gov/connect/twitter.html*) that aggregates Twitter feeds from state and local government (see Figures 34-6 and 34-7).

FIGURE 34-6. Utah.gov multimedia website

Making Data More Accessible

After assessing gaps in what it offered online, in 2009 Utah introduced a groundbreaking new portal (*http://data.utah.gov*). Like others before it, the new portal introduced many new concepts and services into the pattern for how Utah does business online. Following the lead from Federal CIO Vivek Kundra, Utah was the first state government to create a state data portal with the goal of enhancing access to state-provided data. The data portal provides an aggregation point for users to access the data they are looking for.

There are links directly to XML, XLS, RSS, and other types of portable data as well as to sites that provide query capabilities to offer user-defined data sets and information. The intent of providing data on Data.utah.gov is to make it easier for users both in and out of government to purpose the data in productive ways that benefit the Utah economy as well as government itself. Many in Utah government support the effort to become a knowledge-driven, real-time enterprise. To reach this potential, Utah must be able to connect to its citizens and businesses, not only through social media channels but also semantically, through dynamic, real-time, data-driven connections. If government provides reliable, real-time data, third parties in government and in the private sector can provide new added value in all kinds of ways. The state created a Twitter account as a way to provide updates about the site and new data as it became available. After introducing the new site, the state began receiving calls from around the country about how to go about setting up a similar service, and the National Association of State CIOs (NASCIO) set up a working group to identify potential best practices and standards that it could share with its members. Initially, this group wanted to focus on concepts

FIGURE 34-7. Local government Twitter feeds

such as governance structures while Utah kept insisting on the need to keep things simple and "just do whatever you can." Government tends to quickly rise to the level of bureaucracy when implementing projects that are viewed as enterprise in nature or as having a significant impact.

The new portal is an initial step toward what Tim O'Reilly calls "government as a platform" by providing data in formats that developers can use to create their own applications and mashups.

It provides an organized view into government-collected data and is expected to grow over time. The data is categorized into six areas:

State datafiles

These are raw datafiles in formats such as KML and CSV.

State data sources

These are generally queryable sources of large amounts of data where the user can specify the data being searched for through widgets or queries.

Local data sources

As local governments within the state continue to provide more data online, the state will provide an aggregation point to help find these sources.

Data visualizations

These are examples of how state data can be visualized with maps, charts and graphs, and so forth.

Geographic data sources

The state decided to create a separate category for geographic data because of the volume and uniqueness of the data available.

External data sources

Many organizations, including the federal government, accumulate data from the state and then make it available online. Because the state wanted Data.utah.gov to be a one-stop center for locating Utah data, these sources are also included because of their relevance.

Sharing data is an important component in the state's efforts to become more open. With increased emphasis and training, more government agencies are expected to provide data in KML, RSS, and other interoperable formats versus strictly downloadable formats such as CSV (see Figure 34-8).

Concerns About Security and Productivity

Most government entities that engage in Web 2.0-related activities quickly encounter the issues of security and privacy. In Utah, this is no different. Security personnel want to ensure that private data remains that way. One commonly held perspective is that systems outside the state's control may have a tendency to be less secure because the state may not be able to verify what security measures that system or service may have in place. Utah conducts annual online security training which is required for all 23,000 state employees. This training also reinforces proper etiquette and security practices for online activities. The state has also implemented a technical architecture wiki where it shares information on technology standards and practices. Creating standards that address security and privacy concerns has helped Utah ensure that momentum is maintained in its digital government initiatives. Utah's technical standards specifically authorize the use of a set of Internet-based collaboration tools

FIGURE 34-8. Utah.gov data directory

that include services such as Twitter, YouTube, and SlideShare. The state recently approved social media guidelines (*http://www.utahta.wikispaces.net/file/view/State%20of%20Utah%20Social %20Media%20Guidelines%209.22.09.pdf*) to help employees avoid issues as they use these solutions (see Figure 34-9).

Conclusion

In 2006, when the state of Utah completed its previous statewide e-government strategic plan, it identified 50 ways in which state government could use the Internet to improve collaboration with businesses, with federal government, with citizens, and with education, as well as internally within state government. Those strategies included many of the things discussed here. As we complete the next strategic plan, projecting through 2012, collaboration and openness will become even more important, and Utah will continue to be among those states looking to leverage the next wave of technology and web-based services to meet the expectations of its citizens.

FIGURE 34-9. Utah technical architecture wiki

About the Author

DAVID FLETCHER serves as the chief technology officer in the Utah Department of Technology Services, where he has overall responsibility for e-government, innovation, and technical architecture for the State of Utah. During his tenure, Utah has been recognized as the top-performing digital state by the Center for Digital Government. David has also served the state of Utah as the director of general services, the director of information technology services, and the deputy director of the Department of Administrative Services. He has a master's degree in public administration from the University of Washington, and he maintains a blog (*http://davidfletcher.blogspot.com*) on the topic of technology in government.

Memo from President Obama on Transparency and Open Government

Memorandum for the Heads of Executive Departments and Agencies

SUBJECT: Transparency and Open Government

My Administration is committed to creating an unprecedented level of openness in Government. We will work together to ensure the public trust and establish a system of transparency, public participation, and collaboration. Openness will strengthen our democracy and promote efficiency and effectiveness in Government.

Government should be transparent. Transparency promotes accountability and provides information for citizens about what their Government is doing. Information maintained by the Federal Government is a national asset. My Administration will take appropriate action, consistent with law and policy, to disclose information rapidly in forms that the public can readily find and use. Executive departments and agencies should harness new technologies to put information about their operations and decisions online and readily available to the public. Executive departments and agencies should also solicit public feedback to identify information of greatest use to the public.

Government should be participatory. Public engagement enhances the Government's effectiveness and improves the quality of its decisions. Knowledge is widely dispersed in society, and public officials benefit from having access to that dispersed knowledge. Executive departments and agencies should offer Americans increased opportunities to participate in policymaking and to provide their Government with the benefits of their collective expertise and information. Executive departments and agencies should also solicit public input on how we can increase and improve opportunities for public participation in Government.

Government should be collaborative. Collaboration actively engages Americans in the work of their Government. Executive departments and agencies should use innovative tools, methods, and systems to cooperate among themselves, across all levels of Government, and with nonprofit organizations, businesses, and individuals in the private sector. Executive departments and agencies should solicit public feedback to assess and improve their level of collaboration and to identify new opportunities for cooperation.

I direct the Chief Technology Officer, in coordination with the Director of the Office of Management and Budget (OMB) and the Administrator of General Services, to coordinate the development by appropriate executive departments and agencies, within 120 days, of recommendations for an Open Government Directive, to be issued by the Director of OMB, that instructs executive departments and agencies to take specific actions implementing the principles set forth in this memorandum. The independent agencies should comply with the Open Government Directive.

This memorandum is not intended to, and does not, create any right or benefit, substantive or procedural, enforceable at law or in equity by a party against the United States, its departments, agencies, or entities, its officers, employees, or agents, or any other person.

This memorandum shall be published in the Federal Register.

BARACK OBAMA

We'd like to hear your suggestions for improving our indexes. Send email to *index@oreilly.com*.

I

Illinois, Open Book mashup of state contracts and political donors, 216
immutable audit logs, 322
impedance mismatches, 356
inaccuracies in government data, 257–265
information flow about government activities (see government information flow)
information sharing about individuals by government agencies, 312
innovation
    arising from open standards, 15
    bottom-up change through young technologists, 286
    enabling for civic engagement, 83–89
    policy defaults' impact on, 25
insiders (moneyed), influence on government, 193
    rule of insiders, 195
institutional inertia blocking transparency, 276
Intel, duopoly with Microsoft, 31
Intelligence Community platform (BRIDGE), 5, 125
Internet
    democracy, deliberation and, 95–100
    design for participation, 23
    disclosure of government data on, 243
    effectiveness of government transparency goals and, 134
    elimination of limiting factors on democracy, 170
    government data access and, 19
    as information superhighway, 14
    Web 2.0 and importance of data, 31
Internet wave of change, 43
interoperability and portability, encouragement through open standards, 17
Investigative Reporters and Editors, 329
iPhone
    developer platform, 13, 16
    equivalent needed in health care system, 37
    introduction of, 36
    Routesy app, 32
    StationStops app, 30
IT
    antiquated media storing government data, 310
    bottom-up change in government IT through young technologists, 286
    downsizing or eliminating federal organizations' development teams, 284
    federal government, need to develop own software, 1–9
    fragmented IT and one-off apps in DoD, 279
    government IT market, focus on proposals, not products, 280
    government market, pre-Internet mentality, 284
    products, not projects for government IT, 285
    proprietary and antiquated databases storing government data, 310
    setting tone at top for government IT, 286
    transparency for government IT projects, 285
    transparency in government, 276
    user analytics for government IT products, 285
    using 21st-century technology to enable government data transparency, 294
IT Dashboard (IT.usaspending.gov), 119, 295

J

Jonas, Jeff, xxiii, 325
journalism
    failure to ask hard questions, 342
    possibilities in new mediasphere, 339–344
    reporting on government activities, 337
    self-appointed role as intermediaries between government and citizens, 338
journalism organizations, 329

K

Kettl, Donald, 13
Knowledge As Power, 155
Koelkebeck, Tim, xxiii, 287
Krumholz, Sheila, xxii, 239
Kundra, Vivek, 19, 25, 119, 295, 384

L

lack of political will for transparency, 217
law of conservation of attractive profits, 30
Lee, Tim, 247
legal materials, access to, 45
legal restrictions on releasing government data, 307
Legislative Committee Analysis Tool, 215
legislative process, citizens' access to, 153–165
    charges by governments for legislative information, 156
    Constitutional directives on avoiding secrecy, 155
    inadequacy of current tools, 157
    recommendations for improvement, 162–164
    social media and journalism, 160
    Utah state government, 378
Legislative Research Service (LRS), 158
LegiStorm website, 244
Leonhardt, David, 34
Lessig, Lawrence, 144, 229, 251
lethally generous, 128

shift to Web 2.0 principles and tools, 381–384

V

vending machine government, 13
Vermont, virtual corporations, 174
Viégas, Fernanda, xxii, 256
virtual corporations, 174
visual literacy, 254
visualization, 249–256
    of policy, 249
    of politicians, 253
visualization tools for government data, 86
Vogels, Werner, 21
votes of Congress members
    Congress Votes database, 244
voting records in Senate in XML, 209

W

Wall Street Journal, 341
Washington Post, Congress Votes database, 244
Washington Times, 343
Washington's golden rule (see money, influence on government)
Wattenberg, Martin, xxii, 256
Web 2.0, 11
    importance of data and algorithms producing value from it, 31
    lessons for opening process of co-creating government, 121
    Utah state government shift to principles and tools, 381–384
Web 2.0 revolution in government, 294–303
    appointment of first Federal CIO, 295
    deploying 21st-century technology, 294
    encouraging data mashups, 296
webcasting of Congressional hearings, 46
websites (finished) for government data, 88
Weil, David, xxi, 113
White House website, Open For Questions area, 342
White House, Data.gov initiative, 17
wiki, 55
WikiLeaks.org, 246
Wikipedia, 24
    crowdsourcing on, 28
wikis, 86
    enabling collaboration among government employees, 147
Willis, Derek, 244
"Wintel" duopoly of Microsoft and Intel, 31
wisdom of crowds, Barack Obama and, 115–121
    Change.gov transition site, 116
    government spending on economic crisis, watching over, 116

online town hall, 118
open data and open government, 119
opening up process of co-creating government, 121
Recovery.gov site (under construction), 117
word tree visualization, 254
World Wide Web, 16
    implementation by Tim Berners-Lee, 23
    platform enabling participation, 13
    use as tool to revolutionize business, 29
Wyoming, campaign finance disclosure legislation, 214

X

XML
    Congressional voting records in, 244
    roll call voting records in Senate, 209
    using to disseminate government information, 164

Y

YouTube, 24
    use by Republican Congressional members, 186
    video of Condoleezza Rice at Stanford University, 341
    video of Senator George Allen making racial slur, 342
Yu, Harlan, xxi, 20, 90, 247

DANIEL LATHROP is a former investigative projects reporter with the *Seattle Post-Intelligencer*. He has covered politics in Washington state, Iowa, Florida, and Washington D.C. He was a senior researcher on the *New York Times*-bestselling *The Buying of the President 2004* (Harper) by Charles Lewis.

LAUREL RUMA is the Gov 2.0 Evangelist at O'Reilly Media. She is the cochair for the Gov 2.0 Expo. Laurel joined the company in 2005 after being an editor at various IT research/consulting firms in the Boston area. Laurel went to Union College and is a photographer and homebrewer.

COLOPHON

The cover image is from iStockphoto. The cover fonts are Akzidenz Grotesk and Orator. The text font is Adobe's Meridien; the heading font is ITC Bailey.